LIGHTING THE TOWN

LIGHTING THE TOWN

A Study of Management
in the North West
Gas Industry
1805–1880

JOHN F WILSON

Published by Paul Chapman Publishing Ltd
for British Gas plc North Western

P·C·P

Paul Chapman
Publishing Ltd

With love to Barbara.

ACKNOWLEDGEMENTS

'Oldham from Glodwick Field' by J. H. Carse reproduced by kind
permission of Oldham Library Service. The photo of T. A. Fleming
was taken in Manchester Cathedral.

First published 1991 by
Paul Chapman Publishing Ltd
144 Liverpool Road
London N1 1LA

British Library Cataloguing in Publication Data
Wilson, John
  Lighting the town: a study of management in the
  north west gas industry, 1805–1880.
  I. Title
  338.47665709427

  ISBN 1 85396 176 0 cloth
  ISBN 1 85396 181 7 pbk

Typeset by Setrite Typesetters Ltd, Hong Kong
Printed and bound in Great Britain by Athenaeum Press, Newcastle upon Tyne

ABCDEF 654321

Contents

List of Tables and Figures

Abbreviations

When quoting printed sources I have adopted the convention of using only the author's name and the date of publication. Full details of each book can be found in *Sources and Bibliography*. Certain primary source titles and the names of libraries and record depositories have been abbreviated according to the following guidelines.

AGCBM – Altrincham Gas Co. Board Minutes.
BnGLCCMB – Bolton Gas Light & Coke Co. Minute Book.
BGLCMB – Blackburn Gas Light Co. Minute Book.
BnL – Bolton Library.
BlyL – Burnley Library.
BL – Blackburn Library.
BM – Blackburn Museum.
CCWC – Chester Corporation Watch Committee.
CGLCBM – Chester Gas Light Co. Board Minutes.
ChL – Chorley Library.
CnL – Colne Library.
CCRO – Cheshire County Record Office.
CuCRO – Cumbria County Record Office.
ChCRO – Chester City Record Office.
DWGLCBM – Darwen Gas Light Co. Board Minutes.
DwnL – Darwen Library.
GMCRO – Greater Manchester County Record Office.
HGA – Howard Greenfield Archive (Partington).
HGCBM – Hyde Gas Co. Board Minutes.
JADAB – John Abraham's Diary & Account Book.
JOGL – Journal of Gas Lighting.
KGCBM – Kirkham Gas Co. Board Minutes.
LCRO – Lancashire County Record Office.
LplCA – Liverpool City Archives.
LRO – Leigh Record Office.
LrL – Lancaster Library.
MCAD – Manchester City Archives Dept.
MGCM – Manchester Gas Committee Minutes.
NWGHS – North West Gas Historical Society.
OLIC – Oldham Local Interest Centre.
OGLWCMB – Oldham Gas Light & Water Co. Minute Book.
PGLCAB – Preston Gas Light Co. Account Book.
PGLCMB – Preston Gas Light Co. Minute Book.
PGLCSR – Preston Gas Light Co. Share Register.
PP – Parliamentary Papers.
PMPC – Proceedings of the Manchester Police Commissioners.
PRO – Public Record Office.

RGLCBM – Runcorn Gas Light Co. Board Minutes.
RGLCSR – Runcorn Gas Light Co. Share Register.
RtlL – Rawtenstall Library.
RL – Rochdale Library.
RUGCMB – Rossendale Union Gas Co. Minute Book.
SCL – Salford City Library.
SpL – Stockport Library.
StHL – St. Helens Library.
SHGLCBM – St. Helens Gas Light Co. Board Minutes.
WGLCMB – Wigan Gas Light Co. Minute Book.
WL – Warrington Library.

Preface and Acknowledgements

When British Gas North Western first approached the Department of History in 1985 with a view to establishing formal contacts in the field of historical research I had little idea where this would lead. Nineteenth century business history has always fascinated me, and the opportunity to study in detail one of the era's major industries has provided further insights into the subject. In particular, one can discover who exactly was the original 'Sid',(1) and why the undertakings were established in the first place; who was given the responsibility for managing the businesses, and how soon a professional cadre of specialists emerged; and what relationship the utilities forged with their local authorities, especially when the problems of both rapid population expansion and extensive urbanisation were highlighting the inadequate nature of public services. These financial, managerial and political features of the North West gas industry's growth up to 1880 will be the main concerns in this study, demonstrating how businessmen coped with the difficulties of lighting their towns and building an effective and eventually profitable industry from uncertain beginnings.

The gas industry has passed through a series of stages since its emergence at the turn of the eighteenth century: the lighting era up to 1880; diversification into cooking and heating in the face of competition from electricity between 1880 and the 1930s; elimination from the lighting market and relative decline in the mid-twentieth century; and, more recently, a significant recovery in fortunes associated with the conversion to natural gas after 1965. It will be the first of these stages which we shall be examining in the book, when lighting streets, factories, shops and large houses was the principal business of gas undertakings. This was the pioneering phase associated with names like Murdoch, Clegg and Winsor, when the industrialisation of the economy and urbanisation of society were creating new demands for services which in the past had been neglected. It was a period in which new challenges were continually appearing, and an examination of the North West gas industry will illustrate the difficulties experienced by those pioneers in matching supply with demand at a time when technical and managerial disciplines were still in their infancy.

The book itself can be divided into two distinct parts, with the first two chapters tracing the basic chronology, indicating when the major undertakings were formed, by whom, and how they overcame the technical problems associated with building a gas supply system. This provides the background for a detailed analysis of how private ventures were formed, financed and managed, and the study in Chapter 7 of municipalisation. The study will bring out the evolutionary pragmatism which was at the heart of the earlier efforts, and the move towards a more rational and professional approach from the 1830s. A key point to bear in mind when assessing this development is the danger of generalising about the industry, even within a region like the North West, because there was an enormous difference in experience across the size spectrum. The emphasis has naturally been more on the larger businesses, but even here undertakings did not always develop in a standard fashion. In particular, we are faced with such oddities as Manchester, which began as a municipal gasworks at a time when the industry was largely in private hands. Nevertheless, some common features do emerge from the study, throwing light on aspects of business formation, capital-raising and organisational evolution at a time when industrialists were still experimenting with new methods and institutions.

Studying the North West gas industry has involved researching into the records of over 100 businesses. The Howard Greenfield Archive run by British Gas North Western at Partington has been of immense importance in providing some information on many undertakings, but time has not in fact been kind to the historian of gas supply, and because the industry has experienced a series of changes in ownership the records have been dispersed and often lost. Extensive use of local newspapers and municipal records has consequently been vital in filling the gaps created by bad record-keeping in the distant past. Official sources are not much more detailed until 1881, but the various surveys by an increasingly vigilant Board of Trade can be rewarding. Of course, this improvisation is not a completely satisfactory solution to the shortage of business records, but there have been enormous gaps here.

In completing the project I have inevitably run up several large debts, not least to the University of Manchester which provided a two term sabbatical in 1987/88. Most importantly, though, I must thank Mr. R H Greenfield, Chairman of British Gas North Western up to 1989, for the generous financial and administrative support provided between 1986 and 1989, and his successor, Mr. R W Hill, for agreeing to finance this publication. In fact, the region's former Director of Engineering, Mr. F D Wilson, made the initial contact with my Department, and indeed it was mainly because of his perseverance that I was able to make so much progress. The Regional Management Committee has been extremely supportive over the last five years, and I am indebted to them for seeing this project to a conclusion, in particular Mr. Wilson's successor Mr. J Thomas. I must emphasise, however, that this is not a commissioned history, and British Gas North Western bears no responsibility for what has been written.

One of Mr. Wilson's lasting achievements in the historical field will be the North West Gas Historical Society, a body which now has well over 200 members attending regular seminars and outings. It would not be an over-statement to say that my knowledge of, and interest in, gas supply stems directly from the frequent conversations with such friends and supporters as A. S. (Sid) Bennett, Diane Smith, Alan Payne and Martin Lawrence. A special mention should go to Keith Eastwood, who in his role as caretaker archivist in 1987/88 not only guided me through the available records, he also provided me with helpful advice and encouragement. I am much in his debt.

The person, above all, though, who has spent countless hours discussing his boundless interest in the history of North West gas undertakings (especially those in Manchester and Salford) and who must take pride of place in this catalogue of acknowledgements, is Terry Mitchell of British Gas North Western. Without his support and copious comments on various forms of this book the project would have been difficult to complete, and his contributions to Chapters 5—7 have been beyond the calls of friendship and duty.

No list of acknowledgements would be complete without referring to the generous services of both my academic colleagues and the region's librarians and archivists. Professor Bob Millward and Dr. Mike Rose have provided constant encouragement, and the former's expertise in the field has opened up new dimensions to various issues. Dr. Harry Nabb of British Gas South Western and Dr. Derek Matthews of Cardiff Business School have also commented constructively on parts of the manuscript. All mistakes naturally remain my own responsibility, but they have assisted me in developing my studies. Having visited nearly forty libraries and record offices I must express my thanks to those professionals in many parts of the North West for kindly answering my 'Where is the...?' ramblings with courtesy and efficiency, in particular that well-known local oracle, Maggie Watson. The editors of *Business History* and the *Transactions of the Lancashire & Cheshire Antiquarian Society* have also granted permission for me to use excerpts from articles I had published in those journals.(2) Finally, the patient typists at Welman House have produced the book in spite of constant interference from the author. Thank you all.

Accumulating a mass of material and locking yourself away for long periods of deliberation can be a strain on the best domestic arrangements, and in consequence this book is dedicated to my wife, Barbara. She has sustained me through the darker moments and fostered a sense of achievement when light appeared at the end of the tunnel. Words alone cannot express my sense of reliance on her support.

John F. Wilson
Preston, April 1991

(1) 'Sid' featured prominently in the advertising campaign leading up to the privatisation of British Gas in 1986.
(2) See Wilson (1991A) and (1991B).

1
Emergence of Gaslighting, 1805–1826

'The gas-light, too, amazing thought,
So brilliant and clear.
I trust, good sir, 'twill save your purse
Some hundred pounds per year.'

Ralph, *Gas-Light; or the inside of a cotton factory*,
(Manchester, 1818).

Establishing a viable public gas supply industry was one of the more notable achievements of the early nineteenth century. Only a national railway network could claim to have affected as many aspects of Britain's economy and society within such a short time-span, and even though its impact until the 1880s was limited to the field of artificial illumination the gas industry became one of the symbols of urban progress in this era. Indeed, to people living in both large and small urban communities spread right across the country gaslighting must have been one of the most tangible benefits arising from the surge in technological change taking place at that time.(1) The need to supplement natural sources of lighting, to illuminate either business and domestic premises or public highways, had tested the abilities of many engineers and scientists prior to the nineteenth century. Prizes were offered by some of the prestigious scientific societies for the most suitable devices,(2) but it was not until William Murdoch and Samuel Clegg contrived independently to create the gas industry in 1805 that an effective solution was accepted. After 1805, and especially from 1812, gaslighting schemes were started in an ever-increasing number of towns, beginning in London and spreading to all of the regions within a few years of Napoleon's defeat in 1815. The industry's diffusion was naturally not uniform, and several constraints obstructed its progress, not least the availability of competent gas engineers, but by 1826 gaslighting had become a notable feature of urban life.

Our task in this first chapter will be to trace in the story of what is generally regarded as the first construction phase, between 1805 and 1826, introducing some of the interesting characters involved in forming North West gas companies, and explaining how these pioneers overcame the technical problems they faced. We shall see in particular how the story passes through two main phases: the first lasted between 1805 and 1814, when only isolated installations were supplied; and the second started in 1815, when public supply operations first appeared. By 1826 nineteen North West towns were being supplied by twenty-one separate gas undertakings (see Appendix A) illustrating that progress was not exactly spectacular, yet the North West was as well served as any other part of the country outside London. The capital actually played a leading role in establishing the technical viability of public lighting schemes, and it will become apparent that provincial industries benefited enormously from the services rendered by a group of travelling engineers who had learnt their trade after working for or with the big metropolitan companies. This contractor system was at the very heart of gas technology diffusion in the industry's early years, and without it North West towns, like those in most other regions, would have been unable to introduce gaslighting on anything like the same scale as they had achieved by 1826. The years 1805–1826 comprise a vital period in the gas industry's history, laying the basis for a phase of considerable expansion as the nineteenth century unfolded. Later chapters will examine some of the more specialist aspects of the story, like finance, management and municipalisation, but at this stage it is important that we establish the basic chronology and provide the background for more detailed analyses. The study will reveal new information on a variety of different aspects of the industry's evolution in this period, enhancing our grasp of both the regional and national scenes. It will also be possible to test some of the generalisations put forward by other historians, and in making these comparisons we can develop a better understanding of the broader picture.

The region covered by this study has often been described as the cradle of Britain's industrial revolution.(3) It encompasses Lancashire, Cheshire and the southern part of Cumbria (see Figure 1.1, p. 3). Economically, the North West is dominated by Manchester and Liverpool, but there are other towns of significance, from Oldham, Rochdale, Burnley and Ashton-under-Lyne in east Lancashire to Bolton, Blackburn and Preston further to the west. The rise of the cotton industry in the late eighteenth century had been a key factor responsible for the growth of these communities, while the rather earlier development of silk production in Cheshire had stimulated expansion at Stockport and Macclesfield. In places like Wigan and Warrington, on the other hand, the impact of coal and chemicals had been a major influence. The three county towns, Chester, Lancaster and Kendal, had not experienced the full impact of industrialisation, but as administrative, judicial and market centres they were still important communities. Population growth was also obviously another key influence on the region as a whole at this time, with all the major towns undergoing a dramatic process of expansion and change. Lancashire's population alone trebled between 1801 and 1851, to reach almost 2,000,000,(4) reflecting the scale of this experience in one of the major industrial regions of Britain.

It was these dual forces, of industrial expansion and urban population growth, which were setting in motion a vital period of economic and social change, and as the transformation gathered momentum it created multiplier effects which produced an urgent demand for public utilities. Models of this process have been elaborated,(5) describing the emergence of services like transport, water supply and gaslighting as an essential response to the tidal wave of people, bricks and machinery assaulting urban centres at that time. This provides the vital context in which to study the emergence of gas supply in the early nineteenth century, and as the North West was one of the areas most affected by such pressures it is an ideal region in which to examine the interaction between technological innovation and market

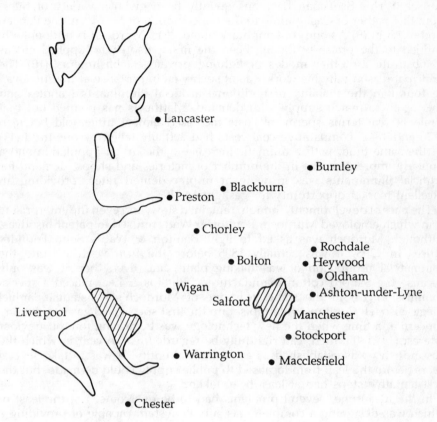

Figure 1.1 The North West Region (indicating towns with public gas supply undertakings by 1826).

pressures. Again, one must emphasise that it was simply as an illuminant that gas was required for much of this period, but even on the basis of such a specialised market the industry was able to build a successful base for later expansion. The North West developed a close affinity with the industry, an affinity which can be traced directly from the earliest experiments with 'inflammable air' and the installation of mill plants through to the establishing of public supply companies, and in this chapter it will become apparent how and when these links were initially forged.

The Pioneers

The early history of gaslighting is by now so widely reported that we do not need to spend much time here going over well-trodden ground.(6) It is firmly documented that, in spite of various scientific investigations in the seventeenth and eighteenth centuries into the phenomenon of an ignitable gas emanating from coal mines,(7) it was only in 1792 that William Murdoch successfully made gas by burning coal in an enclosed chamber to light his house.(8) This Scotsman has consequently been given a variety of titles, from the 'Father of Gaslighting' to the reincarnation of Murdoch, the Persian God of Light.(9) As one contemporary noted: 'Mr. Murdoch is undoubtedly entitled to the praise of having been the first person who applied gas as a substitute for other modes of lighting private establishments'.(10) The principal reason why his work was of such vital importance at that time can be found in the inability of traditional artificial illuminants (candles and sperm oil) to match supply with demand. Matthews has pointed out that while in real terms sperm oil costs increased almost fifteenfold between 1720 and 1841, comparative coal costs had actually fallen by one-third.(11) At the same time, with a dramatic increase in the urban population and a similarly impressive rise in the number of factories and shops, demand for artificial illuminants was growing at unprecedented rates, providing an excellent market opportunity for gaslighting.(12)

The pace of development, though, remained slow, and even the enterprising firm which employed Murdoch, Boulton & Watt, refused to patent his ideas. Although Murdoch was asked to light Boulton & Watt's Soho Foundry offices in 1798, it was actually 1805 before the firm ventured into the commercial production of gas-making plant, and even then it was only because the Salford cotton manufacturers, Phillips & Lee, placed a special commission.(13) In the same year one of Murdoch's assistants, Samuel Clegg, also left Boulton & Watt to set up the first specialised gas engineering concern at a time when the new technology was beginning to arouse wider interest.(14) 1805, then, can rightfully be regarded as the year in which the gas industry was established as a commercial entity. It was to take several years before the leap from localised to public supply could be made, but the first tentative steps had at least been taken.

In the meantime, several problems had to be overcome, not the least of which was designing a complete gas supply system capable of providing a clean, innocuous source of light on demand. The supply of gas can be broken down into three separate processes, after which the product is stored in gasholders and distributed along a mains system. Most of the gas manufactured in the nineteenth century was produced from coal,(15) and Figure 1.2 provides a diagrammatic representation of the main stages. This illustration(16) shows how coal was first of all heated in air-tight retorts and carbonised, after which the crude gas was condensed to remove some of the useful by-products, and then purified as an essential step in the elimination of what Falkus describes as 'the most troublesome. . . .evil-smelling' sulphuretted hydrogen.(17) Having passed through these processes, the resulting coal-gas could then be stored in gasholders until supplied to consumers through an extensive mains and branch-piping network. By 1805 it would be accurate to say that, while Murdoch had succeeded in lighting gas lamps, relatively little had been done either to extract the by-products or eradicate the smell, and the techniques of storing the product and distributing it over a wide area were still awaiting a satisfactory solution. Nevertheless, the potential in gaslighting was being recognised by an increasing number of engineers and businessmen, and even though many of the technical problems had still to be overcome candles and sperm oil were soon to feel the full force of competition in the lighting market.

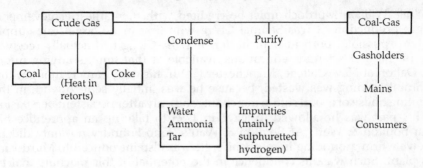

Source: Rowlinson (1984), pp. 10–11.

Figure 1.2 The manufacture of coal-gas

A common denominator linking three of the main public utilities created in the nineteenth century, railways, electricity and gas, was their early experiences with dubious company promoters who sought to persuade investors that here was the technological wonder of the age capable of producing enormous financial returns. The railway manias of the 1830s and 1840s, and the electrical 'bubble' of 1882,(18) were among some of the hardest lessons learnt by British speculators in this era, but they were all predated by F. A. Winsor's attempt to raise £1,000,000 in 1807 on the basis of some wild claims relating to the prospects for gaslighting.(19) Having been introduced to the technology by the French pioneer, Henri Lebon, in 1801, Winsor realised that London would be a good place to sell such an idea. A German by birth, Winsor has been variously described as 'a speculator, an opportunist'(20) and 'a mixture of visionary and charlatan',(21) because after his first demonstration of gaslighting in Pall Mall, London, in 1807, he immediately floated the National Light and Heat Company with a nominal capital of £1,000,000. This venture was eventually to become the first public gas supply company in the world, the Chartered Gas Light & Coke Company (or Chartered Co.), although it was another five years before parliament would sanction its registration.(22)

The legal reasons why Winsor failed to win official approval in 1807 will be examined in Chapter 3, but it is important to stress that even though he made some outlandish claims about the potential profitability of his scheme – he actually anticipated an annual return of £570 on each £5 share(23) – he did succeed in putting gaslighting on to the political agenda and made the new illuminant a focus for popular debate. At the same time, without the work of another key character in this story, Winsor's ambitious plans would have come to nothing. As we have just noted, many of the engineering problems had yet to be tackled and solved, because only plant supplying individual establishments had been produced to date, but after Samuel Clegg had been appointed Resident Engineer to the Chartered Gas Light & Coke Company in January 1813 the industry began to make more significant progress.

While William Murdoch must be credited with the earliest achievements in gas production, it was Samuel Clegg who first made large-scale supply systems possible. Born in Manchester in 1781, Clegg had actually received one of the best scientific educations available at that time, studying under Dr. Dalton at New College, Manchester.(24) In his early career, though, this technical training was wasted, because he was initially sent to work in the counting house of a local cotton merchant, and only after persistent persuasion on his part was he allowed to leave in 1798 to take up an apprenticeship with Boulton & Watt. At Boulton & Watt's Soho Foundry not only did he receive a firm grounding in mechanics, he was also introduced to Murdoch's gas plant. Such was his confidence in the potential of this machine that by 1805 Clegg had ventured off on his own to establish a business in Manchester as a supplier of gas-making equipment. He even claims to have completed the first commercial order, at Lodge's cotton mill in Halifax, just two weeks before Murdoch had installed his plant in the Salford mill of Phillips & Lee.(25) This secured his reputation as one of the two leading gas engineers in the country, as well as a steady stream of orders placed by customers in several different regions. Clegg's status was finally confirmed in January 1813, when he was invited to become the Chartered Company's Resident Engineer, and in his work for that undertaking he laid the basis for the initiation of public supply schemes.

Clegg's career up to 1813 was very much the story of how gaslighting progressed in its first phase of development, but simply to concentrate on his achievements would be to ignore some of the other key influences in the industry's evolution. Indeed, it is important to emphasise that while Clegg may have completed the first commercial contract in Halifax, it was the publicity attendant on Murdoch's success at Phillips & Lee which really gave rise to a surge in orders for gaslighting plant.(26) G. A. Lee had commissioned Murdoch to install gas plant in his Salford cotton mill not only because of his innate fascination with technological innovation, he was also genuinely interested in reducing his lighting costs, and in this aim he was not disappointed. Although capital expenditure exceeded £5,000, Murdoch was able to illustrate that by 1808 he had reduced Phillips & Lee's annual lighting bill from £2,000 (using candles) to approximately £600 for gas.(27) It was this startling revelation which brought home to many potential gas users that this new alternative really could make an impact on business viability. Another consideration was the safety factor, and while there were many sceptics who feared the possibility of explosions, a growing number of millowners were satisfied that gaslighting was less of a fire risk than candles or oil lamps. The first phase in the gas industry's history consequently began to gather some pace only after 1808, but, as Falkus notes, even then progress was hampered by the relatively primitive state of gas technology, and it was several years before significant improvements to the various processes were devised.(28)

In spite of the technical problems facing these pioneers, it would appear that in the North West businessmen were willing to risk placing orders with either Clegg or Boulton & Watt if the kind of savings achieved by Phillips & Lee could be secured. This attitude is reflected in the fortunes of both Clegg's business and Boulton & Watt's gas department, because the bulk of their sales were to customers in the North West. Clegg's first four clients were mills located near Manchester and Bury, while in 1807 the Manchester Police Commissioners asked him to provide a gas-lamp in King Street for an experimental period.(29) It was to be another ten years before this enterprising body was to purchase a full-scale works,(30) but their 1807 trial illustrates how a growing number of people in the region were recognising the potential in gaslighting. By 1811 Boulton & Watt had supplied gas plant to six of the largest cotton manufacturers in the North West,(31) and these sales, amounting to £8,264, accounted for 72% of their gas department's invoice total since 1805.(32) This further emphasises the key role played by the region in stimulating interest in gaslighting, but it would also be fair to say that there is some debate as to the significance of that stimulus in the context of the industry's long-term development.

It is not surprising that the North West was a principal market for gas plant at this time, because the extensive dissatisfaction with existing illuminants like oil and candles went hand-in-hand with a growing demand for artificial lighting from owners of large factory premises in the region. Falkus accepts the view that 'factory demand prompted the earliest experiments with commercial lighting.... especially around Manchester'.(33) This is well supported by the evidence already produced, but in attempting to revise what he calls the 'heroic view of the foundation of gas enterprise, emphasising particularly the work of Murdoch and the introduction of gas into northern factories' Falkus goes on to conclude that it was 'French inventiveness, German entrepreneurship, London "society" capital, and London demand....that provided fertile ground for the new industry'.(34) It is a view which can only be regarded as partially correct. One can accept that Winsor would have pushed forward with his scheme to light London regardless of Murdoch's experiments, because the German had seen Lebon's work in Paris, but Falkus's argument ignores the role played by Samuel Clegg. In its first year, the Chartered Company was prevented from making any progress until Clegg was appointed Resident Engineer in January 1813, and it was only because of his experience supplying equipment to North West customers that he was able to solve the problems and light St. Margaret's, Westminster, in April 1814.(35) Matthews put forward the contemporary view that Clegg made 'the most significant early developments in gas technology',(36) and many of these improvements arose out of the opportunities provided by North West orders to introduce new ideas.

In order to substantiate the claims made here it would be enlightening to examine in brief detail some of Clegg's early contracts. As we have already seen, Manchester and Bury millowners placed his first four orders, and according to Stewart nine of the twelve installations he had completed by 1812 were in the North West.(37) One of the most significant of these came not from a mill but from Stoneyhurst College, near Clitheroe, in 1810–11. Here, Clegg not only improved the design of his retorts and made them more air-tight, he also introduced the first purifying machine to eliminate the noxious sulphuretted hydrogen contained in coal-gas. He had actually tried out his ideas in a plant supplied to Messrs. Harris of Coventry in 1809, but it was only after a series of experiments at Stoneyhurst, conducted in association with Dr. William Henry, a prominent Manchester scientist, that Clegg managed to devise a suitable machine capable of eradicating most of the harmful vapours.(38) It must be noted that this innovation was not capable of removing 100% of the sulphuretted hydrogen,(39) but at least Clegg was beginning to overcome some of the major problems restricting the wider use of gaslighting and when the system came into full-time use in February 1811 gaslighting took a significant step forward.

A similar plant to the Stoneyhurst College installation was later provided for a worsted mill at Dolphinholme, near Lancaster, in 1810, and it is interesting to note that within a few years this was supplying several streets and cottages in the village.(40) Clegg's association with this particular conversion to public supply cannot be confirmed, but it illustrates the range of possibilities opening up to the pioneers after 1810. In other contracts Clegg devised more efficient hydraulic mains and gradually improved the methods employed to store gas and regulate its specific gravity. It was a process of incremental change to different aspects of gas-making, storage and distribution which was typical of his approach, and by 1812, when he lit the house, shop and workroom of a Lithographer in the Strand, London, he had gathered sufficient experience to take on more demanding contracts. It was while completing the Strand contract that the Chartered Company approached him with an offer to take over as their Resident Engineer, and his achievements there are now a matter of common knowledge.(41) One should also note that since 1810 Winsor had been ignored by the Chartered Company, further weakening Falkus's case, and on the basis of this evidence it is clear that a revised view is necessary. It is possible to conclude that Murdoch's pioneering work had inspired Samuel Clegg's entry into the gas industry, and that North West demand stimulated a series of innovations from the Manchester engineer which were vital to the establishment of the Chartered Company as the world's first successful public supply operation.

The Diffusion of Gas Technology

Although Falkus has wrongly underplayed the role of Clegg and his North West customers in the gas industry's initial phase of development up to 1814, he is undoubtedly correct when emphasising how thereafter the relationship was reversed and the Chartered Company encouraged the creation of supply undertakings outside London. This is a vital point in determining the pattern of gas technology diffusion, because having supplied the engineers with a conducive environment in which to improve gas technology when only isolated plants were required up to 1814, in the next phase of expansion based on public supply schemes the North West, and the rest of the United Kingdom, was largely dependent upon London expertise. The combination of 'London "society" capital, and London demand (based on the "urban" needs of commercial establishments and streets)'(42) with Clegg's accumulated technical expertise not only established the technical viability of such an enterprise, it also provided a pool of engineers capable of initiating similar installations. Matthews claims that, along with Clegg, these men — John Grafton, John and James Malam, J. H. Palmer and John Perks — built most of the early public gasworks, and along the way further improved gas technology in that pioneering phase.(43) Nabb concurs with this view, arguing that, as Clegg built the largest works at Bristol, in 1817, the Chartered Company provided the most important engineering contribution to the early development of gas supply in the South West of

England.(44) In Scotland, even by the 1830s 'London ideas still commanded attention',(45) while other contractors also ventured off into the provinces, helping to establish supply operations in Yorkshire and Lancashire.(46) This activity reveals one of the most important features of the gas industry's expansion after 1815, namely, the contractor system, with specialist engineers being called in to plan and supervise the erection of a works. Falkus describes it as an 'economic response ..... maximising the usefulness of these men, and allowing the spread of a scarce resource over a wide area of enterprise',(47) and certainly without such a system the industry's progress would have been much more sluggish.(48)

The direct link between London's pioneering work in public gas supply and the creation of regional gas industries can be clearly illustrated by looking at events in the North West. With Clegg having closed his Manchester business and moved to London in 1813, a serious shortage of expertise was actually emerging. A year earlier Boulton & Watt had also pulled out of this field, preferring to concentrate on their steam engine building rather than compete with specialists like Clegg and Joshua Pemberton.(49) This technical vacuum could have acted as a serious constraint on the evolution of gas supply in the North West as the industry moved from the first phase based on isolated installations on to more ambitious public supply schemes after Clegg's successes in 1814. Fortunately, the vacuum was soon filled by the contractor system, and in Figure 1.3 we can see that of the twenty-one undertakings created in the region by 1826 over half had benefited in some way from the services of an engineer with London experience. As we shall see later, there were also other contractors who operated in the North West, and they were responsible for at least two more undertakings, confirming the undoubted value of the system to the region's emergence as a major centre of gas production after 1815.

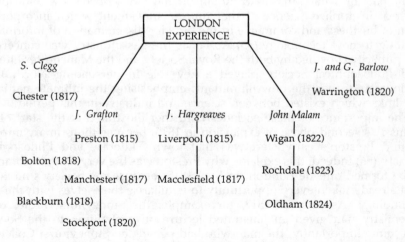

Figure 1.3 The diffusion of gas technology from London to the main North West towns, 1815–24

Once Clegg had succeeded in lighting parts of London by spring 1814, the direction of gas technology was being determined by the need to develop public supply operations, and as far as the provinces were concerned the contractors were an essential vehicle in the diffusion of expertise. But how in the first place did people hear about the benefits arising from gaslighting? In this context, most provincial newspapers were a disappointing source, because they preferred to concentrate on issues of political or military significance. There are notable exceptions to this rule, and as we shall see later some published letters or articles demanding the introduction of better street lighting, but in general this printed medium rarely commented on such matters. There were also no books published on this subject until 1819, other than a comprehensive catalogue describing the process of gas manu-facture by J Maiben & Co.(50) One network did exist, however, and this played an important role in bringing the new technology before a wider audience. The nineteenth century gas industry progressed largely by dint of 'practical experience, painstaking experimentation, and inventive flair, rather than scientific knowledge',(51) but at the same time it would be wrong to say that in the North West individual scientists or scientific societies made only a marginal contribution to the technology. We have already seen how Clegg had been educated by Dr. Dalton up to 1798, while in 1811 he had consulted the leading chemist, Dr. William Henry, on the purification machine. Henry had been working with gas for some years, and in 1804 had lectured to the Manchester Literary and Philosophical Society on the subject of coal-gas. In the audience at that meeting was his close friend George Lee (of Phillips & Lee). Lee has been described as 'one of the most scientific men of his age',(52) and encouraged by what he heard from Dr. Henry proceeded to order gas plant from Boulton & Watt. One should also note that Murdoch's achievements at Phillips & Lee's mill were published in a paper given to the Royal Society of Arts,(53) and the Manchester Literary and Philosophical Society continued to discuss the subject at several meetings during this learning period.(54) The vital point here is that these societies were part of what Musson & Robinson have described as a widespread interest in applied science at that time, a movement which incorporated men of business and commerce in the broader dissemination of information relating to new technology.(55) As far as the gas industry was concerned, the publicity provided by both the Royal Society and the Manchester Literary and Philosophical Society played a key role in persuading North West millowners to use the new illuminant, emphasising the intimate nature of the links which existed between science and industry in this period.

The importance of these societies is further illustrated at the start of the industry's second phase of expansion in 1815, because the primary impetus behind Preston's early start was that town's Literary and Philosophical Society.(56) Indeed, this explains why Preston was the very first gas company to be formed outside London, in May 1815, because the Society's members had already taken every opportunity to familiarise themselves with the new technology. As early as 1812, for example, the Stoneyhurst Professor of Chemistry had given an illustrated lecture on gaslighting to the Society, but, more importantly, the man who had persuaded Stoneyhurst College to adopt the new illuminant in 1810(57) was also both the founder of Preston's Literary and Philosophical Society and the main force behind the movement to start a gas company in 1815. This man was Fr. Joseph Dunn, the head of the catholic mission in the town, and Preston's early lead was largely a result of his work.

For most of the other towns in the region, of course, Literary and Philosophical Societies did not exist, other than the more famous case of Manchester, and it would appear that, as we shall see in Chapter 3, news of gaslighting and its advantages was disseminated largely by word-of-mouth in coffee houses, taverns and in business meetings. The central role of cotton in Lancashire's economic development would have helped here, because textile manufacturers were often the largest single group of Directors in the new gas companies springing up after 1815, and these men would have learnt about the new illuminant from contact with the Manchester pioneers of gaslighting. We shall also examine in Chapter 3 how gas company promoters publicised their schemes, using the informal, localised contacts which were such an important feature of provincial capital formation at this time.(58) These networks, revolving around coffee houses and taverns, provided the medium of communication required for these projects, enabling promoters to recruit all the support they needed. Although isolated installations continued to be supplied and used throughout the nineteenth century,(59) from 1815, as a consequence of Clegg's achievements in London, attention was turning increasingly towards public supplies. In whatever way knowledge of gaslighting was circularised, whether through formal or informal avenues, communities in many parts of the country were slowly beginning to respond to the opportunities made available by that time, pushing gas technology and the leading gas engineers to their limits.

The Contractors

By 1826 twenty-one separate public gas supply undertakings were operating in nineteen North West towns (see Figure 1.1 and Appendix A). In future we shall refer to this group as the First Generation, and not surprisingly it incorporates all the largest urban conglomerations in the region, as well as a few unexpected cases like Chorley and Heywood. There were also some small-scale operations working by the 1820s, for example at Dolphinholme, but these were never intended as public supply operations and consequently have been ignored in our analysis.(60) A simple chronology is provided in Appendix A, and in later chapters an economic analysis of their performance will be attempted,(61) but in this section we shall simply be concerned with examining how the challenge of establishing technically viable public gaslighting schemes was first tackled in the North West. The formation of these enterprises involved a variety of fascinating characters, and it was their vigour and perseverance which ensured that the industry was provided with such a solid base. Above all, though, it was the contractors who performed the central task of building the major systems in the region, as we have seen in Figure 1.3, and by following their progress it is possible to gain some insight into how the public gas supply industry was established in this crucial phase.

The national significance of this contractor system has already been demonstrated, and in the North West these specialist engineers were largely responsible for diffusing the benefits of Clegg's achievements at the Chartered

Company. There are several instances where undertakings relied upon indigenous experts, but even here it is possible to see links between the contractors and local engineers, indicating that either directly or indirectly the specialists were influencing developments in most North West towns. The publication in 1819 of technical treatises on the subject of gaslighting encouraged greater self-help,(62) but in the 1820s the contractor system remained just as important, and without it a technical constraint would have restricted the rate at which undertakings were formed. Some contractors might well have used the works as live test-beds on which to develop their own ideas, but this was an essential aspect of the way gaslighting evolved as a service, and it proved vital to the rate of progress.

(a) *John Grafton*

There is no better example of how the contractors operated after 1815 than John Grafton. His early career illustrates both the demand for such expertise and the impact it made on the provincial diffusion of gaslighting, because apart from his North West contracts it is known that by 1820 he had been directly responsible for gasworks in Carlisle, Edinburgh, Sheffield and Wolverhampton. It is also interesting to note that in 1815 Grafton was only nineteen years old,(63) and like John Malam still employed by the Chartered Company in London. Clegg himself had ventured off on his own in 1805 at the age of twenty-four, indicating that, when one considers their impact, some of the key personnel in the early gas industry were quite young. Perhaps their relative youth blinded them to the difficult engineering problems ahead, but one might argue that a degree of naivety is essential when taking up any technical challenge, otherwise anticipating hurdles by clinging to accepted beliefs would hinder real progress. Certainly, around about the time of Napoleon's defeat in 1815 there still existed a good deal of uncertainty about gaslighting,(64) but the pioneers were still willing to ignore the detractors and push on with their ideas. Clegg was the symbol of this faith, and his able lieutenants assisted him in overcoming the technical and psychological hurdles still in their path.

Grafton's first opportunity to demonstrate his ability to work independently of Clegg came in July 1815, when he was asked by the promoters of Preston Gas Light Company to visit their town and assess the costs and feasibility of building a public gasworks.(65) In fact, the man personally responsible for recruiting Grafton, Fr. Dunn, had actually intended to secure Clegg's services, but as Eastwood surmises it is probable that the criticisms voiced by the Chartered Company's management about their Resident Engineer's consultancy work persuaded him to second Grafton instead.(66) Fr. Dunn had actually been instrumental in bringing Clegg to Stoneyhurst College in 1810,(67) and during the engineer's stay in the North West they struck up a close friendship, a friendship based on their genuine belief in the prospects for gaslighting.

Fr. Dunn had actually been using gas to light his presbytery since the 1790s,(68) and as we noted earlier the Literary and Philosophical Society he founded in the town in 1810 was the inspiration behind the formation of Preston Gas Light Company in May 1815. The Society had actually discussed the possibility of establishing such a venture after listening to a lecture on

Fr. J. ('Daddy') Dunn, S.J. (1746–1827), pioneer of gaslighting at Stoneyhurst College and in Preston.

gaslighting given by the Stoneyhurst College Professor of Chemistry in 1812,(69) but given the problems being experienced by the Chartered Company at that time they presumably decided to await further improvements. By the spring of 1815, after Clegg's successes in London, the Society clearly felt the time was right, and on 25th May the first recorded meeting of Preston Gas Light Company was held.(70) At that meeting a committee of twelve subscribers was appointed, and it is important to note that eight of these men were members of the Literary and Philosophical Society.(71) This committee even met at the home of the Society's Librarian, Isaac Wilcockson, and together with Fr. Dunn this man was to lead the gas undertaking through a difficult first decade. Wilcockson was also the owner and editor of the *Preston Chronicle*, and as Awty reveals this newspaper had frequently agitated for improvements in the town's facilities,(72) reinforcing the work of the Literary and Philosophical Society. It was this activity which led directly to the establishment of Britain's first provincial gas company, and on 8th July the *Preston Chronicle* announced Grafton's arrival in the town, reporting that: 'A young man of ample experience is engaged to superintend the fixing up of the apparatus and laying of pipes.'(73)

It is significant that, even with a scientific society run by an acknowledged expert on gaslighting who had been using the illuminant for over twenty years, Preston Gas Light Company still felt compelled to use the services of a specialist contractor like John Grafton. This confirms the central importance of Clegg's work in London, and without access to this expertise the earliest provincial companies were often reluctant to move ahead. Grafton actually arrived in Preston in July, and from that moment he was involved in every aspect of founding a public gas supply scheme. His duties involved not only finding a suitable site for the works, ordering equipment and installing it, they also included advising on the amount of capital required and persuading local millowners and shopkeepers to use the new service.(74) It was an all-embracing task which, in spite of his youth, Grafton appears to have performed to the satisfaction of the company's management. By February 1816 the *Preston Chronicle* was able to report that a full trial of the system had been completed successfully, and in May it claimed that: 'The excellent manner in which the works have hitherto operated, do great credit to the Engineer, Mr. Grafton, under whose superintendence the whole has been conducted.'(75)

The manner in which Grafton operated at Preston was typical of how the contractor system worked at that time. Preston Gas Light Company was very much at the mercy of their engineer's ability to convert his training under Clegg into practical results, and although Grafton suffered from poor health during the latter part of 1816 he still succeeded in building a technically-viable system. Problems certainly hampered progress, in particular because of leakage problems from both the mains and a gasholder,(76) but in general the work was regarded as a success.(77) It is notable, though, that Grafton used Clegg's basic design for the Preston works, demonstrating that he was yet to develop his own ideas.(78) Nevertheless, it still took almost a year to complete the contract, and while this was not an unduly long period for such an installation at this time, as we shall see, it shows that promoters were obliged to endure a lead-time between hiring an engineer and advertising the availability of a continuous supply.

For his services at Preston, Grafton was paid a total of £505.10s.0d, reflecting the high value placed on such expertise at a time when it was in such short supply. Indeed, the scarcity of gas engineering skills was the reason why Grafton left Preston in February 1817, after the newly formed company in Edinburgh had recruited his services. It is also known that as early as March 1816 Grafton had visited Dublin, presumably to advise on the construction of a gasworks,(79) and after leaving Edinburgh in August 1818 he was appointed Engineer to the Sheffield Gas-Light Company.(80) The Directors at Sheffield were apparently unhappy with his attendance at their works over the twelve months he stayed in that city,(81) and although illness was partly to blame for his absences it is clear that ever since leaving

Preston he was also advising other undertakings as well as taking on the more permanent jobs in Edinburgh and Sheffield. One of the companies which benefited from his advice was at Wolverhampton, but even more important to our study was the gasworks constructed by Manchester's Police Commissioners in 1817.

By the end of the eighteenth century Manchester had grown so rapidly that the Court Leete was experiencing great difficulties in its efforts to govern the township,(82) and in consequence by 1792 an Act had been secured to appoint Police Commissioners with powers to clean, light, watch and regulate the streets.(83) Little of substance was achieved by the Police Commissioners up to 1799, but thereafter under the more inspired leadership of C. S. Brandt, more effort was put into lighting Manchester's streets, and by 1802 2,000 oil lamps had been installed in the township. They even experimented with gaslighting in 1807, when Clegg was invited to install lamps in King Street,(84) but although the *Manchester Mercury* commented that they 'produced a wonderful effect far superior to those lighted with oil'(85) no permanent service was envisaged at that early date.(86)

The first positive steps taken by the Police Commissioners towards constructing their own gasworks were to come nine years later, when in March 1816 a sub-committee was formed of 'several gentlemen of known scientific experience....... to take into consideration the expediency of lighting the whole or any part of the Town of Manchester with Gas'.(87) Clearly, their deliberations were extensive, and only in the early months of 1817 was the Police Commissioners' Agent, Jacob Davies, dispatched to Preston to report on Grafton's work. Davies was obviously impressed, and after further discussions in March and April the Commissioners finally decided at a Special Meeting to construct a similar installation out of the rates. This marked the start of what the Webbs have described as 'the most remarkable of all municipal experiments prior to 1835',(88) placing Manchester at the head of local government developments in that crucial phase.(89)

Although it was natural that, as manager of Police Commissioner affairs, Jacob Davies should play a prominent role in bringing public gas services to Manchester, it would be a mistake to ignore the real driving force behind the scheme, Thomas Fleming (see the photograph on p. 186). Described in the *Manchester Observer* of 1819 as 'Archil Manufacturer; Treasurer of the Commissioners; Treasurer also of the Surveyors of the Highway.... member of the Gas Committee; President of the Blackfriars Bridge Committee; President of the Red Noses at the Turks Head; Church Warden of St. Georges and Aspirant to the Borough Reeveship etc. etc....', Fleming was one of the town's leading early nineteenth century figures.(90) As Treasurer to the Police Commissioners from 1810 he wielded great power in local political circles, the best illustration of which is his ability to persuade his peers to build a gasworks on the rates. It was a master-stroke of political manipulation, and in Chapter 7 we shall examine why, under Fleming's direction, the home of free trade economics decided against private enterprise as the vehicle for providing gas at a time when local government rarely took responsibility for such utilities. The town remained an oddity in this respect for several decades to come,(91) but until the amalgamation of Liverpool's two gas companies in 1848 the Manchester undertaking was the region's largest.(92)

Whether in private or municipal hands, gas undertakings still required specialist advice, and in 1817 the Police Commissioners were anxious to recruit a suitably qualified engineer. Manchester, of course, was particularly well provided with both scientists and businessmen who had gained ample experience of gaslighting, but the requirements of a public supply system demanded different skills. Although the leading firm of engineers, Peel & Williams, was given the contract for building the works, the Gas Committee insisted on the appointment of an engineer 'to superintend the management of the construction of the whole'.(93) Little evidence exists indicating who Peel & Williams appointed to perform this task, but it is clear from Mitchell's detailed research that John Grafton designed the works and advised on its installation.(94) Having seen his work at first hand in Preston, Jacob Davies must have recommended the young engineer to his employers, and between August 1817, when the project was started, and the first continuous supply of gas in March 1818 Grafton was on hand to assist Peel & Williams. The relationship was rather different to the one forged at Preston, because during this period Grafton was also engineer to the Edinburgh Gas Light Company. This explains why he was paid only £105 by the Manchester Gas Committee, compared to over £500 by Preston Gas Light Company. One might also note that Grafton's continued ill-health was probably caused by the constant pressure he must have felt while completing his onerous workload, emphasising the heavy demands placed on gas engineers at this time. In general, though, he appears to have fulfilled his commitments to the satisfaction of those who hired him, and the Manchester gasworks in particular proved extremely successful.

As the late-1810s progressed Grafton continued to take on new challenges, and after being involved in initiating gasworks at Preston, Dublin, Edinburgh, Manchester and Sheffield he then went on to contracts in Carlisle and Stockport. The Stockport Gas Light Company was formed in October 1820, and almost immediately the promotors invited Grafton to design their works.(95) As with Preston and Manchester, Stockport was not short of people who were already conversant with gas technology, a local printer, Thomas Claye, having provided his own gaslighting since 1815. In this case, though, it is not surprising that the company looked to Grafton, because Claye's apparatus consisted of a six inch pipe placed behind his kitchen fire to act as the retort, with the actual light coming from a perforated cruet.(96) The display might well have impressed local inhabitants, but it would hardly have equipped Claye with the expertise to design a public supply operation, making it imperative that the company should turn to Grafton in 1820.

The Stockport contract was Grafton's last direct link with North West gas undertakings, and after what must have been an arduous five years, involving many miles of travelling around the country, he settled in Wolverhampton as the permanent engineer to their gas company. He was regarded as one of the leading gas engineers in the country, and indeed not only had he been responsible for designing and building some of the earliest and largest provincial public gasworks, he also made several important contributions to the technology as his practical experience mounted. Apart from introducing a hand-lamp for lamplighters while working at Preston in 1816, and in 1818 devising a means by which the accumulated tar residue found in hydraulic mains could be siphoned off, his most important patents related to the lining of retorts with fire-clay.(97) Clay retorts later came into general use, replacing the less efficient iron variety,(98) but as early as 1818 Grafton had patented clay-lined retorts which he first tried while at Edinburgh.(99) These designs proved extremely successful, and at Wolverhampton he designed better methods of manufacturing this equipment, by building them up in sections.(100) Indirectly, then, Grafton's impact on North West gas undertakings continued to be felt as these innovations rapidly gained acceptance. He was the archetypical contractor, and the region's gas industry benefited significantly from his pioneering work in these early years.

(b) James Hargreaves

When the Chartered Company was formed in 1812 Frederick Accum and James Hargreaves were charged with the task of building the works,(101) and while their first efforts were so ineffective that Samuel Clegg had to be hired in January 1813, both men still went on to enjoy successful careers in the industry. Accum, of course, continued to work with Samuel Clegg, and in 1819 produced the earliest text-book on gas technology.(102) On the other hand, Hargreaves had left the Chartered Company within a year, and in the next two years it is not clear exactly what he did. In July 1815, however, Hargreaves re-emerges in Liverpool, and by August he was advertising his intention to establish a gas company there.(103) This advertisement, though, is misleading, because Hargreaves was not responsible for initiating the venture: it is more likely that he was acting as the agent for a group of Liverpool businessmen. Falkus has shown how some contractors created gas companies and then sold their interest to local investors,(104) but there is no evidence to indicate that Hargreaves operated in this fashion at Liverpool. On the other hand, it is clear that he must have gained enormously from his contact with Clegg in 1813, because his achievements in the North West stand out in stark contrast to his earlier failure, confirming once again just how influential the Chartered Company's success was to be in the development of provincial gas supply.

Liverpool Gas Light Company was the second such operation to be established in the North West, after Preston, but it soon exceeded in size its earlier counterpart and became the largest private gas company outside London. The inaugural meeting was held in October 1815, the leading promoters being Jonathan Varty, a coach-maker, and Charles Lawrence, a prominent merchant and local politician.(105) Apart from Lawrence, though, no other member of either the Town Council or the wealthy mercantile families of Liverpool chose to support the venture at this stage. Nevertheless, Hargreaves did succeed in persuading the Borough Architect and Surveyor, John Foster, to assist the company's cause. Known locally as 'King' Foster, because of his powerful position within Liverpool Corporation, it was vital to gain his support when seeking permission to lay mains in the streets. The Paving Commissioners actually granted this permission at the end of October 1815, after Foster had personally presented the company's petition, leaving the way open for the construction of a complete gas supply system. It was in fact the late summer of 1816 before the system planned by Hargreaves was working, although as early as January some of the main

J. Varty, coach-maker, co-founder of the Liverpool Gas Light Co. in 1815.

streets were successfully lit. Thereafter, Liverpool Gas Light Company experienced rapid growth, expanding its capital from £6,000 in 1815 to £50,000 in 1818, and demonstrating that gaslighting on a large scale was technically and commercially viable (see Appendix C) in the provinces.

Hargreaves's achievements at Liverpool must have been a source of great pride to him after the humiliation of being replaced by Clegg at the Chartered Company in 1813. His success also meant that, like Grafton, he was much in demand. There is no evidence remaining of how he was persuaded to leave Liverpool Gas Light Company, but by August 1817 Hargreaves had been appointed Engineer to the recently formed gas undertaking in Macclesfield.(106) In fact, a small gaslighting scheme had been started in Macclesfield as early as 1813, but the man responsible for this scheme, a Mr. Hankinson, knew so little about the technology that within two years he had been ruined. It is known, for example, that he used porous material like earthenware for mains, illustrating how important it was to acquire suitable expertise when building a gasworks. Relatively little is known about the company founded in 1817, and even less has been discovered concerning Hargreaves's stay in Macclesfield, but by all accounts the venture was a financial success. As with most North West gas companies, it was five years before a dividend was paid, but between 1822 and 1829 the subscribers received average payments of 12% on their £50 shares, reflecting the profitability of gaslighting after a few years in business.(107) Hargreaves was one of the least-known contractors of this period, but in constructing these two gasworks, and particularly that of Liverpool, he was a significant contributor to the diffusion of gas technology.

(c) *John Malam*

A third engineer who worked directly with Clegg at the Chartered Company, and later built gasworks in the North West, was John Malam. Just like Grafton, Malam had benefited from a sound training, in this case from Boulton & Watt, and when he moved to the Chartered Company in 1814 was immediately appointed foreman at the Peter Street gasworks.(108) This was a unique opportunity at that time, and when he left the company in 1817, after some dispute over rights to ideas he had patented,(109) he found a large market for his services, especially in the North West. Malam was actually one of three brothers who between them influenced the construction of over fifty gas supply operations up to 1846,(110) but it must be emphasised that although they purchased most of their plant from the Sheffield firm of Newton Chambers, each operated independently. Initially, however, after leaving the Chartered Company in 1817, John was actually more interested in developing his gas meter patent, an idea for which the Society of Arts awarded him their prestigious Isis Medal in 1819. A year later he patented further refinements to his patent, but at this stage his ideas did not prove commercially viable,(111) and by 1822 Malam had been persuaded by the failure of a meter market to emerge to turn his attentions towards contracting.

The mid-1820s was a particularly busy time for John Malam. Concentrating largely on Lancashire and Yorkshire, it is known that between 1822 and 1825 he built gasworks in seven different towns,(112) and at the same time made a series of decisive contributions to the design of retorts, purifying machines and gasholders. His first contract was placed by the Wigan Gas Light Company in April 1822, two months after the concern had been formed by a group of local manufacturers and professionals.(113) Malam was invited to tender for the job in March, and his estimate laid down that the cost of his scheme would be £5,497, in addition to which a fee of £825 would be charged for planning and supervising the installation.(114) These prices appear to have been accepted by the Wigan management without any quibble, and as they had already set their capital at £10,000 (see Appendix B) it was well within their means. Over the ensuing twelve months Malam was even provided with progress payments, ranging in size between £500 and £1,000, considerably easing his cash-flow problems. This arrangement was vital to operators like Malam, because unlike Grafton and Hargreaves, who ordered equipment through a gas company, at Wigan the management subcontracted this function to their Engineer. Falkus reveals how in the 1820s he frequently owed over £5,000 to Newton Chambers, emphasising the need for regular payments from customers to maintain liquidity.(115)

It is clear from the Wigan Gas Light Company Board minutes that Malam was given complete responsibility for designing the works, supplying the equipment and putting it to work. The management were in no position to dissent from his estimates, such was their ignorance of gas technology, and in fact by November 1823 they had actually paid him £6,748 for work completed,(116) £426 more than the original estimate. In June 1823 the Directors had attempted to retain £1,000 from his account until the works had proved trouble-free for three consecutive months, but within two weeks of that decision they had given in and Malam was paid in full.(117) The main problem in the relationship was one which emerged when discussing Grafton's career, namely, the contractor's frequent absences while performing similar duties in other towns. Indeed, as early as August 1822 Wigan Gas Light Company was obliged to advertise for an engineer capable of supervising work while Malam was in Wakefield building their gasworks,(118) and it was over six weeks before a suitable candidate could be appointed. This seems to have held up progress, and only in January 1823 was Wigan first provided with a fully operational system. Even then Malam had not completed the contract, and it was the 1824 company meeting when the Directors finally announced: 'The Gas Works are now completed and are considered by competent Judges to be equal if not superior to any Gas Establishments in the country.'(119) This was an inordinately long lead-time between placing a contract with Malam in April 1822 and the successful completion of the works, and it confirms how thinly spread the expertise of these contractors must have been.

The Wigan management's eventual claim that they possessed one of the best designs in the country was clearly well-founded. Ever since his success at the Chartered Company with a new design for retorts, which Peckston regarded as 'decidedly superior to any other at present used',(120) Malam had continued to improve the apparatus. By 1822 experiments with clay-lined retorts had been started, following the ideas of his former colleague, John Grafton, and in 1823 Malam introduced the first of his new retorts at Wigan. Such was the effect they achieved that the Manchester gas undertaking was also equipped with these retorts in 1823,(121) establishing his reputation as one of the leaders in the field. It was also at this time that Malam developed a more effective purifying machine, to reduce further the quantities of sulphuretted hydrogen remaining in gas after its manufacture,(122) and to improve the gasholder he introduced a balancing mechanism which assisted the easier movement of its body. These refinements ensured that his customers were provided with some of the most advanced equipment on the market, and although it is probably true to say that such a process of incremental change may have added to fixed costs at least the undertakings could be sure of their system's technical viability.(123)

Malam's reputation as one of the most accomplished gas engineers of this period secured him a succession of orders, and while completing the systems at Wigan and Wakefield he contracted to perform the same role for Rochdale Gas Light & Coke Company in the summer of 1823.(124) Clearly, his work rate showed no signs of abating, because at this time, apart from building a gasworks at Knaresborough in West Yorkshire, he was also concurrently installing new retorts at Manchester.(125) Although little is known about either the Rochdale or Manchester orders, they demonstrate how he was in great demand in the early 1820s, and this rate of work continued through 1824, when he erected the works at Beverley, West Yorkshire. In the summer of the following year Oldham Gas Light & Water Company also commissioned him to build both aspects of their scheme.(126) There are only a few cases of undertakings in the North West which intended to supply gas and water,(127) and bearing in mind that the Oldham contract took over two years to complete it is possible that Malam had taken on too much. The two systems have obvious technical similarities, and at £48,000 the company's nominal capital was adequate, but by July 1826 the Directors were complaining that the scheme 'is not in a sufficient state of forwardness'.(128) Again, progress payments of up to £1,000 had been provided by the company,(129) but only after the Board had threatened severe financial penalties did Malam step up the rate of construction.(130)

It is difficult to be precise about the reasons why Malam took so long to complete both the Wigan and Oldham contracts, but the tendency to develop machinery as it was installed must have held up progress. Of course, all Malam's contracts were technical successes, in time, and the managements were satisfied with the quality of his work, but the experiments, and absences on other jobs, prevented companies from going into production sooner. We shall be examining in Chapter 5 whether this affected commercial viability, but at least contractors like Grafton, Malam and Hargreaves were establishing technically viable systems at a time when undertakings were heavily dependent upon their advice. Malam, just like Grafton, also left the contracting business in 1826, because by then he preferred to run a gasworks,(131) rather than travel around installing equipment, but he had already made a significant contribution both to the emergence of a North West gas industry, and to various aspects of the production process.

(d) *Other Contractors*

Apart from the series of contracts executed by Grafton, Hargreaves and Malam, several of their counterparts visited the North West to perform individual installations. The most outstanding of these was Samuel Clegg, who built the Chester gasworks. After a series of disputes with the Chartered Company over his consultancy work outside London, Clegg had actually terminated their arrangement in April 1817.(132) He had already designed the Bristol gasworks in 1816, the City of London Gas Light & Coke Company had been provided with some valuable advice on their retorts, and in 1817, in conjunction with Frederick Accum, he had provided equipment for the Royal Mint. When the Chester Gas Light Company promoters contacted him, after establishing the business in October 1817,(133) Clegg had also made several important refinements to his system, most notably in the construction of rotary retorts and telescopic gasholders, continuing the process of incremental change followed since 1805.(134)

Evidence relating to the creation and early management of Chester Gas Light Company has not survived and we are left with occasional references in local papers or city histories to chart its progress. The first Board of Directors, comprising a banker, three attorneys and two unoccupied gentlemen,(135) was evidently in no position to determine how the system should be built, and in consequence their dependence on Clegg was total. This in itself was not unusual, as we have seen above, but what is surprising is that it was fifteen months before the city was being supplied with gas on a regular basis.(136) There was certainly no shortage of finance for the venture, the £6,850 nominal capital having been raised in 1817, and one can only conclude that Clegg's ideas on gas supply were still being refined while he was completing the Chester contract. As we have seen at Preston and Wigan, both Grafton and Malam had not been averse to using those undertakings as live test-beds for their ideas, and obviously they had learnt this practice from their mentor, Samuel Clegg. The companies were in such a dependent state that they could do little to expedite matters. Nevertheless, Chester Gas Light Company actually paid its first dividend in 1821,(137) three operating years after the system had been brought on stream, and thereafter its performance was as consistent as any other North West gas undertaking. Hemingway claimed that by 1831 'every street, row, and avenue is lighted by gas', and although there were the usual complaints about the 'offensive stench produced by the escaping of the gas'(138) there is no evidence that Clegg's engineering contribution had failed to provide a technically sound basis for expansion.

While the county town of Cheshire appears to have been admirably well served by Samuel Clegg, it is less certain how its counterpart in Westmorland fared. Contemporary sources indicate that a London engineer was hired,(139) and we know that his name was West, but further research has failed to determine more about him.(140) The Kendal Gas Light Company had been formed in October 1824, and during its first meeting West had addressed the interested parties on the advantages of gaslighting.(141) This speech was obviously persuasive, because within two days all 300 £20 shares had been taken, allowing West to proceed with his design.(142) Ten months later Kendal was provided with a continuous supply of gas for the first time, bringing the town into line with most of the other main North West communities. West was to enter the annals of popular Kendal history as 'Joe Gas',(143) but it is impossible to say whether he built undertakings elsewhere or stayed there as permanent Engineer.

In sharp contrast to Kendal's gas contractor, the men who built the works of Warrington Gas Light & Coke Company were some of the best known characters in the early British gas industry. Formed in December 1820 by a miscellaneous group of businessmen and professionals, the promoters of Warrington Gas Light & Coke Company had already commissioned Messrs Barlow Bros. to build a public gasworks in the town.(144) The Barlow name, of course, is best known because of T. G. Barlow's achievement in 1849 as founder of what became the industry's main trade journal, the *Journal of Gas Lighting*, but the family's link with gas had started a generation earlier. John Barlow had originally been a Sheffield iron manufacturer, and some time after 1812 he decided to establish a gas equipment business in London in order to exploit the growing demand in this area.(145) Together with his brother George he was responsible for several public gas supply schemes in the south and the Midlands, often building the works and then forming a company with local capital.

The Warrington Gas Light & Coke Company minute books have not survived for this period, but according to the venture's historian Barlow Bros. were in this case responding to the promoters' request for assistance, rather than initiating the scheme themselves.(146) While the contract was being completed, though, the Barlows insisted on complete freedom of action in designing, installing and managing the company until the system was working successfully.(147) This was not unlike the kind of relationship enjoyed by Malam at Wigan, and clearly the Barlows would brook no interference from Directors who would presumably have known little about gas technology. Within a year the contract had been completed and management passed back to the Directors, leaving the company with the supervisory function, but initially Barlow Bros. had complete control of the venture. Paterson does not record any problems with this arrangement, but the Directors were in a weak bargaining position, and like the other North West companies using contractors they were obliged to take a back seat when it came to technical matters.

(e) *Oil-gas*

The reliance of promoters on specialist engineers, which was a feature of the coal-gas undertakings described so far, was even more total when a company chose to use oil-gas apparatus. While Clegg, Grafton and Malam had patented a succession of improvements to coal-gas retorts, purifiers, gasholders and mains, they had been prevented from patenting a whole process because of Murdoch's work. On the other hand, when contemporaries turned to consider using oil(148) they were faced with a monopoly supplier in the form of Taylor & Martineau. The oil-gas process had been available since 1815, having been developed by Phillip Taylor, patented by his brother John, and consequently marketed by the London firm of Taylor & Martineau.(149) We shall be referring to the 'Oil versus Coal' debate at various points in later chapters, but it is important to note at this stage that the former always remained more expensive, and in spite of various refinements to the process no oil-gas undertaking proved capable of competing successfully with a coal-gas supplier. On the other hand, in the 1820s there seemed to be some potential, because not only was oil-gas apparatus more compact, it was also much easier to operate once Taylor & Martineau had installed the system. This, together with the acknowledged superior quality of oil-gas lights,(150) was a big selling point, convincing several groups of promoters in towns all over the United Kingdom that it would be more appropriate to purchase Taylor & Martineau plant.

Taylor & Martineau worked in much the same fashion as the Malams and Barlows, designing and installing a system on the contractor basis, and then passing supervision of production on to the original management. At the same time, there is no suggestion that, in contrast to coal-gas engineers, the oil-gas contractors ever initiated a gas company, preferring instead to sell their equipment to supply undertakings through an agency network covering Edinburgh, Bristol and Dublin.(151) By the early 1820s even some of the established coal-gas undertakings were considering oil as a natural progression, in order to improve the quality of their service,(152) and by 1822 oil-gas companies at Norwich, Hull, Colchester, Taunton and Bristol had been set up in competition with existing suppliers.(153) Taylor & Martineau also supplied plant for use in substantial houses, one of which was the home of Sir John Tobin, a former Mayor of Liverpool and a leading importer of palm oil from West Africa.(154) The oil interests, of course, had been severely rocked by the introduction of coal-gas in the lighting market, but the availability of oil-gas equipment provided an opportunity to win back lost ground, and this new sector of the gas industry benefited enormously from what was essentially a defensive reaction.(155) It was a form of vertical integration in which men like Tobin and other Liverpool merchants were keen to indulge, leading to the creation of an oil-gas company in that city at a meeting held on 27th September 1822.(156)

Such was the confidence in this new venture that all its 300 £100 shares were purchased immediately, and within a week of that inaugural meeting a further 100 had been successfully issued.(157) This allowed construction to go ahead at once, but presumably because Taylor & Martineau were still fulfilling their obligations to the Hull Oil Gas Company it was December before they proceeded with the Liverpool contract, and only in December 1823 was the installation ready to provide a regular service.(158) The main reason why the contract took twelve months to complete was that Taylor & Martineau had also been instructed to lay all the necessary mains and branch pipes, and the original plan was to provide a distribution system seventeen miles in length. Their task was made no easier when, after incorporating the company by Act of Parliament in May 1823, it was stipulated that a four foot gap between their mains and those of the coal-gas operation had to be maintained even in the more cramped parts of the city.(159) The conflicts which arose in Liverpool over this issue, and many other aspects of gas supply, will be examined in Chapter 6, but clearly a bitter rivalry was to emerge as each company sought to eliminate the other. This rivalry intensified after 1834, when the oil-gas operation was converted to coal-gas,(160) and even though Taylor & Martineau failed to sell equipment to any other company in the North West their success at Liverpool was to have important ramifications over the next two decades.

The final case we must consider while discussing the direct role played by gas contractors is the Provincial Portable Gas Co. It was an oddity for two reasons: the venture was founded and managed by businessmen from outside the region; and the gas was supplied in copper bottles, rather than through mains. Although Clegg had 'condensed coalgas in copper globes, in order to form portable lamps, at Stoneyhurst College in 1811',(161) according to Rowlinson this was the only attempt to use coal-gas for this purpose.(162) Eight years later an Edinburgh engineer, D. Gordon, patented a process for condensing oil-gas in copper vessels, and then formed the London Portable Gas Co. to supply houses, shops and other customers who were not connected to a company's mains. Such was the initial success of this venture that subsidiary operations were started in Bristol and Edinburgh,(163) and in 1825 the Provincial Portable Gas Co. was established on a site in Gaythorn (see the photograph on p. 49) to service those potential consumers who lived outside Manchester's township.(164) Mindful of their legal obligations and duties, Manchester's Police Commissioners had restricted their mains to the limits of the town's boundary, leaving new industrial areas like Chorlton-upon-Medlock unconnected. Gordon's company was anxious to fill that obvious gap, and for a time expansion seemed assured. After six years in business, though, the Provincial Portable was suffering as badly as its parent company in London, due largely to the rapid extension of permanent mains by established suppliers. By 1831, the parent company's £100 share was worth no more than 30/- on the open market,(165) inducing Gordon to sell off his Chorlton subsidiary to a local businessman, Mr. Fernley, for £5,650.(166) This marked a decisive change in fortunes for the Gaythorn site, because Fernley converted the operation into a conventional coal-gas supplier using mains and service pipes, and in 1837, as part of their expansionist strategy, Manchester's Police Commissioners acquired the system for £20,000.(167) It is a curious episode in the early history of North West gas supply, and again specialist contractors from London were clearly important in determining the early pattern of technical development.

Self-help?

The contractor system had been of central importance in the establishment of a public gas supply industry in the North West between 1815 and 1826. If we include the Provincial Portable Gas Co., thirteen of the region's undertakings had used the services of a specialist gas engineer to design, construct and start their systems. Even though some delays were experienced as a result of either the contractor's absence on another job or his propensity to experiment, it is clear that without these men even slower progress would have been made. However, twenty-one North West gas undertakings were established in this period, and it is interesting to examine how the remaining eight fared without hiring a Grafton or a Malam. It is doubtful whether they could have survived purely on the basis of home-spun talent, although there is an indication that self-help featured to some extent in this pioneering phase.

When the Bolton Gas Light & Coke Co. was first formed in February 1818, by a local doctor, John Moore, and a group of cotton and engineering manufacturers,(168) no attempt seems to have been made to recruit the services of a specialist gas contractor. Some businesses in the town were already supplying their own gas, among them a firm of tin-plate workers in Moor Lane, Spooner & Worthington, which was to play a key role in the gas company's early development.(169) Although neither Spooner nor Worthington was responsible for forming the new utility, by April 1818 their plans for building a public gas supply system had been accepted by the managing committee.(170) It is also notable that the gasworks was to be built close by Spooner & Worthington's own premises,(171) but even more significant was the appointment of the former's brother, Ralph Spooner, as the Engineer.(172)

It is in the acquisition of Ralph Spooner that we see the Bolton company's first attempt to broaden its search for appropriate technical expertise, because in fact this man had been working for Preston Gas Light Co. since September 1816.(173) Indeed, Spooner had been Grafton's assistant while that town's gasworks was being modified and extended, and when the contractor severed his connections with Preston in February 1817 it was Spooner who took on the position of Engineer.(174) This must have been invaluable experience for him at a time when only a handful of these operations existed, and at Preston he learnt the rudiments of this new trade from one of the industry's acknowledged experts. Spooner was actually a trained engineer by profession, signing himself as a 'Millwright' in the company's share register, and his eighteen months at Preston equipped him with the specialist gaslighting skills which were in growing demand. Bolton's decision to poach Spooner from Preston is an illustration of how acute the shortage of these skills was becoming as more towns decided to build gasworks, and although the latter were extremely annoyed about the situation for the former it proved to be a wise move.

Spooner's appointment as Engineer to the Bolton Gas Light & Coke Co. came at a most unwelcome time for the Preston management. In the short term, they were just about to settle their half-yearly accounts, and at that time the Engineer completed this task, but more importantly his departure deprived them of a member of their team they found difficult to replace.(175) Such was the haste in which Spooner left that he even took Preston's Cash Book to Bolton,(176) and while it is unlikely that any mischief was intended here his new employers were grateful for the assistance it provided in helping them to organise their financial system. In this way, the new operation was acquiring all the expertise it needed to initiate a gas company without the expense of bringing in one of the contractors. Although Spooner had to be tempted with the relatively high salary of £150 per annum, it is clear that this was cheaper than hiring Grafton or Malam. Whether this affected the company's financial viability we shall see in Chapter 5, but it certainly did not expedite construction, because it was the Spring of 1819 before any mains were laid in Bolton's town centre, and the first public lamps were only lit on 1st May.(177) This illustrates that, whether specialist or local engineers were used, there must have been a standard lead-time of at least one year between the formation of a company and the initiation of its service.

In discussing Bolton's case it becomes apparent that some promoters attempted to use local skills wherever possible, Spooner & Worthington designing the system and Ralph Spooner coming from Preston to install it. This technical input was undoubtedly important, but it is important to stress that without Grafton's guidance the latter would have been ill-equipped to take on the demanding role of Engineer to a gas supply company, indicating that the contractor's imprint could still be found on the Bolton operation. Exactly the same could be said about the Blackburn Gas Light Co., because, although never employing a contractor, almost as soon as it was founded in January 1818 this venture used the Manchester under-taking designed by Grafton as its model.(178) In fact, not only did the Blackburn management visit Manchester to inspect Grafton's work, they also purchased burners, mains and tools from the region's largest gas sup-plier.(179) It seems surprising that, by travelling thirty miles to Manchester, the Blackburn management ignored Grafton's system at their closer neigh-bour, Preston, but perhaps they were intending to erect a large supply operation and regarded the Police Commissioners' utility as a better guide.

It was actually three months before the Blackburn management appointed an Engineer to supervise the construction of their works. This man was a Burnley millwright, John Molyneaux, and it is known that in the summer of 1818 he personally inspected Manchester's retort house, advising the Board in September that this equipment was superior to the apparatus recently installed at Birmingham by Samuel Clegg.(180) In spite of this assistance from Manchester, though, it took Molyneaux fourteen months to inaugurate a continuous supply,(181) illustrating how lead-times for such ventures were very similar to those experienced by companies using contractors. Nevertheless, Blackburn Gas Light Co. soon developed into one of the largest businesses of its kind in the region, and as we shall see in Chapter 5 at least three separate extensions were added to the manufacturing capacity in the 1820s to cope with the rapid growth in demand for gaslighting resulting from the management's marketing strategy.(182)

After discussing the cases of Bolton and Blackburn we can now conclude that at least fifteen of the North West gas undertakings established by 1826 had benefited either directly or indirectly from the services of a specialist gas contractor, as we can see in Figure 1.3. Unfortunately, it is impossible to be sure about the undertakings at Salford, Chorley, Burnley, Ashton-under-Lyne, Lancaster and Heywood, because no clues remain relating to who designed and installed their gasworks.(183) Given the extensive publicity accompanying contractors' achievements at this time, however, the failure of their names to appear in association with these companies leads us to believe that other sources of expertise were being tapped. One cannot be too categoric on this issue, but it is essential to examine the surviving information to discover how the early technical problems were overcome in those cases.

Linking at least three of the undertakings just listed as the probable origin of the public supply scheme was the prior use of gaslighting in cotton mills. Of course, Salford can lay claim to the earliest example of this early deployment of gas plant, with Phillips & Lee having placed the first contract in 1805. By 1807 this firm was providing a supply to several gas lamps in nearby Chapel Street, but it was 1819 before a group of local businessmen decided to build a works capable of servicing a wider area.(184) These entrepreneurs, Thomas Appleby, Richard Brain, Edward Fisher and a Mr. Clay, actually chose Clowes Street as their operating base, just one street away from Phillips & Lee's mill,(185) but it is impossible to say whether the two systems were linked in any way. Fisher, described as a 'Patent Gas Manufacturer' in the local trade directory,(186) appears to have been the technical inspiration behind the venture, and under his guidance by the autumn of 1820 Salford was provided with a continuous supply. However, although a second works was completed in the mid-1820s, and mains were laid in several of the town's major thoroughfares, it is important to stress that this undertaking remained one of the smallest in the region until acquired by the Salford Police Commissioners in 1831. Thereafter, more money was spent on the system, but in the 1820s potential gas consumers were poorly served in Salford.(187)

Another of the smaller gas undertakings formed in this period was at Chorley, and here again the public supply service was predated by the provision of gaslighting from a local cotton mill. The Chorley Gas Light Co. was formed in October 1819, and on the original management committee was Thomas Lightoller, a cotton manufacturer who had been supplying a limited service for several years to inhabitants close to his factory. Although he had not originally intended to use his plant as a public supplier, in 1819 Lightoller was persuaded by fellow-manufacturers and local retailers in the town to extend this operation into a full-blown operation.(188) This was also probably the case in Burnley, because in 1823 the Burnley Gas Light

Co.'s first works were set up in the same street as the Howard Mill, and this factory had been using gas for at least five years.(189) One cannot be completely sure that these facts are necessarily linked together, but as we shall see in the next chapter one of the main reasons why from the 1830s gas companies were formed in smaller towns was the realisation by enterprising cotton manufacturers that they could convert their own gasworks into a lucrative source of additional revenue.(190) It is consequently not beyond reason that the small operations at Chorley and Burnley originated in this way, raising capital from other sources to bring the service to a wider audience.

Self-help, then, with local manufacturers converting their private plants into public suppliers, would appear to have accounted for a small number of North West undertakings up to 1826. One cannot be too precise on this matter, because time has not been kind to the records, but given that these were small-scale operations they did not require a significant expansion of capacity meriting the employment of a contractor. For the vast majority of undertakings, though, specialist advice was essential to ensure that a technically viable system was installed. We have seen that the contractor system may have involved some delays, either because the engineer was busy with other customers, or because he insisted on developing new refinements to certain parts of the system, but public supply operations required the kind of specialist advice not generally available. Once completed, though, the gasworks appear to have been as reliable as any installed at that time, providing a sound basis for the expansion to follow as gaslighting gained in popularity. Management were still faced with a difficult technical challenge, particularly as the rate of engineering improvement did not show any signs of abating until much later in the century,(191) but at least the contractors had left them with systems that worked.

The North West Gas Industry by 1826

The North West had provided a conducive environment in the early nineteenth century for gaslighting to flourish, playing host to the first specialised gas engineering concern between 1805 and 1812, and accounting for the bulk of gas equipment sales in that period. Although London became the focal point for technical advance from 1813, North West customers had stimulated many of the early improvements to production and distribution apparatus, allowing Samuel Clegg to go on and initiate the world's first public gas supply for the Chartered Co. in 1814. The region soon responded to this new opportunity, with the first provincial gas companies appearing at Preston and Liverpool in 1815, and because of the large and growing demand for better artificial illuminants in the booming towns of Lancashire, Cheshire and Westmorland the impetus was maintained up to 1826. By that time, nineteen North West towns were beginning to benefit from a public gas supply, and local initiatives had been responsible for all but one of the twenty-one separate undertakings in business (see Figure 1.1 p. 3). Gas was coming to be accepted as the main form of lighting streets, mills, shops, offices and even large houses by the 1820s, and in Chapter 5 we shall examine the general impact of demand on the operation of these ventures as they struggled into life.

While the force of demand was motivating local businessmen and professional people to form gas undertakings, the supply of technical expertise could have acted as a serious constraint preventing the companies from meeting their obligations. It is apparent from what we have seen in this chapter that without the contractor system many promoters would have been reluctant to initiate large public supply schemes, even in towns possessing some expertise in the field. The contractor system was an essential vehicle of diffusion, providing the vital link between Clegg's pioneering work in London and those towns in most parts of the United Kingdom which required specialised skills (see Figure 1.3 p. 9). In the North West thirteen of the undertakings benefited directly from this system, while at least two more were undoubtedly influenced by work completed in other towns. We have noted that the contractors were often prone to extensive experimentation and improvisation while designing and constructing the systems, and we shall discuss in Chapter 5 whether or not this tendency affected financial viability, but technically North West undertakings were well-served by these engineers. One should also emphasise that the contractors were also responding to the efforts of indigenous promoters, indicating how strong the links between the region and the gas industry were becoming by the 1820s. Only the small Provincial Portable Gas Co. was formed by businessmen living outside the North West, and such was the potential demand for gaslighting in the boom towns of the area that local initiative was always to the fore.

When it comes to assessing the size of the North West gas industry in this first phase of expansion up to 1826 major problems exist. Falkus has provided a figure of £3.15 million for the total capital invested in United Kingdom public gasworks by 1826,(192) but the paucity of primary documentation prevents a comprehensive treatment of this subject. There is little doubt, though, that Falkus has under-estimated the total, because, for example, he claimed that the thirteen largest undertakings had spent £1.8 million, but the four London companies alone had already invested £1.5 million,(193) leaving just £300,000 to be distributed around places like Manchester, Liverpool, Birmingham, Bristol, Leeds and Newcastle. A more complete analysis of capital expenditure will be attempted in Chapter 2,(194) but it is evident that the total United Kingdom investment figure must be closer to £4 million for 1826. By that time, as Appendix B reveals, £421,401 had been spent on twenty-one North West gas undertakings, and, remembering that London accounted for at least one-third of the United Kingdom total, this gave the region a position of prime importance as a major centre of gas production.

By 1826 the North West could claim to have one of the largest provincial gas industries. It is extremely difficult to speak with any certainty about the exact number of undertakings operating in the United Kingdom by that date, largely because many failed to apply for parliamentary permission to lay mains or use limited liability,(195) but a figure of 140 seems realistic.(196) Comparable studies on the other major provincial industries (Yorkshire, the Midlands and the North East of England) have yet to be completed, but from the work so far produced the North West appears to have had few rivals. For example, by 1826 there were probably only fifteen undertakings in Yorkshire,(197) in the South West there were ten,(198) while the whole of

Scotland could also claim just ten supply operations.(199) There were naturally some large companies in places like Birmingham (founded in 1817), Leeds (1817), Sheffield (1818), Nottingham(1818), and Leicester (1821),(200) but the North West as a region appears to have been better served. This rapid diffusion of gaslighting is a clear indication of the growing demand for such a service, especially in Lancashire, a demand which continued to spread as the nineteenth century progressed. The struggles of the pioneers were providing a solid basis for expansion, and by the 1820s a technically-viable utility had been created which was becoming an intrinsic feature of urban life in the region.

Footnotes

(1)   Robson (1973), p. 178.
(2)   Falkus (1982), p. 218.
(3)   There is no suitable history of this region as a whole, but see Walton (1987) for a detailed analysis of the North West's heartland.
(4)   Walton (1987), p. 123.
(5)   Robson (1973), pp. 131–143.
(6)   The standard published sources for this subject are Falkus (1982) & (1967), Chandler (1947), and Clegg (1841). The early works of Accum (1819) and Peckston (1819) also provide details on important contracts, while the unpublished theses of Matthews (1983), Nabb (1986), and Rowlinson (1984) deal expertly with a wider range of issues.
(7)   Some of these experiments took place at Wigan, where gas was found to issue from a well. Clegg (1841), pp. 1–4.
(8)   Chandler (1947), pp. 9–11.
(9)   When in 1873 the Shah of Persia discovered the Scotsman's role he immediately associated him with this deity. Mackenzie (1947), p. 12.
(10) Matthews (1832), p. 82.
(11) Matthews (1983), p. 136.
(12) Falkus (1982), p. 224.
(13) Chandler (1947), p. 11.
(14) Falkus (1982), pp. 224–225.
(15) See later, pp. 45 and 171, for an analysis of oil-gas.
(16) I am indebted to Rowlinson (1984), p. 11 for this reference.
(17) Falkus (1982), p. 229.
(18) For a brief description of these events see Evans (1936), pp. 1–10, and Cottrell (1980), p. 189.
(19) For a full history see Matthews (1983), Chapter One.
(20) *Ibid*, p. 13.
(21) Chandler (1947), p. 15. One should also note that in 1807 Winsor was involved in a scheme to raise £5,000,000 for a National Deposit Bank. This venture failed. Hunt (1936), p. 14.
(22) Everard (1949).
(23) Mackenzie (1947), p. 14.
(24) Clegg's early career is described in detail by Bennett (1986B), pp. 2–8. See also Stewart (1962).
(25) Clegg (1841), p. 12.
(26) Falkus (1982), p. 223.
(27) Clegg (1841), pp. 8–12.
(28) Falkus (1982), pp. 229–230.

(29) Bennett (1986B), p. 3.
(30) See later, pp. 15–16.
(31) These were Phillips & Lee, H. H. Birley & Co., J. Kennedy, McConnel & Kennedy, Birley & Hornby and J. Thomas & E. Lewis, all of Manchester or Salford. Falkus (1982), p. 224.
(32) *Ibid.*
(33) *Ibid*, p. 219.
(34) *Ibid*, p. 233.
(35) Everard (1949), pp. 15–25.
(36) Matthews (1832), p. 82.
(37) Stewart (1962), pp. 1–6.
(38) Bennett (1986B), pp. 11–24.
(39) See later, p. 29.
(40) Bennett (1986), pp. 21–52.
(41) Everard (1949), pp. 1–25.
(42) Falkus (1982), p. 233.
(43) Matthews (1983), p. 82.
(44) Nabb (1986), p. 17.
(45) Cotterill (1980–81), p. 20.
(46) Falkus (1967), pp. 506–507.
(47) *Ibid*, p. 506.
(48) For a description of how the system operated elsewhere see Nabb (1986), pp. 60ff.
(49) Falkus (1982), p. 225. Pemberton was a Birmingham engineer who supplied equipment for shopkeepers and small manufacturers.
(50) The first books were by Accum (1819) and Peckston (1819).
(51) Falkus (1982), pp. 233–234.
(52) This label was given to him by Robert Owen. *Ibid*, p. 222.
(53) Clegg (1841), pp. 8–12.
(54) Musson & Robinson (1970), pp. 248–249.
(55) *Ibid*, p. 188.
(56) The following section is taken from Awty (1975), p. 88 and Eastwood (1988), p. 3.
(57) Letter from Fr. J. Dunn to W. Scott, 22/12/23. These letters were discovered by Keith Eastwood and copies can be found in HGA.
(58) See later, pp. 70–79.
(59) For example, the Styal Mill of Greg & Co. was supplied with gas plant in the 1840s, and many of the Manchester cotton mills continued to use their own supply facilities until mid-century.
(60) Bennett (1986). This service consisted of just six street lamps.
(61) See Ch. 3 for a study of capital formation, and Ch. 5 for an analysis of performance.
(62) Accum (1819) and Peckston (1819).
(63) Eastwood (1988), p. 30.
(64) Matthews (1983), p. 53.
(65) PGLCMB, 6 Jul 1815.
(66) Eastwood (1988), p. 12.
(67) Letter from Fr. J. Dunn to W. Scott, 22/12/23.
(68) Eastwood (1988), p. 6.
(69) Awty (1975), p. 91.
(70) PGLCMB, 25 May 1815.
(71) *Ibid.*
(72) Awty (1975), pp. 91–94.
(73) *Preston Chronicle*, 8 Jul 1815, p. 1.
(74) PGLCMB, 17 Jul & 4 Aug 1815, and JADAB 3 Jul and 27 Sept 1815.

(75) *Preston Chronicle*, 24 Feb, p. 1 & 18 May 1816, p. 3.
(76) Eastwood (1988), p. 32.
(77) See later, pp. 131–133, for a fuller analysis.
(78) PGLCMB, 1 May 1818.
(79) *Ibid*, 18 Mar 1816.
(80) Roberts (1979), p. 8.
(81) *Ibid*.
(82) See Redford (1939), Ch. 1.
(83) The sections on Manchester are based on Mitchell (1986).
(84) See above, p. 7.
(85) Quoted in Mitchell (1986), p. 16.
(86) See later, pp. 185–186.
(87) Quoted in Mitchell (1986), p. 25. See later, pp. 186–187, for an analysis of the reasons why the Police Commissioners considered this momentous step.
(88) Webbs (1922), p. 258.
(89) See below, p. 184 for a detailed analysis.
(90) Mitchell (1986), pp. 21–24.
(91) Although it was only 1824 before another local authority built its own gasworks, in Keighley, West Yorkshire, few municipal gasworks existed in 1850. See later, pp. 202–203, and Golisti (1984), p. 39.
(92) See Appendix B.
(93) Mitchell (1986), p. 28. The Gas Committee was formed in Apr 1817, and for many years was dominated by Davies and Fleming. See below, pp. 186–188.
(94) *Ibid*.
(95) The company records have not survived, but see Heginbotham (1890), p. 411.
(96) *Ibid*.
(97) Eastwood (1988), p. 31.
(98) *King's Treatise* (1878), p. 54.
(99) Cotterill (1980–81), pp. 25–26.
(100) Stewart (1962), p. 47.
(101) Everard (1949), p. 27.
(102) He also worked with Clegg on gas plant supplied to the Royal Mint in 1817.
(103) Much of the following is based on the detailed investigations conducted by Harris (1956). Records on Liverpool's two companies are scarce for this period.
(104) Falkus (1967), p. 505.
(105) This paragraph is based on Harris (1956), pp. 9–15. See later, pp. 144–145, for a fuller analysis of this company's performance.
(106) The only information available on this company can be found in *Macclesfield Courier & Herald* (1888), pp. 87–89.
(107) PP (1847). See later, pp. 144–145 for an analysis of NW gas company performance.
(108) Stewart (1962), p. 45.
(109) *Ibid*.
(110) Falkus (1967), p. 506.
(111) See later, pp. 136–137, for the development of pricing policies.
(112) The Yorkshire contracts were in Wakefield (1822), Knaresborough (1823), Beverley (1824) and Gainsborough (1825). Falkus (1967), p. 506.
(113) WGLCMB, 13 Apr 1822 and 15 Mar 1822. Little information has come to light on this company's principal promoters, but prominent on the first committee were Henry Gaskell (solicitor) and Alexander Haliburton (iron-master).
(114) *Ibid*, 23 Mar 1822.
(115) Falkus (1967), p. 507.
(116) WGLCMB, 25 Jul 1822–14 Nov 1823.
(117) *Ibid*, 26 Jun 1823 and 10 Jul 1823.
(118) *Ibid*, 3 Aug 1822.

(119) *Ibid*, 6 May 1824.
(120) Peckston (1819), p. 411.
(121) Stewart (1962), p. 45 and Mitchell (1986), p. 90.
(122) *King's Treatise* (1878), p. 42.
(123) See later, pp. 127–128, for an analysis of this point.
(124) No record of the company's early history has survived.
(125) For the Manchester order see Mitchell (1986), p. 90.
(126) OGLWCMB is only available from 13 Jan 1826, but Malam is mentioned frequently thereafter.
(127) Up to 1826 only the Ashton-under-Lyne undertaking tried to imitate Oldham, but in fact this company never used its authority to build waterworks. Johnes & Clegg (1847), p. 95.
(128) OGLWCMB, 1 Jul 1826.
(129) *Ibid*, 11 Jun 1827.
(130) *Ibid*, 12 Aug 1827.
(131) Falkus (1967), p. 507 describes how he ran the Knaresborough gasworks until 1834.
(132) Everard (1949), p. 30.
(133) The company's records have not survived. See the *Chester Chronicle*, 10 Oct 1817, and Wilson (1991B).
(134) Stewart (1962), p. 10.
(135) Hemingway (1831), p. 337. The prominent local banker, G. B. Granville, appears to have been the leading promoter, along with S. J. Roberts, an attorney. Wilson (1991B).
(136) *Chester Chronicle*, 29 Jan 1819.
(137) *Ibid*, 30 Mar 1850.
(138) Hemingway (1831), p. 338.
(139) The company's early records have not survived.
(140) The only reference to this engineer was discovered in the *Westmorland Advertiser & Kendal Chronicle*, 19 Mar 1825.
(141) *Westmorland Gazette*, 16 Oct 1824.
(142) *Ibid*.
(143) Curwen (1900), p. 199.
(144) Paterson (1877), p. 5, relates how the first committee was made up of a solicitor, a gentleman and three warehouse proprietors, but little material has survived on this company.
(145) For a full description see Nabb (1986), p. 79.
(146) Paterson (1877), p. 5.
(147) *Ibid*, p. 6.
(148) Oil-gas could be made from oil extracted out of vegetables, fish, whale-meat or products like palm kernels. *King's Treatise* (1878), p. 35.
(149) For a full history of this firm see Rowlinson (1984) pp. 26–31.
(150) *Ibid*, p. 45, shows that oil-gas could produce three times as much light as an equal volume of coal-gas.
(151) *Ibid*, p. 31.
(152) This was certainly the case at Preston. Letter from Fr. J. Dunn to W. Scott.
(153) Rowlinson (1984), pp. 31–34.
(154) *Ibid*, p. 34.
(155) *Ibid*, p. 35.
(156) Harris (1956), p. 29.
(157) *Ibid*, p. 30. Even shareholders in the Liverpool Gas Light Co. purchased shares in the new venture.
(158) *Ibid*, pp. 31–32.
(159) *Ibid*.
(160) *Ibid*, pp. 41–42.

(161) Matthews (1832), p. 123.
(162) Rowlinson (1984), p. 46.
(163) *Ibid*, pp. 46−47.
(164) City of Manchester (1949), p. 22.
(165) Rowlinson (1984), p. 47.
(166) City of Manchester (1949), p. 22.
(167) *Ibid*.
(168) BnGLCCMB, 11 Feb 1818. Dr. More was to become Chairman of the Company, reflecting his large holding of 100 shares, but it is not known whether he was familiar with gas technology. Other prominent promoters were John Smith & William Crompton (cotton manufacturers), along with Isaac Dobson of the engineering trade.
(169) Clegg (1872), p. 12.
(170) BnGLCCMB, 14 Apr 1818.
(171) Spooner & Worthington had premises in Moor Lane, and the gasworks were built on land close by in what was to be known as Gas Street. Clegg (1872), p. 11.
(172) BnGLCCMB, 14 Apr 1818.
(173) PGLCMB, 9 Sept 1817.
(174) *Ibid*, 10 Apr 1817.
(175) See below, pp. 128−129.
(176) PGLCMB, 21 Jul 1818.
(177) Clegg (1872), p. 13.
(178) The company documents have not survived in manuscript form, but in Abram (1878) they are reproduced verbatim, and the actual date of each meeting will be quoted in the footnotes.
(179) BGLCMB, 30/3/18, 6/4/18 & 7/8/18.
(180) *Ibid*, 9/9/18.
(181) The first gas was supplied in Mar 1819. *Ibid*, 8/7/19.
(182) See later, pp. 133−135.
(183) It is possible that John Grafton built the Ashton-under-Lyne works, but no corroborating evidence can be found to prove this.
(184) Co Borough of Salford (1920), p. 10.
(185) *Ibid*.
(186) *New Manchester & Salford Directory for 1821/2* (Manchester, 1822).
(187) In 1831 the system was valued at just £6,000. Co Borough of Salford (1920), p. 15.
(188) Baines (1824), pp. 601−602.
(189) Bennett (1948), pp. 179 & 335.
(190) See later, pp. 39−40.
(191) See later, pp. 161−162.
(192) Falkus (1967), p. 503.
(193) Rowlinson (1984), p. 87.
(194) See later, pp. 46−48.
(195) See later, pp. 52−53.
(196) Falkus (1967), p. 503 calculates that 137 public gasworks were operating in the United Kingdom by 1826, while Nabb (1986), p. 214 feels that the upper limit could be as high as 145.
(197) Golisti (1984), Appendix 17.
(198) Nabb (1986), p. 298.
(199) Cotterill (1980−81), pp. 19−21.
(200) For individual case-studies see, respectively, Gill (1948), Lockwood (1980), and Roberts (1979), (1980) and (1978).

2
Growth and Maturity, 1827—1880

*'Tom would talk about his gas plant to everyone .....
He was so pleased with it. Everything about gas was
good and nothing could be bad, and this bubbling enthusi-
asm was infectious.'*

R. S. Neill, *Song of Sunrise* (1958).

After the initial surge in gasworks construction up to 1826, encompassing
towns ranging in size from Manchester and Liverpool down to Chorley and
Heywood, over the ensuing decades supply businesses began to appear in
an ever-increasing number of North West communities. The rush to imitate
the First Generation did not begin immediately, with only three new gas
companies appearing in the following six years (see Appendix A), but
gradually more towns were provided with public supply operations, and by
1880 ninety-six separate systems were in business. Gaslighting was clearly
becoming an essential component of urban life in this era, and communities
of widely differing origins and size were taking advantage of the technological
refinements continually being introduced. Important economic forces were
at play in this process of diffusion, but as in the last chapter we shall leave
the study of timing, motivation and financing till later, concentrating here
on describing when and how gaslighting came to many of the North West's
towns. This was a period of rapid growth for the British gas industry,(1)
and the region's undertakings certainly remained among the leading suppliers as they responded to the continued increase in demand for their
products. A feature of this growth was the diversification into extracting
more of the by-products from coal-gas, and by the mid-nineteenth century
significant revenue was being earned from a variety of residuals which in
the past had been allowed to run off as waste. It is a measure of their
growing sophistication as business ventures that the gas undertakings
were able to exploit these new markets, but one must not forget that until
the 1880s their income and profits were heavily dependent on the market
for gaslighting, and on this basis they enjoyed a lucrative period of expansion.

The commercial viability of gas supply was to attract the attention of two
potentially influential bodies, local government and parliament. While the
effects of the latter's interference in gas matters were not as damaging as
some contemporaries would have us believe,(2) it will become clear that as
far as the ownership of North West gasworks was concerned the impact of
the former was far-reaching as more towns copied the Manchester lead in
operating their own gasworks. Indeed, purely in terms of ownership patterns,
it is possible to see a sharp north/south divide emerging within the British
gas industry by the 1870s, by which time many North West gas companies

had been municipalised, and while the reasons behind this trend will be the main subject of Chapter 7 we shall examine here how it evolves. The influence of both local and central government is an essential aspect of the North West gas industry's nineteenth century history, and by providing this background material now it will be easier to understand some of the more detailed sections of later chapters.

Recounting the story of this interference also helps to reflect the industry's increasing industrial, financial and political significance after the earlier struggles to establish the industry between 1805 and 1826. A mature, profitable industry gradually emerged from that pioneering work, and such was gas-lighting's entrenched position by 1880 that it was well prepared for the imminent introduction of its most potent long-term rival, electricity. The struggle between these two energy sources lies outside our prescribed period, but it is important to state that, although problems undoubtedly lay in store for gas producers after 1900, during the nineteenth century their supremacy in the lighting market was barely dinted. In the North West the gas industry continued to flourish in a highly conducive environment, as the First Generation of undertakings built on the firm foundations laid by the early pioneers and new operations were established in communities all over the region. Even though ownership patterns do change markedly, it is a story of growth and financial viability to match any other utility in this period.

The Spread of Gaslighting

By the mid-1820s gaslighting in the North West was to be found mainly in the industrial and commercial towns of Lancashire. Only Kendal had the benefit of a public supply in Westmorland by this time, while in Cheshire the service was limited to Stockport, Macclesfield and Chester. Size of population was obviously an important determinant of where gas under-takings were established,(3) and for this reason one could hardly expect more North West towns outside Lancashire to feature in Appendix A up to 1826. On a nation-wide basis, by 1821 all towns with a population exceeding 50,000 had a public gasworks, and by 1826 only two with more than 10,000 (Lincoln and Whitehaven) were excluded.(4) This indicates that size was indeed a key consideration, and it was not until the 1830s and 1840s that the majority of medium and small-sized towns started to introduce gaslighting.

Appendix A illustrates how the North West was typical of the country as a whole, with communities of ever-decreasing magnitude beginning to build gasworks, from Bury (15,086) and Stalybridge (14,216) in the late 1820s to Clitheroe (5,213) and Leigh (3,000) in the 1830s.(5) Falkus speaks of the 'generality of gaslighting by the mid-nineteenth century' in the United Kingdom,(6) and in 1849 the *Journal of Gas Lighting* listed 760 towns having a public gas supply.(7) Table 2.1 has been compiled to give a clearer picture of the number of North West gas undertakings operating at various points within our period,(8) demonstrating that by 1847 this utility existed in forty-nine North West towns. The period 1815–1880 has been divided into four different phases for ease of reference, and this illustrates how after the late 1840s progress continued. Indeed, between 1848 and 1880 almost as many towns were added to the list (forty-seven) as had been provided with

Table 2.1 Number of gas undertakings and towns supplied in the North West, 1826–1880

	Private		Public		Total	
	A	B	A	B	A	B
1826	20	19	1	1	21	19
1847	45	44	5	5	50	49
1865	61	61	18	18	79	79
1880	51	51	45	45	96	96

Key: A = Undertakings; B = Towns

a public supply up to 1847 (forty-nine), indicating the extent to which gaslighting spread across the region.

Although gaslighting experienced a continuous process of diffusion within the North West after 1826, the geographical direction of this activity remained heavily oriented towards Lancashire's expanding towns. Over the next two decades Lancashire accounted for twenty-one of the thirty new undertakings formed in the region (see Appendix A), reflecting that county's dynamic growth in this period of industrialisation and urbanisation,(9) while nine operations appeared in Cheshire and none at all in Cumbria. This trend is only to be expected,(10) given Lancashire's larger population and greater economic significance, but to concentrate on geography is to ignore some of the more important features of the industry's dispersion across the region.

Up to 1826 the towns with a public gas supply could be broken down into two groups: firstly, the industrial and commercial centres like Manchester, Liverpool, Bolton, Blackburn and Preston; and secondly, the administrative centres like Chester, Lancaster and Kendal. These distinctions hide many similarities which existed linking all these towns, but in broad terms they are sufficient to allow some differentiation between the types of community possessing a gasworks. The first type was naturally predominant in 1826, and because of the North West's economic characteristics it remained so throughout our period, but increasingly after 1830 towns with widely differing functions were beginning to take advantage of the new illuminant. It is with this theme in mind that we can discuss the North West industry's progress, bringing in the equally important subjects of an undertaking's exact origin and its source of technical expertise. This approach will provide us with a detailed insight into the basic chronology revealed in Table 2.1 and Appendix A, and explain how gaslighting spread across the region in a period of rapid urban expansion.

(a) Industrial and Commercial Centres

By far the most dominant characteristic of those North West towns building public gas supply operations both before and after 1826 was their role as industrial and commercial centres. There are naturally many problems with this definition, in particular the tendency of most towns to have some

manufacturing and marketing functions. As the nineteenth century progressed, however, industrialisation was responsible for either the expansion
of relatively small communities or even the creation of new centres, allowing
an easier determination of function. This type of growth provided a fertile
breeding ground for the gas industry, and even though the first use of
gaslighting might have been in private premises often these operations
evolved into complete public services.

We noted in the last chapter that it was a common feature of many First
Generation gas undertakings that some of the original promoters would
have developed an interest in the new illuminant before persuading others
to finance a public works. From Fr. Dunn at Preston and the Police Commissioners at Manchester, many of the pioneers had already experimented
with gaslighting themselves, while at Chorley and Burnley cotton mill
plants provided the basis for the town's system.(11) After 1826 this continued
to be a fruitful source of initiative, and a succession of undertakings benefited
from the work of private suppliers. An illustration of this is provided by
one of the first companies established after 1826, once the early surge in
construction had been completed, at Stalybridge (see Appendix A). The gas
company here was formed in 1829 by five local cotton manufacturers, two of
whom, D. Harrison and G. Cheetham, were partners in a firm which had
been using gas for several years.(12) It should be noted that two other
millowners in the town had also been supplying their own gas since 1818,
but their names do not feature in the Stalybridge Gas Light Co. list of
promoters.(13) Nevertheless, gaslighting was already a common sight in the
town, and this would have facilitated the efforts of Harrison, Cheetham and
associates in establishing the venture.

This kind of connection between private use and public service was also
prominent in the formation of Bury Gas Light and Coke Co. in 1828. It is
well known that in 1806 Samuel Clegg had supplied plant to two Bury
mills,(14) and in 1818 an iron founder also started to manufacture his own
gas.(15) Given the town's size by the 1820s,(16) it is surprising that Bury did
not feature among the First Generation discussed in the last chapter, a
puzzle further deepened by the knowledge that at least three businesses
were lit with gas by 1818. Few records survive from this period, but it is
apparent that none of the private users were involved in the gas supply
operation's promotion or funding.(17) Nevertheless, others in the town
would have been made aware of the benefits arising from the new illuminant
by watching developments in those factories, and the decision to form a
public supply undertaking was probably influenced by the desire to gain
access to these benefits.

A more detailed illustration of this pattern of causation is provided by
Colne, where a gas company was created largely as a result of interest in
equipment used by a local cotton manufacturer. In fact, the source in this
case is a novel by Robert Neill, *Song of Sunrise*, and while generally historians
must be wary when relying on fictionalised accounts of real events it would
appear that this particular story line is based largely on hard facts.(18)
Admittedly, the book is a love-story set among the thrusting cotton manufacturers of east Lancashire, but an important sub-plot describes how one of
this group contrives to interest his neighbours in a public gas supply and
eventually forms the Colne Gas Light & Coke Co. It is a fascinating glimpse

into how promoters operated in the smaller industrial communities of the nineteenth century, bringing to the fore how important it was for potential subscribers and consumers to witness at first hand the advantages of gas-lighting. This was the strategy pursued by Nicholas England, one of the town's leading cotton manufacturers. He was not actually using gas at the time, but when a local rival, Thomas Thornber, brought gaslighting to Colne in the mid-1830s England realised that once the rest of the business community saw how this allowed him to increase his working day at a relatively cheap cost then they would all be clamouring for a supply.(19) The quotation at the head of this chapter indicates how extensively Thornber publicised the benefits of gaslighting, and within a year England was able to form the Colne Gas Light & Coke Co. after selling 150 £20 shares to forty-seven local investors.(20)

England's successful manipulation of his fellow citizens would not have been too dissimilar to the kind of practices pursued by influential business-men in communities all over the United Kingdom. We shall be examining these methods more thoroughly in Chapter 3, as well as the economic motivation behind such actions,(21) but they clearly reflect the growing acceptance of gaslighting once potential consumers had seen the illuminant at work. Certainly, just as at Bury and Stalybridge, Colne Gas Light & Coke Co. benefited from this interest, and although it did not evolve directly out of a private gas plant the venture was indirectly the result of Thornber's initiative. This demonstrates how local private gas users were instrumental in the construction of public supply systems in many North West towns, both before and after 1826.

Another case to illustrate how gas undertakings often emerged from the activities of individual gas manufacturers is Hyde Gas Co. As early as 1812, just prior to leaving the North West for London, Samuel Clegg had installed gas plant in the extensive Hyde cotton mill of Samuel Ashton & Bros.,(22) but it was 1844 before the town was given even a limited public supply. This service was provided by Isaac Booth, a local cotton manufacturer who has been described as 'a man of enterprise and public spirit'.(23) By the 1850s, though, at least ten separate gas suppliers existed in the town,(24) and while evidence on gas prices has not survived this anarchic situation would not have been conducive to efficiency. All the suppliers were actually millowners who appeared to vie with each other over the quality of their service to streets in the immediate vicinity of each factory. Booth was the largest supplier, but even he only covered a small area of Hyde, and the remainder rendered a limited service. Judging from their role in the early management of Hyde Gas Co., and from their substantial shareholding, it would appear to have been the Hibberts who were responsible for the rationalisation of gas supply in the town when in 1854 they entered into negotiations with the ten private suppliers.(25) They too were cotton manu-facturers and recognised the vital importance of integrating the systems and supplying from a central works in order to reduce costs. Booth, on the other hand, was not quite as public-spirited as his reputation implies, and he refused to sell his works unless in addition to its market value a payment of £2,000 was made for the goodwill associated with his gaslighting business.(26) The Hibberts eventually gave in to his demands, rather than have their scheme undermined by wasteful competition,(27) and by April 1855 £25,000 had been raised from local investors for the integration of the various systems.

On a slightly smaller scale from the Hyde Gas Co., but nevertheless demonstrating the growing awareness that centralised, integrated supply systems could offer cheaper prices, was the Droylsden New Gas Co. formed in 1857. The promoters stated in their memorandum of association that their aim was 'the supply of Gas to the mill-owners and inhabitants of Droylsden',(28) and it is revealing that they should prioritise their potential consumers in this way. In fact, the company was created by four groups of cotton millowners, all of whom had their own gas plant, and each sold this plant to the new supply company. The total price paid for the four works was £2,514, accounting for one-quarter of the venture's start-up capital,(29) but by 1865 £16,000 had been invested in the centralised system,(30) and clearly Manchester Corporation regarded this as a viable operation because in 1869 they purchased Droylsden New Gas Co. for £25,000. This was part of the town's expansionist strategy, to be described in Chapter 7,(31) but the key point here is how the private gas suppliers in Droylsden were moving towards more rationalised systems by the mid-century in order to reduce gas prices.

(b) *Interconnections*

The formation of gas companies at Hyde and Droylsden out of a group of private suppliers was symptomatic of the need for co-ordinated manufacturing and distribution systems to ensure that industrialists could take advantage of economies of scale, and that consumers could be offered lower prices. As we shall see in Chapters 5 & 6, this became one of the main strategic considerations as Directors strove to improve performance.(32) At the same time, though, it will also become apparent that their horizons were limited by political boundaries when planning extensions. Apart from Manchester and Liverpool, which will be discussed later,(33) there are very few cases of communities co-operating to provide a single supply for more than one town, and those examples which do exist were among the smaller industrial centres. Technological and financial constraints could well have combined to prevent more inter-connections, but these factors would only have been influential in the first two decades and it is more likely that the desire for political hegemony was the key reason why towns rarely co-operated on this issue. This discussion encroaches on what will be examined in Chapter 7, but it is important to understand that in the nineteenth century contemporaries regarded with great suspicion any interference with local independence, whether from central government or neighbouring towns,(34) and only in isolated cases can we find evidence of mutual assistance.

The earliest case of two towns building a single gasworks was at New Mills and Hayfield in 1836, followed by Radcliffe and Pilkington in 1845. In both cases the close proximity of each partner provided a strong logic for the co-operation, but unfortunately hardly any records have survived to explain how the companies coped with the problems of building such systems. We are better informed about two further cases of integration which occurred in the 1850s, at Farnworth and Kearsley and in the Rossendale valley. In the early-1850s, Farnworth cotton manufacturers had initially attempted to secure a supply from Bolton Gas Co., but such was the strength of local feeling against any possible assimilation into their larger neighbour that efforts were made to establish a new company. A gas supply had in fact been available since 1833, when a retailer, Thomas Berry, had extended his own personal system to cover the centre of Farnworth, but his prices were far too high at 9/- (45p) per thousand cubic feet.(35) By 1854 the Farnworth business community had also been successful in persuading their Kearsley counterparts to join them in creating a public gas supplier, and in August the Farnworth & Kearsley Gas Co. held its first public meeting.(36)

The Rossendale Union Gas Co., also formed in 1854, was another ambitious scheme, linking Bacup, Rawtenstall and several surrounding villages. A Bacup Gas Light & Coke Co. had been in business since 1835, but when in 1853 a group of Rawtenstall cotton manufacturers, led by James Whittaker, decided to form an undertaking in their town the logic of collaborating with their neighbours in Bacup persuaded them to seek a merger. The Bacup operation was just at that time applying for powers to incorporate the company and expand its system, making Whittaker's arguments especially convincing, and by October an agreement had been signed which led to the creation of Rossendale Union Gas Co. in 1854.(37)

In the early stages this new undertaking supplied the bulk of its gas either from private gasworks run by millowners or from the Bacup plant. The main private source was Ashworth's factory at Clough Fold, and for two years several private plants were linked together until the new system had been completed.(38) A brand new works was actually being built, in Rawtenstall, and by the autumn of 1856 the company was in a position to commence regular service.(39) In the meantime, all the private gas manufacturers had agreed to sell their plant to the company, and when the Rawtenstall works became operational an expanding market was placed at its disposal. However, while the Rossendale Union Gas Co. management was clearly able to cope with the technological and organisational problems associated with building such a system,(40) the Directors could do little to obviate any of the legal hold-ups which plagued the incorporating Bill's progress. No less than five petitions were lodged against their Bill in 1854, and in consequence £2,300 had to be spent by the company on attorneys and advisors while defending their scheme.(41) Some of the millowners also exacted a high price for their plant,(42) bringing the formation costs to a level which might have been prohibitive had the promoters been able to predict what was to happen. These legal and financial problems might also have discouraged other promoters from proceeding with similar rationalisation policies, although it is probable that the desire for local independence would have been a more important reason why mergers of this kind were so unusual. We shall return to this subject in later chapters, because it has such an important bearing on how companies devised their marketing strategies, but the Rossendale Union Gas Co. provides an illustration of both the possibilities for integrated systems by the mid-nineteenth century and the obstacles which prevented more combinations.

(c) New Industrial Towns

If few towns were willing to envisage sharing a gas supply in the nineteenth century, then the emphasis was placed even more heavily on local initiative. In certain places local government provided the stimulus,(43) but for the most part private businessmen were the main source of enterprise and relatively few copied the much earlier example of municipal action at Manchester. The need for private enterprise would have been particularly acute in the new towns emerging as a result of either the work of an individual or the introduction of industries into green-field sites. This was evidently the case at Fleetwood, because in the late-1830s Sir Peter Fleetwood converted 'a wild and desolate warren' on his Rossall estate into a thriving seaport.(44) The first building was only inhabited in 1836, but by 1840 the new town had been connected by railway to Preston, a market had been opened and the Fleetwood Gas Co. established. This undertaking was never a major supplier, but neither the town nor the company would have existed without the vision of Sir Peter Fleetwood, and operating through an agent he supervised the rapid growth of this port over the next two decades.

In a similar vein one might also categorise St. Helens and Widnes alongside Fleetwood. Although not created by individuals they owed their expansion to two families which encouraged both industrial and municipal improvement, infusing new life into what had been small communities up to the 1830s. At St. Helens it was Peter Greenall, the head of the local brewing business, who was the moving spirit behind the town's development, dominating its early administrative life and introducing coach services, railways, a water supply and gaslighting.(45) He was actually Chairman of the St. Helens Gas Light Co., formed in 1832, and until his death in 1846 he managed to ensure healthy relations were maintained between the utility and the local business community.(46) While Greenall dominated St. Helens up to 1846, in Widnes the main influence was John Hutchinson, the man who founded the chemical industry in that town when moving into the area in 1847.(47) In 1856 Hutchinson was also responsible for establishing the Widnes Gas and Water Co., and, although he continued to operate his own private gas plant supplying the village of Appleton, the undertaking was able to attract customers from the expanding number of chemical manufacturers attracted into the town.(48) The influence of Greenall at St. Helens and Hutchinson at Widnes proved vital in bringing services like gaslighting to these communites, and while neither could be described as company towns it is clear that they depended heavily on certain personalities to provide the necessary leadership.

The most obvious examples of company towns in the North West are those like Barrow and Crewe which sprang up as a result of railway activity. As Marshall has noted, Barrow 'was railway-inspired and railway-dominated' in the mid-nineteenth century,(49) with the Furness Railway Co. taking responsibility for the supply of water and gas sometime in the 1840s.(50) The management of these utilities was later passed to a subsidiary, the Barrow Gas & Water Co., created in 1863, and under James Ramsden, Furness Railway Co.'s resident administrator, the service became a highly profitable sideline. In similar fashion, the Crewe gasworks was constructed by the Grand Junction Railway Co. in 1842.(51) Although originally intended only for use in its engineering works, by the 1850s the company was supplying the town as a public service, demonstrating how reliant Crewe was on the paternalistic practices of such businesses.(52) This was also true of another company town, Poynton, where after 1845 the Vernon collieries provided gas from plant built within the confines of their own premises.(53) Here, too, the community was reliant upon its major employer, but one must remember that each of these towns was only supplied as a direct spin-off from the commercial considerations of the companies concerned, emphasising how paternalism was heavily tinged with economic motives in this era.

Barrow, Crewe and Poynton highlight in the extreme how important local initiative was to the establishment of gas undertakings in nineteenth century industrial towns. One must also notice how the industrialisation of North West communities and the dispersion of gaslighting were intimately connected, the latter benefiting from the impact of the former as the region's industries continued to expand. It would appear to have been the case that, after the 1830s, once a community was gripped by the industrial forces of the time a public gas supply would soon follow, indicating how gaslighting had become an essential feature of urban life in these towns. Nelson could be regarded as a microcosm of this relationship, because it grew from little more than a single public house in 1849 into a small industrial town within twenty years. In fact, in 1849 'Nelson' was the Nelson Inn at the junction of two turnpikes connecting Colne and Barrowford, but in that year the East Lancashire Railway Co. built a station nearby, and within a decade a range of shops, industries and workers had been attracted to the location.(54) In 1860, largely as a result of a local engineer's encouragement, the Nelson Gas Co. was created to supply this community,(55) and although the early supplies were provided from the Ecroyd mill plant,(56) by 1863 a central gas-works had been constructed. Nelson Gas Co. was naturally one of the smaller gas suppliers in the North West at this time, but its formation and early development illustrates how vital a relationship existed in the nineteenth century between industrialisation and the gas industry's progress. The two trends were intimately connected, and in later chapters we shall see how this relationship affected gas company financing, management and growth.

(d) *Market, Tourist and Residential Towns*

While the increased use of gaslighting in the North West was closely linked with the industrial and commercial progress of the time, it is also clear that from the late 1830s towns based on a variety of functions were beginning to recognise the need for a public supply. This was not altogether a new trend, because featuring among the First Generation of undertakings had been administrative and marketing centres like Chester, Lancaster and Kendal, but apart from these county towns none of their smaller counterparts had been as quick as the industrial communities to introduce gaslighting. The earliest market towns to have a public gas supply, Clitheroe (1836) and Kirkham (1838), were also developing a range of manufacturing indus-tries,(57) bringing up the problem of categorising towns once again. In fact, though, both of these companies were formed as a result of pressure from

commercial interests, and only at Clitheroe was a significant proportion of
the first share issue purchased by cotton millowners.(58)

The main impetus behind the creation of Clitheroe Gas Light Co. in 1836
would appear to have come from the town's professional people, small
workshop-owners and retailers, and the original prospectus showed more
concern about 'the dangerous state of the streets, resulting from the many
buildings which were then going forward', rather than supplying cotton
mills in the town.(59) At Kirkham, on the other hand, the powerful family
of cotton merchants headed by Edmund Birley was instrumental in bringing
gas to the town, buying 37% of the original shares and managing the
company in its early years.(60) They had evidently witnessed the benefits of
gaslighting at first hand in Manchester, because most of their extensive
business interests were based in that town,(61) and as a result the Kirkham
Gas Co. was created in 1838.

The introduction of gaslighting into towns like Clitheroe and Kirkham
was symptomatic of the illuminant's broader dispersion by this time, and
from the 1840s more of these communities copied the larger industrial
centres. Just as with Bolton, Burnley and Stockport, in some cases the
establishment of a public gas supply was also influenced by the prior use of
gaslighting in private installations. This was certainly the case at Altrincham,
where in 1844 the landlord of the Unicorn Hotel, George Massey, put down
a small works to light his premises and added a few street lamps to attract
customers.(62) Such was the impression he created on local retailers, merchants and professional people that within two years the Altrincham Gas
Light Co. had been formed with a capital of £5,000. Massey must not have
played any direct role in actually promoting this venture, because his name
appears in neither the list of shareholders nor the first Board of Directors,(63)
but indirectly he had been the instigator, and until the construction of a
new works in 1847 his plant also provided all the gas used in Altrincham.(64) It
was a pattern of development which became common in the nineteenth
century — the Wilmslow and Alderley Edge Gas Co. (1872) was preceded by
a service based on Bower's cotton mill(65) — continuing a theme we developed
in the last chapter.

Not only were the small market towns beginning to take advantage of
gaslighting from the late-1830s, by the 1840s some of the region's tourist
resorts were considering the introduction of this service to improve facilities
for their visitors. The earliest illustration of this trend was at Lytham, where
'the delightful and invigorating influences of the climate and sea were well
and widely appreciated by the populace of the large inland towns'.(66)
Once connected to the expanding railway system, in 1846, its future as an
important resort on the Fylde coast was assured, and by 1847 a gasworks
had been built to light the streets, hotels, shops, taverns and offices of the
town.(67) Interestingly, it was the local Improvement Commissioners who
initiated this utility, a feature this resort shares with its larger neighbour,
Blackpool, and the resort one can see across the Ribble estuary from Lytham,
Southport. Why the local authorities should be so active in these places we
shall see in Chapter 7,(68) but clearly private enterprise was not as keen to
invest in such services at resorts.(69)

Although in 1853 the Blackpool Improvement Commissioners erected the
town's coal-gas plant, in fact two years earlier a group of tar and turpentine

distillers based in Hull had formed the Vegetable Oil Gas Light Co. to provide gaslighting in towns not yet supplied. They introduced their first oil-gas plant in 1851 at Settle, Yorkshire,(70) and in the same year installed a system on the outskirts of Blackpool.(71) Hardly anything is known about these businessmen, but it is notable that this was only the second time a gas company had been formed in the North West by entrepreneurs based outside the region. One should also indicate that, just like its earlier counterpart, the Provincial Portable Gas Co.,(72) it soon failed, emphasising how uncompetitive oil-gas remained when compared to the much cheaper coal-gas. The Blackpool Improvement Commissioners were consequently obliged to step in and build the coal-gas plant in order to supply gaslighting at a lower price, bringing the resort into line with its rivals along the Lancashire coastline.

The role played by local government in starting a public gas service links the towns of Lytham, Blackpool and Southport, but strangely the latter two share another common feature, in that oil-gas plant was used in the first stages. Of course, Blackpool's unsuccessful experiment with oil-gas was imposed upon the town by outsiders, but at Southport it was the local Improvement Commissioners who initially chose Stephen White's hydrocarbon gas plant for the public undertaking.(73) White's process, using resin as the main raw material, had created general interest in the late-1840s,(74) and his sale of some plant to the Assembly Rooms in Southport persuaded the Commissioners to use this equipment. Bailey claims that the town had been reluctant to introduce coal-gas because the hoteliers had 'certain qualms as to its possible effects on the atmosphere',(75) but the hydrocarbon plant offered a better quality of lighting free from the odorous nature of coal-gas.(76) The Southport Improvement Commissioners had been established in 1846 principally to enhance conditions in the resort, but in opting for White's process they had unwittingly imposed high prices on the local business community, and by 1852 they were being pressured into converting to coal-gas.(77) It was calculated that the oil-gas price would have to be at least 10/- (50p) per thousand cubic feet in order to break even,(78) and as by this time coal-gas prices in the region had fallen to around 6/6d (32.5p) the Commissioners were forced to reassess the position.(79) King concluded that the hydrocarbon process 'was eventually condemned, chiefly on the ground of its uncertainty and wastefulness',(80) and at Southport prices had been reduced to 5/6d (27.5p) after going over to coal-gas in 1852, demonstrating that there is little doubt which method was most cost-effective.(81)

Southport's experiment with hydrocarbon gas, and Blackpool's equally brief liaison with the Vegetable Oil Gas Co., were extremely unusual for the time, because after the earlier flurry of excitement over oil-gas in the 1820s coal-gas had dominated the British scene. The resorts were obviously attempting to create a comfortable environment for tourists by using the better quality oil-gas, but their conversion to coal-gas indicates that the operation of such utilities was firmly based on commercial considerations. The local authorities were indeed anxious that gaslighting should not become a drain on the rates, a point we shall consider again in Chapter 7.(82) Nevertheless, the supply of gas was clearly no longer the preserve of industrial or commercial centres, with residential towns and resorts building systems by the

1840s. This dispersion continued throughout our period, covering the spa-town of Buxton (1850) and the emerging spots like Ambleside (1868), St. Annes (1876) and Formby (1877). Even small suburbs like Woolton (1856), Rainhill (1870) and Hoylake (1878) were initiating gas companies, along with the villages of Kirkby Lonsdale (1849), Lymm (1861) and Blackrod (1861). A detailed economic analysis of the industry's progress is necessary before this process of dispersion can be fully understood,(83) but at least we are now aware of the background, and in later pages we can follow the discussion with some knowledge of the chronology.

Expansion and Investment

Simply tracing the number of gas undertakings operating in the North West, and examining the economic character of towns responsible for the utilities is an instructive method of charting the industry's expansion up to 1880, but this only tells part of the story. A brief scan of Appendix B indicates that not only did the number of public gasworks increase rapidly from the 1820s, the scale of their operations also grew at an impressive rate. Indeed, especially for the large First Generation undertakings, demand for gaslighting accelerated so quickly that continual pressure was placed on their capacity and greater levels of fixed investment were required. Table 2.2 is the first attempt at calculating the gross historical cost of this investment by North West gas undertakings, showing clearly how between the 1820s and 1870s the amount spent on plant and mains rose to almost £8.5 million. A particularly revealing feature of Table 2.2 is the average investment figure, because this indicates how the scale of operations jumped markedly from 1847: the average undertaking had increased in size by just £6,600 between 1826 and 1847, but in the next eighteen years it rose by over £24,000, and from 1865 to 1880 the mean reached £88,465, over three times the 1847 figure. Of course, averages hide the enormous differences in size within the region,(84) but clearly from mid-century growth was demon-strably greater than in the first decades, and as we shall see in Chapter 6 this story is paralleled by the expansion in sales.

Examining Table 2.2 (and Appendix B) gives a detailed insight into how the North West gas industry evolved up to 1880. The reasons for this expansion, and how it was managed, will be discussed in Chapters 5 & 6, but we can give some indications here of the basic stimuli. Above all, it was the growth in demand for gaslighting which underpinned the whole story, and especiall from the 1830s management was able to exploit the highly price elastic nature of the demand for gas to stimulate consumption. In simple terms,(85) this meant that prices were reduced significantly from an average of around 10/- (50p) per thousand cubic feet in 1830 to approxi-mately 6/6d (32.5p) by 1847, encouraging both traditional (millowners, local authorities, shopkeepers, publicans and offices) and new (domestic) consumers either to take more gas or to apply for a supply. As the price fell even further, to about 3/6d (17.5p) by 1880, the undertakings were able to attract even more custom, giving rise to the increase in investment charted in Table 2.2. At the same time, even though the more significant phases of growth evidently came after 1847, when the average investment per under-taking increased almost three-fold, even in the earlier decades, especially for the larger First Generation businesses at Manchester, Liverpool, Bolton,

Table 2.2 Capital invested in North West gas undertakings, 1826–1880 (£)

	PRIVATE			MUNICIPAL			TOTAL		
	Capital Invested	Number of Undertakings	Average Investment	Capital Invested	Number of Undertakings	Average Investment	Capital Invested	Number of Undertakings	Average Investment
1826	373,701	20	18,685	55,014	1	55,014	421,401	21	20,067
1847	977,747	45	21,727	355,428	5	71,086	1,333,175	50	26,663
1865	2,597,728	61	42,585	1,406,936	18	78,163	4,004,664	79	50,692
1880	2,923,327	51	57,320	5,569,286	45	123,762	8,492,613	96	88,465

Sources: See Appendix B

Blackburn and Preston, steady progress was being made (see Appendix B).

Although the sensitivity of gas consumption to successive price reductions provided the basis for expansion after 1830, it is important to remember that running in parallel with this trend was the diversification of output. From the very outset, as the names of companies like the Bolton Gas Light & Coke Co. indicate, promoters had recognised the possibility that income could be earned not only from gaslighting, but also from the coke produced after coal had been carbonised in the retorts. This was an especially valuable by-product, because in towns located at a distance from coalfields, for example Kendal, their main raw material could be expensive, yet some of this increased cost could be recouped from sales of coke which would command a higher price than in places like Wigan. Carbonised coke could also be used as a substitute for coal to heat up the retorts, reducing costs even further. The main problem with coal-gas coke, though, was that to manufacture good quality, luminous gas this meant producing a poor quality, soft coke.(86) This would have reduced the value of coke as a by-product, because management were naturally more concerned about their staple source of income, and consequently only low quality material was produced. The price of coke was also extremely variable − at Liverpool, for example, in 1850 it was sold at 5/- (25p) per ton, but four years later this had risen to 15/- (75p)(87) making it an unreliable revenue earner.

In fact, until the 1840s by-product sales represented only a small proportion of total income, and in the early decades most residuals were actually allowed either to dissipate into the air or were disposed of as waste.(88) Only slowly did supply undertakings recognise the potential in this business, and in Manchester's case it was a matter of responding to the pressures imposed by a consumer. Coal-gas consists of many valuable chemical components which in turn can be used to extract other materials.(89) The tar, for example, which accumulated in retorts, holders and mains can produce naphtha, a compound which Charles Mackintosh used to treat cloth in order to manufacture water-resistant coats, and in 1834 he was negotiating with the Manchester Gas Committee for a regular supply of this derivative.(90) Mackintosh's factory had been built alongside Fernley's gasworks at Gaythorn but at this stage he could not buy enough naphtha from that small business, and Manchester's gasworks was consequently asked to develop new plant for producing this compound.(91)

Mackintosh's relationship with the Manchester gasworks was extremely unusual in the commercialisation of by-product manufacture, although by the 1840s a greater awareness of the possibilities in this field had emerged generally. The coke, tar, ammonia, sulphur and naphtha income had consequently started to grow by mid-century, and as Appendix D reveals some companies were able to generate a good business in these areas. However, one must not forget that the manufacture of by-products was entirely dependent upon the amount of coal carbonised, subjugating the whole operation to the lighting market. It would have been uneconomical to have produced gas just for the by-products, and in this context one must be wary when describing gasworks as diversified businesses, because they could not turn to alternative markets when demand for gaslighting slumped. By-products never even approached becoming the lifeblood of any undertaking, and management relied principally on the gaslighting market for the bulk of their business.

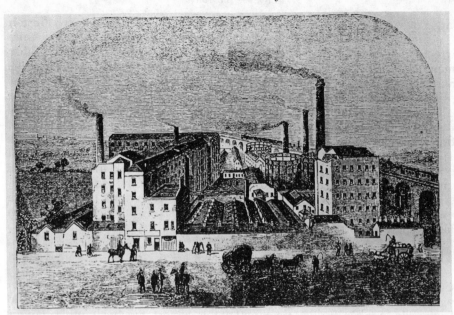

The Gaythorn site in Manchester, with the gasworks on the right (formerly that of the Provincial Portable Gas Co.) and Mackintosh's factory on the left.

By-and-large, the growth depicted in Table 2.2 was internally generated, businesses adding to capacity as the levels of consumption dictated. Few opportunities existed within North West towns for expanding externally through acquisitions or mergers, firstly because in only a few communities were rival operations established to compete with entrenched suppliers,(92) and secondly because only a small number of inter-connections were attempted at this time.(93) The whole subject of competition will be discussed in Chapter 6, but in contrast to London individual North West companies rarely faced much opposition from new challengers, and where they did combination was always the solution. Liverpool was the most celebrated example of a market where two companies vied for the available custom, resulting in the merger of 1848,(94) while Manchester also expanded territorially by acquiring neighbouring companies.(95) Kendal, Chester, Haslingden and Accrington are rather different cases where competition existed for a brief period, and we shall see in Chapter 6 how their problems were created and settled, but while the latent threat of competition could influence management strategy, in the main the existence of a rival was not a major concern for most North West gas companies.(96)

In the North West one of the key considerations of gas companies in this respect was a proliferation of private plants, some of which supplied neighbouring streets and premises. We saw in the last section how often these small operations either formed the nucleus of a public supply business or encouraged others to initiate a service, but for established suppliers they could also hamper expansion plans. The easiest solution to this predicament was to purchase the plant and incorporate any mains which existed into the larger system, creating a more stable environment for future growth. Preston Gas Light Co. pursued this very strategy in 1839, absorbing a small venture which had been started twelve years earlier by a group of four cotton manufacturers located in a part of the town not then supplied with gas.(97) Similar instances can be found in other places: at Accrington the Oakenshaw printworks gas plant was bought in 1862;(98) the Wigan Gas Light Co. paid £200 to a cotton millowner 'to do away with their gasworks and take all their gas from the company';(99) and in 1863 the Widnes Gas and Water Co. finally acquired Hutchinson's private plant supplying Appleton Village.(100) These external strategies were very much the exception, of course, and because of the localised nature of gas manufacture and distribution internal growth remained the dynamic force behind most of the expansion experienced in the North West. Again, both Manchester and Liverpool were exceptional in some of the strategies they pursued, but few undertakings had access to the scale of demand generated in those towns.

The Gas Engineer

Central to the expansion of North West gas undertakings described so far was the ability of management to organise this growth technologically and financially. A more detailed treatment of this subject must wait until Chapters 5 and 6,(101) but it is essential to emphasise how the Engineer slowly gained in status and eventually became the focus of strategic decision-making. We saw in the last chapter that the contractor system had acted as the crucial vehicle helping to diffuse gas technology in the industry's early years, with engineers like Grafton, Malam, the Barlows and even Samuel Clegg travelling around the region designing and installing supply systems. By the 1820s this profession of gas engineer had become much more stable, and individuals were more likely to base themselves in one particular town and act as both Engineer to an undertaking and consultant to smaller operations elsewhere. This is an indication of the profession's growing maturity, and even John Grafton and John Malam settled down to this new role.(102) Within the North West the Engineers to larger supply operations took on the mantle once held by contractors as the source of technical expertise, and companies formed after 1826 frequently called on the services of these experts.

Probably the most famous North West gas engineer of this period was Thomas Newbigging. Born in 1833, he had started a distinguished career as engineering apprentice in Blackburn, and by 1857 had risen to the post of Engineer and Secretary to the Rossendale Union Gas Co. Newbigging stayed there until 1870, when he left the country to take up a position as Engineer to the Pernambuco Gasworks in Brazil, returning to England in 1875 and setting up a consulting business in Manchester.(103) His most notable achievement was the publication of *The Gas Managers' Handbook* in 1870, in which he laid down basic guidelines on how a supply undertaking should be managed and advising Engineers on the mounting number of legal controls imposed on the industry.(104) Other books and articles of his covered the detailed organisation of a company's operations, providing the kind of advice in written form which a travelling contractor would have provided in the earlier years.

Not quite rivalling Newbigging for national impact, but nevertheless influencing the process of diffusion within the North West, was a group of Engineers who advised several undertakings on the type of plant to install. John Rofe, for example, the Preston Gas Light Co. Engineer between 1839 and 1861, was responsible for either the original design or the extension of works at Hyde, Warrington, Kirkham and Wigan. He later moved to London as a consultant, and his successor at Preston, H. Green, also inherited his advisory role at Wigan.(105) Orlando Brothers of Blackburn was similarly in great demand at Wigan and Darwen, and other prominent local Engineers included George Emmott at Oldham and the Kings at Liverpool. Their names are often mentioned in the client company's Board minutes whenever major engineering issues arose, continuing the traditions established by the pioneering contractors of the industry's first years. Only rarely did North West companies look outside the region for technical advice,(106) indicating how well they were served by this time, in contrast to the earlier period when a dire shortage of expertise could have constrained the diffusion process. After the 1820s the Engineers, along with many specialist engineering firms,(107) provided all the services required in this important period of expansion, and such was the growth in gaslighting that men like Rofe, Brothers, Emmott and the Kings were constantly in demand. It was a system which evolved naturally from the one which had been so instrumental in creating provincial gas industries between 1815 and 1826, and the only complaints voiced about the new breed was their tendency to form manufacturing concerns through which most of their designs were supplied.(108)

The continuous expansion of capacity revealed in Table 2.2 demonstrates that the pool of technical talent in the region was capable of effectively answering the calls made by companies on their services. We shall also see in Chapter 6 that these Engineers gained such a position of influence over management that by the 1840s Directors were dominated by the advice coming from their technical staff. Indeed, it was the Engineer who orchestrated the growth illustrated in Table 2.2, and on the basis of his calculations and plans decisions were made affecting the course of gaslighting's progress in this era. At the same time, greater political interference in gas affairs was experienced from the 1840s, and management was obliged to monitor closely both local and central government's attitude towards the industry

Political Interference

As a public utility it was inevitable that the gas industry should be regulated by central government, and certainly in the nineteenth century a series of controls was introduced to ensure that consumers were not exploited by what could often be an outright monopoly. In this context, we take as our definition of the term 'public utility' that offered by Chantler, which states that 'the public utilities are a group of economic undertakings of recognised social importance, which are subject to special measures of intervention by public authority'.(109) These controls ranged over prices and profits, as well as standards of service and later even an obligation to supply. As we shall see, though, only slowly did the gas industry fall strictly within this definition, because measures were only introduced in a piecemeal fashion spanning the whole of our period, but in providing a service to the public, often as a monopoly, the undertakings were always seen by legislators as potential sources of difficulty. The details relating to each particular regulation will be discussed at length where appropriate in the following chapters, but it is important to understand that gas supply was the subject of much parliamentary debate in the nineteenth century, and politicians used a variety of methods to protect consumers.

Until the late—1840s direct competition was regarded as the most effective method of controlling gas companies, contemporaries arguing that prices and profits would find their 'natural' level if two or more systems were allowed to supply a community.(110) Detailed controls relating to numbers of Directors, company meetings, presentations of accounts and an obligation to supply street lamps at a cheaper price than oil were from 1812 always included in private Acts secured by gas companies, but as we shall see in the next chapter by no means all applied for such statutes, and many were run on the basis of deeds of settlement drawn up by local attorneys.(111) Statutory incorporation was the best guarantee of securing rights to break open the streets for main-laying purposes, not to mention providing shareholders with limited liability, but such Acts never guaranteed sole access to a particular market and often in large towns companies faced severe competition. The situation was most problematic in London, where by mid-century thirteen separate companies had been established, and it was not unusual for the mains of three or four systems to run down the same street in the more affluent areas.(112) In the North West there was less of a problem, but even in towns with only one supplier the threat of competition always existed, and we shall see later how local authorities frequently used this threat to secure cheaper street lighting.

Although as early as 1818 the companies at Oxford and Nottingham had been limited to paying a maximum dividend of 10% on their shares,(113) only rarely did parliament impose such restrictions over the next twenty-five years. Both companies at Liverpool were actually affected by this particular regulation when applying for statutory authority to raise extra capital between 1834 and 1841,(114) but no other North West undertaking was controlled in this way until the 1847 Gasworks Clauses Act was passed. The detailed operation of this measure will be examined in the next chapters,(115) but in short it consolidated all 'provisions usually contained in Acts authorising the making of gasworks for supplying towns with gas' into a single Act which could then be included in any statute sought by a gas company.(116) This new Act also specified a 10% maximum dividend, and at the same time laid down that a maximum price should also be imposed. It was a decisive switch in direction away from the earlier belief in competition as the most effective form of regulation, and while the control would only be applied to companies when they sought another private Act, the Gasworks Clauses Act in time became a central feature of most gas company constitutions. However, as we shall see later, these controls were largely ineffective, mainly because the maxima set were too generous to encourage companies either to extend their systems or reduce their prices much further, and in any case most managements were able to manipulate pricing levels in order to guarantee regular 10% dividends by the 1840s.(117) Matthews argues that the main forces operating on London gas companies were those relating to costs, rather than parliamentary controls or consumer pressures on prices,(118) and although for the North West one must stress the influence of potential or actual competition, as well as local government interference, management operated in a relatively unfettered environment free from the impact of statutory regulations.

In the three decades following parliament's first consolidated attempt to introduce effective controls on all gas companies through the 1847 Act, successive modifications were attached to private statutes. The most notable of these changes was a reduction in the maximum dividends to be paid on new capital to 7%, introduced from the mid-1850s. The capital raised earlier, of course, was still allowed to earn 10%, but fresh issues could only pay predetermined lower returns.(119) In 1871 the government revised and standardised the miscellany of controls by passing a Gasworks Clauses Amendment Act to update its 1847 predecessor. This new legislation retained all the regulations on maximum dividends and prices, thus perpetuating the problems which had existed for several decades, but in insisting on an obligation to supply any consumers living within fifty yards of a company's mains it broke new ground. By introducing such obligations, along with more regulations on the quality of gaslighting and compelling companies to supply gas continuously,(120) the state was consequently bringing the industry within the definition of a public utility offered earlier, providing controls which carried a sense of social duty. At the same time, while central government controls on dividends and prices were initially not very effective,(121) North West gas companies faced increasingly powerful bodies at local government level which were far more instrumental in affecting management strategy and control.

One of the main reasons why statutory regulations were tightened and broadened in the 1860s and 1870s was the growing level of municipal interest in gaslighting. Local authorities were at that time experiencing a major change in emphasis with regard to their responsibilities as providers of certain services, and in areas north of a line stretching from Cardiff to King's Lynn there was a move towards municipalisation of industries like gas supply.(122) An obvious feature of Tables 2.1 and 2.2 (and Appendix A) which has so far been purposely ignored is how within the North West there was a significant growth in the number of municipal gasworks after 1847. Indeed, as we demonstrated in the last chapter, Manchester is the very home of municipal trading, its Police Commissioners having built and managed a utility since 1817, and later passing the works on to Manchester Corporation in 1843.(123) Only in Yorkshire, at Keighley (1824) and Beverley (1825), did local authorities attempt to imitate Manchester in those early years,(124) because private enterprise was then regarded as the natural vehicle for public utilities. Slowly, though, this attitude was modified and municipal trading by the 1860s came to be accepted in the Midlands, Wales, the north of England and Scotland as an acceptable feature of a local authority's duties. Why this change occurred, and what effect it had on the North West gas industry, we shall discuss in Chapter 7, but it was one of the most far-reaching aspects of the nineteenth century growth in local government.

In the North West, beginning at Manchester and later spreading to some of that town's larger neighbours (see Appendix A), municipal trading made a slow start, affecting just five systems by 1847. Their average investment was much higher than the private operations, as Table 2.2 reveals, but this comparison is misleading because in 1847 Manchester constituted two-thirds of the municipal total capital (see Appendix B). Appendix A illustrates how the main surge in local authority acquisitions came after 1860, and by 1880 there were forty-five municipal gasworks. This trend can be further highlighted by examining Table 2.2, which shows that, although it had taken almost forty years to increase its share of total capital invested in the North West gas industry from 12.8% to 35.1% in 1865, by 1880 the municipal sector accounted for almost two-thirds of this total.

Municipalisation was clearly catching on quickly in the North West by mid-century, and when one compares the average investment of private and municipal gas suppliers in Table 2.2 this reveals how particularly in the larger industrial towns the policy was extremely popular. Indeed, although there are more private undertakings in 1880, the municipal sector is almost twice as large when measured in terms of sales or capital. Table 2.3 provides a breakdown of the top twenty businesses in each sector measured by sales, and again there is a big difference in the scale of operations. The most striking feature of Table 2.3 is that, while the companies at Liverpool and Preston were comparable in size with the top ten municipal undertakings, only the first nine private operations would have fitted into the top twenty municipal suppliers. This contrast is further emphasised when we take an

Table 2.3 Top twenty private and municipal undertakings in the North West by 1881 (sales in million cubic feet)

	Private			Municipal	
1)	Liverpool United	2,220.1	1)	Manchester	2,181.7
2)	Preston	317.0	2)	Salford	659.3
3)	Ashton	142.8	3)	Oldham	547.6
4)	Stalybridge	141.7	4)	Bolton	449.5
5)	Accrington	125.8	5)	Blackburn	316.7
6)	Rossendale	118.0	6)	Stockport	252.7
7)	Chester United	109.2	7)	Birkenhead	247.5
8)	Stretford	75.4	8)	Rochdale	246.5
9)	Hyde	70.0	9)	Bury	194.1
10)	Radcliffe & Pilkington	62.9	10)	Burnley	194.1
11)	Farnworth & Kearsley	59.4	11)	Wigan	172.3
12)	Altrincham	57.6	12)	Southport	151.3
13)	Ramsbottom	41.2	13)	Warrington	125.2
14)	Runcorn	33.3	14)	St. Helens	114.7
15)	Haslingden Union	30.7	15)	Darwen	86.0
16)	Kendal Union	27.6	16)	Barrow	81.3
17)	Todmorden	25.8	17)	Macclesfield	79.5
18)	Littleborough	24.8	18)	Wallasey	67.4
19)	Ormskirk	16.2	19)	Dukinfield	67.3
20)	Wilmslow & Alderley Edge	15.9	20)	Widnes	66.1
	TOTAL	3,715.4		TOTAL	6,300.8

Source: PP, *1881 Return*

average sales figure for each column: the figure for the twenty companies would be 185.5 million cubic feet, and that for the municipal sector 70% greater at 315 million. If we were to exclude the distorting influences of Liverpool United and Manchester from each column, the averages would then be 78.7 million and 216.8 million, respectively, confirming the size of the gap which emerged between the two groups.

Municipal trading had become an established feature of North West local government by the 1860s and 1870s, and especially in the larger towns where the impact of urbanisation and industrialisation was felt greatest. Why this was the case, and why such important companies as Liverpool United and Preston remained in private hands, we shall attempt to explain in Chapter 7. Of course, the North West was not unusual in this respect, and in most regions outside the south of England municipalisation continued apace, albeit in a rather patternless fashion, throughout this period. However, at no time did the state provide local authorities with powers to build or purchase gasworks without the prior permission of a company's shareholders. Local improvement Acts were passed sanctioning the construction of gasworks, but in these cases no private operation had been established in the towns affected. Even when the powers and finances of local government were strengthened by the 1872 Borough Funds Act and the 1875 Public Health Act,(125) companies were still not faced with compulsory purchase orders. We shall also see in Chapter 7 that, as Matthews comments, 'municipal ownership involved no interference with the rights of property',(126) because shareholders were generously compensated for passing control to local authorities.(127) It is a fascinating story which requires a detailed understanding of how government at the local level evolved out of the chaos prevailing in the early nineteenth century into a system capable of dealing with the wide range of challenges facing communities as a result of urbanisation and industrialisation. The North West gas industry was affected by all these forces, and they provide an essential part of the backcloth to our study.

The North West Gas Industry by 1880

The North West gas industry had passed through a period of considerable expansion up to 1880, with growth particularly marked from the late-1840s. Table 2.2 reveals the extent and pace of this increase in activity, illustrating how capital investment had risen to almost £8.5 million by the end of our period, compared to £421,401 in 1826. This was an impressive rate of progress based on the widespread use of gaslighting across the region in towns with a wide variety of economic and social functions. By 1881, as Table 2.4 shows, almost half a million consumers were being supplied in the region, and total consumption exceeded 10,600 million cubic feet. Unfortunately, it is extremely difficult to compare this performance with that in other regions, partly because few comparable studies have been concluded to date,(128) and partly because official returns were woefully inadequate. There were two surveys by the Board of Trade, in 1847 and 1866, but they were only intended to cover those companies incorporated by a private Act, and in any case some failed to comply with requests for information. Regular official returns were only instituted by the Board of Trade in 1881, and even

Table 2.4   Capital, sales and consumers for A) England and Wales, and B) North
           West, by 1881

A: England and Wales

	Issued Capital and Loans (£)	Number of Undertakings	Sales (in million cubic feet)	Consumers (Number)
Private	30,586,622	338	42,263	946,997
Municipal	14,039,583	121	16,613	634,657
Total	44,626,205	459	58,876	1,581,654

B: North West

Private	2,865,867	40	3,843	155,389
Municipal	5,564,286	44	6,848	289,063
Total	8,430,153	84	10,691	444,452

Source: PP, *1881 Return*

then many non-statutory gas companies were excluded. This is why in
Table 2.4 only eighty-four North West gas undertakings are covered, leaving
out twelve (admittedly small) operations.(129)

Although Table 2.4 has some weaknesses, it is nevertheless useful as an
illustration of both the size of the gas industry by that time and the
divisions in ownership which had emerged since the 1850s. In England and
Wales as a whole, the private sector accounted for 68.5% of issued capital
and loans and 71.8% of sales, while in the North West the positions were
almost reversed, the municipal sector providing 66% and 64.2%, respectively.
This reveals the large municipal bias which had emerged in regions north
of that Cardiff—King's Lynn line, but one might well ask whether the
figures for England and Wales are distorted by the inclusion of London's
huge private companies. If the four London undertakings were excluded
from Section A of Table 2.4 then the municipal sector would have contributed
45.6% of the capital and 41.5% of the sales. This would give a better
indication of how public ownership was advancing in England and Wales
generally, and even though non-statutory companies are not covered by the
survey they would not have altered the balance significantly.(130)

A more detailed examination of the 1881 Board of Trade returns also
reveals another feature which had in fact always been a characteristic of the
gas industry. In fact, by 1826 a pyramidical hierarchy had already emerged,
with the London companies at the peak and the tiny enterprises of Chorley
and Heywood at the base,(131) and in 1881 this hierarchy was still evident
on both national and regional scales. In the North West, judged simply on
sales, two undertakings could claim sales in excess of 2,000 million cubic
feet, five sold between 300 and 2,000 million cubic feet, twenty-eight sold
between 50 and 299 million cubic feet, and forty-nine sold less than 50
million cubic feet.(132) This structure was an inevitable consequence of the
localised nature of gas supply, with size depending on the area within a
business's franchise. Civic independence, and large start-up costs, had

prevented many cases of interconnections between different towns, as we saw earlier, and in any case only in smaller communities were such links forged in an attempt to pool resources and provide a more cost-effective service. Municipalisation reinforced the trend towards a localisation of gas supply by strengthening the control of local authorities over their districts, and although Manchester's undertaking expanded by acquiring neighbouring companies this was an exceptional case. The hierarchical structure remained a permanent feature of the gas industry right up to nationalisation in 1949, and only in the last thirty years has an integrated supply system emerged with the introduction of natural gas.

Another conclusion we can draw from the 1881 Board of Trade return was that the North West gas industry probably exceeded in size any outside London. The capital was still the dominant force it had been since 1812, but if in 1881 the four London companies had invested £13.8 million, and the North West undertakings £8.4 million, this leaves just over £22 million for the rest of England and Wales.(133) The figures on gas consumption would not provide a different picture, London and the North West contributing approximately 29,500 million cubic feet to the total of 58,876 million cubic feet. Table 2.5 can also be used to indicate how individual North West gas undertakings were among the largest in the United Kingdom outside London. One must put this into perspective by pointing out that by 1881 the Gas Light & Coke Co. (formerly the Chartered Co.) and the South Metropolitan Co. were recording sales of 12,169 million cubic feet and 3,645 million cubic feet, respectively, putting them well ahead of any other British operation, but two North West undertakings were among the three leading provincial

Table 2.5 Top twenty provincial gas undertakings by sales in 1881 (million cubic feet)

(1)	Birmingham Corporation	2,726.2
(2)	Liverpool United	2,220.1
(3)	Manchester Corporation	2,181.7
(4)	Glasgow	1,975.0
(5)	Leeds Corporation	1,342.3
(6)	Sheffield Corporation	1,131.7
(7)	Dublin	1,019.0
(8)	Nottingham Corporation	956.4
(9)	Bristol United	947.0
(10)	Newcastle & Gateshead	927.2
(11)	Bradford Corporation	882.5
(12)	Salford Corporation	659.3
(13)	Edinburgh	585.0
(14)	Belfast	572.0
(15)	Leicester Corporation	571.4
(16)	Oldham Corporation	547.6
(17)	Bolton Corporation	449.5
(18)	Portsea Island	371.0
(19)	Hull (part of British Gas Light Co.)	368.8
(20)	Brighton & Hove	360.5

Source: PP, *1881 Return*

gas suppliers, and another three featured in the top twenty. It is also revealing to note that just outside this group we can find Preston Gas Co. (317 million) and Blackburn Corporation (316.7 million), indicating the industry's size across the region.(134) Indeed, with two of the largest towns in the country (Manchester and Liverpool) and the leading British industry (cotton) stimulating growth in other centres, the North West provided an expanding market for gaslighting, and it is for these reasons that the region produced such a large gas industry.

Having played a leading role in the gas industry's early evolution after 1805, the North West retained its position of importance by stimulating the creation of the largest group of undertakings outside London. Expanding initially with the general impact of increasing industrialisation and population growth, as we shall see in Chapter 6 by the 1840s the domestic market was beginning to feature more prominently in marketing strategy as better technology and cheaper raw materials allowed reductions in gas prices.(135) Management also slowly realised that demand for gaslighting was extremely price sensitive, and as this elasticity precipitated an almost continuous increase in consumption then ever-greater investment in capacity ensued, resulting in the rapid expansion charted in Table 2.2. Although the balance of gas undertaking ownership swung from private into public hands, no political obstacles were placed in the way of gas supply becoming one of the major public utilities in the nineteenth century. In the North West the industry received every encouragement from both private and municipal supporters, producing a utility of strength and vitality which proved capable of exploiting an expanding market. In the next chapters we shall add substance to the issues outlined briefly in these introductory pages, bringing to life a story which is both fascinating in itself and relevant to so many issues in British economic and social history.

Footnotes

(1) See Falkus (1967), pp. 496−505, for the period up to 1850. No adequate history of the late nineteenth century exists, but see Matthews (1983) and Nabb (1986) for views of individual regions.

(2) The *Journal of Gas Lighting* complained bitterly about, for example, the introduction of auction clauses and the sliding scale system. JOGL, 1 May 1877, p. 657.

(3) See Robson (1973) for a study of this subject.

(4) Falkus (1967), p. 496.

(5) The population figures are taken from the 1831 Census.

(6) Falkus (1967), p. 499.

(7) JOGL, 10 Mar 1849, pp. 25−26.

(8) The problem with Appendix A is that all the public supply businesses established between 1815 and 1880 are listed, and some were derived from earlier businesses.

(9) Useful background to this story can be found in Walton (1987), pp. 103−124 and 198−220.

(10) Lancaster was still an important port in the early nineteenth century, and Kendal had substantial manufacturing businesses. See Schofield (1946), pp. 36−52.

(11) See above, pp. 26−27.

(12) March (1957), pp. 104–5.
(13) The other private gas users were J. Leech at his Grosvenor Street mill, and George Adshead in Stayley St. *Ibid*, p. 104.
(14) Stewart (1962), p. 3.
(15) Barton (1973), p. 101. The iron founder was Benjamin Bassett of Rochdale Road.
(16) The town had a population of 15,086 in 1831.
(17) The names of these private users do not appear in the list of shareholders. Bury Gas Act, 9 Geo. IV, 1928, p. 2.
(18) Neill (1958). The story concurs with evidence found relating to the company's original promoters and subscribers. See Articles of Agreement of Colne Gas Light & Coke Co., 17 Dec 1838.
(19) *Ibid*, pp. 152–173. England is quoted as saying: 'It's no good talking to 'em yet, not till Thornber's running till seven each night and they're shutting down at three. That'll work their money loose. It'll drive 'em mad.'
(20) England purchased ten of these shares himself, and at the company's first meeting was appointed Chairman. See Appendix C for a view of the company's profits, and pp. 152–153 for a brief analysis of its performance.
(21) See later, pp. 86–88.
(22) Stewart (1962), p. 5.
(23) Middleton (1932), p. 196.
(24) HGCBM, 12 Feb. 1855.
(25) The Hibbert family held 245 of the 2,464 £10 shares issued in 1854, Samuel Hibbert was appointed Chairman of the company, and Joseph and John Hibbert also sat on the Board. HGCBM, 12 Feb and 18 Jun 1855.
(26) *Ibid*.
(27) *Ibid*.
(28) Droylsden New Gas Co. Memorandum of Association, 1857, p. 3. It is claimed that the first gas company in Droylsden, formed in 1851, had failed by 1856, but no information can be found to corroborate this story. See City of Manchester (1949), p. 34.
(29) Droylsden New Gas Co. Memorandum of Association, 1857, pp. 3–6.
(30) PP, (1866).
(31) See later, pp. 191–194.
(32) See later, pp. 131–134.
(33) For Liverpool see pp. 171–173, and for Manchester see p. 194.
(34) For a general discussion of this subject see Fraser (1976), pp. 1–10.
(35) See later, pp. 163–165, for a study of prices.
(36) This story is related in Barton (1887), pp. 60–67, but nothing further is known about the company.
(37) Rossendale Union Gas Act, 17 Vict., Cap xxvi, 1854.
(38) RUGCMB, 10 Feb 1854–11 Nov 1855.
(39) *Ibid*, 18 Oct 1856.
(40) They hired the services of Thomas Hawkesley, the Nottingham Gas Light Co. Engineer. See *Ibid*, 21 Aug 1854, and Roberts (1980), pp. 10–12.
(41) RUGCMB, 21 Aug 1854. The main objectors were a group of Bacup ratepayers, a Bacup cotton manufacturer, Haslingden & Rawtenstall Waterworks Co., and Haslingden Gas Light & Coke Co.
(42) One millowner was paid £3,000. *Ibid*, 1 Aug 1854.
(43) See later, pp. 204–206.
(44) This story is told in Porter (1876), p. 227.
(45) See Barker & Harris (1954), pp. 91–103 and 290–313. In 1831 St. Helens had a population of 6,500, but by 1845 this had grown to 11,800.
(46) SHGLCBM, 9 Apr 1832. See later, pp. 152–154.
(47) See Hunt (1958).

(48) *Ibid* (1958), pp. 177–179.

(49) Marshall (1958), p. 281.

(50) It has not proved possible to establish the exact date when a gasworks was built in Barrow, but the ordnance survey map drawn in 1849 indicates the existence of this utility on exactly the same site as that used by the Barrow Gas & Water Co. from 1863.

(51) Chaloner (1950), p. 54.

(52) *Ibid*, Chapter Four.

(53) Shercliffe, Kitching & Ryan (1983), p. 32.

(54) Smith (1921) and Bennett (1957) provide a detailed history of these towns.

(55) John Landless, a Nelson millwright, was largely responsible for creating this company. Nelson Gas Co. Memorandum of Association, 27 July 1860, p. 5.

(56) Bennett (1957), p. 175. The Ecroyds were the leading cotton manufacturers in the town, and later agreed to take their gas from the company.

(57) For a study of Clitheroe see Thompson (n.d.), pp. 1–11.

(58) See later, p. 146.

(59) Thompson (n.d.), p. 13.

(60) KGCBM, 23 Apr 1840, and see later, p. 146.

(61) The Birleys were leading Manchester cotton manufacturers, and in fact had purchased gas plant for their mills from Boulton & Watt in 1807. Falkus (1982), p. 224.

(62) Ingham (1879), p. 178.

(63) AGCBM for 1846.

(64) Ingham (1879), pp. 178–179.

(65) Hodson (1974), p. 46.

(66) Porter (1876), p. 443.

(67) *Ibid*, p. 447.

(68) See later, pp. 204–206.

(69) See later, pp. 224–226.

(70) Golisti (1984), p. 37.

(71) Turner & Palmer (1981), p. 18.

(72) See earlier, pp. 24–25.

(73) Bailey (1955), p. 129. See also Harris (1956), pp. 169–174 for a more detailed description.

(74) JOGL, 10 Oct 1850, pp. 302–303, and 11 Nov 1850, pp. 317–318.

(75) Bailey (1955), p. 129. See also later, pp. 85–86.

(76) See earlier, pp. 7–8, for a discussion of this subject.

(77) Bland (1887), pp. 111 & 129.

(78) JOGL, 11 Nov 1850, p. 318.

(79) See later, p. 164, for the source of this information.

(80) *King's Treatise* (1878), p. 342.

(81) Bland (1887), p. 129.

(82) See later, pp. 210–211.

(83) See later, pp. 160–163.

(84) This subject will be discussed on pp. 54–55.

(85) See later, pp. 163–166, for an analysis of price trends.

(86) Rowlinson (1984), pp. 10–12.

(87) Harris (1956), p. 64.

(88) At Bolton the tar was burnt in a plant erected outside the town, and the ammoniacal liquor was run off into a brook. Clegg (1872), p. 28.

(89) The major constituents of coal-gas are hydrogen (47%), methane (23.5%), carbon monoxide (14%), nitrogen (9%), unsaturated hydrocarbon (3%), carbon dioxide (2.5%), and oxygen (1%). Smith & Lefevre (1932), p. 26.

(90) MGCM 16/5/34.

(91) City of Manchester (1949), p. 49.

(92)   See later, pp. 170−171.
(93)   See earlier, pp. 40−41.
(94)   Harris (1956), pp. 29−57.
(95)   City of Manchester (1949), pp. 16−35.
(96)   See later, pp. 170−177.
(97)   Eastwood (1988), p. 62. This venture was created mainly by the Rodgetts, and their factories were located in Bow Lane. See later, pp. 138−139.
(98)   Singleton (1928), p. 114.
(99)   WGLCMB, 3 Apr 1851.
(100) Hunt (1958), p. 179. See earlier, p. 42.
(101) See later, pp. 154−159.
(102) Grafton was based in Wolverhampton, and later moved to Cambridge. Stewart (1962), p. 47.
(103) Information kindly supplied by Rawtenstall Library.
(104) This book went through seven editions.
(105) WGLCMB, 6 Feb 1862.
(106) Rossendale Union Gas Co. hired the Nottingham Engineer, Thomas Hawkesley. RUGCMB, 21 Aug 1854.
(107) See later, pp. 154−159.
(108) For example, Orlando Brothers manufactured retorts and mains, and Blackburn Gas Light Co. Directors felt that this business sometimes distracted his attentions.
(109) Chantler (1939), p. 60.
(110) *Ibid*, pp. 60−66.
(111) See later, pp. 74−77.
(112) Matthews (1986), p. 256.
(113) Chantler (1939), p. 66.
(114) The Liverpool New Gas & Coke Co. was limited to 10% dividends in 1834, and in 1840 the same restriction was imposed on the Liverpool Gas Light Co. Harris (1956), pp. 42 and 53.
(115) See later, pp. 101−102.
(116) Gasworks Clauses Act, 1847.
(117) See later, pp. 109−111, and Chantler (1939), pp. 67−72, and Rowlinson (1984), pp. 99−104.
(118) Matthews (1986), p. 246.
(119) Chantler (1939), p. 68.
(120) *Ibid*, pp. 75−79.
(121) See later, pp. 108−109, for a discussion of auction clauses and sliding scale regulations introduced in the 1870s.
(122) PP (1945). See also later, pp. 203−204.
(123) See Mitchell (1986).
(124) Golisti (1984), p. 39.
(125) See later, pp. 204−206.
(126) Matthews (1986), p. 261.
(127) See later, pp. 208−209.
(128) See Nabb (1986) for a study of the South West, London is covered by Matthews (1983), and Cotterill (1980−81) has examined Scotland. The only other known attempt to cover a region is the work by Golisti (1984) on North Yorkshire, but this does not provide information on either investment or sales.
(129) The one municipal operation excluded was the small works at Dalton, and the eleven companies were at Northwich, Crewe, Poynton, Marple, Sandbach, Kirkby Lonsdale, Cheadle, Middlewich, Milnthorpe, Ambleside and Carnforth. All the latter were either unincorporated ventures or were owned by railway and coal companies.

(130) The eleven North West private companies excluded from the 1881 Return had invested an estimated total of just £57,460 by 1881. See Appendix B.
(131) See earlier, pp. 28–29.
(132) PP, 1881 Return.
(133) *Ibid.*
(134) *Ibid.*
(135) See later, pp. 160–163.

3

Company Creation and Capital Formation to 1826

> 'The original shareholders in the undertaking...were
> afforded a sufficient opportunity of exercising those
> virtues, so necessary for men who embark in trading
> enterprise in all generations — faith and patience.'

> W. A. Abram, *History of the Blackburn Gas Light Co.*
> (Blackburn, 1878), p. 3.

It has been firmly established in the previous chapters that local initiative and capital were responsible for the creation of public gas supply operations in almost all North West towns. Although much of the technical expertise had been recruited from London in the early years, and two short-lived ventures at Manchester and Blackpool were formed by businessmen based outside the region,(1) all the other companies emerged principally out of the willingness of manufacturers, retailers and professional people living and working within a particular community to form their own supply operation and finance its start-up. Of course, in contrast to utilities like turnpike trusts, canals and railways, which connected at least two, and often many more, towns, gas undertakings supplied only one community, and for this reason they were entirely dependent upon local support. This is a vital feature of the pattern in which North West gas companies appeared throughout the nineteenth century, and in this chapter we shall examine in detail how it affected the creation and financing of First Generation undertakings up to 1826. How were the businesses promoted? What type of constitution did they adopt? Why did investors risk their money in such ventures? And what impact did all this activity have on general developments in these areas? Each question will be discussed at length, providing not only a closer view of early nineteenth century provincial capital formation, but also a basis for the later analysis of management strategy. There will inevitably be some overlap here, because before we can understand why shares were purchased by certain groups it is essential that the market for gaslighting is discussed, but in performing this brief analysis of early consumption patterns we will reveal the main motives for investing in North West gas companies, as well as explain the common ownership structures which emerged at that time. It is also important to note that we are here primarily concerned with private enterprise, and Manchester will be excluded from our deliberations in an attempt to show how venture capital was raised in a crucial period for the gas industry.

The first half of the nineteenth century was an important learning phase in the development of investment practices. As relatively large businesses gas companies needed to raise capital by selling shares, but company law was only just beginning to emerge from over a century of stagnation, and the general legal situation regarding limited liability was shrouded in uncertainty. Company promoters had already improvised with a range of devices to protect shareholders' interests, and although from 1825 parliament started to repair some of the damage done to company law in the eighteenth century, it was several decades before the situation was clarified and wider use of the joint stock company form made possible.(2) Railway investment in the 1830s and 1840s played a leading role in precipitating these improvements, but one should not forget that the practice of financing companies had been evolving for at least sixty years, and both canal and gas undertakings had played important parts in preparing the ground for the later reforms.(3)

A central figure in this story will be the company's attorney. Not only was he responsible for guiding management through the legal difficulties of the time and drafting the requisite articles of association, he also acted as subscription and share transfer agent, raising all the fixed capital required in this period of steady expansion. The provincial attorney had grown in stature as a financial intermediary during the eighteenth century, and when the early North West gas companies were created promoters used the extensive local contacts built up by the legal profession to sell shares. This was by no means unique to gas companies, because both canals and railways used attorneys in exactly the same way,(4) but it will become apparent how for the region's private gas undertakings this relationship endured longer than in other sectors. The story will be continued into the next chapter, but it is important to establish just how vital this bond became during the promotion and financing of First Generation ventures. Above all, the process was a localised phenomenon revolving around the attorney, and while coffee houses and taverns might have been the main channels for this activity the system proved capable of satisfying the capital requirements of each company over at least seven decades. How this situation evolved will be the main subject here, and why it retained its strength will be discussed in Chapter 4, helping to explain how in the nineteenth century gas shares became such a staple feature of the provincial investment scene.

Legal and Financial Background

When F. A. Winsor floated the National Light and Heat Co. in 1807 he and his supporters were ill-prepared for the five-year struggle which lay ahead in securing a Royal Charter to incorporate the business as a joint stock company.(5) Ever since 1720, when the Bubble Act was passed, incorporation had been granted sparingly by a parliament which felt that promoters and financiers could not be trusted with unfettered access to limited liability.(6) The Bubble Act had been drafted after a fierce bout of speculation in ventures of dubious viability, ranging from the manufacture of perpetual motion machines to the extraction of silver from lead. This frenzy culminated in the spectacular collapse of a company formed in 1710 to fund £10 million of the National Debt. Known as the South Sea Co., but with precious little knowledge of overseas trading, by 1720 its share price had declined in value by 85%. A secret parliamentary committee was set up to investigate the situation, and this revealed not only serious accounting irregularities in the company's books, but also corruption at the highest levels of government with regard to its stock. At the same time, another 190 unsuccessful companies were formed in a short period of excited behaviour in 1719–1720, during which shares to the value of £220 million were issued.(7) To bring the speculative fever to a halt, and stabilise public confidence in an unpopular government, the 1720 Bubble Act was enacted. In short, this measure stipulated that, unless firms were incorporated by Royal Charter or Act of Parliament, they had no rights to transfer their shares or have more than six partners, effectively ending the general use of the joint stock company form in England for over a century.(8)

The main problem with this pernicious legislation was that it made incorporation expensive,(9) while arising out of the early eighteenth century speculative mania, during which large losses were made, the joint stock company became associated with 'a malign perversion of industry, destructive of commercial probity, [and] of a well-ordered social life'.(10) Later, influential economists like Adam Smith also made this form of organisation synonymous with monopoly and inefficient management, reinforcing the widespread feelings of animosity felt towards limited liability.(11) As a consequence, well into the nineteenth century English business was pervaded by strong individualistic tendencies, and the partnership system remained the basic organisational form. This was especially the case in manufacturing industry, where small-scale operations dominated and the expense of incorporating a business was prohibitive. During the eighteenth century insurance, utility and trading operations were the only sectors to take advantage of full incorporation, and it is no coincidence that these contained some of the largest businesses in the country at that time.(12)

The joint stock company form provides promoters with the opportunity to raise large amounts of capital by selling shares in their venture to an unspecified number of subscribers. This spreads the risk of starting a company, while limited liability ensures that the shareholder would lose only his or her investment if the business was liquidated. On the other hand, simple partnerships offered no such security, all partners being liable to pay a company's debts from their personal resources. For large businesses in particular, limited liability was essential if sufficient capital was to be raised, and in the eighteenth century canal promoters had recognised the strength of this argument. By 1800, over 100 Canal Acts had been passed, beginning in 1766 with the Duke of Bridgewater's scheme and peaking in the 'canal mania' of 1791–1794, when eighty-one were enacted.(13) The canals, more than any other sector, were responsible for popularising the joint stock company form as a vehicle for raising significant sums, one contemporary noting in 1808 that 'the frequency of subscriptions for making canals had showed the facility of raising large sums in this manner for any public undertaking'.(14) Another key point about these ventures was that much of the capital came from local businessmen whose operations would be directly affected by their creation, and as Ward demonstrates this familiarised large numbers of manufacturers and commercial men with the practice of investing in companies other than their own.(15)

The Chartered Co. and Alternatives

Although canals had achieved much in overcoming some of the popular prejudices associated with joint stock companies, and in the process raised

over £20 million,(16) contemporaries were still wary when faced with highly
speculative manias like that of 1807 and 1808. Tooke described these years
as a 'period of almost universal excitement, leading as usual to hazardous
adventure',(17) and one of the ventures for which many had little respect
was Winsor's £1 million National Light & Heat Co. of 1807. There was
natural caution about his claim that investors could earn £570 per annum on
each £5 invested,(18) and Wilberforce was not far wrong when he described
the scheme as 'one of the greatest bubbles ever imposed upon public
credulity'.(19) This was an inauspicious start for the public gas supply
industry, especially when in 1809 the Bill was rejected after detailed investigations had been completed by a parliamentary Select Committee.

It must be emphasised that Winsor's Bill had failed because his outlandish
claims could not be supported, not because the authorities were averse to
granting limited liability to gaslighting companies. One can confirm this by
noting how in 1810 the forceful James L. Grant revamped the scheme,
reduced the capital to £200,000, excluded Winsor from the new organisation,
and successfully re-applied for parliamentary permission to incorporate the
company.(20) Of course, it was only in 1812 that a Royal Charter was finally
granted to the Chartered Gas Light & Coke Co. (or Chartered Co., as it was
more commonly known), but this further delay was a measure of the
damage Winsor had done to the cause of public gas supplying, rather than a
reflection on the revised prospectus. The German entrepreneur had destroyed
public gas supply's technical and commercial credibility, and it was only
after Clegg's successes in 1814 that the Chartered Co. was able to restore
some of this lost confidence.(21)

The incorporation of the Chartered Co. in 1812 was a significant milestone in
the history of gas supply, not least because this brought into existence the
world's first public gaslighting company. In an organisational sense, the
company's 1812 Act was also to become a model for the industry, setting
down a wide range of regulations which later came to be accepted as
standard practice when provincial gas undertakings were deciding on their
constitution. Many of the general joint stock company regulations had
actually been devised as means of controlling how canal operations should
raise their capital,(22) when their meetings should be called, the manner in
which shares should be transferred, and the pattern of land acquisition.
This illustrates how company formation had already been evolving for
several decades,(23) but it is important to note that the Chartered Co. did
pioneer one aspect of company law which came into general use after 1812,
preventing management paying dividends out of capital raised from share
issues.(24) In general terms, though, its constitution was similar to that of a
canal company, providing the management with a clear legal status for their
operations.

Where the Chartered Co.'s Act would differ, of course, was in the clauses
specifically relating to gas supply, and in this respect it certainly did introduce
the ground-rules for early gas companies. The most fundamental of these
controls, and one which in the nineteenth century parliament steadfastly
refused to change, was that no monopoly was granted to any gas supplier,
reflecting the contemporary antipathy towards this level of market control.(25)
Although no maximum prices, or dividends, were imposed, street lighting
contracts could be nullified if gaslighting became more expensive than oil,

and they were even obliged to supply public lamps in streets where mains had been laid. The obligation to supply was regarded as one of the prices the Chartered Co. had to pay for permission to break open the streets and lay its mains, but it is interesting to note that while the early North West gas companies copied many of the other regulations they were reluctant to abide by this particular stipulation, the majority preferring to negotiate with the local authority on the subject of street lighting.(26)

By 1812, then, the joint stock company form had become an acceptable vehicle for organising and financing public gas supply businesses which required large amounts of capital. The Chartered Co.'s 1812 Act had set a crucial precedent in this respect, not only in securing access to limited liability, but also in having statutory main-laying rights included in the constitution. These were to be two of the most important reasons why gas companies sought full incorporation by Act of Parliament, providing security for their shareholders and access to the streets, and although parliament resisted pleas for the monopolistic control of a district promoters were still able to promise some guarantees when floating their schemes. Another advantage of being a joint stock company was that as a corporate body they could then sue for damages, and this was vital in protecting company funds in cases of fraud or theft.(27) However, applying for a private Bill was still expensive and long-winded. Of course, no company had to wait as long as the Chartered Co. for its sanctioning Act, but the cost of hiring legal and parliamentary advisors, and following a Bill through both Houses, could materially affect initial viability by raising formation costs to prohibitively high levels.(28) Businessmen in other sectors had also baulked at incurring all this expense, and consequently in the late eighteenth century an unincorporated form of organisation emerged which substituted a deed of settlement for the Act and provided subscribers with the same rights.

The unincorporated company, as Cottrell notes, was 'in a grey area of the law',(29) because it combined different aspects of the law relating to both partnerships and land ownership. Technically, because of the ability to transfer shares in these businesses it contravened the 1720 Bubble Act, and in fact between 1807 and 1825 several unincorporated ventures were actually deemed illegal by the courts for this reason.(30) These judgements naturally caused some alarm in business circles, but such was the widespread use of deeds of settlement by the 1810s that in general they were allowed to co-exist with their incorporated counterparts. Hunt argues that this unincorporated form 'was one of the main lines of advance towards freedom of incorporation' in the early nineteenth century,(31) and for many small and medium-sized North West gas companies it offered the security of limited liability without the expense of securing an Act of Parliament. We shall see later how in certain cases the failure to incorporate a company, and consequently gain statutory permission to lay mains in the streets, could create difficulties when management negotiated with local authorities,(32) but organisationally the unincorporated form obviated many of the difficulties facing promoters at that time. Indeed, one could well argue that company law could have forestalled the entry of several small ventures into the gaslighting market, by raising high financial barriers at the time of incorporation, but this possibility is too hypothetical to consider seriously. It is sufficient to say that, in spite of the limitations imposed by the 1720 Bubble

Act, both incorporated and unincorporated gas companies were regarded
by promoters of public utilities as acceptable forms of organisation by the
1810s, and these legal instruments facilitated the expansion of the North
West gas industry over the following seventy years.(33)

Once gas companies were beginning to appear in larger numbers after
1812, whether incorporated or not their promotion and creation took on a
standardised format. Again, reflecting their pioneering role in this field, it
was the canals which had been responsible for developing a system that
survived into the 1840s and was widely used by the early railway industry.
Evans has described how the promoters, who were usually locals themselves,(34) publicised their schemes by posting adverts either in local newspapers or in popular meeting places like coffee houses and taverns located
in the communities to be directly affected by the project. A public meeting
was then called of the town's 'prominent citizens' (landowners, manufacturers, bankers and attorneys) to discuss the prospectus. If sufficient interest
could be generated a committee was appointed from within the assembled
group to raise the initial subscription fund, and once the project was
supported by a significant number of these 'prominent citizens' a general
share issue was announced at a second public meeting. This would be
followed by a period of frenzied activity involving promoters and potential
subscribers, and after most of the shares had been sold permission would
be sought from the local authorities to go ahead with the project. It was at
this stage that some deviation can be discerned, some companies deciding
on full incorporation by private Act, some choosing to use the deed of
settlement, but in all cases the promoters needed to promise investors that
their liability for any of the company's debts was limited only to the
amount they had spent on shares. This was a vital aspect of the relationship
between promoters and shareholders, and whichever legal path was taken
the companies always used limited liability. The process also shows how
company creation was highly localised at this time, and in this context it is
important to understand how the provincial capital market operated in
response to these demands.

The 1720 Bubble Act had aimed a devastating blow at the emerging
London capital market of the early eighteenth century.(35) By making illegal
the transfer of shares in all but a few incorporated ventures, it forced
investors and financiers, operating mainly out of the coffee houses around
Exchange Alley in the City of London, to concentrate on the areas of state
funding, mortgages and trade credit. There is evidence that a highly complex
structure of financial services evolved after 1720,(36) and in 1773 the London
Stock Exchange was formally established, but such was the scarcity of
company shares that only rarely were they traded in this expanding market.
Another feature of the City's specialisation in the eighteenth century was
the gulf which existed between this activity and provincial capital formation.
It is too dangerous to speculate on whether the City would have supported
provincial companies had the 1720 Bubble Act not been passed, although
the spread of joint stock enterprises could well have forged links between
the financial centre and manufacturing areas, but what is certain is how,
outside London, capital markets became informal and localised, based on
kinship or personal contacts and local knowledge.(37) As late as 1850 a

parliamentary Select Committee noted how 'the advantage of local investments in the immediate vicinity of shareholders must not be overlooked',
contemporaries being more interested in 'enterprises...managed by those
whom they have long known and trusted, and whom they have chosen'.(38)
This was the prevailing situation when gaslighting first came on the scene,
illustrating how local business communities were essentially self-supporting
when it came to financing projects affecting their own towns, and in the
following pages we shall see how the industry exploited this system to the
full.

While we have demonstrated the central role played by local initiative
and capital in this scenario, one cannot discuss the subject fully without
emphasising the linchpin in the system, 'the familiar and trusted figure of
their local attorney'.(39) In the absence of specialist financial intermediaries,
the attorney had been drawn into the field of capital formation through his
work in the land and mortgage markets, acting as the intermediary in an
increasing number of financial transactions during the eighteenth century.
Pressnell has described the attorney as 'the key man' in provincial financial
matters by this time,(40) and Evans shows how both canals and railways
benefited from their services.(41) One might not go as far as Anderson in
describing a typical Lancashire attorney's office as 'in all important respects,
a capital market',(42) but certainly they were widely regarded as effective
mobilisers of local capital resources. There was some contemporary criticism
of 'scheming attorneys' promoting dubious railway companies in the
1820s,(43) but in general their reputation was entirely suited to the delicate
task of persuading potential investors to purchase shares in an enterprise.
In fact, the attorneys would have had a dual importance, because their legal
expertise was also essential in drafting the requisite articles of association
for the new company and unravelling the intricacies of early nineteenth
century company law. This advisory role was just as important as their
ability to raise capital, and we shall see in the next section that without the
advice and contacts of a prominent local attorney few North West gas
companies would have survived the often traumatic inception process.

The localised nature of investment practices and the central role of attorneys
were the two distinguishing characteristics of provincial capital formation
which most benefited North West gas companies. Restrictions imposed
upon joint stock ventures by the 1720 Bubble Act complicated the legal
process of constituting businesses, but by the time supply operations were
beginning to appear in the region not only had a standardised format
evolved for creating companies, there was also an unincorporated variant
which significantly reduced the cost of acquiring limited liability status.
The early nineteenth century was a period of improvisation and experimentation in these areas, and gas companies were very much in the mainstream
of attempts to improve the methods of forming and financing provincial
utility businesses. Their experiences were by no means unique, and canals
had in fact pioneered many of the techniques in vogue by the 1810s, but by
exploiting the system successfully gas company promoters were able to
raise all the capital they needed, and at the same time reinforce the strength
of arguments advocating both reform of company law and improvements in
methods of capital mobilisation.

Inaugural Procedures

When it comes to surveying the manner of gas company creation up to 1826, and discussing how they decided on which legal status to adopt, we are provided with a fascinating glimpse into contemporary practices. There are cases which must be excluded from our survey, in particular the municipal venture at Manchester, the private plant at Salford, and the Provincial Portable Gas Co.,(44) but the other eighteen companies are still an interesting sample. Unfortunately, time has been unkind to the historian, and while for some businesses a wealth of information has survived several left hardly anything. This creates unwanted gaps in our database, but by searching through what remains it is possible to discern a series of common features which support the view that both company creation and capital formation in the provinces were beginning to conform to a set pattern. As we saw earlier, the canals had been mainly responsible for laying down ground-rules in these areas, as well as introducing such practices to a large number of local business communities, while attorneys had also developed some familiarity with the techniques required for a successful promotion. These were vital features of the provincial scene by the early nineteenth century, and the North West's earliest gas companies benefited enormously from tapping into this rich seam of experience. Space prevents a detailed review of each case, but by pointing to certain features we can highlight the essential characteristics of the industry. Table 3.1 has also been compiled to reveal basic information on all eighteen companies, where it exists, and on this basis a general overview can be produced.

Once a group of promoters had decided to introduce gaslighting into their community, either by converting private plant into a public system or, more commonly, by building gasworks and laying mains designed by specialist contractors, they were then obliged to follow the series of steps described earlier in order to raise capital and constitute the business on legally acceptable lines. The first task was to interest what Evans called the town's 'prominent citizens' in the project,(45) and press them to attend a meeting at which a prospectus would be discussed. In Preston's case the instigator of the scheme, Fr. Dunn, used the Literary & Philosophical Society he had created in 1810 to recruit supporters for his ideas.(46) The Treasurer of the Society, Isaac Wilcockson, was also owner-editor of the *Preston Chronicle*, and he used this medium to expose the glaring inadequacies of oil lamps in order to publicise the advantages of gaslighting. Liverpool's coal-gas company promoters, headed by Jonathan Varty and Charles Lawrence, did not benefit from the existence of a scientific network like the one influencing events in Preston, but the *Liverpool Mercury* had been as critical as the *Preston Chronicle* of poor street lighting, reporting on 'the accidents which are perpetually occurring by night in such towns as this, when alterations are so frequently making in buildings, paving etc'.(47) The *Mercury* also took a close interest in gaslighting once the Liverpool Gas Light Co. had been created in August 1815, and in March 1816 its editor even purchased a share in the undertaking.(48)

The support of local newspaper proprietors was clearly of great assistance to the region's first gas company promoters at Preston and Liverpool, and some potential investors would have been attracted to these ventures by

Table 3.1 Capital of early North West gas companies 1815–26

	Year of Creation	Year of Incorporation	Issued Capital A	Issued Capital B	Share Value A	Share Value B	First Dividend	Venue of First Meeting
Preston	1815	1839	2,000	17,100	10	15	1821	Red Lion
Liverpool (Coal)	1815	1818	6,000	50,000	30	100	1819	Crown Inn
Macclesfield	1817	1824	N/A	N/A	N/A	N/A	1822	N/A
Chester	1817	1845	13,700	13,700	20	20	1821	N/A
Bolton	1818	1820	7,300	15,000	10	10	1823	Commercial Inn
Blackburn	1818	1838	5,000	13,120	10	10	1823	The Hotel
Chorley	1819	1850	1,300	1,300	10	10	N/A	N/A
Warrington	1820	1822	7,060	15,000	20	20	1830	Nag's Head
Stockport	1820	1825	5,000	15,000	N/A	N/A	1824	Angel Inn
Wigan	1822	1822	10,000	12,500	10	10	1825	Town Hall
Rochdale	1823	1823	12,000	12,000	25	25	N/A	N/A
Burnley	1823	1826	4,500	5,400	10	12	1827	N/A
Liverpool (Oil)	1823	1823	30,000	40,000	100	100	1830	King's Arms
Kendal	1824	1846	6,000	6,000	20	20	1827	Town Hall
Ashton	1824	1826	30,000	30,000	25	25	1829	N/A
Oldham	1825	1826	48,000	48,000	10	10	N/A (a)	Angel Inn
Lancaster	1826	1856	8,000	8,000	20	20	N/A	Town Hall
Heywood	1826	1826	2,700	2,700	10	10	N/A	N/A

Key: A: Year of creation B: 1826 (N/A: not available)
(a) At Oldham no dividend had been paid at least by 1833 (OGLWCMB)
Sources: See Appendices A and B

reading articles on the schemes. However, it is difficult finding other examples where this medium of communication played an influential part in proceedings. Indeed, in several towns local newspapers had yet to be established,(49) and even where they existed companies were only mentioned after the first meeting had occurred. Of course, advertising the promoters' intentions was extremely important, but the companies would not have relied on newspapers to attract a town's 'prominent citizens', and as Evans has demonstrated most of the canvassing would have been done in the local coffee houses and taverns.(50) It was largely through personal contact in these popular meeting places that promoters recruited an audience to listen to their proposals. We can also see from Table 3.1 that eight of the eleven inaugural meetings about which any information survives were held in public houses, and it is more than likely that most of the seven unknown cases would have occurred in the same type of venue. Why three companies were formed in a Town Hall we shall examine in Chapter 7,(51) but the public house obviously had a central position in provincial company creation, and it will become clear later that this function was extended into the closely connected field of capital formation.

Having attracted potential investors to a meeting, the promoters were then faced with the more difficult task of persuading them to purchase shares in the new venture. It has still not been established, though, who made up this amorphous band of promoters, but apart from the well-documented cases like Fr. Dunn at Preston it is impossible to be specific when categorising them by occupations because the information does not

'Oldham from Glodwick Field' by J. H. Carse (1831). The gasworks is the construction in the left-centre.

exist. When the management of North West gas undertakings is discussed in Chapter 5, an occupational analysis of the first Directors will be presented,(52) and the promoters usually appeared among this group, but the Boards also included many other men who had not been responsible for starting the company. It is nevertheless possible to say that the initiators were men of some status in local business and professional circles, a point which will be substantiated in Chapter 7,(53) and this in itself was sufficient to ensure that the inaugural meetings were well-populated.

When these inaugural meetings were called a subscription list was passed around the assembled group to gauge the extent of their interest, requiring individuals to sign their name and intimate how many of the shares they might buy. There is little evidence to suggest that promoters had any problems filling these lists: at Kendal, so quickly were the 300 £20 shares taken that 'a great many were obliged to leave the Hall disappointed, so great was the anxiety to become shareholders'.(54) This kind of frenzied activity was unusual, but in general, as the *Blackburn Mail* noted of that town's first gas company meeting, promoters 'met with no difficulty in procuring subscriptions'.(55) A managing committee was then appointed from the subscribers present, and at the same time the services of a prominent local attorney were secured to provide the company with legal advice on matters relating to its constitution.

Constitutional Matters

Apart from having to decide on how the gasworks and mains system ought to be built, and negotiating a street lighting contract with the town's local authorities, tasks which were demanding enough,(56) the managing committee was also responsible for charting a path through the legal minefield of early nineteenth century company law. Subscribers in utilities were also anxious that they would lose only their investment if the venture failed, rather than have creditors claiming compensation out of promoters' personal wealth. It was the attorney's function to ensure adequate legal protection was built into the constitution, bearing in mind the financial resources at the management's disposal. One must remember that it took the Chartered Co. until 1817 to pay a dividend on the £200,000 raised in 1812,(57) and the commercial viability of provincial gas undertakings was still far from assured even in the 1820s.(58) This discussion is beginning to impinge on the subject of our next two sections, but whether subscribers were motivated by the possible financial rewards or the need for access to a supply of gas it was still essential that they should be offered the security of limited liability. This would involve the managing committee in a debate on the merits of incorporation, and it is evident from Table 3.1 that there is little consistency in the solutions arising from these deliberations.

When the very earliest North West gas companies came to consider on what legal basis they ought to be constituted, they immediately cast around for guidance from similar companies, and of course only the Chartered Co. had directly relevant experience. At Preston, where their attorney, John Abraham, was asked in September 1815 'to furnish the best possible means to prepare an instrument by which the Trustees and Proprietors should be governed', he noted in his diary that information on 'the London Company' had to be collected.(59) Four days later he was advising Preston Gas Light Co. that it should be governed by a deed of settlement, rather than a private Act, but at the same time in drafting this document he copied many of the clauses from the Chartered Co.'s 1812 statute, linking the two ventures technically and legally.(60) Abraham actually excluded the sections imposing an obligation to supply street lamps in all places where mains had been laid, but in most other respects — company meetings, raising capital, share transfers, elections and duties of Directors, presentation of half-yearly accounts, and appointment of auditors — the deed of settlement bore a close resemblance to the Chartered Co.'s constitution.(61) Clause XVI provided the all-important security for investors, stating that: 'The Proprietaries shall, in no case, be responsible to a greater amount than the amount of their respective subscriptions.' However, one major difference between the two constitutions is evident, in that Abraham did not include the clause preventing management from paying dividends out of the share capital. As we shall see later, nothing sinister should be read into this, because there are good reasons why the regulation was ignored. It is also important to note that the Directors were tightly controlled by Clause XV. This stated that:

'The Trustees shall not contract any debt to a greater amount than the funds in their hands will be sufficient to satisfy, and if they contract any such debts, they shall be themselves alone personally liable for the amount.'

It was an important discipline on the activities of senior management, providing additional security for shareholders against the possibility of fraud, and forcing the Board to keep a careful eye on their cash-flow.

Preston Gas Light Co. shareholders were all satisfied with Abraham's draft, and by the end of September each person had signed the deed of settlement as an indication of their agreement to abide by the regulations. Indeed, not only was Abraham's deed of settlement suitable for Preston's venture — it remained in force there for twenty-four years (see Table 3.1) — a similar form was also used by several of the North West's early gas companies. At Liverpool it was March 1816 before the managing committee adopted a deed of settlement drawn up by a prominent local attorney, Charles Rawlinson.(62) No evidence survives to suggest that Rawlinson was in contact with Abraham, but it is too much of a coincidence that, from the preamble naming the first Board of Directors, to the early clauses dealing with share transfers and the duties of management, and the granting of limited liability to all subscribers, the two documents are identical.(63) There is even the same clause which prevented the Board from contracting 'any debts to a greater amount than the funds in the hands of Treasurer', indicating the extent to which the formation of unincorporated gas companies was being standardised. This can be further substantiated by referring to the other surviving deeds of settlement from this period,(64) drafted for the Blackburn, Bolton,(65) Chorley and Warrington undertakings, which were also structured along the lines adopted by Abraham. Again, we cannot link the respective attorneys directly by quoting a series of communications, but there seems little doubt that the deed of settlement had achieved a conventional format after 1815, providing companies with a relatively inexpensive means of safeguarding shareholders' interests.

The ready acceptance of unincorporated status by many First Generation North West gas undertakings is reflected in Table 3.1, with twelve of the eighteen cases listed using a deed of settlement until eventually incorporated. They clearly regarded applying for incorporation by private Act as unnecessary in their earliest years, but a puzzling feature of Table 3.1 is that some companies soon decided to seek statutory powers, while others remained unincorporated for twenty or even thirty years. An added source of confusion are the six companies which sought incorporation in the same year they were formed, including the tiny business at Heywood and the larger companies at Oldham, Ashton and Liverpool (oil). Why should there be such a disparity in this area? What obliged companies to apply for a private Act? And how did management decide on the timing of this conversion? These are difficult questions to answer if one looks only at Table 3.1, because the size of a company's issued capital was obviously not a decisive factor. Had size been a determinant of incorporation, Preston and Blackburn would have sought an Act much sooner than the late-1830s,(66) yet the smaller undertakings at Heywood, Burnley, Wigan and Rochdale had received statutory powers many years earlier. The crucial point to remember here is that in securing these statutory powers the companies were not simply incorporating themselves, they were also gaining access to the streets for main-laying purposes and having their rights to supply certain districts confirmed. Of course, limited liability was important, especially for the larger capitals of Liverpool (coal and oil) and Oldham, but other factors pressured management into spending money on a private Act.

An illustration of the forces influencing these decisions can be found in the conversion of Liverpool Gas Light Co. into a fully incorporated company in 1818. The Board had raised £12,000 in £30 shares by this time,(67) but the demand for gaslighting was growing so rapidly that in the winter of 1817–1818 it was almost exceeding capacity. This would have necessitated the issue of more capital, a move accommodated by Clause XVII of their deed of settlement,(68) but as Harris notes the management's main problem was not financial, it was 'the chaotic state of local government at that period'.(69) The organisation of local government will be examined at length in Chapter 7,(70) but in simple terms the Liverpool Gas Light Co. experienced great difficulty in negotiating with both the council and the vestry for rights to break open the streets. These problems were further exacerbated when districts outside Liverpool's boundaries started demanding a supply, and at the end of 1817 it was finally decided that the company required a private Act to provide statutory authority for their operations.

It took Liverpool Gas Light Co. six months to secure their first Act, and in that period £696 was spent on legal advice. This was regarded as the price of security, and the Board was obviously willing to sanction such expenditure. £696 was in fact a small proportion of the company's equity by the summer of 1818, because its Act also empowered management to increase the nominal value of their existing 400 shares from £30 to £100, and issue 100 new £100 shares, bringing the nominal capital to £50,000. This would have been another important reason why the company was incorporated, but in itself it was not sufficient to prompt such a move because the deed of settlement provided adequate legal protection. Above all, it was the need to ensure unfettered access to streets in Liverpool and surrounding districts which was much more influential in determining the change in legal status.

Having statutory authority to lay mains was a vital right for gas companies, and as we shall see in Chapters 5 and 6 effective planning was only possible when management was confident of its position. Events at Liverpool support this view, and at Bolton a similar situation developed. The town of Bolton was at that time made up of Great Bolton and Little Bolton, both of which had their body of Trustees with powers to regulate matters like street lighting.(71) The first gas undertaking formed in 1818 was actually called the Great Bolton Gas Light Co., and its deed of settlement specified that it was set up just to supply that part of the town.(72) Permission was duly gained from the Great Bolton Improvement Commissioners to lay mains there, but when manufacturers and retailers in Little Bolton started requesting a supply the Commissioners in this area were not as supportive, fearing assimilation and domination by their larger neighbours. To resolve this situation, in October 1819 the Great Bolton Gas Light Co. decided to incorporate the business and gain statutory rights to supply all parts of the town. By July 1820 an Act had been passed which granted both these wishes, and the Bolton Gas Light & Coke Co. consequently came into existence. The management had also taken this opportunity to double their capital to £15,000 (see Table 3.1), but as with the Liverpool Gas Light Co. they had sought an Act largely to ensure local political rivalries could not hamper their expansion plans.

The situation in which Great Bolton Gas Light Co.'s management had found itself in 1818 was exactly paralleled at Burnley, where the town was divided into two self-governing townships of Burnley and Habergham Eaves.(73) When the Burnley Gas Light Co. was formed in 1823 it was in fact only intended as a service to the business community in Habergham Eaves, but such was the pressure of demand from Burnley that by 1826 statutory authority to supply both townships was gained.(74) Again, the management was side-stepping the need to engage in negotiations with both bodies of Improvement Commissioners, and at the same time they increased their capital by adding £2 to the nominal value of the company's £10 shares to finance the system's expansion.

The need for unrestrained access to their local market was the main reason why North West Gas companies were incorporated either when they were formed, or within a few years of inception. This was certainly the case at Liverpool, Bolton and Burnley, while at Macclesfield in 1824 the management sought a private Act because a rival operation was being promoted in the town.(75) We noted in the last section that monopolistic control of a market was never sanctioned for any supplier in the nineteenth century,(76) but by securing statutory powers the Macclesfield Gas Light Co. could prevent a competitor from excluding them from laying mains in the streets.(77) In a similar vein, the Liverpool Oil Gas Co. was obliged to seek incorporation immediately, because the Liverpool Gas Light Co. had already gained statutory rights in the town and surrounding district.(78) At Preston, Blackburn, Chorley, Lancaster, Chester and Kendal (see Table 3.1) such difficulties did not affect management strategy in the early years, and these companies waited on average twenty-five years before applying for parliamentary authorisation. The unincorporated companies will be examined in greater detail at a later stage, when the general issue of relations with local government is discussed,(79) but it is nevertheless possible to conclude that these ventures did not need further powers at this early stage because they were not threatened by either local authority obstruction or competition. The choice of constitution was determined largely by such considerations, and although securing limited liability on an increased capital was also of importance this was a secondary consideration in view of the adequate protection given by deeds of settlement at this time.

Early Financial Structures

It is clear from what we have seen so far that the methods used to form and constitute North West gas companies were similar to those which Evans describes as standard practice for canal and railway undertakings by the early nineteenth century. Although substantial differences emerged in the legal character of the gas ventures, some preferring incorporation, some remaining unincorporated for many years, their early organisational experiences conformed to a set pattern. The attorney and meeting places like coffee houses and taverns had played leading roles in this process, and when we come to consider the methods adopted to raise capital for the gas companies these features do not diminish in importance. We saw earlier how the provincial capital market of this period was an informal and localised network eschewing any need for specialised institutions or personnel, and North West gas undertakings illustrate how effective this system had become in satisfying a constant demand for capital. The attorneys were at times hard pressed to convert subscription list signatures into hard cash, and when dividends were initially slow in coming these agents were obliged to use all their experience and contacts in order that new issues were placed speedily, but in general such problems did not constrain the industry's expansion. The companies were also willing to use sources of finance other than share issues, in particular ploughed-back profits, and this money was often vital to the survival of these businesses in their unprofitable first years of trading.

While none of the eighteen companies listed in Table 3.1 even approached bankruptcy, such was their rate of expansion that management had to keep a watchful eye on capital requirements and the business's liquidity, giving the subscription agent some difficult periods when cash had to be raised at short notice. The subscription lists passed around at the inaugural meetings of North West gas companies were, as we noted in the last section, usually signed by enough people to warrant the managing committee proceeding with the scheme. We shall examine who purchased the early share issues, and the equally important subject of why, in the next section, but whatever the status of these subscribers, or their motivation for investing in a gas supply venture, the managing committee was initially entirely reliant on their financial support. However, it was one thing to gain a signature, but quite another to extract even a deposit on the shares from some subscribers, and much time and energy was expended by senior management persuading the more recalcitrant to answer the early calls for capital. Once again, it was the company's legal advisor who provided the vital expertise in this area, extending his role as a financial intermediary in the local money markets into subscription agent for gas undertakings. As we saw earlier, attorneys were one of the main cornerstones in provincial capital formation, and for a new venture it was essential that promoters should have access to a wide range of contacts in the local community. This was particularly the case when additional capital was required soon after an undertaking had been launched, because in those early years (see Table 3.1 and Appendix C) profitability was poor and shareholders might not have been as anxious to pump in more money.

In these circumstances, management relied entirely on their subscription agents to raise the much-needed capital, and especially in the first years experience in these matters was essential if the ventures were to make progress. A feature of gas company capitalisation which helped promoters and attorneys sell shares was the typically small denominations into which they were divided. Canal company shares usually had a nominal value of at least £100,(80) while, apart from the two Liverpool businesses, Table 3.1 shows how most North West gas shares were valued at between £10 and £25. There are two main reasons why they were kept at such a low value: in the first place, gas supply operations required less capital than canals, allowing the creation of small shares to attract more investors; and secondly, the companies were reliant on only a single business community for their capital. The latter is particularly relevant, because, while canal and railway companies advertised and sold shares in several towns along their intended route,(81) as utilities which were only servicing individual communities gas companies relied almost entirely on the people living in their planned distribution area to purchase shares. This reveals the very nature of provincial capital formation, contemporaries preferring to invest in businesses and promoters they knew, and we shall see in the next section just how localised gas company shareholding became.

A low share denomination was an important way of persuading some investors to sign subscription lists, fearful as many were of companies making large calls on their subscribers at frequent intervals. Yet, the subscription agent was still faced with the task of persuading subscribers to pay over money to the company, and to ease the burden payment for shares was usually spread over several months.(82) In the case of Oldham Gas & Water Co. the £10 shares were actually raised in calls of £1 or £1.10s. between January 1825 and January 1828,(83) but such a time-span was exceptionally long and most followed the practice at Preston where the £10 share was raised in two equal instalments within a year.(84) The subscription agent was assisted in this task by the customary practice, started by canal companies,(85) of including forfeiture clauses in articles of association. This regulation was designed to give subscribers a certain amount of leeway when answering calls, but failure to pay the instalments by an agreed date would result in the share being forfeited to the company. At Oldham, for example, by January 1828 204 of the 960 shares had been forfeited in this way, and the company's subscription agent, Henry Barlow, was obliged to sell these 'by private contract' through his network of contacts.(86) This was an inordinate number of forfeited shares for North West gas companies, but the enforcement of such regulations was essential if subscription agents were to raise all the capital required.

There is an acute shortage of information revealing just how North West gas company subscription agents operated in the early nineteenth century, most board minutes, where they exist at all,(87) simply mentioning how many shares had been sold, or forfeited, and whether additional capital was to be raised. Fortunately, though, John Abraham at Preston wrote down his experiences in a diary,(88) and this has survived to reveal how an attorney used his contacts to generate sufficient capital for that company's first construction phase. One of Abraham's first tasks was to collect the £5 call made on the shares in July 1815, and this was performed by personally visiting most of the subscribers himself between July 6 and 29.(89) The management also decided in August 1815 to issue another 50 £10 shares, and Abraham responded to this by posting lists 'at about a dozen places likely for subscriptions to be made at'.(90) These 'places' were the principal coffee houses and taverns in the town-centre, where the businessmen and professionals of Preston met socially, and over the following months he was often visiting such institutions to see 'persons likely to take considerable shares' as the company's capital requirements increased.(91) By the spring of 1816 Preston Gas Light Co. was considering a further issue of 600 £10 shares, and Abraham continued to canvass potential investors 'at the Coffee Houses and Taverns at this Town', as well as advertising in the *Preston Chronicle*.(92) He also wrote to several people for support,(93) and it is clear from his correspondence that Abraham was not averse to indulging in hyperbole. Evans has described how some attorneys resorted to 'high-pressure salesmanship' when selling shares,(94) and this can be illustrated by quoting a letter from Abraham written in May 1816 claiming that: 'I doubt not the concern even if only extended to the extremities of the three main streets here will pay from 10−20%'.(95) It was actually 1821 before Preston Gas Light Co. paid its first dividend, of 6%, and only in 1844 did this reach 10%,(96) emphasising the dubious nature of Abraham's tactics. Nevertheless, by exploiting his extensive network of contacts, by the end of 1818 176 shareholders had invested a total of £11,690 in the company, preventing an early liquidity crisis from halting expansion.

The manner in which Abraham sold Preston Gas Light Co. shares would have resembled closely the pattern of capital formation in early North West gas ventures. Of the businesses listed in Table 3.1 which left any information, each employed a prominent local attorney as their subscription agent,(97) and their reliance on this influential individual was total. In most cases the inaugural meetings were successful in selling the first issue of shares,(98) but the subscription agent would still have to chase up the signatories for the money, and when more capital was required he would also be responsible for generating interest in the scrip and persuading existing and new share-holders to invest more. We shall see in the next section that many subscribers bought shares for reasons unconnected with the financial viability of gaslighting, but such was the need for fresh capital in the early years that subscription agents were obliged to tap a wide range of sources when selling shares, and in securing this money an attorney's network was often stretched to the limit. This was certainly the case at Preston, where Abraham regularly toured the town's social institutions or visited individuals personally, emphasising the importance of the informal contact system as an essential feature of the industry's growth, and illustrating the increasingly standardised methods used in raising finance at that time.(99)

Capital Extensions

It is clear from Table 3.1 that several First Generation undertakings seriously underestimated their capital requirements, in particular the larger companies established before 1820.(100) This cautious policy was pursued because it was extremely difficult to predict accurately the level of demand for gaslighting, and while the specialist gas contractors hired by most businesses were capable of designing technically viable systems these men were ill-equipped to advise on commercial matters. For the subscription agents at Preston, Liverpool, Blackburn, Bolton, Stockport, Wigan and Warrington further pressure was imposed on their networks by the need to sell extra shares soon after the first issue. Ward has noted of canal finance that the 'most frequently recurrent and most intractable problem.... was that of raising additional funds to cover an increase in the cost of the works over the original estimate',(101) and while underfunding occurred on a smaller scale in the North West gas industry it could still test the abilities of subscription agents to meet capital requirements. At the same time, certain clauses written into North West gas company constitutions undoubtedly assisted the attorneys when they came to sell new issues, and to ignore these regulations would be to miss a vital element in the development of such concerns.

An important aspect of the early constitutions which has not yet been explained, but which clearly influenced the methods employed to raise extra finance, was that existing proprietors were always given the first opportunity to buy any new issues. This was regarded as an inalienable right to which investors must be eligible, otherwise new investors would be able to benefit from the enterprise of the originals without having shared that initial risk. More importantly, the original shareholders would also be able to prevent any dilution of their control over pricing and investment strategies, revealing how the ownership pattern of early North West gas companies was often representative of local power structures. After all, these were a town's 'prominent citizens',(102) and controlling local utilities was another manifestation of their political and economic status within the community. We shall be examining this issue further in Chapter 7,(103) but it is vital to remember that the undertakings were an intrinsic feature of the local economic and political scenes, and for this reason most of a town's leading businessmen and professionals regarded it as essential to be linked to such ventures.

Another important clause frequently included in these constitutions was the limitation of voting rights.(104) These restrictions had been pioneered by the canal undertakings,(105) and the 1844 Companies Act later made them compulsory for all incorporated businesses.(106) However, they could not prevent interest groups from banding together to determine strategy, and it will become apparent in Chapter 5 that some sectors dictated important elements of management decision-making.(107) By giving shareholders the right to purchase all new issues, the constitutions also ensured that control would be retained within a closed circle, and as a consequence new investors were only brought in when shares were forfeited. Having risked their money on a gas company, and, as we shall see in the next section, having agreed to pass their dividends for several years, the original shareholders were therefore anxious to purchase any new issues which management created, in order to retain control over the business and prevent any dilution of ownership. For these reasons, the First Generation companies were able to finance their early expansion largely through the issue of shares, and in doing so they built up a close relationship, through the legal profession, with the local business and investing communities.

Raising additional capital was consequently never a major problem for North West gas companies and their subscription agents. There is evidence of both defaulting and frenzied activity on the part of attorneys, but in general existing proprietors usually preferred to invest more money rather than see control and ownership diluted by the introduction of new share-holders. One should not minimise the task facing subscription agents too much, and clearly John Abraham had his problems in Preston, but by 1826 eight of the companies listed in Table 3.1 had been able to increase their capital in spite of generally poor levels of profitability. More needs to be said here about the motivation behind original share purchases, but this will come in the next section, and it is sufficient to say at this stage that proprietors were anxious to retain control over the venture in which they had a stake. Burnley Gas Light Company was rather unusual, in that extra capital was raised by increasing the value of their £10 shares by £2 when the business was incorporated, but in the other seven cases almost £100,000 was added to issued capital by selling new shares to existing proprietors. This was not a vast sum when compared with the quantities invested in canal or insurance companies at this time,(108) but it was a vital lifeline to the gas undertakings in a period of uncertainty. It also demonstrates how efficiently the informal provincial capital market operated when local businesses demanded extra finance.

Although a share issue was the main method of satisfying the fixed investment needs of North West gas companies, other means were sometimes used to ease short-term liquidity problems. One of these alternatives was the fixed-term loan bearing between four and five per cent interest, and while articles of association always limited the management's borrowing powers in this respect, it was a useful expedient in pressing circumstances. In two notable examples, at Preston in 1826 and at Blackburn in 1819, loans of £6,000 and £3,000, respectively, were raised to shore up acute liquidity crises at times of rapid expansion.(109) On the other hand, most of the other First Generation companies survived without loans in the early decades of their existence, and the Liverpool Gas Act of 1818 expressly forbade manage-ment from raising money in this fashion.(110) In fact, loans were not a crucial means of financing until the 1840s, by which time credit-worthiness was such that the companies were able to attract a lot of support from short-term investors. The main reason why loans were not important in the early years was that interest had to be paid whether or not the company was profitable, while on expiration the loan had to be redeemed in full. At a time when management was experiencing great difficulties paying regular dividends, the potentially onerous burden of these loans could have exacer-bated problems in the medium term, and only in unusually pressing circum-stances were Directors willing to envisage this method of financing.

If the fixed-term loan was regarded as a dangerous form of funding, for similar reasons North West gas companies were equally wary when it came to relying on bank overdrafts. Pressnell has claimed that eighteenth century country banks were active in the promotion of utilities like turnpike trusts and canals,(111) but as far as North West gas undertakings were concerned their role was supportive, rather than creative. Ward has since discredited Pressnell's argument and stated that 'the part played by banks in the finance of canals was modest',(112) a statement which would act as an adequate summary of their relationship with gas suppliers. Indeed, in only two cases up to 1826 did banks provide any assistance, and these were at Preston and Blackburn where the Directors had also been obliged by their expansionist strategies to take out fixed-term loans.(113) The sums involved were never large, in neither case exceeding £1,100 in the 1820's, and while it would have been useful for the companies even this level of support was unusual for the region as a whole.(114)

Ultimately, it was a gas company's ability to sell all of its shares to local investors which determined whether or not it was going to survive and grow. Fixed-term loans and overdrafts were important only on the margin, reflecting the need for a judicious use of financial resources at a time when profitability was uncertain or inconsistent. It is at this stage that we must emphasise one of the more striking conclusions of Table 3.1, namely, that for those where the evidence is available, it took North West gas companies on average almost five years to pay a dividend. There are obvious contrasts, with Warrington taking ten years and Kendal only three, but the early dividend performance was in general uninspiring. As the quotation at the top of this chapter indicated, 'faith and patience' were virtues shareholders frequently needed to possess in abundance,(115) and as Appendix C reveals, only Liverpool Gas Light Company performed creditably in this respect, paying 10% dividends from 1824. Of course, the region's gas undertakings were not unusual of the industry as a whole, and in many other parts of the country returns were just as poor in the 1820's. Indeed, one could argue that many provincial gas companies, and in particular those set up in the North West, were never initially intended as profit-generators, and we shall see in both the next section and Chapter 5 that there is much to be said in support of this convention. At the same time, although dividends were often not paid for several years, the companies were still making some profit, and it is interesting to note that management chose to re-invest this in the business, rather than squander it on the shareholders.(116)

Self-finance has a central position in English business finance in this period. Crouzet has described how there was an 'overwhelming predominance of self-finance', with firms 'ploughing back immediately, regularly and almost automatically the greater part, or even the whole of their profits.'(117) From the surviving evidence on North West gas companies, it is apparent that their Directors, coming as they predominantly did from manufacturing industry and commerce,(118) brought with them a keen appreciation of the need to plough back profits into the business whenever possible, and in particular when finance was urgently needed. Fixed capital was supplemented frequently by that part of the profits which management decided not to distribute as dividends, and in the early years this amounted to the whole surplus. At Preston, for example, before a dividend was declared in 1821, £2,760 in retained earnings had been spent on new plant and mains, and in the following five years, while £4,346 was paid out in dividends, a further £6,163 was invested out of profits.(119) Detailed accounting information like this is not available for the other enterprises, but it is clear from later events that self-finance was an ubiquitous practice and provided a useful source of capital for management.

The ubiquity of self-finance can be clearly traced from the series of capitalisations which occurred in the 1840s. This trend was started by Liverpool Gas Light Company in 1841, when management applied for statutory powers to increase their capital by £50,000. After a detailed investigation of its finances, a parliamentary Select Committee was informed that since 1818 £143,000 had been invested out of undistributed profits, and management was granted permission to capitalise £100,000 of this sum by giving two bonus shares to all existing proprietors for every one held.(120) In 1843, Bolton Gas Light & Coke Company followed this precedent, by increasing the nominal value of its £10 shares by £6.10s, 'profits amounting to £6.10s and upwards [on each share having] been created and expended ... in the extension of the works'.(121) Chorley Gas Light Company also took advantage of this lucrative means by which shareholders received additional income from their original investment, by doubling the nominal value of its £10 shares in 1849,(122) and in 1847 the Ashton Gas Company Directors were empowered to add £5 to their £25 shares in recognition of deferred profits spent on the business.(123)

These examples indicate the early importance of self-finance to North West gas companies, with management following conventional contemporary practice in ploughing back money which was not paid out in dividends. However, it was not simply a matter of pursuing the same kind of financial strategies as those employed by a typical cotton manufacturer; the policy also helps to reveal why gas companies were established in the first place. In the early years management was clearly under no pressure to pay dividends, illustrating that investing in these ventures was not determined by the desire to reap rich financial rewards in the short term. One should never ascribe altruistic motives to the investment, because the majority of subscribers were purchasing shares for soundly based economic reasons, but, as we shall in the next section, speculative intentions do not seem to have been significant.

When the financing of early North West gas ventures is considered as a whole, it is clear that the methods used and sources tapped were similar to those pioneered by the canals. By the 1810s and 1820s business and professional communities in the region had become familiar with the process of forming joint stock utility companies, and from what we have seen in this section they showed no aversion to investing in limited liability undertakings. There is something of a paradox here, because both contemporary sources and historical analysis of early nineteenth century business finance reveal a widespread antipathy towards the joint stock form of organisation. This animosity was based on the general assumption that such devices were synonymous with monopoly and managerial inefficiency, and in the highly individualistic business climate of that era these were regarded as symptoms of industrial malaise.(124) However, public utilities were obviously regarded in a different light, and contemporaries were sufficiently pragmatic to overcome any philosophical reservations they might have held to purchase shares in canal, water and gas companies. This was vital to the emergence of a provincial capital market, because when the railways came along with their huge capital requirements it was important that a system for raising large amounts of money was available. The organisation might have been informal and reliant to a considerable extent on attorneys, but for gas companies it proved to be capable of supplying all the capital they needed. Any financial problems these utilities faced were those associated with expansion, and because existing proprietors were allowed to purchase all new issues they eagerly took up the opportunity to extend their holdings. But who were the original shareholders, and why did they invest in gas companies? These are the key questions we shall now go on to consider.

Motivation and Ownership

The reasons why different groups, or even people within those groups, invested in North West gas companies are difficult to discern precisely. To understand this issue fully we would need access to records of private discussions or communications which have long since been forgotten or lost. All we are left with is fragmentary evidence on shareholdings, as well as knowledge relating to both the markets for gaslighting at this time and the poor early returns made on gas shares. Falkus has concluded that 'economic motivation (expectation of demand) was paramount in the intro- duction of gas lighting',(125) but while this was undoubtedly an accurate reflection of promoters' intentions it fails to indicate that until the 1840s those sectors which financed, managed and owned gas companies were also those which used most of the gas. A more suitable terminology which encompasses various reasons for buying gas shares is required in order to clarify the situation.

When analysing why late eighteenth century investors purchased canal shares, Ward distinguished between 'economic' motives, based on 'the desire to reduce transport costs', and those with a 'financial' origin, deter- mined by 'the expectation of financial advantage'.(126) He actually concluded that, while 'unimpeded access to wide markets' was a key influence on share-buying by industrialists and merchants, the main motive behind canal company investment for all groups was 'financial',(127) 'inspirited by the enormous profits (30 and 40%) made by the proprietors of old canals'.(128) This distinction helps to differentiate between the various motives which stimulated public utility investment, identifying those groups which were likely to buy shares in the interests of establishing a public gas supply for example, and those which anticipated monetary returns. In our study the terms 'strategic' and 'speculative' will be used to describe these reasons: the former relates to investors who were interested in the service a gas under- taking would provide; and the latter categorises proprietors who expected to make money directly and immediately from their shares. To help us draw this distinction an analysis of ownership patterns is required, together with an understanding of the closely connected subject of gaslighting demand patterns, bringing to light the main reasons why gas companies were so well supported in the North West.

Before we go on to consider who bought gas shares, it would be interesting to examine the pattern of investment in other utilities at this time. In his detailed study of the capital raised for twelve northern railways, Broadbridge has calculated that 63% of the subscriptions came from the broad categories 'Industry' and 'Trade'.(129) These manufacturers, merchants and retailers were persuaded to invest only partially by 'the desire for improved communications, and the wish to break the costly monopoly of the canals',(130) but mainly because railway investment was regarded as one of the most lucrative of the era.(131) Similarly, in the late eighteenth century canals were seen as a good risk, and we noted earlier how what Ward describes as 'financial' motives were the main reason for buying their shares. Ward reveals that 53.7% of the canal capital raised between 1755 and 1815 came from the industrial and commercial sectors,(132) demonstrating that not only was a significant proportion of the money raised for transport utilities provided by businessmen in the same occupations, but 'financial' motives would also appear to have been prevalent in determining this activity. Were these characteristics also to be found in the financing of North West gas companies? To answer this question we must first examine the market for gaslighting in order that greater clarity might be brought to a picture which is often clouded by inaccurate generalisations.

A full analysis of consumption patterns must await Chapters 5 & 6,(133) but it is possible at this stage to highlight the basic features of a market structure which remained unchanged for several decades. Until the 1850s there were three main markets for gaslighting: firstly, the growing number of factories and workshops; secondly, the retailing, public house and office sectors; and thirdly, street lighting. The larger homes of wealthy inhabitants were frequently connected up to the mains from the outset, but domestic demand would have come a very poor fourth on the list of markets in the early years, and only around mid-century did it even begin to expand. One should also note that, while the need for improved street lighting was an important consideration in the minds of many gas company promoters, this service was paid for by the local authorities, and with the obvious exception of Manchester, no North West undertaking received any financial support from the rates. The first two markets were consequently the focus of promoters' attentions when publicising a scheme. This was essential not only to secure customers, but also to sell the company's shares, and in general the weight of evidence suggests a close correlation between the use of gaslighting and the original subscribers in supply undertakings.

Such was the growing interest in gaslighting by the 1810s that an increasing number of businessmen and professionals were beginning to recognise the need for a public supply system. Some of the large millowners could have afforded their own plant, while a few publicans and shopkeepers had also experimented with primitive apparatus to enhance their premises, but for most it was better to purchase shares in a gas company. Rowlinson has described this activity as a form of vertical integration, with 'large shopkeepers and factory owners wanting to secure a better and cheaper form of light' by buying an interest in the local utility to help its launch and early development.(134) It was certainly a rational policy to pursue for those without the resources to provide their own supply, and many millowners also recognised that by pooling resources the community could both share the cost of construction and at the same time take advantage of economies of scale in production and distribution to reduce the price. By exploiting these ideas promoters were able to attract a range of interested parties to the inaugural meetings, and once there potential investors could be converted into subscribers by stressing the advantages of co-operation.(135) It is consequently possible to see how the motivation behind gas share purchases was essentially 'strategic' in origin, determined in large part by the burgeoning demand for gaslighting and the needs of a local community. In effect, the subscription lists were dominated by those with the greatest interest in building a public gas supply system, and 'speculative' motives were rarely of much influence.

Early Shareholders

Primary documentation on North West gas company shareholders is either scarce or incomplete, but in Table 3.2 the original investors in five of the First Generation have been analysed according to occupations. The information has been sorted to demonstrate principal economic function within that town, putting for example the large land owning manufacturers, merchants and bankers into Sections 1, 2 or 3 respectively, rather than into Section 4, to reflect their local significance. On the other hand, small workshop owners like ironmongers, braziers and watchmakers have been categorised along with the 'Retailers' in Section 2, because their income levels and consumption of gas would have been similar to those of shopkeepers. Of course, the largest consumers were manufacturers, and in differentiating between textile (principally cotton) and other types of factory owners, it is possible to see how dominant the former had become in the North West. The 'Miscellaneous' category in Section 3 refers to a wide range of occupations, from teachers and military personnel to agents, surveyors and accountants, and we shall discuss later whether their reasons for buying gas shares were similar to those in Section 5, 'the intangible mass of gentlemen'(136) and unoccupied women. Trade directories and local histories have been consulted extensively to ascertain the occupation of those who signed themselves as 'Gentleman' or 'Esquire', because many prominent attorneys, bankers, merchants and manufacturers often used these signs of status. The task was made easier by the high level of geographical concentration among these shareholders, a point to which we shall return later, indicating again the localised nature of provincial capital formation.

The occupational analysis provided in Table 3.2 leads us to a closer understanding of the reasons why investors supported these ventures. One must remember that, apart from street lighting, the main markets for gaslighting at this time were mills and large workshops, together with shops, pubs and offices, and if the 'strategic' motives were to be predominant then one would expect those sectors to have purchased most of the shares. In fact, the final column of Table 3.2 reveals that 'Manufacturers' and 'Services' accounted for 63.6% of all the shares issued by these five companies, while at Blackburn and Warrington the two sections actually contributed as much as 71.4% and 72.2%, respectively.

The largest individual category of shareholders was the textile manufacturers, contributing 18.2% of the capital. It is also interesting to note that, although 'Manufacturers' held a smaller proportion of the capital than 'Services', the former held a much larger number of shares per subscriber than the other sectors. This reflected both the greater financial resources of

Table 3.2 Occupational breakdown of shareholders at inception of five companies, 1818–1822

	PRESTON (1818)			BLACKBURN (1818)			BOLTON (1818)			CHORLEY (1819)			WARRINGTON (1822)			ALL FIVE		
	A	B	C%	A	B	C%	A	B	C%	A	B	C%	A	B	C%	A	B	C%
1. MANUFACTURERS																		
Textile	23	241	20.2	25	172	34.4	6	156	14.1	7	12	9.2	2	15	4.2	63	596	18.2
Others	7	78	6.5	5	9	1.8	4	199	18.0	0	0	0	7	43	12.2	23	329	10.0
Sub-Total	30	319	26.7	30	181	36.2	10	355	32.1	7	12	9.2	9	58	16.4	86	925	28.2
2. SERVICES																		
Textile Merchants	18	95	8.0	8	56	11.2	2	35	3.2	3	7	5.4	6	46	13.0	37	239	7.3
Other Merchants	13	84	7.0	8	34	6.8	1	20	1.8	2	4	3.1	5	24	6.7	29	166	5.1
Retailers	23	130	10.9	26	69	13.8	10	257	23.3	20	42	32.0	11	94	26.6	90	592	18.0
Publicans	7	12	1.0	5	7	1.4	1	20	1.8	10	16	12.2	3	18	5.1	26	73	2.2
Transport	3	7	0.6	1	2	0.4	0	0	0	0	0	0	0	0	0	4	9	0.3
Builders	6	38	3.2	6	8	1.6	1	20	1.8	2	2	1.5	3	15	4.2	18	83	2.5
Sub-Total	70	366	30.7	54	176	35.2	15	352	31.9	37	71	54.2	28	197	55.8	204	1162	35.4
3. PROFESSIONS																		
Legal	24	169	14.2	11	60	12.0	1	28	2.5	3	4	3.1	3	20	5.7	42	281	8.6
Banking	6	78	6.5	1	5	1.0	0	0	0	0	0	0	2	15	4.2	9	98	3.0
Medical	4	19	1.6	3	13	2.6	2	250	22.6	1	1	0.8	0	0	0	10	283	8.6
Clerics	7	58	4.9	2	5	1.0	1	10	0.9	2	2	1.5	0	0	0	11	75	2.3
Gas Engineers	3	6	0.5	1	2	0.4	0	0	0	0	0	0	0	0	0	4	8	0.2
Miscellaneous	7	31	2.6	4	20	4.0	2	30	2.7	4	9	6.9	2	11	3.1	19	101	3.1
Sub-Total	51	361	30.3	22	105	21.0	6	318	28.8	9	16	12.2	7	46	13.0	95	846	25.8
4. FARMERS	2	10	0.8	0	0	0	0	0	0	5	10	7.6	0	0	0	7	20	0.6
5. UNOCCUPIED																		
Gentlemen	9	112	9.4	2	6	1.2	1	20	1.8	5	11	8.9	5	35	9.9	22	184	5.6
Ladies	10	26	2.2	7	32	6.4	4	59	5.3	6	11	8.9	4	17	4.8	31	145	4.4
Sub-Total	19	138	11.6	9	38	7.6	5	79	7.1	11	22	17.8	9	52	14.7	53	329	10.0
TOTALS	172	1194	–	115	500	–	36	1104	–	69	131	–	53	353	–	445	3282	–

Key: A: Number of shareholders   B: Number of shares purchased   C: Proportion of total shares issued

these men and, more importantly, their interest in using gas to improve the performance of mills. At Preston, the town's most prominent cotton manufacturers, run by the Horrocks family, purchased eighty-nine of the 1,194 shares (7.4%), and clearly many of their counterparts shared the same feelings on this matter. Blackburn millowners were even more supportive of their local gas company, and in Chorley 'Others' were not represented at all. On the other hand, 'Textile' was actually overtaken by 'Others' in the Manufacturers' section at Bolton and Warrington. In the former's case, this was because several engineering firms had played leading roles in forming that company,(137) while textiles was not a major industry in the latter where chemical and soap production dominated. In general, though, the textile (mainly cotton) industry was well represented among North West gas shareholders, and we shall see in Chapters 5 & 6 how this affected early pricing policy.

While textile manufacturers were the largest single category of shareholders, the most important section was 'Services', providing as much as 54.2% and 55.8% at Chorley and Warrington, respectively, and 35.4% overall. Within this section it is, of course, the shopkeepers and small proprietors categorised under 'Retailers' who provided most of the money. This link between retailing and gas companies was to become very strong in the ensuing decades, because shops were the main consumers of gas for much of the nineteenth century, and their purchase of gas shares was entirely rational.(138) On the other hand, it is surprising that publicans were so poorly represented, because they too were among the best consumers, but probably their lower income levels prevented them from spending what might have seemed large sums on gas shares. The two categories of merchants were certainly important investors, accounting for 12.4% of the capital overall, and they would have wanted gas to light warehouses and offices. It should be emphasised, though, that while there is some evidence of coal merchants buying shares they did not purchase significant quantities as means of securing bulk contracts.(139) Similarly, few builders showed much interest in the ventures, and neither did coal carriers, largely because they could not perceive any economic advantage from investing in utilities which would hardly have affected their business. Overall, though, share purchases and gas consumption were closely linked, if one accepts the evidence in Table 3.2, and particularly for those in the 'Manufacturers' and 'Services' sections becoming subscribers was a pragmatic response to the opportunities created by the innovation.

If 'strategic' motives were more important as far as factory-owners, merchants and retailers were concerned, it is much more difficult to be precise about the reasons why groups 3, 4 and 5 invested in early gas companies. The 'Professions' section actually accounted for 25.8% of the total capital in Table 3.2, but one must remember that clerics, doctors, attorneys and bankers were often among the promoters of the First Generation companies,(140) and in these cases they were mainly interested in bringing the benefits of gaslighting to their communities. One must be wary when ascribing altruistic intentions to this activity, because they would also have needed to light their churches, offices and streets, but 'speculative' motives do not seem to have had a major influence in Section 3 as a whole. As far as 'Gentlemen' were concerned, their presence at inaugural meetings was often used as a means of adding a degree of credibility and status to the venture, encouraging others in the community to sign the subscription lists. Clearly, though, unoccupied people would only invest in joint stock companies for 'speculative' reasons, and we shall see in the next chapter how this section in particular contributed an ever-increasing proportion of North West gas share capital once the companies started paying better dividends. In the first years, the financial incentives were not strong enough to attract much support from *rentiers*, but in time, for reasons which will become obvious, they came to dominate shareholders' registers.

It is unfortunate that similar evidence to Table 3.2's contents cannot be produced for the other thirteen companies in Table 3.1. Relatively few of the registers have survived, but where simply a list of subscribers can be found it can be used as further support for the points made above: fifty-one of the 132 Oldham Gas Light & Water Co. subscribers were cotton manufacturers,(141) and twenty-one of the sixty-two Lancaster Gas Light Co. subscribers would have come under Section 2 of Table 3.2.(142) Of course, such lists could be highly misleading, because they reveal nothing about actual shareholdings, but taken in conjunction with what we know about the five companies analysed in Table 3.2 they support the point that 'strategic' motivation was the primary impetus behind North West gas company investment. In short, there was an intimate relationship between those sectors which bought most of the shares and those which used most of the gas, leading us to conclude that the financing of First Generation public supply undertakings was related directly to functional, rather than to financial, matters.

A final point to make about the contents of Table 3.2 is the level of geographical concentration revealed by shareholders' addresses. It is vitally important to our argument that most of the proprietors should have lived or worked within the distribution area of the gas company concerned, otherwise their businesses would not have benefited from the system. Again, many of the more successful businessmen often lived outside the towns, and detailed searches of trade directories have been conducted to locate their premises. This has revealed that on average only 5% of those shares issued by the five companies were purchased by outsiders,(143) and consequently the vast majority were owned by locals who were investing in a local service. The shareholders were mainly concerned with providing a better source of artificial lighting for their own use, and even though dividends were by no means assured they were anxious to build a gasworks which would service their business needs.

The poor performance of North West gas company investments was one of the key conclusions arising from the last section. We noted in particular that, for twelve of the eighteen undertakings analysed in Table 3.1, it took on average almost five trading years to pay a dividend, while Appendix C indicates that only the Liverpool Gas Light Co. recorded consistently high returns in the 1820s. Indeed, in London and many other parts of the country, dividends were poor,(144) where they were earned at all, indicating that investors could hardly look on gas companies with the same kind of feelings with which new canals were apparently greeted. We have already seen how, especially in the 'canal mania' of 1791–1794, promoters had been able to raise capital by pointing to the highly lucrative nature of mid-eighteenth century canal construction.(145) In sharp contrast, however, the first North West gas company promoters could not realistically offer the prospect of high dividends to potential shareholders, because there was little evidence that gaslighting schemes were financially viable, especially in the provinces.(146) This would force them to put the emphasis much more on the economic benefits arising from a public gas supply, and as manufacturers, merchants and retailers were eager to introduce the new illuminant into their poorly lit premises such an incentive was often sufficient to persuade them that purchasing shares would produce positive gains. The possibility that financial returns could eventually be made on these investments would not be completely ignored, and in time, of course, the shareholders were to reap a rich reward, but initially the main reason for participating centred on 'strategic' factors closely associated with the needs of their own businesses.

While it is possible to say with some certainty that, from what we have seen so far, 'speculative' motives were a relatively insignificant influence on most shareholders' decisions to assist the launch and early development of a North West gas company, another interesting indication of intentions was the pressure exerted on management to pay dividends. Had original shareholders been concerned with financial returns they would have clamoured for dividends, but complaints from proprietors were noticeably absent from the reports of annual general meetings and Board minutes, and management was generally left to its own resorts. Naturally, criticisms of the Directors would probably have been excluded from the company's records by the Board, wherever possible, and in fact only rarely was any discussion reported, but nothing was heard about the lack of dividends. One might well argue, indeed, that the reluctance of many North West gas company Boards to include a regulation imposed on the Chartered Co. in 1812, preventing Directors from paying dividends out of share capital, was another indication that promoters and early shareholders were not creating the utility with the intention of making direct financial returns on their investments.(147) It is also important to remember that Directors ploughed significant sums back into the business in those early years, as we saw earlier, emphasising further the value placed on establishing a technically viable service capable of serving the needs of a limited market.

North West gas companies do not appear to have been intended as 'speculative' projects, and the bulk of the capital was provided mainly to ensure that the premises of local manufacturers, merchants, retailers and some professionals would be able to secure a regular supply of gas. We shall see in Chapter 5(148) how certain interests consequently managed to manipulate both investment strategy and the pricing structure to their advantage, but even for those shareholders who were unable to exercise any influence over prices the public supply would have been cheaper than any product manufactured from small private plants. The creation and financing of North West gas companies was 'strategically' motivated, and proprietors were willing to see any profits made in the first years reinvested in the works and mains in order to build a technically viable system capable of satisfying local business needs. Dividends were earned in time, to such an extent that parliament eventually intervened to stipulate maximum levels, but they were not anticipated initially. Buying original gas shares was clearly regarded by most as 'a long-term investment'.

Conclusions

North West gas company creation and financing conformed closely to a common set of procedures which were well established by 1800. Local businessmen and professional people were already familiar with the practice of purchasing shares in joint stock companies after the earlier surge in canal investment, and attorneys had become the central figures in provincial capital mobilisation. Both incorporated and unincorporated forms had also evolved by the turn of the century, and the latter in particular proved to be a useful means of constituting businesses and avoiding all the expense and delay involved in seeking a private Act for the former. Gas company promoters were able to exploit all these features of the North West financial scene, and as locals were willing to invest in projects which offered largely 'strategic', rather than financial, benefits the undertakings did not experience a financial constraint on their early growth. The undertakings were seen as utilities which would bring general advantages to the local community, and as such they were different in character from the canal and railway companies created in this era, because they offered only a limited attraction as speculative investments.

An important concluding point to make about investment in provincial gas companies is that this activity did not precipitate any significant changes to either company law or capital market organisation. Just as with canal companies,(149) gas undertakings relied on informal, localised capital markets, and because the system worked so effectively there was no pressure to insist on radical change. It took the 'railway manias' of the 1830s and 1840s to bring in any significant innovations, with the sheer scale of this investment leading to the establishment of provincial stock exchanges and decisive reforms of company law. In the next chapter we shall examine the extent to which North West gas companies benefited from these changes, but it is relevant to point out that the First Generation had been so well served by the informal methods of raising capital that in many cases only parliamentary intervention forced them to change, while for most of the companies created after 1826 traditional practices remained in use throughout the nineteenth century.

Footnotes

(1) See earlier, pp. 45 & 24.
(2) For a fuller description of this subject see Cottrell (1980), Ch. 3.
(3) See later, pp. 96—99, for a detailed analysis of this subject.
(4) Evans (1936), pp. 12—15. See also Hudson (1988) for the attorney's role in the West Riding woollen industry.
(5) See Matthews (1983), pp. 13—17, and Chandler (1947), pp. 16—27.
(6) This section is based on Hunt (1936), pp. 6—9. See also Chatfield (1977), pp. 80—81.
(7) Thomas (1973), p. 6.
(8) Hunt (1936), p. 9.
(9) Some of the early railway companies paid up to £70,000 in legal costs, but according to Hunt (1936), p. 64, the average cost in the 1820s was around £600.
(10) Hunt (1936), p. 12.
(11) See Pollard (1968), p. 24.
(12) Hunt (1936), pp. 16—21.

(13) Thomas (1973), p. 5.
(14) Quoted in Hunt (1936), p. 10.
(15) Ward (1974), pp. 97—105.
(16) *Ibid*, pp. 74—75.
(17) Quoted in Hunt (1936), p. 15.
(18) Quoted in a pamphlet issued by Winsor in 1807. See Chandler (1947), p. 19.
(19) Quoted in Hunt (1936), p. 26.
(20) Everard (1949), p. 31.
(21) See earlier, pp. 6—8.
(22) For example, the Act stipulated that all the capital had to be raised within three years of incorporation, otherwise the shareholders would not be granted limited liability.
(23) Hunt (1936), p. 10 shows how many of the regulations supervising canal companies were later used in railway company private Acts.
(24) *Ibid* , p. 26.
(25) Chantler (1939), pp. 65—66.
(26) See later, pp. 139—141.
(27) Rowlinson (1984), pp. 98 & 155—157.
(28) Early provincial private gas Acts were to cost up to £700. See later, pp. 101—102.
(29) Cottrell (1980), p. 39.
(30) The authorities were particularly concerned about the propensity of unincorporated companies to allow shareholders to transfer their stock and thus defeat one of the 1720 Act's main aims. Hunt (1936), pp. 17—21.
(31) *Ibid* , p. 29.
(32) See later, pp. 173—175.
(33) See later, pp. 101—102.
(34) This description is based on Evans (1936), pp. 12—15.
(35) For a more detailed study see Morgan & Thomas (1962), pp. 10—15.
(36) Dickson (1967).
(37) Cottrell (1980), pp. 7—10.
(38) PP (1850).
(39) Hudson (1988), p. 212.
(40) Pressnell (1956), p. 126.
(41) Evans (1936), p. 18. See also Hudson (1988) and Ward (1974), p. 108.
(42) Anderson (1969), p. 83.
(43) Evans (1936), p. 13.
(44) The plants at Salford and Chorlton-upon-Medlock were privately owned (see earlier, pp. 27 & 24) and the Police Commissioners owned the Manchester gasworks.
(45) Evans (1936), pp. 12—15.
(46) See earlier, pp. 10—11.
(47) Quoted in Harris (1956), p. 5.
(48) *Ibid* , p. 14.
(49) No local newspapers were produced in Oldham, Stockport, Burnley, Bury and Rochdale until mid-century.
(50) Evans (1936), p. 13.
(51) See later, pp. 204—206.
(52) See later, p. 125.
(53) See later, pp. 194—197.
(54) *Westmorland Gazette*, 16 Oct 1824, p. 1.
(55) *Blackburn Mail*, 21 Jan 1818, p. 3.
(56) See later, pp. 139—141.
(57) Matthews (1983), p. 53.
(58) See Nabb (1986), pp. 50—52 for a view of fortunes in the South West.
(59) JADAB, 15 Sept 1815.

(60) *Ibid*, 19 Sept 1815. See earlier, pp. 12–13.
(61) This section is based on a comparison of Eastwood (1988) and Hunt (1936), p. 23.
(62) Harris (1956), p. 14.
(63) See Eastwood (1988) and Harris (1956), pp. 235ff.
(64) See *Sources* in Section D for location of these records.
(65) This particular deed of settlement does not survive, but Clegg (1872), pp. 9–10, provides some details.
(66) By 1839 the capitals of Preston Gas Light Co. and Blackburn Gas Light Co. were £24,000 and £20,000, respectively.
(67) This section is taken from Harris (1956), pp. 13–21.
(68) *Ibid*, p. 237.
(69) *Ibid*, p. 20.
(70) See later, pp. 194–197.
(71) For a review of Bolton's political scene, see Garrard (1983), pp. 159–207.
(72) Clegg (1872), p. 9.
(73) See Bennett (1948), pp. 350ff.
(74) See the preamble to Burnley Gas Act (1826), Cap. xxxvi.
(75) *Macclesfield Courier* (1888), p. 88.
(76) See earlier, pp. 52–53.
(77) The rival company never actually went into business. *Macclesfield Courier* (1888), p. 88.
(78) Harris (1956), pp. 29–32.
(79) See later, pp. 173–177.
(80) See Ward (1974), pp. 26–78.
(81) Evans (1936), pp. 15–16, and Ward (1974), pp. 97–113.
(82) This was another practice commonly followed by canal companies. Ward (1974), pp. 113–121.
(83) OGLWCMB, 27 March 1825 & 6–9 Jan 1828.
(84) PGLCMB, 6 July 1815 and 22 June 1816.
(85) Ward (1974), p. 118.
(86) OGLWCMB, 9 Jan 1828.
(87) At Preston, for example, only two shares were forfeited. PGLCAB, 1818–1825.
(88) JADAB, 1815–1817.
(89) *Ibid*, 6 July 1815, 28 July 1815, and 16 Aug 1815.
(90) *Ibid*, 29 Aug 1815.
(91) *Ibid*, 15 May 1816.
(92) *Ibid*, 8 June 1816.
(93) Letters to J. Horrocks, 8 May 1816, and to a Lancaster gentleman, 2 Sept 1815.
(94) Evans (1936), p. 19.
(95) J. Abraham to J. Horrocks, 8 May 1816, JADAB.
(96) See Appendix C.
(97) There is no relevant information on companies at Rochdale, Macclesfield, Stockport, Burnley, Chorley, Lancaster, Chester, Ashton and Heywood.
(98) Most of the shares were usually sold at the meetings. See earlier, pp. 70–73.
(99) This was also true of the share certificates used at that time, because similar designs have been discovered in Preston, Blackburn and Bolton.
(100) Liverpool Gas Light Co., for example started with a capital of just £6,000. Harris (1956), p. 13.
(101) Ward (1974), p. 113.
(102) Evans (1936), p. 13.
(103) See later, pp. 194–197.
(104) For example, at Wigan proprietors with up to three shares had one vote, between three and six shares two votes, between seven and ten shares three votes, between eleven and fifteen shares four votes, between sixteen and twenty shares five votes etc. WGLCMB, 6 Mar 1822.

(105) Ward (1974), p. 115.
(106) Joint Stock Companies Registration and Regulation Act (1844).
(107) See later, pp. 130–136.
(108) Hunt (1936), pp. 46–47.
(109) See PGLCAB, 1820–1826, and Abram (1878), p. 28.
(110) Harris (1956), p. 20.
(111) Pressnell, (1956), p. 398.
(112) Ward (1974), p. 109.
(113) PGLCAB, 1820–1826, and Abram (1878), pp. 28–45.
(114) The municipal undertaking at Manchester also relied on loans during the 1820s. See later, p. 189.
(115) Abram (1878), p. 3.
(116) Nabb (1986), pp. 65ff.
(117) Crouzet (1972), p. 188.
(118) See later, p. 125.
(119) PGLCAB, 1815–1826.
(120) Harris (1956), pp. 52–53.
(121) Bolton Gas Act (1843), Cap xiv, clause VIII.
(122) Chorley Gas Light Co. Deed of Settlement 9 Apr 1849.
(123) Ashton Gas Act (1847), Cap cci, clause XV. See later also the case of Chester on pp. 173–174.
(124) Pollard (1968), pp. 24–25.
(125) Falkus (1982), p. 234.
(126) Ward (1974), pp. 126–127.
(127) *Ibid*, p. 138.
(128) Quoted in *Ibid*, p. 135 from *Universal British Directory of Trade, Commerce and Manufacturers* (1793), p. 204.
(129) Broadbridge (1970), p. 140.
(130) *Ibid*.
(131) Thomas (1973), pp. 10ff.
(132) Ward (1974), pp. 74–75.
(133) See later, pp. 183–185. See also Falkus (1967), pp. 499–502 and Rowlinson (1984), pp. 63–77.
(134) Rowlinson (1984), p. 65.
(135) See earlier, pp. 38–39, for a study of Colne.
(136) Killick and Thomas (1970), p. 100.
(137) See earlier, pp. 25–26.
(138) Rowlinson (1984), pp. 63–77.
(139) See later, pp. 173–174, for a study of Chester.
(140) See earlier, pp. 12 & 25, for examples of clerics and doctors involved on early managing committees.
(141) Preamble to Oldham Gas Act (1825).
(142) Report on proceedings in *Lancaster Guardian*, 24 Sept 1925.
(143) The actual proportions are: Blackburn 2.4%; Preston 5.3%, Bolton 3.6%, Warrington 8.2% and Chorley 5.4%.
(144) *King's Treatise* (1878), p. 48 reports how, although the Chartered Co. paid dividends of between 6.5% and 8% from 1817 to 1830, two other London gas companies (the City of London, and the Imperial) paid no returns for their first ten years of trading, and concluded that 'in the commencement of their history, gas companies were by no means commercially successful'.
(145) See earlier, p. 65.
(146) They could, like Abraham at Preston, exaggerate the potential profitability of gaslighting schemes. See earlier, p. 79.
(147) See earlier, pp. 73–74.
(148) See later, pp. 130–135.
(149) Ward (1974), p. 97.

4

Gas Shares and Government Controls

'For many years the company have enjoyed such an unexampled degree of prosperity, and have paid such handsome dividends, that it is considered to be hardly the thing for a capitalist not be connected with it.'

Bacup Times, 13 June 1874, p. 8 (Commenting on the Rossendale Union Gas Company).

The informal and highly localised methods of raising capital prevailing in the provinces had satisfied the constantly increasing fixed capital requirements of early North West gas companies. Promoters had initially pursued the cautious policy of selling only enough shares to build a system capable of supplying a relatively limited market, but as the business expanded and a larger number of customers started to appear management was obliged to supplement capacity by issuing more equity to existing shareholders. By 1826, almost £375,000 had been invested in twenty companies and in spite of the poor dividend performance attorneys acting as subscription agents had experienced relatively few difficulties when placing the issues. Proprietors clearly regarded their gas shares as long-term investments, anticipating only meagre financial returns in view of the intended benefits arising from the establishment of such a utility. These 'strategic' motives had eased the burden imposed on subscription agents, because otherwise their network of contacts would have come under severe pressure had they been obliged to tempt investors with the inducement of high dividends. At the same time, gas companies exploited all the features of provincial capital formation which had evolved mainly out of the practices of canal promoters, and in this respect they were very much in the mainstream of developments in the areas of company law and financing large-scale business. This had not led to any fundamental changes to either of these fields, but at least canal, water and gas companies were preparing the way for what was to happen as a result of the railway manias in the 1830s and 1840s.

The formation of stock exchanges at Liverpool and Manchester in 1836, and the greater accessibility of limited liability after the 1844 and 1856 reforms of company law were two of the most far-reaching changes to provincial capital formation in the nineteenth century. Although it was several decades before manufacturing industry started to take advantage of these basic features of a mature economy,(1) they were vitally important in providing both an improved mechanism for transferring financial resources between sectors, and greater security for investors. They were certainly vital to their principal initiators, the railways, and in time other industries realised the benefits of the new system. However, it is equally apparent that most North West gas companies largely ignored the refinements precipitated by railway investment, and unless obliged by government regulations to follow a different path they clung to the traditional methods of financing and organising operations which had been so effective in the first decades of growth. Indeed, only the introduction of auction clauses forced managements to abandon the intimate relationship they had enjoyed with their local communities. In the meantime, although contacts might have been forged informally either through legal dealings or in coffee houses and taverns, and an attorney, rather than a specialist share broker, acted as the investment intermediary, several million pounds had been raised for the region's private gas undertakings by the 1880s, illustrating how successful these traditional practices could remain.

One of the main reasons why North West gas companies did not need to change their methods of raising capital was that, after the initial struggles, by the 1830s gas shares were synonymous with regularity and respectability, and proprietors proved eager to purchase any new issues managements were disposed to create. Indeed, such was the profitability of gas investments that increasingly government was forced by various pressures to limit dividends. The attractiveness of gas shares also facilitated a decisive change in ownership patterns, with the original shareholders transferring ownership to a different type of investor. Interestingly, though, even the companies created after the 1820s were financed in the first stages by the same type of investor as those who had supported the earlier ventures, and only once a company had become financially viable did the ownership structure change. Gas shares became one of the staple features of provincial investment portfolios after the 1820s, but in no case did this by itself prompt management to seek a quotation on the Manchester or Liverpool stock exchanges. Even though ownership patterns changed, the market in these commodities remained local in character and extent. The main aims of this chapter will be to examine how this system evolved, charting the legal, institutional and financial pressures which influenced the way North West gas companies were funded. A localised clique continued to dominate the management and ownership of these businesses, and at a time when other industries were either pioneering or copying a wider range of devices for raising capital the region's private gas suppliers stuck rigidly to traditional practices unless forced to change by government regulations. These controls were a vital part of the changing environment in which the industry was obliged to operate from the 1840s, and we shall see what kind of role they came to play in determining certain aspects of the businesses' development.

Legal and Financial Background

The complete overhaul of company law between 1825 and 1856 was an indication of the growing importance attached to limited liability in this period. Up to the 1820s, many contemporaries refused to envisage the joint stock company as anything other than a dubious means of financing speculative enterprises, while those businesses which had taken advantage of this device were regarded as monopolistic organisations run by managers who had little interest in efficiency.(2) Of course, these popular prejudices failed to reflect the significant benefits gained from joint stock companies, in particular the ability to raise large amounts of capital for big business, the security of limited liability, and the corporate status endowing powers to sue debtors. For utilities like canals, railways and gas undertakings, an incorporating Act could also be used to seek statutory powers for building their systems, obviating potentially difficult negotiations with local authorities over rights, for example, to lay mains in public highways. There may well have been, as Hunt argues, 'a strong commercial prejudice in favour of "individualistic" enterprise' at this time,(3) but many people in commerce, industry or the professions were willing to invest in utility companies, for a variety of reasons. In addition, company promoters had also experimented with an unincorporated form of organisation which provided limited liability by obliging shareholders and trustees to sign a deed of settlement. This 'product of opportunism'(4) was regarded by the legal establishment as a dubious means of avoiding the limitations on share transfers introduced as long ago as 1720, but such was the widespread use of the unincorporated form, and so loud were the cries for corporate status by the 1820s, that parliament was forced to accept the need for reform.

There had been several recent speculative manias prior to the 1820s, in particular between 1791 and 1794, and again in 1807–1808, but the 'veritable avalanche of extravagant promotions and general speculation'(5) which took place in 1824 and 1825 precipitated the first attempt in over one hundred years to interfere with company law. The 1720 Bubble Act had restricted joint stock company use mainly to the largest trading, transport and insurance enterprises, principally because it made incorporation expensive and time-consuming, but when in 1824 and 1825 624 companies were created with a capitalisation of over £372 million the authorities decided to repeal the statute.(6) This was something of a triumph for company promoters and investors, but at the same time one must remember that incorporation still required a private Act, and in the 1830s several unincorporated companies were again deemed illegal because of their failure to secure parliamentary ratification.(7) In effect, the legal situation had hardly changed, and although there was wider recognition of the role joint stock companies could play in the financing of large-scale business no government was willing to remove the legal barriers preventing greater use of corporate status until the 1840s.

It was argued at the end of the last chapter that neither the canal nor the gas companies created up to 1825 had influenced the reform of company law. They were certainly an important part of the general groundswell of opinion forcing parliament to intervene in 1825, but it was only as part of this movement that they influenced events. We have also claimed that, with the exception of the two oil-gas companies mooted in Manchester and Blackpool,(8) North West gas companies were not linked with speculative investment activity. Although some of the London supply undertakings were rather more dubious in character,(9) in general the provincial gas industry did not attract the attentions of unscrupulous company promoters. The Bubble Act's repeal in 1825 would have had little impact on this activity, and even though improvements to the process of registration were introduced in 1834 and 1837(10) the insistence on Acts or Charters as a record of incorporation still proved to be a prohibitively expensive feature of company law.

The refinements of the mid-1830s were forced on parliament by yet another investment mania. Joint stock banks were among the most prominent features of this 'rage', but the years 1835–1837 mark the first significant interest in railways, and by the end of the boom eighty-eight of these ventures had been formed with a nominal capital of £70 million.(11) In the following years, there were several unsuccessful attempts to provide investors with greater security and prevent fraudulent promotions, but only in 1844, after a Select Committee investigation, was the Joint Stock Companies Registration and Regulation Act passed.(12) This was the most significant reform of company law to date, initiating what W. E. Gladstone described as the policy of 'publicity'.(13) The main aim of the policy was to protect shareholders' interests by introducing minimum levels of subscribed capital, audited balance sheets, half-yearly returns, and compulsory registration for all companies with more than twenty-five members. On the other hand, registration secured only unlimited liability, and an incorporating Act was still required if promoters wanted full protection of investors' money.

It was in 1856 that the simple process of registering a company by seven people brought full limited liability status, and although this Companies Act made auditing voluntary, rather than compulsory, and the clause stipulating minimum levels of subscribed capital was discarded, this created an extremely liberal framework within which company promoters could operate. In the meantime, over £200 million had been raised for railway ventures by 1848, providing a severe test for the 1844 Act, and even though several weaknesses were revealed by the schemes of promoters like George Hudson there remained a general consensus that limited liability was essential as a means of financing large-scale businesses.(14) The 1856 Act, and the later codification of all regulations relating to joint stock companies in 1862, were a reflection of this consensus, freeing promoters and management from the constraints which had prevented wider use of incorporation. Several influences had combined to produce the succession of reforms to company law between 1825 and 1856, not the least of which was the huge surge in interest shown by investors in buying shares, and especially railway shares, after 1835. Classical economists demanding the end of all government restrictions on investment had created a conducive philosophical environment in which these reforms could take place, replacing the prejudicial attitudes of their eighteenth century counterparts,(15) but in the main parliament was reacting to the economic realities of an expansionary era. Another important point one should make about the desire to invest in joint stock companies is that the movement included both the money markets of London and the informal provincial networks arising out of canal construction. The initial interest in railways was actually a provincial phenomenon, and in this respect the industry not only introduced more effective means of organising new ventures, it also precipitated a significant overhaul of the disparate capital markets which had been a feature of company financing up to the 1830s.

Provincial company formation and the associated task of raising finance had largely revolved around canal, water and gas companies in the late-eighteenth and early-nineteenth centuries,(16) but as we saw in the last chapter the process was localised and informal, and attorneys were regarded as the principal financial intermediaries. Thomas has argued that this activity had not led to the emergence of a well organised system with full-time specialists because 'the necessary conditions' had not yet been fulfilled. These 'conditions' he defines as 'a large number of securities with dispersed ownership among a wealthy investor class, together with a developed legal and banking framework to assist the process of transfer',(17) and from what we have already seen in this chapter clearly the latter in particular had hardly started developing. It was the railway and joint stock bank mania of the mid-1830s which was to prompt the creation of stock exchanges in Manchester and Liverpool, as a growing number of people were attracted into the stockbroking trade by the opening up of new investment opportunities.(18) Both institutions were constituted in 1836, at the peak of the first 'railway mania', and particularly in the late-nineteenth century, assisted by refinements in company law, they grew into important features of the provincial capital market, raising significant sums of money for ventures in a wide range of industries.(19)

The reform of company law and the establishment of provincial stock exchanges had facilitated the creation and financing of joint stock ventures, allowing promoters the opportunity to bring schemes before a wider audience which was better protected by regulations controlling many aspects of this process. Of course, problems still existed, especially with the presentation of financial information to prospective or actual shareholders,(20) but progressively facilities improved up to the 1850s and gradually Thomas's 'conditions' were fulfilled. But did these developments have any impact on the way North West gas companies were organised and financed? In general, the gas industry was one of the most frequent users of joint stock company status, and between 1844 and 1868 in total 678 British supply undertakings were incorporated.(21) It is also true to say that, as a proportion of those formed, more gas companies survived than in any other sector, and most of those which were liquidated would probably have been municipalised. In fact, only 15% of the 678 gas companies created in this period had disappeared by 1868, compared to 28% of the water companies, 59% of the railway companies, 66% of the manufacturing companies, and 70% of the mining companies.(22) One should not forget that mergers could have accounted for some of the liquidations in these sectors, but the sharp differences reflect accurately how, while speculation had featured prominently in the creation of many mining, manufacturing and railway undertakings, it was rarely a factor in provincial gas company formation. However, this reveals little about the North West gas industry, and a detailed analysis of how supply operations fared in the changing legal and financial climates of the mid-nineteenth century is necessary before we can come to any firm conclusions on the subject.

Incorporation and Gas Companies

The reform of company law and the establishment of stock exchanges at Manchester and Liverpool could have assisted the means by which North West gas companies were created and financed, opening up new opportunities for promoters and management when securing either start-up or additional capital. Although the informal, localised methods of raising funds had been successful, and no undertaking had suffered from a cash constraint on its expansion, from the 1840s in particular it was becoming much easier to organise joint stock companies and sell shares to a wider audience through specialist brokers working in stock exchanges. Canal and gas companies had contributed to this movement, and by the 1820s, as a result of investment in such schemes, there was an 'increased public willingness to hold shares'.(23) This trend was accelerated by the railways, providing an even larger pool of potential investors willing to support utility ventures.(24) Given that gas shares by the 1830s were increasingly being recognised as reliable and remunerative, public supply undertakings would have experienced little difficulty selling their equities in stock exchanges. Had they exploited these new opportunities one might expect their ownership structures to be different from those of the First Generation gas companies, while the motivation for investing would have been more 'speculative' in character, rather than 'strategic'. The scenario appears logical, especially when one considers the profitability of gaslighting after the early sacrifices,(25) but a series of questions must be discussed before accepting anything. Were new companies automatically registered as joint stock organisations? Did both the older and more recent undertakings use stock exchanges from the 1830s? How did ownership structures differ when comparing shareholders' registers in the 1820s and 1860s? And, if companies did change their methods of financing operations, what factors prompted management to adopt new practices?

In the early years of development several North West gas companies had used the fully incorporated form of organisation, but although by 1826 twelve had secured a private Act this belies the inconsistent pattern of development. In fact, as Table 3.1 reveals, only seven of these businesses were incorporated at the time of their inception, six applied for corporate status after a few years in business, and the remainder continued to be governed by deeds of settlement, in some cases for up to thirty years. We argued in the last chapter that the main reason why managements decided to seek statutory powers was the need to establish their rights to lay mains in certain districts.(26) Size in itself was not initially a principal determinant of legal status, and in the unsettled situation prevailing up to 1844 the deed of settlement provided adequate protection for shareholders, including the all-important limiting of liability for a company's debts. It was vital, though, that management should be assured of its distribution rights, and only an Act of Parliament could guarantee these, forcing twelve of the First Generation to go through what was an expensive and time-consuming business of applying for ratification. In contrast, until the 1840s the companies at Preston, Blackburn, Chorley, Lancaster, Chester and Kendal experienced neither local authority obstructions nor competition from rival suppliers, and consequently the respective managements felt sufficiently confident of their position to ignore the need for incorporation.

In time, of course, all the First Generation were incorporated, and it is interesting to note that the Preston, Blackburn, Chorley, Lancaster, Chester and Kendal companies were motivated to take this step by an acceptance of the need to ensure full legal protection of shareholders' investments, rather than any worry over distribution rights. At Blackburn, in June 1837, after the issued capital had recently been increased to £19,640, and plans were being drawn up to extend capacity further, a Special General Meeting decided 'to apply to Parliament in the next session for an Act to Incorporate the Proprietors of Shares in this company with powers usually granted in such cases'.(27) A similar expansion of capital by Preston Gas Light Company in the 1830s, from £18,000 to £24,000, was also prompting a reconsideration of the business's legal status. A local barrister had actually advised the Preston Directors in 1836 that unless additional finance was raised they were in danger of overextending themselves and contravening the clause preventing them from contracting 'any debts to a greater amount than the funds in their hands'.(28) They were prevented from making progress on their application 'by the determination of the public functionaries.... to postpone the grant until the passing of a Bill.... for regulating Chartered Companies',(29) but once the law had been reformed the business was fully incorporated.(30) In the cases of Chester (1845), Kendal (1846), Chorley (1850) and Lancaster (1856) they were simply taking advantage of the easier registration procedures introduced in 1844, and again the Directors were concerned to protect their expanded share capitals.(31)

There is an obvious contrast in motives between those First Generation companies seeking incorporation almost immediately, and those which relied on a deed of settlement for several years, the former acting as a result of problems with their distribution area, the latter responding to the changing legal scene. Once bound by the regulations imposed by parliament, though, a gas company was obliged to seek another Act every time the Directors wanted to raise extra capital or extend the distribution area, and this would usually entail both further expense and the inclusion of additional controls.(32) When a Bill passed through parliament it was possible for anyone who objected to its proposals to lodge a petition insisting on certain modifications. The company would then be forced to defend its claims, adding to the legal costs with no guarantee of victory.(33) This issue will be discussed again in Chapters 5 and 6, but an important point to remember is that often gas companies were reluctant to seek extra statutory powers because their operations could be materially affected by regulations imposed while the Bill was being debated.(34)

Another aspect of incorporation which may also have discouraged managements from imitating the larger incorporated suppliers was the growing number of regulations imposed on gas companies after the 1840s. Indeed such was the volume of controls that in 1847 the Gasworks Clauses Act was passed.(35) One of the definite improvements arising out of this Act was the significant reduction it introduced to the length of private statutes. By the 1840s an incorporating Act could be up to eighty pages long, with clauses referring to a wide range of issues like land purchases, environmental problems, trading rights and the whole panoply of limited liability controls and reporting procedures. To obviate all these legal niceties, and consequently reduce the cost of drafting legislation, the Gasworks Clauses Act was passed.(36) Thereafter, each private Bill would simply have to include this Act as one of its clauses and all the current regulations relating to such undertakings would then be applied to that company. In 1845, a similar Act consolidating joint stock company law had also been passed,(37) and again a clause referring to this statute would simply be added to bring any undertaking within those regulations. This, in conjunction with other refinements in the registration process introduced as a result of the 1844 Companies Act, drastically reduced the size of private bills down to ten pages, and at the same time cheapened incorporation by up to 40%.(38) However, while this facilitated the process of raising extra capital, and many of the older companies would have seen the imposition of further regulations as one of the inevitable costs of expansion, for companies established after the 1830's the decision on legal status was still by no means clear-cut.

Although by 1826 twelve of the North West's eighteen gas companies had been incorporated (see Table 3.1) and eventually the remainder applied for private Bills, it is clear from Table 4.1 that in the region as a whole, especially after the 1820s, most managements preferred the deed of settlement as the legal basis for their operations. Only twenty-six of the ninety-seven companies analysed were incorporated within three years of inception, and even after the reforms to company law in 1844 and 1856 the unincorporated form remained extremely popular in the region. By 1880, most of these businesses had in fact been incorporated, and just eleven non-statutory operations remained,(39) but over two-thirds of the companies used a deed of settlement for several years after their formation. The promoters and management would have regarded both the cost of incorporation and the imposition of parliamentary regulations as too high a price to pay, and as with the unincorporated First Generation companies like Preston and Blackburn they preferred to negotiate with local authorities or rival suppliers in order to establish a firm foothold in their market.(40)

Size, of course, would have been another important consideration, because many of the undertakings formed after 1830 relied in the first years on small issues of shares (see Appendix B), and only as they expanded did it become feasible to spend money and time applying for a private Act. The relatively large businesses formed in the 1840s and 1850s, at Accrington (£10,000), Farnworth & Kearsley (£20,000), Hyde (£25,000), and Birkenhead (£50,000), were incorporated immediately, but these were unusually large for that period. The more typical were those at Ormskirk (£5,000), Radcliffe & Pilkington (£9,000), Colne (£5,000), Nelson (£6,500), and Prescot (£6,000), where promoters would prefer to keep formation costs to a minimum. The deed of settlement consequently remained in vogue throughout our period, and many of the smaller undertakings would have regarded incorporation as wasteful expenditure as long as their distribution area was not in doubt.

Table 4.1 Legal status of North West gas companies, 1815–1880

	Incorporation within three years	Unincorporated for four years or more	Municipally created undertakings	Total
1815–1826	10	10	1	21
1827–1847	6	23	1	30
1848–1865	8	19	7	34
1866–1880	2	14	3	19

Sources: See Appendix A

The unincorporated company consequently remained a popular feature of North West gas undertaking formation procedures, promoters ignoring the refinements in company law even in the 1850s and 1860s. Of course, the older companies and those created later with large capitals took advantage of the reforms either to provide shareholders with limited liability, or secure authority for their supply operations, but the majority preferred the tried-and-trusted method of hiring an attorney to draft a deed of settlement. These attorneys had also acted as subscription agents for most of the early supply undertakings, raising the increasing quantities of capital required by exploiting their informal network of local contacts. They were assisted in this task by both the 'strategic' motivation driving people to invest in gaslighting schemes, and the clauses inserted in all constitutions which guaranteed existing shareholders first chance to purchase new issues. As we saw in the last chapter,(41) this combination of factors ensured an adequate supply of capital in the first phase of expansion up to 1826, and there is very little evidence to indicate that in the following decades North West gas companies were formed and financed in markedly different ways.

Raising the Capital

If, in general, North West gas companies were reluctant to use incorporated status in their first years of business, it is equally clear that undertakings established after the 1820s continued to rely on both the methods of forming companies and the sources of finance which had served the First Generation so well. Indeed, the whole process remained a local affair, with the promoters, management and shareholders coming from the business community to be supplied by an undertaking. We saw in Chapter 2 how gaslighting was being used in towns with a wider variety of economic functions from the 1830s, and with the exception of Blackpool's Vegetable Oil Gas Company all the undertakings were created as a result of local initiative.(42) It is also apparent that the methods of organising public meetings to discuss such a scheme were similar to those employed in the 1810s and 1820s, while the legal profession continued to play a key role in drafting company constitutions and raising the capital. The motivation behind investing in gas companies formed after the 1820s might well have changed, given the improved profitability of the industry by that time, but the techniques used to establish a public lighting venture were not much different from those which had been so effective for the First Generation.

When we examined the issues of ownership and motivation in the last chapter, it was demonstrated that the bulk of the First Generation's equity was purchased by manufacturers, merchants and retailers who were primarily interested in establishing a public gas supply for their own use. These 'strategic' motives overrode any preconceived notions that financial returns could be made on their investment, and proprietors continued to answer calls for new capital, even though dividends were poor, because they were anxious to construct a technically viable system. By the 1830s, though, in contrast to ten or twenty years earlier, it was common knowledge that gaslighting schemes could be made to pay once demand had responded to the price reductions of this era. There would consequently appear to have been a combination of 'strategic' and 'speculative' reasons why investors supported the later North West gas companies, because while the former did not diminish in importance the latter must have been an additional source of attraction once the older companies started to produce regular returns.

The continued importance of 'strategic' motives can be illustrated by examining the occupational breakdown of shareholders in eleven North West gas companies created between 1836 and 1860. This evidence can be found in Table 4.2, where the sections and categories employed are identical to those used in Table 3.2.(43) Almost two-thirds of the capital invested in five First Generation companies had been provided by 'Manufacturers' and 'Services' (see Table 3.2), and although Table 4.2 shows that there was a slight reduction in the proportion purchased by the former, the latter increased to such an extent that the two sections together accounted for 70.3% of the equity issued by these eleven companies. In fact, if one excluded the market and residential towns of Kirkham, Altrincham and Buxton then the manufacturers would have contributed as much to their local gas companies as their counterparts in Table 3.2, and for the eight industrial towns of Table 4.2 the two sections would have been responsible for 71.4% of the equity. It is also apparent that, as in Table 3.2, 'Services' was the largest section, and 'Retailers' was the largest individual category. This demonstrates the continued importance of 'strategic' motivations, because shopkeepers, merchants and publicans were the major consumers of gas up to the 1880s,(44) and they were as anxious as anybody to see a gas company established in their community. Manufacturers were obviously also significant investors in the industrial centres for exactly the same reasons, especially at Colne, Hyde and at Radcliffe & Pilkington, and in these cases they had played a leading role in starting the ventures.

There are consequently several important similarities in Tables 3.2 and 4.2, but an obvious contrast is the significantly smaller proportion of the shares bought by 'Professions'. This difference can be explained by pointing out that the five companies covered in Table 3.2 were much older than those analysed in Table 4.2, and the former's administrative, judicial and financial communities were in a more sophisticated state of development. We also saw in Chapters 1 and 2 how clerics, doctors and attorneys frequently played prominent roles in gas company formation, while the later undertakings were more commonly initiated by local manufacturers, merchants and retailers. Only at Altrincham, Clitheroe and Buxton were professionals significant investors, and these were more residential or commercial centres than the industrial towns like Colne and Haslingden. On the other hand, there is a small increase in the 'Unoccupied' share of total issues, but this was largely due to the unusual cases of Northwich, Nelson, Hyde and Altrincham, where significant proportions were purchased by 'Gentlemen' and 'Ladies'. This trend can be partially explained by the growing importance of domestic demand for gaslighting from the late 1840s, but principally one must remember that gas shares were also coming to be seen as both lucrative and relatively risk-free, and for unoccupied people living off investment income the attraction must have been strong. At the same time, manufacturers, merchants and retailers would have been aware of these monetary inducements, and clearly, as we argued earlier, North West gas companies established after the 1820s were supported for a combination of 'strategic' and 'speculative' reasons.

When the commercial viability of gaslighting ventures was added to the more general benefits bestowed on industry and commerce by such a scheme, it is apparent that promoters and their subscription agents would have encountered few difficulties in selling sufficient shares. To substantiate this one need only point out that people living outside the distributing area of the company in which they had invested held on average only 6.5% of the shares issued by the eleven companies in Table 4.2.(45) This mean, however, hides some oddities within the sample, in particular Runcorn and Buxton, where outsiders held 25.2% and 20%, respectively. Runcorn, of course, was at the heart of Merseyside's salt-coal trading network, and as such was populated by Liverpool and Warrington merchants who had some interest in a gas company providing better lighting for their offices and warehouses in the town.(46) The Buxton Gas, Coke & Coal Company on the other hand, was supported by a Manchester attorney, Edmund Buckley, who had purchased 20% of the stock, while the remainder was owned by the town's business and professional people.

Apart from these unusual cases, the average investment by outsiders in the other nine companies would have been 3% of the equity, demonstrating how, as with the First Generation, it was predominantly a case of locals financing their local gas supplier. The motivation may have taken on a more 'speculative' character, but 'strategic' reasons were still important in helping to explain why so many manufacturers, merchants and retailers were willing to support the company in the riskier start-up phase. This subject will be discussed again in the next section, but it is clear that the initial financing was undertaken by people interested in gaslighting as both a public service and an investment producing direct monetary rewards. The evidence also suggests that the process of company creation and capital formation remained a highly localised phenomenon throughout our period, and this has important implications for the industry's relationship with developments in the provincial capital markets.(47)

Gas Companies and Stock Exchanges

Arising out of the first major 'railway mania' of 1835–1837, when eighty-eight projects were started with a nominal capital of £70 million, the two stock exchanges at Manchester and Liverpool were to become significant new features of the provincial capital market.(48) The sheer volume of demand for both capital and the expertise required to raise large amounts of money had led to the formalisation of share dealing, but it is essential to remember that these were specialist brokers leading the movement, and their main interest was railway construction. Although gas shares had been traded in the financial communities of both towns, commodities of this kind were relatively insignificant when compared to railway scrip, and in the ensuing decades the former hardly featured at all in provincial stock exchange dealings.(49) In fact, up to 1880 the two institutions had quoted only Liverpool's gas companies,(50) and, as we shall see later, even those undertakings had only been listed because of government regulations controlling the way capital was issued by some managements. There was a general reluctance on the part of North West gas companies to use stock exchanges, but while this might appear to have been an opportunity ignored by the Directors, it is vital to remember that no supply operation experienced

Table 4.2 Occupational breakdown of shareholders at inception of eleven companies 1836–1860

	Clitheroe (1836)			Runcorn (1836)			Kirkham (1838)			Colne (1838)			Northwich (1839)			Haslingden (1841)		
	A	B	C%	A	B	C%	A	B	C%	A	B	C%	A	B	C%	A	B	C%
1. Manufacturers																		
Textile	12	45	18.0	0	0	0	2	6	1.8	16	59	39.3	0	0	0	18	161	29.2
Others	2	3	1.2	10	225	27.9	0	0	0	2	2	1.3	14	75	20.8	0	0	0
Sub-Total	14	48	19.2	10	225	27.9	2	6	1.8	18	61	40.6	14	75	20.8	18	161	29.2
2. Services																		
Textile Merchants	4	11	4.4	2	31	3.8	12	123	37.2	1	3	2.0	1	10	2.8	4	25	4.5
Other Merchants	3	9	3.6	10	205	25.4	3	8	2.4	2	8	5.3	6	37	10.2	3	35	6.4
Retailers	30	68	27.2	8	120	14.9	17	56	16.9	17	54	36.0	18	76	21.1	23	209	37.9
Publicans	6	19	7.6	3	45	5.5	9	26	7.8	2	8	5.3	0	0	0	3	20	3.6
Transport	0	0	0	2	30	3.7	1	6	1.8	0	0	0	0	0	0	1	5	0.9
Builders	1	1	0.4	1	20	2.4	3	14	4.2	0	0	0	3	9	2.5	1	10	1.8
Sub-Total	44	108	43.2	26	451	55.7	45	233	70.3	22	73	48.6	28	132	36.6	35	304	55.1
3. Professions																		
Legal	5	23	9.2	1	50	6.2	1	4	1.2	2	8	5.3	1	10	2.8	1	5	0.9
Banking	0	0	0	0	0	0	0	0	0	1	3	2.0	0	0	0	0	0	0
Medical	4	9	3.6	0	0	0	3	16	4.8	0	0	0	1	5	1.4	2	14	2.5
Clerics	2	8	3.2	0	0	0	0	0	0	1	1	0.7	1	2	0.5	2	13	2.4
Gas Engineers	0	0	0	0	0	0	0	0	0	0	0	0	0	0	0	0	0	0
Miscellaneous	6	19	7.6	2	14	1.7	4	9	2.7	1	1	0.7	2	13	3.6	0	0	0
Sub-Total	17	59	23.6	3	64	7.9	8	29	8.7	5	13	8.7	5	30	8.3	5	32	5.8
4. Farmers	3	8	3.2	0	0	0	3	15	4.5	0	0	0	10	32	8.9	0	0	0
5. Unoccupied																		
Gentlemen	6	26	10.4	1	45	5.5	14	41	12.4	0	0	0	11	47	13.0	8	51	9.3
Ladies	1	1	0.4	2	20	2.4	2	7	2.1	2	3	2.0	18	45	12.5	1	3	0.5
Sub-Total	7	27	10.8	3	65	7.9	16	48	14.5	2	3	2.0	29	92	25.5	9	54	9.8
Totals	85	250	—	42	805	—	74	331	—	47	150	—	86	361	—	67	551	—

	Altrincham (1844)			Radcliffe & Pilkington (1845)			Buxton (1850)			Hyde (1855)			Nelson (1860)			Total		
	A	B	C %	A	B	C %	A	B	C %	A	B	C %	A	B	C %	A	B	C %
1. Manufacturers																		
Textile	0	0	0	17	290	34.5	0	0	0	14	698	28.3	12	96	10.7	81	1355	17
Others	1	10	1.3	2	30	3.6	0	0	0	4	187	7.6	3	26	2.9	38	558	7
Sub-Total	1	10	1.3	19	320	38.1	0	0	0	18	885	35.9	15	122	13.6	119	1913	25
2. Services																		
Textile Merchants	3	35	4.4	4	80	9.5	1	5	2.5	7	99	4.0	8	95	10.6	44	517	6
Other Merchants	7	110	13.8	0	0	0	2	7	3.5	0	0	0	2	11	1.2	38	430	5
Retailers	20	208	26.0	11	170	20.2	5	18	9.0	32	652	26.5	48	152	16.9	219	1783	23
Publicans	0	0	0	4	70	8.3	3	39	19.5	5	130	5.3	1	20	2.2	37	377	4
Transport	0	0	0	0	0	0	0	0	0	0	0	0	1	2	0.2	5	43	0
Builders	2	11	1.3	4	80	9.5	4	13	6.5	2	31	1.3	14	86	9.6	35	275	3
Sub-Total	32	364	45.5	23	400	47.5	15	82	41.0	46	912	37.0	75	366	40.8	378	3425	41
3. Professions																		
Legal	3	45	5.6	0	0	0	2	50	25.0	3	136	5.5	1	10	1.1	20	341	4
Banking	0	0	0	0	0	0	0	0	0	0	0	0	1	4	0.4	2	7	0
Medical	5	70	8.7	1	20	2.4	1	5	2.5	2	124	5.0	1	2	0.2	20	265	3
Clerics	1	10	1.3	0	0	0	0	0	0	0	0	0	1	40	4.5	8	74	1
Gas Engineers	0	0	0	0	0	0	0	0	0	0	0	0	1	40	4.5	1	40	0
Miscellaneous	12	92	11.5	1	20	2.4	2	28	14.0	1	4	0.2	12	73	8.1	43	273	3
Sub-Total	21	227	27.1	2	40	4.8	5	83	41.5	6	264	10.7	17	169	18.8	94	1000	11
4. Farmers	1	15	1.8	4	70	8.3	3	11	5.5	2	31	1.3	4	55	6.1	30	237	3
5. Unoccupied																		
Gentlemen	12	70	8.7	1	10	1.2	4	24	12.0	13	163	6.6	15	143	15.9	43	443	5
Ladies	4	114	14.3	0	0	0	0	0	0	13	209	8.5	0	0	0	85	579	7
Sub-Total	16	184	23.0	1	10	1.2	4	24	12.0	26	372	15.1	15	143	15.9	128	1022	13
Totals	71	800	–	49	840	–	27	200	–	98	2464	–	126	855	–	749	7597	–

Key: A: Number of shareholders   B: Number of shares   C: Proportion of shares issued

severe financial difficulties in the nineteenth century, and the traditional methods of raising additional finance proved just as effective in the 1870s as they had been in the 1820s. Why they clung rigidly to the tried-and-tested, rather than change over to new practices, reveals a good deal about the nature of gas companies, and in examining these developments we are also led on to tracing other important aspects of their financing which are indicative of the growing prosperity of these businesses.

The traditional method of raising capital for expansion purposes revolved around a clause inserted in all North West gas company constitutions guaranteeing existing shareholders the right to purchase all new share issues at par. We noted in the last chapter how this had helped subscription agents sell the additional shares several undertakings were obliged to create as a result of underestimating their initial capital requirements,(51) because, in effect, purchasing issues at par provided proprietors with additional income when the market value of these equities had risen progressively from the 1820s. Proprietors jealously protected this right, providing all the capital required by management in the period of expansion up to 1880. It was seen as both a reward for the risk involved in the early stages and a means of preventing the dilution of ownership, ensuring a localised clique not only controlled investment and pricing policies, they also had exclusive access to the shares once dividends reached respectable and consistent levels after the 1820s. The retention of this system made seeking a stock exchange quotation irrelevant, and until the 1880s, with the exception of Liverpool's two companies, no gas share flotation took place at either of the two institutions in the region. In 1834, though, when the Liverpool Oil Gas Company was seeking permission to convert to coal-gas, parliament insisted that a clause be inserted into the ensuing private Act which was to undermine the traditional system of conducting share issues for that venture. This clause, hereafter referred to as the auction clause, stipulated that 300 of the newly authorised 1,000 £100 shares had to be sold at a public auction, preventing current proprietors from acquiring the whole issue at par. Six years later an auction clause was also included in the Act empowering Liverpool Gas Light Company to create another 500 £100 shares, and when the two companies merged into the Liverpool United Company in 1848 all their new 4,000 shares were to be sold in this way.(52)

It is not clear why the Liverpool undertakings were chosen as the first British gas companies to have an auction clause incorporated into their constitutions. The regulation was later justified, at a time when dividend controls were much more rigid, as a means of preventing companies from making indirect payments to shareholders in the form of a premium which they could make on shares issued at par,(53) but up to 1834 Liverpool Oil Gas Company had been a commercial disaster (see Appendix C). Admittedly, Liverpool Gas Light Company had been paying 10% dividends since 1824, but then so had other bulk suppliers, and the auction clause was not applied generally until 1877.(54) Having imposed an auction clause on one of the town's gas companies, the authorities must have concluded that it was only fair to insist on its rival conducting share issues in the same fashion. Not until 1865 was another North West gas company affected by the auction clause,(55) although from the 1840s it was becoming a standard provision of private gas Acts in other regions.(56) In 1877, a Standing Order of parliament finally made it compulsory for all future gas share issues to be sold at auction, and over the following decade another five North West undertakings were forced to go along the path pioneered at Liverpool.(57) The *Journal of Gas Lighting* characteristically described the auction clause as 'a distinct violation of the established rights of existing shareholders',(58) but whatever its justification the regulation was certainly to have a significant impact in the long term. In the period up to 1880, however, it affected relatively few companies, and the majority continued to use the traditional methods of raising capital confident in the knowledge that they worked so well.(59)

Auction clauses were intended as a device for transferring any premiums to be earned on the sale of new shares from existing proprietors to the companies concerned, as well as ensuring that the stock was sold at a realistic price. Management was consequently obliged to ascertain an accurate market valuation in order to abide fully with the clause. This would not necessarily involve a quotation on a local stock exchange, because, as we shall see in the next section, gas shares were traded at healthy premiums through the informal networks controlled by attorneys, but in the cases of Liverpool's two companies their respective Boards opted for formalised dealing on the Liverpool Stock Exchange. Liverpool Gas Light Company was actually able to sell its 250 £100 shares for over £45,000 through this institution, bringing an additional £20,000 into the company's reserves, compared to the traditional method of allocating them at par to existing shareholders.(60) It is not known how the less profitable Liverpool New Gas & Coke Company fared with its share auctions, but given the potentially lucrative nature of coal-gas supply in that town it is rational to presume that the sale would have been a success.(61)

The reluctance of any other North West gas companies to use either the Manchester or Liverpool stock exchanges until required to sell shares by public auction is hardly surprising. Shareholders would have been acting irrationally had they voted to replace the lucrative issue of stock at par to themselves with a public auction at a time when their companies were so profitable. They could not be expected to have shown such altruism, and for this reason share issues continued to be an exercise in self-remuneration conducted by proprietors. In short, provincial stock exchanges were un-necessary as long as the traditional system was allowed to prevail, such was the desire of existing shareholders to retain ownership within a localised clique organised by prominent local attorneys. Furthermore, the strength of these traditional methods was a testimony to the remunerative nature of gas shares after the 1820s, and in the next section we shall see what other implications this had for gas companies and their proprietors.

Controls and Profits

Auction clauses were one of the most effective means by which parliament controlled distributed gas profits in the nineteenth century.(62) Although the first use of this regulation on Liverpool's former oil-gas undertaking is at first sight puzzling, in time the authorities recognised how important it was in curbing shareholders' rights to such lucrative extra sources of income. This view had emerged as a result of the general feeling by the 1840s that attempts to limit dividends paid on gas shares had not produced the desired results. As with so many regulations relating to utilities, maximum dividends had been introduced to control canal companies because contemporaries regarded this kind of business as monopolistic, and parliament felt obliged to impose a 10% limit in order to prevent exploitative pricing.(63) This view was only applied to the gas industry as a whole after several decades spent experimenting with indirect methods of controlling private supply companies,(64) but even when maximum dividends were finally introduced as a compulsory feature of private Acts little was achieved.

As early as 1818 the Oxford and Nottingham gas companies had been restricted by their incorporating statutes to paying 10% on all original shares, the intention of parliament being to provide both a downward pressure on prices and a fund for local authority improvement purposes.(65) Reserve accounts could also be established by these companies, of up to £4,000, to be used either in topping up the dividends when profits were insufficient for a 10% dividend, or to pay arrears, and anything in excess of that £4,000 ceiling would then have to be paid over to the town's Treasurer. At Nottingham, however, the company failed to comply with this section of the Act, and instead of creating a reserve account management reinvested surplus profits in the business. By 1841, a total of £24,000 had been used in this way, but according to Roberts little effort had gone into reducing prices by improving production techniques.(66) At Oxford, a similar situation prevailed, demonstrating the ease with which gas companies were able to side-step the early measures aimed at controlling profits and pursue their own financial strategies. Neither company ever paid more than a 10% dividend in the 1820s, and indeed Oxford only achieved this level in 1835, but neither did they follow a policy of reducing prices in line with their improved profitability, defeating one of the regulation's main aims.(67)

The reluctance of parliament to impose maximum dividends on all gas companies after 1818 was a reflection of the industry's relatively poor commercial record in those early years. It was only in the 1830s and 1840s that more of the larger, profitable concerns were forced to accept a 10% limit on the dividend payments as a condition of being allowed to raise more capital. In the North West, not surprisingly perhaps, the two Liverpool companies were the first to be affected by this trend when they applied for new powers in 1834 and 1841, but after the 1847 Gasworks Clauses Act standardised this provision for companies seeking additional capital all the leading suppliers were limited to 10%.(68) The 1847 Act also allowed the Court of Quarter Sessions, if petitioned by two gas consumers, to investigate the accounts of any company controlled in this way, and if excess profits were discovered then the price of gas would have to be reduced, but there are no documented cases in the North West where these powers were ever used.

Gas prices had actually been falling considerably since the early 1830s, largely because of lower production costs, better metering and more efficient planning, allowing management the opportunity to manipulate charges to such an extent that, as Chantler argues, 'this would amount virtually to a guaranteed 10% per annum'.(69) Shareholders would consequently be willing to purchase any new issues at par because this would provide additional income from the handsome premiums to be made on most gas stocks by the 1840s, and in fact companies would no longer need to plough undistributed profits back into the business when they were so confident of selling any shares to existing proprietors. Indeed, the 1840s marked a watershed in this respect, North West companies no longer converting reinvested profits into new equities from this period, relying instead on their well-rewarded shareholders for all the expansion capital required. The legislation also allowed them to create reserve accounts from which money could be transferred to keep up dividends in times of local trading difficulties, providing further evidence that these new controls were easily by-passed.

There is general consensus that dividend controls were both ineffective and unduly generous, and by the 1850s many companies, when applying for powers to raise new capital, were being obliged to accept limits of 7.5 or even 6%. Experiences varied, for example in 1854 the Bolton Gas Co. was instructed to pay just 6.5% on the 7,466 shares created by their Act,(70) while only a year earlier Blackburn Gas Co. had been allowed to increase the nominal value of its original shares from £10 to £15, create 3,000 new shares, and continue to pay 10% on all those issued.(71) In 1860, however, another Blackburn Gas Act restricted the dividends on 6,000 fresh shares to 7.5%, and when further powers to increase the capital were sanctioned in 1876 a maximum of 7% was imposed.(72) The tightening of dividend controls consequently created a complicated capital structure for many expanding companies — in 1876 Blackburn Gas Co. had 6,000 shares paying 10%, 6,000 shares paying 7.5%, and 11,607 shares paying 7% — but it was the only way contemporaries felt confident of imposing some restraint on profitability. Blackburn was also far from unusual among the North West's First Generation gas companies, and by the 1850s most were operating a two-tier capital structure, paying 10% on their original capital and 6 to 7.5% on the more recent issues.(73) Nevertheless, until the introduction of compulsory auction clauses in 1877, shareholders were not actually limited to these levels, because management could still pay out excess profits in the form of premiums on shares issued at par, and by allowing companies to build reserve accounts this ensured consistent dividend returns even in the most difficult of circumstances.(74)

One of the main conclusions to be derived from this discussion of dividend constraints, apart from the point that they could only work effectively in conjunction with an auction clause, was that from the 1830s gas supply companies were capable of producing lucrative returns. Initially, as we saw in the last chapter, dividend performance had been inconsistent, but once technically viable systems had been developed and demand was encouraged by progressive price reductions the shareholders were amply rewarded for their patience. A full explanation of this turn-round will be offered in the next chapters,(75) but there is little doubt that by the 1830s gas undertakings were being regarded as monopolies capable of commercial exploitation. Appendix C gives a full list of the dividends paid by companies of varying size, and with the exception of Darwen and St. Helens it is evident that shareholders were receiving healthy returns from the late-1820s. The Liverpool Gas Light Co. was by far the most consistent, but that town's oil-gas company also proved to be a good investment after its conversion to coal-gas production in 1834, paying an average dividend of 10.1% until the merger in 1848.(76) As the quotation at the head of this chapter indicates, even the smaller suppliers were held in extremely high regard, and when we remember that between 1842 and 1873 northern railway companies produced 'far from princely returns' of 5 or 6%,(77) investors were well advised to look to gas shares for a better source of income. Clearly, the general consensus concerning gas companies was that: 'No public undertakings have been such uniformly safe and good investments.'(78)

Another indication of the gas industry's remunerative nature after the 1820s was the appreciable premiums to be earned on selling shares in the region's supply companies. Initially, of course, these premiums were negligible, and there is even evidence that at Preston, for example, shares were being transferred at a discount of £1 while dividends remained poor.(79) This situation was to improve markedly, though, principally as a result of the combination of better dividends with a general strategy of reducing prices to stimulate greater consumption. By the late 1820s the shares of profitable ventures like Liverpool Gas Light Co. were already trading at a premium of up to 75%,(80) and shares in the Preston Gas Light Co. were selling for up to £5 above their £20 nominal value.(81) Table 4.3 has been constructed from the monthly returns provided by the *Journal of Gas Lighting*,(82) demonstrating how by the mid-nineteenth century North West gas shares were regarded as extremely rewarding investments. The figures reveal that the average premiums for all the companies listed rose from £14.14s in 1855 to £42.16s in 1870, but because nominal share values differed in size one can only gain a true impression of the premiums by examining each individual case. An obvious conclusion is that the large First Generation companies (Liverpool United, Bolton, Preston, Blackburn, Warrington, Wigan and Ashton) provided the best premiums, often approaching, and even exceeding, 100% of their nominal share values, and even smaller businesses (Kendal, Chester, Lancaster and Rochdale) could produce healthy returns. The Prescot Gas Co. appears to have been an exception to the general rule, that holding on to North West gas shares would not only earn an investor the maximum dividends available (see Appendix C), it would also lead to an appreciable increase in the market value of that holding, and there was little parliament could do to control this aspect of the industry.

Limiting gas company dividends had clearly not affected the premiums earned on these shares, and indeed the increases in market value recorded in Table 4.3 demonstrate that investors were not affected by parliamentary controls. A full analysis of the industry's expansion in this period is necessary before we can understand why the region's gas companies became such popular investments, but this will have to wait until the next chapters.(83) It is sufficient to note in this context that statutory controls had not tarnished the reputation of gas shares, and even where auction clauses applied, for example at Liverpool, there was still a strong demand for what were widely regarded as reliable investments. Shareholders were consequently acting completely rationally when exploiting their right to take all new issues at par, and as we noted earlier this prevented gas stocks from featuring on provincial stock exchange lists. There was simply no need for North West gas companies to seek a formal quotation when their capital requirements were satisfied so adequately by calling on the support of existing proprietors, and unless an auction clause applied to a new issue then subscription agents were left with the relatively easy task of placing shares within the local investing community. For this reason the gas industry played hardly

Table 4.3 Market price of North West gas company shares in 1855, 1865 and 1870

A = nominal price B = market price

	1855		1865		1870	
	A	B	A	B	A	B
Accrington	10	15.10s	10	15	10	15
Altrincham	5	6	5	6	5	6
Ashton-under-Lyne	30	60	30	60	30	60
Birkenhead	35	37	35	?	35	?
Blackburn	15	25	15	27	15	27
Bolton	16.10s	35	16.10s	40	16.10s	35
Congleton	25	31	25	31	25	?
Dukinfield	?	?	18	27	18	36.10s
Liverpool	100	186	100	213	100	208
Prescot	9	7	9	?	9	?
Preston	20	44	20	208	20	210
Rossendale	10	?	10	15.10s	10	16
Sandbach	10	12	10	?	10	12.10s
Todmorden	5	6	5	?	5	?
Warrington	20	29	20	39.10s	20	37
Wigan	10	22	10	20	10	20
Heywood	25	?	25	40	25	?
Hyde	9	?	9	10.15s	9	10.15s
Kendal	9	?	9	17	10	19.10s
Lancaster	31.10s	?	31.10s	38	31.10s	38
St. Helens	10	?	10	18.10s	?	?
Chester	20	?	20	?	20	174
Chorley	20	?	20	?	20	27
Average premium		14.14s		27.8s		42.16s

Source: *Journal of Gas Lighting*, Oct 1855, Jan 1865, and Jan 1870.

any part in the emergence of a formalised provincial capital market, and until auction clauses were imposed on all companies management stuck rigidly to the traditional practices while they worked so effectively.

The Rise of the 'Rentier'

The informal, localised methods of raising finance were an intrinsic feature of North West gas company expansion which built an intimate and mutually – supportive bond between investors and supply operations. Only one case can be found of a company failing to place an entire issue of new shares with existing proprietors, when in 1846 the unprofitable St. Helens Gas Light Co. was left with 102 of the 400 £5 shares it had just created.(84) The company's subscription agent, John Ansdell,(85) was then asked to dispose of the remainder, and within a few months he had been able to sell the whole issue through his network of contacts.(86) In every other documented example of share placement, new issues appear to have been eagerly snapped up by existing proprietors keen to share in the industry's prosperity. At the same time, while this particular process of capital formation did not make much of a contribution to the refinements in capital mobilisation taking place in the provinces, some interesting developments occurred with regard to North West gas company ownership structures which indicate that expansion capital was provided by sectors of a local community which had not participated extensively in the riskier start-up phase. These changes require some explanation, because they demonstrate just how lucrative gas shares had become during the nineteenth century.

In the early years of a typical North West gas company's development most of the capital would have come from local manufacturers, merchants and retailers. As we saw in Table 3.2, 'Manufacturers' and 'Services' purchased 63.6% of the shares issued by five First Generation companies, while for eleven supply operations (see Table 4.2) established between 1836 and 1860 these sectors provided 70.3% of the equity. In neither case did unoccupied gentlemen or ladies invest significantly in these businesses, the proportion being 10.0% and 13.4%, respectively, reflecting the high risk factor involved in the start-up phase. We also rejected the notion that 'speculative' motives influenced decisions to buy gas shares at the inception of North West gas companies, and even though after the 1830s gaslighting had established a reputation as a commercially viable business the primary reason for supporting these utilities remained the need to gain access to a regular supply of the illuminant. In any case, unoccupied people were generally not interested in risk-taking, and as *rentiers* they depended upon a reliable source of income from their investments. By the 1830s, though one could state conclusively that provincial gas share dividends were regarded as both regular and remunerative, encouraging *rentiers* to acquire an ever-larger proportion of these equities, and at the same time financing the rapid expansion of gas supply thereafter.(87)

The consequences of all these developments for North West gas company ownership structures can be seen in Table 4.4. It is important to remember that the eight companies analysed here had been in existence for an average of forty-three years at the point of sampling, and as a result their capitals were much larger than at their inception. At the same time, only those shares paying the maximum dividend of 10% have been examined, because not only were these commodities most in demand, but ownership of such equities would also ensure that proprietors would have been given the first chance to purchase new issues at par. For these reasons the shares paying between 6 and 7.5% have been excluded from our analysis, but one must not forget that, as new issues were purchased in quantities bearing a direct relation to the number of 10% shares owned,(88) then the breakdown in Table 4.4 bears a close resemblance to the actual ownership structure for the whole capital. This gives the evidence presented a fair degree of accuracy in reflecting who had acquired North West gas shares once performance had started to improve, bringing to light a radical turn-round in the balance of ownership.

If 'Manufacturers' and 'Services' had accounted for approximately two-thirds of the start-up capital for North West gas companies (see Tables 3.2 and 4.2), after several decades in business these two sections only owned around one-quarter of the equity in Table 4.4's eight undertakings. Of course, the picture is not uniform, and at Preston, Colne, St. Helens and

Table 4.4 Occupational breakdown of North West gas company shareholders 1865–1879 (10% shares only)

	Preston (1865)			Buxton (1870)			Chorley (1871)			St. Helens (1871)			Bolton (1872)			Warrington (1872)			Colne (1875)			Lancaster (1879)			Totals		
	A	B	C%	A	B	C%	A	B	C%	A	B	C%	A	B	C%	A	B	C%	A	B	C%	A	B	C%	A	B	C%
1. Manufacturers																											
Textile	14	431	14.4	0	0	0	13	168	10.0	0	0	0	30	1941	26.0	2	77	5.3	8	91	6.9	1	142	0.5	38	2396	4.9
Others	1	24	0.8	0	0	0	2	20	1.2	15	1197	26.0	7	289	3.9	3	142	7.7	0	0	0	0	0	0	21	1672	3.4
Sub-Total	15	455	15.2	0	0	0	15	188	11.2	15	1197	26.0	37	2230	29.9	5	219	13.0	8	91	6.9	1	142	0.5	59	4068	8.3
2. Services																											
Textile Merchants	4	108	3.6	2	35	4.8	4	52	3.1	0	0	0	12	248	3.3	3	94	6.4	4	425	32.6	2	320	1.1	19	900	1.8
Other Merchants	6	193	6.4	6	59	8.0	4	100	6.0	0	0	0	6	73	1.0	4	257	17.6	3	285	21.8	6	2541	8.5	29	3252	6.6
Retailers	25	523	17.4	1	5	0.7	21	297	17.7	11	558	12.1	14	557	7.5	6	65	4.4	21	155	11.9	7	1065	3.5	92	3238	6.6
Publicans	2	12	0.4	4	144	19.6	3	26	1.5	1	48	1.0	3	62	0.8	1	7	0.5	2	14	1.0	0	0	0	13	314	0.6
Transport	0	0	0	0	0	0	0	0	0	0	0	0	0	0	0	0	0	0	0	0	0	0	0	0	3	27	0.1
Builders	5	38	1.3	3	27	3.7	0	0	0	2	109	2.4	3	59	0.8	2	39	2.7	1	5	0.3	0	0	0	10	250	0.5
Sub-Total	42	874	29.1	16	270	36.7	32	475	28.3	14	715	15.5	38	999	13.4	16	462	31.7	31	884	67.6	15	3926	13.1	166	7981	16.3
3. Professions																											
Legal	19	328	10.9	2	105	14.3	2	14	0.8	3	671	14.6	5	197	2.6	6	141	9.7	3	25	3.7	13	6369	21.2	48	7850	15.9
Banking	1	9	0.3	0	0	0	0	0	0	0	0	0	2	6	0.4	1	6	0.4	0	0	0	0	0	0	2	15	0.1
Medical	2	14	0.5	1	10	1.4	2	44	2.6	1	89	1.9	2	29	0.4	3	46	3.2	1	2	0.3	0	0	0	10	234	0.4
Clerics	5	135	4.5	0	0	0	5	57	3.4	1	9	0.2	3	274	3.7	7	109	7.5	0	0	0	1	100	0.3	19	692	1.4
Gas Engineers	0	0	0	0	8	1.1	0	0	0	0	0	0	0	7	0.1	0	0	0	1	7	1.0	1	600	2.0	3	660	1.3
Miscellaneous	9	138	4.6	4	46	6.2	4	19	1.1	4	60	1.3	17	348	4.7	3	39	2.7	2	9	1.3	6	1895	6.3	28	2448	4.9
Sub-Total	36	624	20.8	8	169	23.0	13	134	8.0	9	829	18.0	28	855	11.4	20	341	23.5	7	43	6.4	21	8964	29.9	110	11899	24.2
4. Farmers	0	0	0	3	29	3.9	24	442	26.4	0	0	0	4	140	1.9	0	0	0	2	12	1.8	2	452	1.5	31	1075	2.2
5. Unoccupied																											
Gentlemen	17	264	8.8	10	126	17.1	6	104	6.2	4	169	3.7	28	1316	17.6	10	200	13.7	20	130	19.5	16	5637	18.8	87	7961	16.2
Ladies	62	783	26.1	11	141	19.2	27	331	19.7	37	1690	36.7	58	1914	25.6	16	235	16.1	21	142	21.3	45	10879	36.3	218	16100	32.8
Sub-Total	79	1047	34.9	21	267	36.3	33	435	26.0	41	1859	40.4	86	3230	43.3	26	435	29.8	41	272	40.8	61	16516	55.1	305	24061	49.0
Totals	172	3000	–	48	735	–	117	1674	–	79	4600	–	193	7454	–	67	1459	–	89	1302	–	100	30000	–	671	49084	–

Key: A: Number of shareholders   B: Number of shares   C: Proportion of total number of shares

Bolton manufacturers, merchants and retailers were still well represented, holding over 40% of the shares, while at Warrington and Chorley their proportion was only slightly lower. Nevertheless, when one compares these figures with those in Tables 3.2 and 4.2, it is clear that there had been a significant reduction in the representation of groups which had been among the driving forces behind the establishment of public gas supply operations in the region. At Colne, for example, 'Manufacturers' and 'Services' still owned 50.9% of the 10% shares, but in 1838 they had contributed 89.4% of the start-up capital, while at Warrington the figures were 37.9% and 72.2%, respectively. Only four manufacturers had been among the sixty-two signatories of Lancaster Gas Light Co.'s original deed of settlement in 1826, but a further twenty-one were merchants, retailers and publicans, and by 1879 these categories could claim just 13.6% of the 10% shares. The balance of ownership had clearly altered dramatically in all the companies analysed, and in particular, there was a decisive shift away from 'Manufacturers' and 'Services' towards sectors which were attracted by the earning power of gas shares.

The most obvious feature of Table 4.4, when compared with our earlier analyses of shareholders' occupations, is the way 'Manufacturers' and 'Services' gave way to the 'Unoccupied' categories and attorneys as the largest groups of investors. Although *rentiers* had purchased at least 10% of the early North West gas company shares (see Tables 3.2 and 4.2), by the 1860s and 1870s their importance had grown beyond recognition and they accounted for 48.5% of the 10% equities issued by these eight undertakings. This growth was particularly marked among 'Ladies', because in Table 4.4 the category provides both the largest number of shareholders (277) and the largest proportion (32.5%). It is a trend worth examining, because we need to understand exactly why the 'Unoccupied' sectors gained in importance. Most significantly, as the companies were over forty years old, it is probable that many of the manufacturers, merchants and retailers who had purchased a large proportion of the original gas shares could well have died by the 1860s and 1870s, and, while their businesses were usually passed on to male members of the family, it was common in this era for their female relatives to inherit any investment portfolios. It is extremely difficult to illustrate the relevance of this convention, but at Preston, for example, no less than thirty-two of the sixty-two 'Ladies' listed as proprietors in 1865 had the same name as those shareholders who had invested when the company was first established. The test is hazardous, and indeed figures for other companies are not as striking,(89) possibly because names had changed due to marriage, but it is more than likely that some of the 'Ladies' in Table 4.4 would have inherited shares formerly owned by businessmen who featured in Sections 1 and 2 of Tables 3.2 and 4.2.

The whole issue of share transfers is clouded in uncertainty because so little information has survived to indicate how and when ownership structures changed so dramatically. It is clear that the company subscription agent was responsible for the transfer process, and consequently he would have tapped his local contacts when an existing proprietor wished to dispose of a holding, but few share registers remain to chart the actual pattern of transfers. Given the performance of gas shares as investments after 1830, the subscription agent would have been able to interest alternative local investors in these equities, and from the evidence presented in Table 4.4 it is evident that *rentiers* were eager to purchase those which came available. Inheritances and retirements accounted for some of the increase recorded in 'Unoccupied' shareholders, but the very fact that 'Ladies' and 'Gentlemen' retained their holdings provides clear evidence that gas stocks were secure investments. Similarly, attorneys owned many more North West gas shares than they had done in the start-up phase, almost doubling their proportion from 8.6% in Table 3.2 to 15.8% in Table 4.4, and as the legal profession was closely associated with gas company financing it says much for the value attached to these shares by the mid-nineteenth century.

Although most North West gas companies had adhered to the traditional methods of raising capital throughout our period, it is vital to note that, as a result of the changing ownership structure revealed in Table 4.4, the sources of start-up and later expansion capital were markedly different. In the riskier period, when dividends were poor and irregular, 'strategic' motives prompted manufacturers and retailers to provide the bulk of the start-up capital, but once commercial viability was assured and the shares became marketable commodities *rentiers* acquired a growing interest in the equity, and in the process financed the more rapid expansion of this period.(90) Table 4.4 reveals that together 'Professions' and 'Unoccupied' owned 72.5% of the 10% shares issued by those eight companies, while in Table 3.2 'Manufacturers' and 'Services' had accounted for 63.6% of the stock first created by five early companies, emphasising the decisive change in owner-ship structures over this period.

North West gas undertakings were consequently well served by their local communities in the nineteenth century, different sectors contributing funds for different reasons at different times. One must also emphasise that, in spite of the growing importance of *rentiers*, a high level of geographical concentration was still a key feature of the ownership pattern: the five First Generation companies featuring in Table 3.2 had on average 5% of their equity owned by people living outside the distribution area, and the figure for Table 4.4 is 9.6%.(91) This reaffirms the views put forward earlier, that ownership was still dominated by a localised clique which was controlled by the company's subscription agent. There was, as we saw in the last section, no need to formalise this system by seeking a quotation on the Manchester or Liverpool stock exchanges, and as long as gas shares remained a remunerative form of investment the shareholders were equally happy with these arrangements.

Conclusions

After having been in the mainstream of developments leading to an im-provement in the ways joint stock companies were formed and financed, from the 1830s North West gas companies became isolated from the main innovations in these areas which were introduced largely as a result of 'railway mania'. The gas industry's promoters, management and shareholders would have argued that their traditional methods of creating ventures and raising either start-up or expansion capital were effective enough in providing the finance to satisfy the growing demand for gaslighting in the region, and it is hard to find evidence to contradict such a view. By 1881 the official

returns indicate that almost £3 million had been raised by private North
West gas companies (see Table 2.2), but for the period 1815—1880 as a whole
this certainly understates the actual amount because so many of the operations
had been municipalised. It is, indeed, impossible to state exactly just how
much the region's investors had provided for private gas suppliers, but one
could estimate the figure at approximately £5.5 million.(92) This is remarkable
testimony to both the industry's expansion and its attractiveness as an
investment, especially from the 1830s. Statutory controls on dividends (and
prices) did little to diminish the demand for gas shares, and localised
cliques steadfastly refused to allow outsiders any opportunity to participate
in new issues, eagerly taking up all the stock created by management.
Ownership structures certainly altered, with regular dividends and handsome
premiums attracting *rentiers* when on the rare occasions gas shares came on
the market, but at the same time there was no attempt at formalising
investment practices, and attorneys acting as subscription agents were able
to place any shares which came available with their local contacts.

In the main, then, there is no evidence to support the contention that
difficulties raising capital constrained the expansion of North West gas
companies up to 1880. The remunerative nature of gas shares ensured a
steady flow of capital into the business from a variety of sources: in the
riskier start-up phase local businessmen supported the ventures because of
their need for gaslighting; and once gas shares earned a good reputation as
investments *rentiers* snapped them up. This enabled management to continue
expanding the business in line with market projections, and indeed by the
1840s ploughed-back profits were of much lesser importance as a result of
the improved marketability of these commodities. At the same time, this
begs the question whether gas suppliers were more interested in maximising
profits or providing a cheaper, better quality service to the local community.
Of course, they were commercial ventures, not philanthropic institutions,
and management had a duty to look after the interests of their shareholders,
but in constructing their price lists and conducting their sales strategies it is
vital to understand by what criteria they were governed, and who determined
the policies. This is the area to which we must now turn, examining how
gaslighting was made to pay, and whether management made the best of its
market opportunities to build up businesses capable of producing both
adequate returns and an improved service.

Footnotes

(1)   Cottrell (1980), pp. 162ff.
(2)   Hunt (1936), pp. 3—29.
(3)   *Ibid*, p. 13.
(4)   Cottrell (1980), p. 39.
(5)   Hunt (1936), p. 30.
(6)   Thomas (1973), p. 8.
(7)   Hunt (1936), pp. 41—44.
(8)   See earlier, pp. 24 & 45.
(9)   Matthews (1985), pp. 39—48.
(10) Cottrell (1980), p. 43.
(11) Hunt (1936), pp. 61—76.
(12) For a more detailed study see *Ibid*, pp. 90—101, and Cottrell (1980), pp. 43—45.
(13) This section is based on Hunt (1936), p. 105. W. E. Gladstone was the Minister
      at the Board of Trade.

(14) For a review of Hudson's career see Mountfield (1979), Ch. 2.
(15) Cottrell (1980), p. 45.
(16) Thomas (1973), p. 8.
(17) *Ibid*, p. 5.
(18) Stockbroking attracted a wide range of people, including insurance agents, commission agents, accountants and merchants. Killick and Thomas (1970), p. 103.
(19) Thomas (1973), pp. 11−24; Killick and Thomas (1970), pp. 101−103.
(20) Chatfield (1977), pp. 114−116.
(21) In contrast, 186 railway companies, 1,016 manufacturing companies and 1,419 mining companies appeared in this period. Hunt (1936), p. 157.
(22) *Ibid*.
(23) Killick & Thomas (1970), p. 102.
(24) On railway investment and investors see Broadbridge (1970).
(25) See earlier, p. 71.
(26) See earlier, pp. 75−77.
(27) Abram (1878), p. 60.
(28) PGLCMB, 3 May 1836. See earlier, pp. 74−75.
(29) *Ibid*, 1 Jan 1838.
(30) Preston Gas Act, 1839, cap. 3.
(31) For an examination of the Chester and Kendal companies see later, pp. 173−177.
(32) Rowlinson (1984), pp. 98−142. See also later, pp. 110−111.
(33) Rossendale Union Gas Co. had been forced to spend £2,300 on legal costs in 1853. See earlier, p. 41.
(34) See later, pp. 110−111.
(35) For a review of government controls see earlier, pp. 51−55, as well as Chantler (1939), pp. 60−84, and Rowlinson (1984), Ch. 3 and 4.
(36) Gasworks Clauses Act, 1847, Cap. XV.
(37) Chatfield (1977), p. 113.
(38) The costs for Preston Gas Light Co. were £866 in 1839, and £451 in 1853, while those for Blackburn Gas Light Co. fell from £730 in 1838 to £604 in 1853.
(39) See earlier, pp. 55−56.
(40) See earlier, pp. 54−55.
(41) See earlier, pp. 80−86.
(42) This paragraph is based on p. 45.
(43) See earlier, pp. 86−87.
(44) See later, pp. 166−168.
(45) The proportions were: Colne 0%; Runcorn 25.2%; Radcliffe & Pilkington 3.6%; Northwich 6.6%; Kirkham 0%; Altrincham 0.6%; Clitheroe 7.6%; Haslingden 0%.
(46) Some of the Liverpool businessmen who invested were G W Tobias, J Bartlett, I Fisher, W Stock and J Fletcher. It should be emphasised, though, that the company was dominated by local soap manufacturers. See later, p. 152.
(47) Buxton Gas Light & Coke Co. Registration document, 3 Dec 1850.
(48) Thomas (1973), pp. 11−24.
(49) *Ibid*, pp. 11 & 22.
(50) Killick & Thomas (1970), p. 105 and *Manchester Stock Exchange Daily Lists*, 1836−90.
(51) See earlier, pp. 80−81.
(52) See earlier, p. 27.
(53) Chantler (1939), p. 69. See later, p. 113, for the appreciable premiums to be earned on gas shares.
(54) Harris (1956), p. 42.
(55) This was the much smaller Littleborough Gas Co. which was obliged under a private Act to auction £9,870 of its £30,000 start-up capital. PP, 1881 Return.
(56) Chantler (1939), p. 69.

(57) These were the companies at Chester, Preston, Prescot, Radcliffe and Pilkington, and Stretford. PP, 1881 Return. These companies only operated auction clauses in the 1880s, and so fall out of our period for consideration.
(58) JOGL, 1 May 1877, p. 657.
(59) The only gas company quoted on the Manchester and Liverpool stock exchanges in 1880 was the Liverpool United Gas Light Co., and by 1890 only Stretford, Altrincham and Chester had been added to the lists. See *Manchester Stock Exchange Daily Lists* (1880; 1890) and *Burdett's Official Intelligence*, 1890.
(60) The company held three separate auctions between 1841 and 1845. Harris (1956), p. 53.
(61) Even after an auction clause was imposed, a company could still simply invite tenders without securing a stock exchange listing.
(62) Chantler (1939), p. 63.
(63) Rowlinson (1984), p. 172.
(64) See earlier, pp. 52−53
(65) Chantler (1939), p. 66.
(66) Roberts (1980), pp. 6−11.
(67) Rowlinson (1984), pp. 172−173.
(68) Chantler (1939), p. 67.
(69) *Ibid*, p. 68. See later, pp. 163−166, for a discussion of prices.
(70) Bolton Gas Act, 1854, Cap xx.
(71) Abram (1878), p. 113.
(72) *Ibid*. pp. 155 and 224.
(73) PP, 1881 Return.
(74) See later, pp. 228−229.
(75) See later, pp. 160−163.
(76) PP, 1847 Return.
(77) Broadbridge (1970), p. 63.
(78) This was quoted in the provisional registration documents for Kendal Union Gas & Water Co. from a meeting held in November 1845 of the shareholders in that enterprise.
(79) See Preston Gas Light Co. Transfer documents, HGA.
(80) Thomas (1973), p. 11, shows that a Liverpool Gas Light Co. £100 share could sell for up to £380, but in view of the evidence in Table 4.2 a premium of 75% was more likely.
(81) Preston Gas Light Co. Transfer document, HGA.
(82) Each week the JOGL published a comprehensive list of share prices.
(83) See later, pp. 160−163.
(84) SHGLCBM, 28 Sept 1846. See later, pp. 152−154, for an explanation of the company's troubles.
(85) Barker & Harris (1954), p. 203 claim that he was 'the town's first successful solicitor' who wrote many of St. Helens' early legal documents in his capacity of clerk to the Improvement Commissioners.
(86) SHGLCBM, 1 Dec 1846.
(87) For a review of the industry's growth see earlier, pp. 46−49.
(88) Proprietors were only allowed to buy new shares in quantities which bore a direct relation to the number of 10% shares they possessed.
(89) The available information shows that comparable figures for other towns were: Bolton 10; Chorley 10; Colne 7; and St. Helens 4.
(90) See earlier, pp. 46−49.
(91) Where adequate information is available we can see that the proportion of equity held by outsiders was: Preston 5.7%; Lancaster 13.7%; Chorley 11%; Colne 17.5%; and St. Helens 10.3%.
(92) See earlier, p. 47.

5
Management Strategy and Business Development to 1830

> 'The Public have obtained so great, and so rapidly in-
> creasing a means of adding to the convenience and
> comfort of society, as the use of gas, under due manage-
> ment, must afford.'
>
> Report from the Select Committee on Gas-Light
> Establishments PP, 1823, v, 233.

Although sufficient evidence has been produced to dismiss any notion that North West gas companies were prevented from expanding by a shortage of capital, and promoters were able to overcome the legal obstacles imposed by company law at that time, business development up to 1830 was by no means trouble-free. There may well not have been a financial constraint on company inception, and in time shareholders were well rewarded for the risks taken in those first years of trading, but it is still true to say that initially most First Generation companies performed badly. Much was made of gaslighting's superiority over other forms of artificial illumination, in terms of both safety and price, and logically one might expect management to have exploited the full potential of these advantages by building profitable businesses. Most undertakings were also granted sole access to their local markets, yet in the first years of trading this monopolistic position did not provide high, or even regular, profits.(1) The limited market for gaslighting at that time would have held up more significant progress, while the service itself was usually only available for up to seven hours each day, but these were only two of the problems facing management, and in this chapter we shall assess how the first private gas company Directors met these challenges and established commercially viable businesses.

An examination of early management must necessarily provide a detailed analysis of who was responsible for taking the key decisions on such matters as investment and prices. The services of a specialist contractor had been recruited by many companies, for the purposes of building a technically viable system, but rarely did these engineers stay in one town after the works had been commissioned, and in any case their mode of operating usually resulted in long lead-times which placed additional strains on finances.(2) In the absence of a body of professional gas managers, major shareholders were consequently obliged to take on the demanding task of running the business, and any explanation for the poor performance must revolve around the policies and procedures arising from this management system. To a large extent, the first Directors were victims of circumstances, in that management techniques were poorly developed in the early-nineteenth century, and gaslighting was a new type of business to these

men. Problems with contractors, equipment manufacturers and major consumers also dogged progress, but the relationship between ownership
patterns and management control were influential features of early company
results, and the ineffective planning methods instituted by part-time
Directors only compounded the situation.

Gaslighting as a commercial operation posed a series of problems for
management up to 1830, and there was much that contemporaries failed to
grasp about the economics involved. On the other hand, while highlighting
the possible existence of a managerial constraint on company growth, it is
vital to remember the 'strategic' motives which lay behind the decisions to
invest in these ventures. This helps to rationalise the actions of Directors,
especially when the limited market for gaslighting is also considered, and
in assessing the ability of management to exploit the commercial potential
in their new product, a sense of perspective is essential. One must not fall
into the obvious trap of regarding all North West gas companies simply
as profit-making enterprises, and whilst the concern at Liverpool (and
Manchester) may well have operated by different criteria, it is apparent that
dividends were initially not a top priority for management. Nevertheless, in
the pursuit of their general aims they devised strategies which were to have
longer-term implications for the industry's expansion after 1830, and while
the issues are often by no means clear-cut, what we shall have to say about
early performance is vital to an understanding of the story up to 1880.

Senior Management

Local initiative and capital had been responsible for establishing almost all
North West gas undertakings, and inevitably this resulted in prominent
members of a community being elected on to a committee which took the
burden of running a business few understood. Typifying the embryonic
state of management at that time, these committees used a variety of titles
('committee of management' or 'committee of trustees') to describe their
status, but they were in effect acting as a Board of Directors, and in the
early years of a company's development this body took all the decisions.
The Board planned the works and mains system, and decided on such
matters as legal status, investment strategy, pricing, raw material purchases,
staff recruitment and dividend policy. Routine functions were often delegated
to the few employees hired to run either the works or the office, as we shall
see in the next chapter,(3) but even here Directors were expected to visit the
premises on a regular basis, extending their role from strategic into functional
management.(4) Furthermore, in the early months Board meetings were
held on a weekly basis, and while this burden would eventually be relaxed
the Directors were clearly expected to commit themselves wholeheartedly to
the task of building a business capable of satisfying proprietors' expectations.

Although a Director's burden was initially time-consuming, it is important
to stress the unremunerative nature of senior management. Rowlinson has
likened this to 'the eighteenth century system of government by unpaid
squires and gentlemen',(5) and certainly it is difficult finding evidence that
in the early years a Board member was allocated regular salaries or fees. Of
course, the post was nominally held on a part-time basis, and the Directors
were mostly in business themselves, but they did not regard this position

as an opportunity to increase their personal incomes directly. It was 1824 before the Preston Gas Light Co. Board received any honorarium, and even then they were simply given the thirty shares forfeited by former proprietors to distribute amongst themselves,(6) while up to 1831 their counterparts in Bolton were allowed only an annual meal financed from the fines levied on Directors for non-attendance.(7) Above all, it is important to emphasise that there was no conspiracy to defraud local investors, because the promoters and Directors were usually the same people, and their hopes for the venture were clearly explained. The enterprises were Director-led from the outset, the same individuals often having been responsible for promoting the schemes, and in the pursuit of their broader aims they ensured that decision-making followed a path commensurate with most of the shareholders' aims.

When considering the payment of senior management, it is also important to add that deeds of settlement or incorporating Acts included a series of regulations intended to avoid certain abuses. They were especially prevented from contracting 'any debts to a greater amount than the funds in the hands of the Treasurer'.(8) Some articles of association, like those of canal companies, even prevented Directors from using their privileged position to supply the gasworks with equipment or raw materials, and in Wigan Gas Co.'s case this resulted in the resignation of six of the thirteen-man Board within a year of the business's creation.(9) On the whole, however, this kind of abuse was rare, and there are no known cases of any North West Directors being prosecuted for fraud or any other dubious practices. This re-emphasises the non-speculative nature of gas supply in the region,(10) and while the collection of 'rogues' and 'speculators' who sat on certain London Boards might have run their businesses 'crookedly and incompetently',(11) in the North West participation at that level was linked to a range of alternative influences.

Contemporary opinion was in fact divided over the trustworthiness of joint stock company Directors. There were those who, like Adam Smith, believed that 'being the managers of other people's money.... it cannot well be expected that they should watch over it with the same anxious vigilance with which partners in a private copartnery watch over their own'.(12) Pollard has demonstrated that the evidence to support such views was plentiful,(13) and clearly some London gas companies were badly served by their elected officers. On the other hand, the joint stock company form was growing in popularity after 1790, and more investors were willing to risk money in this type of venture, regardless of the warnings from eminent economists and politicians.(14) The reasoning behind this trend also reveals one of the fallacies perpetrated by people like Smith, because it was often assumed that an automatic divorce between control and ownership took place in joint stock companies, but rarely did this actually occur in provincial utilities. The late-eighteenth century canal undertakings had invariably included large shareholders as Directors,(15) and North West gas companies were controlled and managed by those responsible for initiating the schemes, and buying shares, from the outset. Notwithstanding this point, though, there was also clearly an obvious purpose behind the decision of prominent local people to associate themselves with these ventures, highlighting once again the whole issue of motivation which was so central to our discussion of investment.

The intimate relationship between control and ownership at Board level was in part an inevitable result of the informal and localised provincial investment system. We saw in the last two chapters how joint stock companies would usually only receive sufficient finance when supported by well-known and trusted local businessmen, and as the gas promoters were often prominent members of a community they were able to convince potential investors that the venture was not a 'bubble'.(16) The success of most capital issues demonstrates how well they achieved these aims, but when explaining the reasons why important residents were linked with gas companies one must also remember that utilities became another extension of the urban power structure. Joyce describes how the North West's Tory-Anglican elite led local society 'by divine right of precedence' at that time, and they saw ownership and control of the gas supply as a further manifestation of their grip on a town's institutions.(17) It is consequently no coincidence that the dominant Tory families were all major shareholders in the region's gas companies, and in many cases they were also actively involved in their management.(18)

A more detailed discussion of early-nineteenth century urban power networks will be incorporated into Chapter 7's analysis of municipalisation, but it is vital to understand the status of gas company Directors and the socio-political reasons why they were so closely involved in gas supply. Having identified influences of this kind, one can then begin to place in a wider perspective the 'strategic' motives which lay behind most decisions to purchase the first share issues.(19) The desire to extend their influence over every aspect of a community's economic, social and political life was clearly a central driving force behind the willingness to finance and manage local utilities. With regard to gas investments specifically, they were anxious not only to secure a regular source of supply, they also wanted to exert as much control as possible over pricing and investment policies, and in view of their status these aims were often fulfilled. It was largely a matter of ensuring effective representation at the highest managerial levels, and as a result we shall see that the early development of most North West gas companies was dominated by the needs of certain interest groups which had played leading roles in forming and financing the operations.

When we examined the issue of ownership it was established that industrial and commercial groups contributed most of the riskier start-up capital, whether the companies were created before or after 1826. Although the profitability of gaslighting was uncertain in the first years of trading, local manufacturers, retailers and merchants were anxious to secure a regular supply of the new illuminant, and consequently they were willing to pump money into the businesses in order to achieve these 'strategic' aims. Of course, buying shares was no guarantee that the company would act in their interests, and the most effective means of ensuring that policy was favourable would be to acquire influence at Board level. Indeed, the purchase of shares for 'strategic' reasons can only be proven by examining the composition of early Boards and the policies they pursued, and in revealing the close links which existed between control and ownership it is possible to understand why certain priorities were pursued.

If this thesis is to be substantiated, it is to be expected that the dominant groups identified in Table 3.2 should have provided most of the Directors

Table 5.1 Composition of North West gas company Boards at the time of their creation, 1815–1826

		No.	% of Total
1.	*Manufacturers*		
	Textiles	32	21.9
	Others	6	4.1
	Sub-total	38	26.0
2.	*Services*		
	Textile Merchants	12	8.3
	Other Merchants	18	12.3
	Retailers	23	15.7
	Publicans	6	4.1
	Transport	0	0
	Builders	4	2.7
	Sub-Total	63	43.2
3.	*Professions*		
	Legal	15	10.3
	Bankers	3	2.1
	Clerics	3	2.1
	Medical	5	3.4
	Gas Engineers	0	0
	Miscellaneous	9	6.2
	Sub-Total	35	24.0
4.	*Farmers*	0	0
5.	*Unoccupied*		
	Gentlemen	10	6.8
	Ladies	0	0
	Sub-Total	10	6.8
	Total	146	–

Companies analysed: Ashton-under-Lyne, Preston, Bolton, Blackburn, Chester, Rochdale, Kendal, Wigan, Warrington, Chorley, Oldham, Macclesfield and the two Liverpool undertakings.

while the mains systems were being planned and the pricing structure determined. The available evidence is not always enlightening on matters of shareholders' occupations, but in Table 5.1 it has been possible to analyse the composition of fourteen Boards at the time of their creation. Every effort has been made to identify occupations on the same basis as that undertaken when examining shareholders,(20) but it is important to remember that Table 5.1 includes a larger number of companies than Table 3.2, broadening the sample to cover over half of the North West ventures formed up to 1826 (see Appendix A).

A striking conclusion to be drawn from comparing Table 5.1 with Table 3.2 is the close relationship between the proportions of share capital purchased and the corresponding representation of those groups on early Boards. The largest group in both Tables is 'Textile Manufacturers', and although there was a smaller proportion of Directors than shareholders in the 'Services' section in Table 3.2, together with 'Manufacturers' they still accounted for 69.2% of the Directors, compared to 63.6% of the capital. The number of

'Other Merchants' has been boosted by the twelve Directors of Liverpool Oil-Gas Co. who represented the oil trade, but this again indicates the manner in which Boards were initially dominated by those sectors most responsible for establishing the ventures.(21) The major groups of share-holders, and particularly the larger manufacturers, were simply converting their roles as initiators and financiers into one of active management. In addition, one must remember that control of urban society was still very much the preserve of a privileged minority, and the management of North West gas companies was an extension of this hierarchical system, allowing prominent local businessmen to reinforce their control over structure and strategy.

The analysis of early Directors in Table 5.1 confirms the existence of close links between ownership and management, but before we go on to demon-strate how this was extended to consumption through the bias in certain policies it would be helpful to reveal how the system worked on the ground. On average the Directors of companies featuring in Table 3.2 owned 17.3% of the issued share capital in their respective companies, but this inevitably hides significant variations, from the unusually low figure of 5% at Preston to 28.3% at Warrington.(22) Preston Gas Light Co. is actually an exceptional case in this respect, because none of the partners in Horrockses, the town's leading cotton firm, sat on the Board, even though their collective holdings would have comfortably exceeded those of the Directors.(23) There were, however, two cotton manufacturers on that Board, both of whom were closely connected with Horrockses,(24) and later passages will confirm that the firm was able to play a leading role in determining key aspects of company policy. At Blackburn and Bolton the main millowners preferred to participate directly in the management of their gas undertakings, with prominent local manufacturers like John Fleming, Thomas Livesey and James Pilkington sitting on the Board of Blackburn Gas Light Co.,(25) and John Smith, James Ormrod and William Crompton taking similar positions in Bolton Gas Light & Coke Co.(26)

Of course, describing the representation of leading local businessmen is only providing part of the story, because neither individuals nor groups were majority owners of capital, and ownership was in general extensively dispersed. There are even cases of people from Sections 3 and 5 taking prominent positions within some companies, but they were often passion-ately interested in gas lighting, having been closely involved in the venture's promotion.(27) The key additional considerations were the amount of gas a group might consume, and the threat posed to a company's monopoly, emphasising the close links which existed in the early development of most companies between management, strategy and consumption. It is only by examining this relationship that a complete understanding of the industry's first hesitant efforts can be achieved, and in the following sections evidence will be produced to demonstrate how in those years the interests of large consumers remained paramount. One must be especially wary of making the dangerous assumption that most North West gas companies were initially managed as profit-making ventures, and while a careful eye was always kept on the marginal costs of expansion, rewarding shareholders out of the surpluses generated from this cautious strategy was rarely regarded as a top priority until other matters had been settled.

Early Problems and Solutions

An obvious conclusion to draw from the performance of early gas suppliers is that most experienced severe difficulties paying dividends, even though a monopoly of the local lighting market was normally assured. Table 3.1 illustrates how for fourteen of the First Generation there was an average delay of four years before shareholders received any return, and when profits were made management normally ploughed them back into the venture.(28) There are naturally many reasons which help to explain this trend, but above all management was concerned principally with the development of a technically viable system which would provide a regular and safe supply of gas, and the reinvestment of profits can be seen as evidence of the 'strategic' motives behind their actions. They were also concerned to maintain high prices which would cover costs and provide a surplus for works extensions, but before analysing these issues it is necessary to consider how the Directors tackled the mundane features of building a new business in this pioneering phase.

One of the first tasks facing promoters and Directors was to convince contemporaries that gaslighting was safe. In London, Samuel Clegg had been forced to resort to the extreme of piercing a gasholder, in order to convince sceptics that an explosion would not ensue after an accident of this kind.(29) Nothing as expensive was attempted in the North West, but the official launch of a service would be accompanied by some ceremony as a means of overcoming any scepticism, as well as advertising the capabilities of gaslighting. The fictionalised account of Colne Gas Co.'s inauguration describes how beer, pies and music were laid on for the curious audience,(30) and a Bolton Gas Light Co. employee remembered how on a similar occasion in his town the streets were 'thronged with sightseers, who eagerly debated the merits of the new light'.(31) Preston Gas Light Co. installed lamps on the obelisk located in the market-place (see the photograph on p. 133), and the *Preston Chronicle* reported how: 'The street lights shone with an effulgence that at once annihilated every doubtful presage [sic].'(32) The *Westmorland Gazette* similarly reported that, when Kendal Gas Co. first lit the Town Hall and main streets: 'A beautiful Gas Star . . . shone conspicuously and dazzled the wondering bewildered eyes of the numerous groups assembled to witness the interesting spectacle.'(33)

Management was evidently successful in securing good publicity at the time the service was launched, bringing to the attention of potential consumers just exactly what the company had to offer. As we shall see later, a street lighting contract was also essential at this stage if the service was to be advertised, providing a natural shop-window for the business, and, most importantly, demonstrating both the safety aspect and the regularity of supply. In this context, the companies were very much at the mercy of their Engineer, and although it was common to have lead-times of at least a year when the systems were built, and contractors were prone to extensive plant modifications, the apparatus installed in the North West does not appear to have caused any concern over safety.(34) Only at Manchester was there a serious explosion,(35) and although it caused sufficient concern for a Select Committee of 1823 to request details of the incident, most accepted that human error was the cause, rather than any engineering flaw.(36)

The construction of North West gasworks was in general an engineering success. Contractors might well have experimented with new ideas, extending the lead-times inordinately in some cases, but at least this proved technically effective, and the systems supplied on a regular basis. At the same time, it is important to point out that all the blame for delays cannot be heaped on contractors' shoulders, because not only were they obliged to improvise with an evolving technology, they in turn were dependent upon their own suppliers for equipment delivered promptly and to specification. The Chairman of Blackburn Gas Light Co. had to report in January 1819 that the inability to light the town by the date promised (September 1818) was entirely attributable to 'the failure of the Contractors for the Buildings to complete their work'.(37) Of course, apart from the gas supply operations, there was no gas engineering industry at that time, and management was obliged to place orders with general suppliers inexperienced in the fabrication of equipment like retorts. In 1826 Wigan Gas Co. rejected four out of the nine retorts it had just received from a local engineering business,(38) and problems of this kind would severely handicap any attempt to match supply with demand. For branch piping they were even obliged to use surplus gun barrels left over from the Napoleonic Wars, emphasising the extent to which improvisation was an important asset for the pioneers when building their systems.(39)

If arranging the provision of suitable materials could cause problems for the gas contractors specially hired to build gasworks, then these difficulties would have been compounded by the technical vacuum many left after completing the installation. Not only was there an undeveloped gas engineering industry, there was also only a handful of specialist gas engineers in the country, and as we saw in Chapter 1 they were hard pressed to meet the demands placed on their skills. Bolton Gas Co.'s poaching of Ralph Spooner from Preston encapsulates the situation,(40) and the experience he had gained as John Grafton's assistant would have been the only recognisable form of training available at that time. Permanent staff were often hired while the contractor was still completing the system, in order that certain essential techniques might be learnt,(41) and neighbouring gasworks could also be visited as a means of picking up new ideas,(42) but serious problems still remained.

The acute shortage of suitably qualified engineering staff prompted Directors into making imaginative use of local skills. Spooner's departure from Preston resulted in Horrocks seconding one of their mill engineers, William Elsworth, to act as full-time Engineer,(43) and he actually remained in that post until 1839. There was some logic in this appointment, particularly as that gas company supplied many of the cotton mills in the vicinity, but, as we shall see, at first Elsworth clearly lacked expertise in key areas. Liverpool Gas Light Co. was rather more fortunate in finding a replacement for James Hargreaves when he left in 1817, because they were able to recruit William Sadler, the son of a famous balloonist who had used gas to inflate his flying craft. In fact, Sadler had received some scientific training from his father, an Inspector of Chemistry to the Admiralty, and up to 1821 he was responsible for the successful expansion of the largest private gas company in the region. Only an argument with the Treasurer caused Sadler's resignation, but this heralded the accession of the King family to the post of Engineer, and their contribution to gas engineering and management proved extremely effective.(44)

The long lead-times between company inception and first regular supply, the inconsistent service provided by equipment manufacturers and suppliers, and the scarcity of experienced gas engineers, were all endemic features of a nascent industry, but while the pioneers were willing to improvise with the resources available, there is clear evidence that this organisational environment was not conducive to effective commercial performance. One of the principal reasons given by the Directors of Preston Gas Light Co. for their failure to report a dividend after four years of trading was that 'the experience of the persons best acquainted with the business of these establishments was extremely limited for a considerable time after the formation of the company'. They went on to bemoan how 'the additions which were in such rapid succession called for by the progressive demands for the new illuminating power rendered it frequently necessary to lay aside or materially alter implements... which had cost considerable sums of money'.(45) This demonstrates how seriously they felt the loss of Spooner, and highlights the grave shortcomings in the planning procedures employed at that time.

The weaknesses in Preston's managerial team were by no means unique; it was a predicament in which most provincial gas undertakings were placed. As the *Journal of Gas Lighting* later reflected, early managers exhibited an 'inexperience and ignorance of the advantages of a systematic control over their daily operations'.(46) Again, the generally embryonic nature of early-nineteenth century management techniques would have explained some of these weaknesses,(47) but the responses of early gas company Directors to this situation appear to have been at least *ad hoc*, if not frequently inadequate. In the smaller operations, matters were further exacerbated by the tendency to hire engineering staff on a part-time basis, and as we shall see in the case of St. Helens Gas Co., this led to major problems in the supervision of both production and office procedures.(48)

Newbigging, in one of his influential publications on the subject of gasworks management, argued that: 'One of the evidences of good administrative skill in the conduct of a gasworks is the ensuring that extensions are carried out systematically and with foresight.'(49) Written in the 1860s, this advice was based on several decades of experience in the field,(50) and it must have been heavily influenced by the knowledge that in the early years systematic planning was rarely used. As Johnes and Clegg noted in 1847, a major contributor to the poor performance of gas companies in their first years of operation was the 'errors, and consequent loss of capital which have often occurred, both in the first erection of gas-works, and also in the modes of making gas adopted at these establishments'.(51) It is difficult to disagree with these views, and reading the Board minutes of those pioneering businesses one is given the impression that Directors worked largely on a hand-to-mouth basis, responding to problems as they arose, rather than planning strategy to obviate any predictable difficulties.

The most fundamental aspect of this pragmatic approach to planning was the general tendency to underestimate the demand for gaslighting, leading to the 'errors' noted by both Johnes and Clegg and the Directors of Preston Gas Light Co., and forcing swift reassessments of capacity and loading at short notice. There were clearly extenuating circumstances which deflect some of this criticism, particularly with regard to the availability of materials and qualified managerial staff, but an initial conservatism undoubtedly prevented companies from fully exploiting the commercial potential in gaslighting, and this managerial constraint would help to explain why the dividends were so poor in the early years. At the same time, however, this assessment ignores the 'strategic' motives analysed in Chapter 3, and before drawing any negative conclusions on the quality of early management, it is important to remember why the companies were created and in whose interest they were run.

Investment and Marketing Strategies

Planning and constructing a gas supply network in the early-nineteenth century was dictated by a variety of influences, but principally these can be identified as the cost of buying plant and mains, the predilections of management, and the market for gaslighting. The first two factors have already been discussed, and they will be considered again, but the latter has received scant treatment. It was briefly noted in Chapter 3 that up to the 1850s, gaslighting was used mainly in shops, public houses, offices, factories, streets, and a small number of large homes,(52) yet little mention has been made of the reasons why the market was predominantly commercial and industrial in character. Above all, one must remember that, although it was cheaper and safer than oil or candles, gaslighting was still prone to emit the unwanted by-products of heat, smell and even sulphuric acid,(53) and for domestic consumers this was too much to bear. In the more spacious premises of mills, shops, taverns and offices, as well as in the streets, these by-products were less obvious, giving the companies an identifiable group of markets to exploit. The method of charging customers on a rental basis (often three months in advance) also proved unsatisfactory for householders, because they might not be in one room all the time, while in commercial or industrial premises the system provided at least a basis for calculating usage.

Another prime consideration for potential customers would have been the price of gas, and in spite of gaslighting's relative cheapness, companies were initially obliged to charge between 12/6 (62.5p) and 15/- (75p) per thousand cubic feet.(54) This put the product beyond the means of the mass market, and in fact it was only in the 1880s, after prepayment meters and incandescent burners had been introduced, that the majority of town-dwellers were connected up to the mains. Of course, companies were obliged to cover their costs and provide funds for further plant extensions, and the prices prevailing up to 1830 were only a reflection of these harsh economic realities. One should also remember that dividends were slow in coming, indicating that the prices were not set at levels which exploited consumers, while most of the early profits were actually ploughed back into the business in order to improve the service.

The largest nineteenth century market for gaslighting was in the retail sector, and with the number of shops increasing at a faster rate than the population, companies were faced with a rising demand for their product. Publicans also competed for custom by offering more attractive premises, and shopkeepers used the artificial light as a means of advertising their stocks, helping to accelerate the major changes taking place in this sector at that time.(55) Even greater expansion was to come from the 1850s with the advent of plate glass (and cheaper gas),(56) but in the early years companies relied on retailers for their perennial source of custom. Mills and street lamps were also major users of gas, of course, but these markets were seasonal in nature, and, as we shall see later, other factors could affect demand from these customers.

Gaslighting was consequently limited principally to commercial, industrial and local government sectors, leading to the concentration of main-laying in the town-centre where most of these consumers would have been located in the early-nineteenth century. The service itself was also initially limited to around seven hours of supply per day, further constraining hopes of rapid expansion. In terms of control over investment strategy, though, while retailers were important as both shareholders and consumers, it was the prominent local manufacturers who dominated decision-making. Indeed, confirming our earlier claim that ownership, management and consumption were all closely linked, the pattern of main-laying in those first years was dictated by the requirements of larger consumers. There are exceptional cases where different policies were pursued, and certainly the largest undertakings (in Liverpool and Manchester) did not follow the same pattern of development, but in the medium-sized industrial centres especially a high level of standardisation can be discerned from the way management focused on the needs of some groups at the expense of others.

The relationship between ownership, management and consumption can be illustrated by referring to developments in some of the main towns. Awty's comment, that 'the requirements of the cotton mills were the consideration that influenced the Preston company' in its first decade of trading, would be typical,(57) and it is apparent how, with one exception, by 1820 each of that undertaking's branch mains terminated at a factory. This system is illustrated in Figure 5.1, demonstrating how the works of Horrocks & Jackson's, Horrockses in Frenchwood and Cotton Court, Collinson & Watson, the Canal factory, and Riley & Paley's were all connected to the gasworks from the outset.(58) The Chapel Street branch had been laid at the behest of the company's principal founder, Fr. Dunn, and within two years another main had been laid to his school in Fox Street, but otherwise main-laying in Preston was initially a matter of focusing on the needs of substantial cotton manufacturers. By the early months of 1821, the works of Park & Oxendale in Pitt Street had also been lit,(59) and throughout the period up to 1830 mains extensions were planned and executed in response to the mill-building trend.(60)

Reflecting this concern with potentially large consumers, Bolton Gas Co. pursued a remarkably similar strategy. This venture's first experimental trial was conducted on the premises of Dixon & Smith,(61) one of the town's largest cotton mills, and part-owned by an early Chairman of the gas undertaking, John Smith.(62) By 1821, the system had been extended to connect all the similar-sized establishments, like those of William Crompton, Ormrod & Hardcastle, Bolling, Wingfield, and Lum,(63) and it is revealing to note that most of these businessmen were all shareholders in the gas company, and some sat on the Board.(64) At Blackburn, the Board even decided in 1825 to build a second gasworks, because, due to 'the low

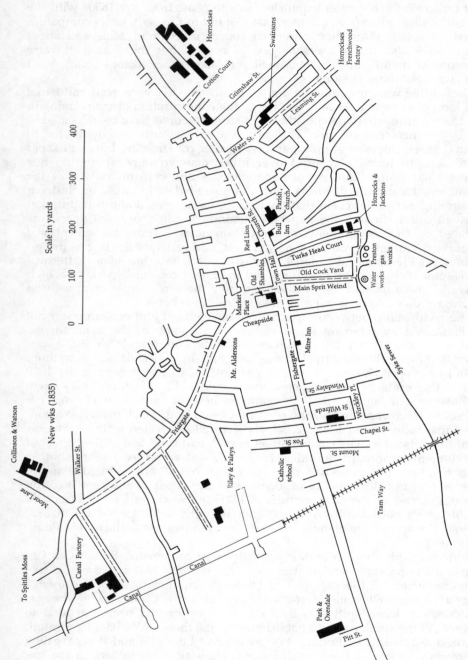

Figure 5.1 Preston Gas Light Co. distribution system (1820).

A view of the market-place in Preston (c.1820), showing the gaslamp at the top of the obelisk.

situation of the cotton factories at the bottom of King Street, the company are unable to supply such factories with gas to the satisfaction of their proprietors'.(65) The large mills of John & Thomas Livesey & Co., John Fleming, Messrs. Fielden & Co., William Throp, Robert Townley, and James Rodgett had already been supplied for several years by that time, and as all of these businessmen were also Blackburn Gas Light Co. shareholders, and several were Directors,(66) they were making sure that their interests were being given top priority. Ashton-under-Lyne's gasworks was also built within sight of fourteen cotton mills and two foundries, reflecting the desire of the six industrialists on the Board to maximise the value of their investment.(67)

Management was naturally acting rationally when showing such a concern for the requirements of prominent local manufacturers, because expansion was dependent upon the marginal costs of connecting new consumers. Laying mains and supplementing both production and storage capacity were an expensive business, and as marginal costs were so high it was vital that a guaranteed source of custom like a factory should be assured as a means of recouping investment. In addition, as we shall see in the next section, gas companies were also aware of the potential threat from manufacturers who could afford to supply themselves, and it was vital that any competition for custom should be stifled instantly. Once a system had been established it was then relatively cheap to install branch pipes to feed new consumers off the principal mains, keeping marginal costs low and providing the basis for a reduction in average costs by exploiting any economies of scale as consumption started to rise.

In evaluating these fundamental economics of gas supply, it is important to stress that, while production was subject to decreasing costs over a certain range of output, these economies of scale were extremely limited,(68) and companies were more concerned to control marginal costs. In fact, gas companies can reap greater economies of scale in the distribution system, where a well-planned system allows the extensive exploitation of a market. This is well illustrated in the pattern of main-laying Preston Gas Light Co. embarked on up to 1820 (see Figure 5.1), covering the town's central streets (Fishergate, Friargate and Church Street) as a means of linking the mills with any shops, taverns, offices, workshops and street lights located in that vicinity. A central location for the gasworks was crucial to the success of this strategy, because in the early-nineteenth century a town-centre was the commercial and industrial hub of the local economy, and any gas company wishing to reduce its marginal costs would need to be situated in the same area. In spite of the environmental problems this would cause, most gasworks were consequently based close to the heart of a town, and of the First Generation only the works at Oldham (see the photograph on p. 72) and Rochdale were constructed in relatively isolated locations.(69) Another important determining factor in this respect was the need to establish the plant at the lowest point in a town, in order that gas could be supplied using its natural pressure, rather than having to be pumped around the town, reducing the cost of distributing the product.

Although there was evidently a strong bias in early investment strategy towards the needs of large consumers, Directors certainly tried to encourage retailers especially to take a supply. This relates closely to a point just made, because having laid mains in the streets where most of the shops and taverns were located the companies could connect up new consumers, keep marginal costs to a minimum, and reduce total average costs. There were indeed attempts at conducting simple marketing exercises, in order to ascertain the potential size of the gaslighting market, and while these often proved inadequate, at least management was making some effort to match supply with demand. The Blackburn management, for example, estimated in February 1818 that 'supposing every shop, warehouse and factory be supplied with gas, the number of jets would be near 3,500',(70) and although they initially planned to lay down sufficient capacity to supply 2,000 in the first year, by 1819 2,484 had been connected, as well as 161 street lamps.(71) Due to delays in completing the system, however, it was March before a regular supply could be guaranteed, 'but as the winter was then very far advanced, it was thought most advisable not to make any charge for the use of it' until July, and they discovered that 'allowing the gratuitous use of the Gas. . . . had the effect of causing nearly 200 shops, etc., to be fitted up'.(72) On the other hand, as well as stretching the company's finances, this put an added strain on the existing capacity, indicating just how ineffective these planning procedures could be.

The decision of Blackburn Gas Light Co. to provide free gas for three months was extremely unusual, but in many other respects their experiences were typical of the early problem of development in most North West gas undertakings. Before building their works, Manchester's Gas Committee canvassed all the town-centre 'shops, counting houses, etc.', encouraging occupiers to sign a book deposited for that purpose at the Police Commission office if they intended to take a supply. This book has not survived, and it is not known whether the exercise was of much help, but management still experienced great difficulties keeping pace with the growth in demand.(73) John Abraham, a Director of Preston Gas Light Co., records in his diary how in the early months of 1816 he was frequently questioning the occupants of centrally located business premises 'as to their inclination to have the Gas',(74) but the Board was obliged to admit in 1820 that 'the cost [of the system] has exceeded by a considerable sum the estimates which were from time to time submitted to them'.(75) Directors were consequently aware of the need to extend their custom-base, and some marketing was attempted, but the shortcomings in their planning procedures, combined with a tendency to underestimate demand, resulted in an investment strategy which lacked any clear direction other than the desire to serve large factories.

Pragmatism and expediency appear to have been the by-words of North West gas company management in coping with their market. The need to control marginal costs also built an innate conservatism into investment strategy, forcing them to concentrate on serving the needs of central districts, but in view of the problems recorded earlier, in terms of equipment suppliers and the vagaries of gas engineering at that time, companies could still find themselves hard pressed to satisfy even that limited market. Irrespective of this cautious approach, however, most were slow to produce any direct financial rewards for shareholders, and although policy was more attuned to ploughing back any surpluses into plant extensions and improvements, the poor dividend performance reveals a good deal about the inability of management to maximise the full potential in gaslighting's superiority over its main rivals. The lack of qualified staff and the problems with contractors and suppliers were major burdens with which Directors had to deal in this pioneering phase, but there does appear to be strong evidence to support the claim that a managerial constraint existed in the early phase, and this seems to have affected adversely the development of both investment strategy and effective planning.

Of course, the ultimate defence one can produce to explain the logic behind these policies is that most North West gas companies were created and financed for 'strategic' reasons. Management's principal mission was to build a technically viable system capable of serving the needs of those who had helped to found the ventures, and as long as this aim was fulfilled then few complaints could be voiced. The Chairman of Blackburn Gas Light Co. even went as far as to claim in 1819 that 'the company was originally intended more as an accommodation to the public, than to put an extravagant profit into the hands of the proprietors'.(76) Likewise, at Preston the Board reported that 'one of the principal designs of those who first projected the establishment of the company was to confer a public benefit on the town',(77) and in 1823 they were still playing down 'any very sanguine hope of it proving a profitable speculation'.(78) These were attempts at justifying the lack of dividends, but nevertheless shareholders did not cavil at the statements, and if we bear in mind the qualification that 'public' and 'town' were loose euphemisms for 'business community' then we come closer to understanding the inner workings of these businesses.

Having noted these qualifications to our earlier critical analysis, there are other matters to be considered, in particular the longer-term implications of policy decisions. This is especially true when we come to discuss pricing structures, because while management might legitimately have secured the custom of large mills as a matter of priority, and provided generous incentives for remaining loyal to the gas company, these policies could have limited the potential for future growth. One must be wary of using excessive hindsight to assess managerial performance, but it is vital to see how Directors operated, and examine what impact their investment and pricing policies had on the industry's long-term development.

The Price Structure

Calculating prices was a major challenge to early Directors, and such were the complexities involved that some companies simply copied the list of charges used by neighbouring operations in the hope that their production and distribution costs were similar.(79) The difficulty was further compounded by an inability to monitor consumption accurately, because until the 1830s reliable meters were not available and management was obliged to fall back on the vague system of charging customers a fixed sum for permission to light a certain type and number of lamps over a pre-set period. An example of this rental method can be found in Figure 5.2, which is the earliest example of its kind in the region. This demonstrates the problems companies would have experienced in checking that consumers were turning off their lights at the agreed time. Some latitude was allowed if the light was extinguished within fifteen minutes of that time, and publicans could negotiate special terms if they opened at irregular hours, but the onus was placed mainly on the customer to abide by these regulations.

Abuse of this system was in fact rife, with customers either widening the jets on their burners or simply lighting premises irrespective of the terms laid down. Companies hired inspectors to walk the streets by night as a deterrent to such irregularities, but judging from the frequency with which one reads comments that 'a great number of persons... burn gas by contract... beyond the time for which they contract' they were largely unsuccessful.(80) One Board guessed that some consumers took twice as much gas as that for which they paid, and they were no doubt correct in asserting that one of the chief causes of their poor dividend performance was 'the immense quantity of gas being consumed more than the contractor for it had a right to have used [sic]'.(81) Even publishing the names of persistent offenders,(82) cutting off their supply,(83) or increasing their prices until compensation had been received,(84) were all ineffective. Only the mass introduction of meters in the mid-1830s brought greater stability to this crucial area, and we shall see later how the replacement of a contractual system was fundamental to various developments in the pricing structure.

Unreliable though it may have been, however, the contractual system did not create many problems over customers refusing to settle bills, because most companies insisted on payments in advance on either a quarterly or half-yearly basis. This provided the ultimate security of being able to disconnect recalcitrant users, and although prepayment might have led to complaints when the supply was interrupted due to essential maintenance,

PRESTON GAS LIGHT COMPANY
Scale of Charges Per Annum
For Burners of Various Sizes
Calculated for
Lighting to the Hours Below Mentioned.

Cockspur	Till 7 o'clock	Till 8 o'clock	Till 9 o'clock	Till 10 o'clock	Till 11 o'clock
No. 1 Jets(2)	16-	£1.1s.	£1.6s.	£1.11s.6d.	£1.16s.6d.
No. 2 Jets(3)	£1.3s.6d.	£1.11s.6d.	£1.19s.6d.	£2.7s.	£2.15s.
Argand					
No. 1	£1.5s.6d.	£1.11s.6d.	£1.19s.6d.	£2.7s	£2.16s.
No. 4	£3.12s.6d.	£5.5s.	£6.11s.	£7.17s.6d.	£9.6s.6d.

Persons wishing to take the Light make applications to the Foreman, at the Works (for the present) who will give them for information respecting their fitting up, etc. – Shortly the Trustees will have a Clerk in the Counting House adjoining the Works to house them, to whom all applications must be made.

Innkeepers and others whose hours of lighting are irregular, may be accommodated by making a special Agreement with the Trustees.

No-one will be charged an extra sum, if he extinguishes his light within a Quarter of an Hour after the Time for which he has contracted to use it, and, on Saturday evenings, in all cases, the Company will allow the privilege of burning to the latest hours, if required.

The Rents will be collected 1st. May and 1st. November, and those who begin to take it at any other time a Proportionable charge will be made up to each rent day, varying according to the time of the year from which they have begun.

By the Direction of the Trustees,
(Signed,)
JNO. ABRAHAM,
Secretary.

Figure 5.2 Verbatim copy of Preston Gas Light Co. price sheet, 1817

or inefficient works management, income was usually forthcoming. On the other hand, this does not mean that consumers, actual or potential, gladly accepted the charges imposed by companies, and here again policy was influenced by the same pressures which dictated the basic pattern of investment strategy.

Pricing policy was a key tool for stimulating sales, but it is interesting to see how the bias towards large consumers exhibited in investment strategy was maintained, leading to a structure which some contemporaries regarded as unfair and unambitious.(85) As we noted earlier, the need to cover start-up costs and fund refurbishments ensured that prices were kept at levels which most people could not afford, but for the large consumers connected up as a top priority incentives were provided to ensure their loyalty. Directors were well aware that manufacturers could afford to install gas-making plant in their premises, and indeed many of the largest factories were already making their own illuminant, but if a gas company offered supplies at a cheaper price industrialists would find it inadvisable to provide an alternative source. In consequence, a range of substantial discounts was devised, particularly in towns dominated by industrial interests, confirming the influence of this sector over yet another crucial instrument of management strategy.

The first price schedule to be formulated in the region was at Preston, where after detailed negotiations with the town's two major cotton producers, Horrockses and Ainsworth, Cottrell, it was decided that, on the prices quoted in Figure 5.2, for argand lamps a 10% discount should be granted to those using more than twenty lights, while for the smaller cockspur lamps a discount of 43% was offered.(86) Prices at Preston were reduced in 1822, and the Directors explained that this decision was made 'in consequence of an understanding made with the proprietors of factories at the time the prices of the lights were advertised that if at any time the [company] could with propriety diminish the charges... they would do so'.(87) Wigan Gas Light Co. did not initially offer any discounts when their first prices were announced in June 1822, even though they had copied the Preston schedule verbatim,(88) but after pressure from several cotton manufacturers a differential of 15% was introduced in 1825.(89) Thereafter, separate price lists for each type of consumer were published,(90) and in 1829 an additional discount of 2.5% was extended to all spending more than £100 annually on gas,(91) reflecting the preferential treatment given to the industrial interests in this town.

As Table 5.2 demonstrates, the price schedules of Preston and Wigan were typical for the region's industrial towns, to the extent that discounts were offered to large consumers. Manufacturers regarded this generous treatment as a natural right, one noting that: 'If I were to find the price charged to me was such that the shopkeepers had it at the same rate, I would put down my own gasworks; the large discounts allowed to me, however, makes me (sic) take my gas from the company'.(92) This vigorous defence of the discount system came from Alfred Rayner, and it is interesting to see that he was both a prominent shareholder in, and a Director of, Ashton-under-Lyne Gas Light Co.,(93) the smaller consumers of which paid one-third more for their gas than substantial manufacturers.(94) His comments reveal the threat faced by Directors when considering their prices, and on the evidence produced in Table 5.2 it is apparent how far most were willing to go to prevent the loss of these customers.(95)

An illustration of how industrialists could respond if they thought the gas company was not treating their sector with the generosity they felt was deserved actually comes from Preston, where the first set of discounts had been negotiated. Even though in 1823 these discounts had been increased by a further 10%, by 1828 four millowners located to the west of Lancaster canal had put down their own gas-making plant because they regarded the company's prices as excessive.(96) This syndicate was headed by the Rodgetts, and Preston Gas Light Co. calculated that it cost them £300 in lost income per annum, or approximately 7.5% of the annual lighting rents. The Directors claimed that the disruption would not affect the business in any other way, because the Rodgetts did not intend to supply other customers,(97) but they

Table 5.2 Gas prices in the North West, 1815–1830 (shillings per thousand cubic feet)

	Price at start-up	Price in 1830
Ashton-under-Lyne	12/-*	10/6*
Blackburn	12/-*	10/-*
Bolton	12/-*	10/-*
Burnley	12/6	8/9*
Chester	12/6	10/-
Kendal	12/6	12/6
Liverpool (Coal)	15/-	12/6
Macclesfield	12/-	10/-
Manchester	14/-	12/-*
Oldham	12/6*	12/6*
Preston	15/-*	12/6*
Stockport	12/-*	12/-*
Warrington	15/-	12/-
Wigan	12/6	10/6*
Average	13/-	11/1

Key: *Indicates that discounts were offered to large consumers.
1/- was equivalent to 5 pence.

Sources: Company records and PP (1847a).

could not afford to lose too many of these large consumers without suffering heavily.(98) It also cost the gas company £4,750 in 1839 to purchase the gasworks installed by Rodgett and his associates,(99) demonstrating how expensive such a development could be.

The discount system became an essential feature of gas company pricing policy in the North West, and the industrialists who dominated the Boards of most undertakings made sure their interests were protected. There was strong economic justification for attracting this kind of custom, and as we noted in the last section, connecting up mills could help to maintain tight control over marginal costs. On the other hand, many contemporaries, and especially the smaller consumers, regarded the preferential treatment accorded this group as of dubious validity. In particular, Johnes and Clegg noted that, as the prices charged to shopkeepers and publicans were higher, this was acting as a significant obstacle to any further increase in sales.(100) Moreover, on the issue of marginal costs, they argued that it was not essential to have factories as consumers, because it would have been possible to supply most of the town-centre shops, taverns and offices which took the bulk of gas used in the 1820s from the mains laid to feed street lamps.

Acquiring a contract to light the streets was an essential starting-point for all undertakings, and often one of the first acts of a Board was to persuade local councillors or improvement commissioners to convert from oil to gaslighting. Securing local authority support was naturally vital, because only by gaining permission to lay mains in the public highway could a business supply its customers. Although only a few streets would be lit initially, these were in the middle of the town where most shops, taverns, offices and factories were located. However, while few problems seem to have been experienced in gaining this approval, and only in one case was payment exacted,(101) the companies were obliged to concede any profit on street lighting because the typical price of local authority complicity was a cheap supply. One might wonder why the companies did not negotiate a fee for the use of the public highway and charge local authorities a realistic price for their service, but as Directors and shareholders were usually also a town's leading ratepayers they were anxious to keep down the cost,(102) resulting in a system which posed some problems for early management.

The claim made by Johnes and Clegg that 'very commonly the gas for the public lights is sold for less than the cost of production' is echoed in many contemporary sources,(103) but it is difficult to illustrate the point with hard factual evidence. One London company estimated that in the 1820s a street lamp would use about 20,000 cubic feet of gas per year, and if the standard price to private consumers of 12/6 (62.5p) per thousand cubic feet was charged then each lamp should have yielded an annual income of £12.50.(104) In fact, only £5 per lamp was received from London authorities, and on top of the substantial outlay on mains and lamps this indicates the unprofitable nature of street lighting in the metropolitan districts. Over a similar period, Paterson calculated that in Warrington the street lamps consumed 12,500 cubic feet, but as the company was paid just £3 per lamp, they were losing £4.80 annually on each street lamp, compared with income earned from private consumers of 12/6 (62.5p).(105) Furthermore, the street lighting prices at Warrington were higher than the standard price of £2−£2.75 per lamp in the North West.(106) Comparisons are hazardous, because the lighting times varied enormously and no standard form of burner had yet come into general use, but few Directors would have disagreed with the conclusion drawn by the Board of Bolton Gas Light Co. that street lamp 'prices are below prime cost'.(107)

Not only were street lighting prices unremunerative, there were also other drawbacks to this contract. Johnes and Clegg drew attention to the excessive waste of gas involved, claiming that 'of the leakage in the main pipes... a very large proportion must be exclusively attributed to the street lamps, and must be considered to form part of the expense of feeding that particular class of burners'.(108) This would have been impossible to prove, because relatively little was known about monitoring or controlling seepage at that time, but as the mains were charged with gas simply to light the street lamps for much of the night then Johnes and Clegg would not have been overstating the case. Installing mains and lamps, and hiring lamp-lighters, would have further added to the cost of servicing this contract, confirming the general impression that indirectly companies paid a high price for their supposedly free access to roads for main-laying purposes.

Having noted these disadvantages, it is important to emphasise that public lighting was by no means completely negative in its impact on early gas companies, because Directors granted the concessions 'with the sole view of obtaining the privilege of breaking up the streets, and preventing opposition, local or parliamentary'.(109) Failure to deal favourably with local authorities could have calamitous consequences, especially if a rival was granted access to the same market, and, as we shall see in the next chapter, Chester Gas Light Co. was unable to withstand the competition arising from this situation.(110) Moreover, having laid the mains along the central thoroughfares of a town, where most of the potential consumers were located, it was then relatively cheap to connect up shopkeepers, publicans and even millowners, keeping marginal costs tightly under control, while at the same time providing a base load from the street lamps. The contract might well have been unremunerative, in terms of direct earnings, but clearly it was an essential springboard for any company's future development, justifying economically and politically the generous treatment accorded local authorities. Directors and other commentators might have complained frequently about the direct commercial implications of cheap street lighting, and in negotiations with councillors or commissioners they rarely missed an opportunity to stress how much was lost on this business, but quite simply the contract was vital to a company's welfare.

The pressures imposed by various pressure groups were consequently leading to the emergence of a three-tier price structure in the North West: local authorities received gas at or below cost price; manufacturers benefited from substantial discounts; and the remainder paid a higher, standard price. Some companies were able to avoid introducing discounts, because industrial interests were not as dominant in their towns,(111) but most were constrained by the prevailing economic and political realities. This situation cast considerable doubt on the ability of the region's gas companies to operate as monopolies capable of dictating their own pricing and investment strategies, and in addressing the issue of performance it is important to bear in mind the conditions in which they were obliged to function. Monopoly conditions may in theory have existed in the early North West gas industry, but monopoly profits were certainly not earned, and a complete assessment of performance is required to comprehend why companies were unable to maximise the full potential of their market position.

Company Performance

It is above all clear that most of the First Generation were established principally to serve the needs of their owners, and especially the influential industrial classes. Manufacturers were not only the largest group of shareholders (see Table 3.2) and Directors (see Table 5.1), they were also the major consumers of gas, and they used this position to manipulate pricing and investment strategies in their interests. Gas undertakings would also have been keen to secure custom from factories, because while the overhead costs of connecting large consumers were not much different from laying mains to those who would use only a few lights, the average cost of supplying the former would be substantially lower. Another commercially sound reason for pursuing this priority was the threat posed by manufacturers, with their financial ability to build private plants, forcing prices down through the use of discounts to the point where markets would not be contested. Even though by 1830 shopkeepers and publicans purchased most of the gas sold, their interests were subsumed under those of industrialists because small consumers were much more dependent on the gas company, and it would have been prohibitively expensive for them to have supplied their own gas. One should also stress the vital role played by mills in bringing down the average cost of supplying gas to all consumers, and as industrialists often played a central role in creating the companies this underlines the dependence of smaller consumers on their larger counterparts.

Having noted the strong justifications for targeting millowners as consumers, one must also mention some of the commercial drawbacks of giving them such a priority position in company strategy. We have already noted how most of the early users of gaslighting were located in the town-centre, and they could easily and cheaply have been supplied from the street lamps, keeping marginal costs within manageable limits. Moreover, just as with street lighting, the mills only took gas between September and March, resulting in a substantial proportion of a company's plant remaining idle for almost half the year. Demand from manufacturers was also much more vulnerable to swings in the trade cycle, and at times of industrial depression gas companies often reported a substantial reduction in consumption.(112) This brings into question the economic viability of investment and pricing strategies designed to suit industrialists, because the average cost of supplying a seasonal consumer must inevitably be higher than those for the larger group of small consumers who used gas all year round. On balance, though, it is important to stress that gas companies would have been foolish had they neglected the industrial sector because the market was so small at that time. The management structure also ensured that this sector received favourable treatment and given the cost of gaslighting and its limited use in confined premises the early companies would have struggled without the contributions of local manufacturers.

Unfortunately, it is extremely difficult to illustrate this argument by referring to evidence on market breakdown, because little of this has survived.(113) Street lighting typically accounted for one-fifth of sales,(114) but how the rest was distributed can only be vaguely estimated. In the early years, given the priorities pursued by most undertakings, factories would probably have taken more gas than any other private sector group, but as we described earlier Directors encouraged retailers located near the mains to take gas, and by 1830 smaller consumers probably outnumbered the large. On the other hand, the amount of gas used by a factory would have been considerably greater than in a shop or tavern, and even after a large number of small consumers had been connected to the network in towns like Warrington and Ashton-under-Lyne the industrial sector still accounted for well over one-third of sales in 1847.(115) Retailers provided staple, perennial business, but without local manufacturers most North West gas companies would have operated with much higher average costs, and by laying mains to these large consumers management was keeping to a minimum the marginal costs of connecting up new customers.

The rate of growth in gas sales arising from this market, however, was certainly unspectacular up to 1830. After the initial rush to match supply with demand, it is apparent that most companies were content to service a limited market without taking many risks by extending the network too far from the town centre. Even at Preston, Bolton and Blackburn, by 1830 total income had reached just £5,288, £5,182 and £2,824, respectively,(116) and as Appendix D demonstrates the more rapid phases of expansion for two of these companies came later (when prices started to fall). Johnes and Clegg claimed that the main reason for the sluggish growth in demand for gaslighting was the preferential treatment accorded manufacturers and local authorities, forcing standard prices to a level which most could not afford. They wanted companies to abolish this system, on the grounds that smaller consumers were subsidising the larger, but this argument ignores the points already made above relating to the commercial logic behind the discounts. In effect, early gas companies were obliged to favour their larger consumers, otherwise the implementation of the threats voiced by people like Reyner could have serious consequences for company performance. One should also add that the general level of prices was determined by costs and technological capabilities, and it was only after 1830 that these factors assisted a significant reduction in charges, while the poor early returns left management with little room for manoeuvre in this respect.(117)

Having noted these features of early performance, it is important to reiterate that most of the First Generation did not operate by orthodox commercial criteria; they were more interested initially in establishing technically viable systems capable of serving the needs of predetermined groups of customers, rather than rewarding shareholders directly with dividends. At the same time, management was constantly aware of the need to control marginal costs, and Directors rarely invested in new plant and mains to supply a district of limited commercial potential. This can be seen at Blackburn Gas Light Co., where in 1829 the Board resolved, after refusing to supply a factory outside the town in Wensley Fold, 'that any person wishing gas to be carried out of town do lay the additional pipes at his own expense, and that he then take the gas by contract'.(118) This concern with marginal costs remained of paramount importance throughout the nineteenth century, and by controlling what could be the prohibitively high costs of expansion, management was slowly beginning to learn how gaslighting could be made to pay. Most companies were in fact beginning to produce some dividends by the late-1820s (see Appendix C), and although the growth of income was still limited (see Appendix D) shareholders were at last being rewarded directly for their 'faith and patience'.(119) In most cases it was several years before returns reached 10%, but Directors were finding out how to balance the various aspects of their commercial scene by following essentially cautious strategies which built on the initial successes of the scheme and generated better profits.

This analysis of company performance is based on a generalised interpretation of developments within the region, and inevitably there are several notable exceptions to the problems just outlined. The most successful companies outside the two main towns were at Macclesfield and Chester, demonstrating that it was possible to produce good dividends from an early date. Both groups of shareholders had been obliged to wait until the fifth year of trading before receiving a financial return on their investments (see Appendix C), but in Macclesfield Gas Light Co.'s case in particular thereafter they received a generous return which averaged 11.5% between 1822 and 1830. Relatively little is known about this undertaking's early history other than that James Hargreaves built the gasworks, but the Directors were able to hold out against demands to introduce discounts for large consumers until 1833, and the price of gas was held at 12/- (60p) per thousand cubic feet up to 1830.(120) This indicates that the company had a strong hold over its gaslighting market, and as we shall see in Chapter 7, it survived as an

unincorporated firm until 1860. In the same vein, although Chester Gas
Light Co.'s published dividends do not match those of the Macclesfield
venture, they averaged 7.1% between 1822 and 1830. In fact, in 1827 the
shares were actually doubled in value by the capitalisation of £6,850 from
reinvested profits, effectively doubling the return on the initial investments
from that date. This company was also able to charge a standard price of 10/-
(50p) to all customers up to 1842, confirming again the ability of some
managements to exploit the monopolistic position they had gained. At neither
Macclesfield nor Chester did sales expand rapidly until the 1840s,(121)
highlighting the general propensity to pursue limited investment strategies,
but their dividend performance confirms the view that in some circumstances
gas companies did enjoy monopolies which produced consistently high
returns.

To substantiate this point further it is interesting to examine the most
successful First Generation venture, Liverpool Gas Light Co. This undertaking had been the first to record a dividend in 1819 (see Appendix C), and
from 1824 returns of 10% were regularly produced as income expanded
from £4,755 in 1818 to £27,137 in 1830.(122) The sales and dividend performances combined actually outstripped those of any other North West gas
company, and although the market for gaslighting in Liverpool was naturally
much larger than in places like Blackburn, Preston and Bolton,(123) it is
important to remember that a rival oil-gas company had been competing for
the business from 1823. Rowlinson has estimated that most of the 1,168
shops in Liverpool in 1822 were already lit by coal-gas,(124) and the Liverpool
Oil Gas Co. was certainly able to capture some of these customers, but the
relatively high price of oil-gas militated against a significant incursion into
the market.(125) Liverpool Corporation had also built a small gasworks in
1819 to supply the Town Hall,(126) but the Liverpool Gas Light Co. still
supplied the street lamps, and in general its monopoly of coal-gas in the
city allowed management to maintain a standard price of 12/6 (62.5p) for all
consumers up to 1830, providing the foundations for a highly successful
business.(127)

Conclusions

The policies and performances of these three companies at Macclesfield,
Chester and Liverpool illustrate the commercial potential in the early gaslighting market. In most North West towns, however, the latent threat of
competition posed by local manufacturers, and the limited market for gaslighting while prices were so high, prevented Directors from recording
similar returns. One must reject the claims of Johnes and Clegg, that the
discount system prevented further growth in demand, but it is certainly fair
to emphasise both the shortcomings in early planning procedures and the
highly cautious investment strategies as major contributors to the generally
poor dividend record. Above all, though, it was the organisational and
economic realities prevailing in any particular town which determined the
extent of a company's monopoly, and the kind of policies management was
able to pursue, and only in the less industrialised towns did an actual
monopoly exist which was capable of producing good returns.(128) We shall
continue this discussion in the next chapters, but it is apparent from what

we have seen so far that most undertakings were prevented from exploiting their theoretical monopoly by the nature of their circumstances, and in consequence profitability was disappointing.

In the final analysis, the region's gas companies were mostly formed and financed to bring the new artificial light to business communities, and as 'strategic' motives lay behind the involvement of most investors, then Directors were achieving their initial objective once a technically viable business had been established. This success must be regarded as vindication for their actions, and in securing a regular supply of gas the shareholders were reaping indirect gains from what were widely regarded as long-term investments. Only slowly did Boards begin to exploit the commercial potential in gaslighting, but in the first stages most of the profits were ploughed back into the ventures in order to improve the service. By the late-1820s an increasingly profitable industry was beginning to emerge, based on a highly conservative approach towards investment and a pricing policy designed to favour large consumers, and in the next chapter we shall examine how this legacy affected performance at a time of more rapid expansion. Liverpool Gas Light Co. demonstrated the possibilities in gas supply, albeit in a much larger commercial community, but in other towns strategy was severely constrained by both the fear of competition and the interests of those who dominated the decision-making process, and this legacy was to have significant long-term influences on the development of gas supply in the post-1830 era.

Footnotes

(1) See Wilson (1991A) for another view of this subject.
(2) See earlier, p. 11ff, for a survey of this activity.
(3) For a discussion of management see pp. 154–157.
(4) The five Directors at Preston were actually allocated a weekday each for this visit, while at weekends they were all expected to be in regular attendance. PGLCMB, 9/9/16.
(5) Rowlinson (1984), p. 186.
(6) PGLCMB, 5/7/24.
(7) Clegg (1872), p. 22.
(8) See earlier, pp. 73–74.
(9) WGLCMB, 7/11/22.
(10) See earlier, pp. 86–89 for a discussion of this issue.
(11) Matthews (1985), p. 39.
(12) Quoted in Pollard (1968), p. 24.
(13) *Ibid*, p. 25.
(14) See Hunt (1936), Ch. 3, and earlier, p. 65.
(15) Ward (1974), pp. 26–78.
(16) See above, pp. 68–69. A 'bubble' was the contemporary term for a speculative venture or mania.
(17) Joyce (1980), p. 2.
(18) See later, p. 195, for further evidence on this matter.
(19) For an analysis of 'strategic' motives see above, pp. 86–89.
(20) See above, p. 86.
(21) Harris (1956), p. 30. See earlier, p. 23.
(22) The figures for each company are: Preston, 5%; Blackburn, 16%; Bolton, 25%; Chorley, 12.3%; and Warrington, 28.3%.

(23) The partners in Horrockses owned eighty-nine shares, compared to the forty-nine of the Directors. PGLCSR.

(24) They were William Taylor, who ran one of Horrocks's factories, and Thomas German, who had formerly worked for Horrockses. Awty (1975), p. 94.

(25) BGLCMB, 16/1/18.

(26) Clegg (1872), p. 10.

(27) A doctor, John Moore, became the Chairman of Bolton Gas Light Co., in recognition of the 150 shares he owned, and another doctor, Abraham Chew, was Chairman of Blackburn Gas Light Co. until his death in 1819. See earlier, pp. 25–26.

(28) See above, pp. 82–83, for a discussion of this policy.

(29) Everard (1949). p. 26.

(30) Neill (1958), p. 244.

(31) Clegg (1872), p. 13.

(32) Quoted in Eastwood (1988), p. 29.

(33) *Westmorland Gazette*, 6/8/25, p. 1.

(34) See above, p. 28, for a description of this work.

(35) See Mitchell (1986), pp. 66–71.

(36) Evidence given by Jacob Davies to the Select Committee on Gas Establishments (1823).

(37) BGLCMB, 14/1/19.

(38) WGLCMB, 4/5/26.

(39) The Preston Directors were even duped into placing an order with a supplier whose name was the same as their usual source, leading to several months' delay in completing the works. PGLCMB, 25/7/16.

(40) Clegg (1872), pp. 10–11. See also earlier, pp. 25–26.

(41) This happened at Wigan, Warrington and Oldham, where, respectively, George Richardson, John Rushton and George Emmott were hired while the Contractor was still on site.

(42) WGLCMB, 10/12/26, and BGLCMB, 13/3/18.

(43) PGLCMB, 5/5/18.

(44) Harris (1956), pp. 18–25. See later, pp. 156–157, for a study of the King regime.

(45) PGLCMB, 30/4/20.

(46) JOGL, 10/2/49, p. 8.

(47) Pollard (1968), Ch. 4.

(48) See later, pp. 152–154. Cotterill (1980–81) also explains how this was a problem in Scottish gas undertakings.

(49) Newbigging (1883), p. 3.

(50) See earlier for Newbigging's career, pp. 50–51.

(51) Johnes & Clegg Report, 1847, p. 96.

(52) See earlier, pp. 85–86.

(53) The sulphuric acid would come from gas of a low purity. Rowlinson (1984), pp. 14–16.

(54) These prices were not used at the time, because customers were charged on the rental basis, but in evidence to PP (1847a) the companies later calculated these levels. See later, pp. 162–163.

(55) Rowlinson (1984), p. 66.

(56) Winstanley (1983), pp. 1–4.

(57) Awty (1975), p. 110.

(58) All these manufacturers owned shares in Preston Gas Light Co. PGLCSR, 1818–39.

(59) PGLCMB, 1/1/21.

(60) See *Ibid*, 14/4/23 and 2/1/26.

(61) Clegg (1872), p. 13.

(62) Smith held ten shares in Bolton Gas Light Co. and chaired the early meetings in 1818. BnGLCCMB, 20/2/18.

(63) *Ibid*, 21/8/21 and 26/4/22, and Clegg (1872), p. 17.

(64) James Ormrod and William Crompton were among the first Directors appointed in 1818, and only Lum had not subscribed to the company's share capital. Clegg (1872), pp. 10–16.

(65) BGLCMB, 21/1/25.

(66) All of these businessmen had bought shares in 1817, and Thomas Liversey, William Throp and John Fleming were Directors. BGLCMB, 20/2/18.

(67) No shareholding information is available for Ashton-under-Lyne, but the six industrialists on the eleven-man Board were Charles Buckley, James Lees, John Cheetham, Alfred and Frederick Reyner (all cotton manufacturers), and John Booth (coalmine-owner). Ashton Gas Act, Cap. cci, 1847.

(68) Matthews (1986), p. 255.

(69) It is not known why the companies were pushed out of the town, but the works were located over a mile from the town-centre.

(70) BGLCMB, 20/2/18.

(71) *Ibid*, 13/1/20.

(72) *Ibid*, 8/7/19.

(73) Mitchell (1986), pp. 25–32.

(74) JADAB, 11/5/16. See also 3/1/16.

(75) PGLCMB, 3/7/20.

(76) BGLCMB, 14/1/19.

(77) PGLCMB, 4/1/19.

(78) *Ibid*, 6/1/23.

(79) Wigan Gas Co. copied the Preston schedule in 1822. WGLCMB, 13/6/22.

(80) SHGLCBM, 18/1/43.

(81) PGLCMB, 5/1/18.

(82) *Ibid*, 4/8/18.

(83) See Clegg (1872), p. 18, for Bolton Gas Light Co.'s response.

(84) BGLCMB, 13/1/20.

(85) Johnes & Clegg (1847), pp. 94–97.

(86) PGLCMB, 1/7/16 and JADAB, 5/3/16.

(87) PGLCMB, 23/12/22.

(88) WGLCMB, 13/6/22.

(89) *Ibid*, 5/5/25.

(90) PP (1847a).

(91) WGLCMB, 1/10/29.

(92) Quoted in Johnes & Clegg (1847), p. 138.

(93) Ashton Gas Act, Cap. cci, 1847.

(94) Johnes & Clegg (1847), pp. 137–139.

(95) In the 1830s both Warrington and Liverpool (coal) introduced discounts for large consumers. See Paterson (1879), p. 11, for Warrington, and later, p. 168, for Liverpool.

(96) No evidence survives to indicate whether the Rodgett gas was cheaper than that of Preston Gas Light Co.

(97) PGLCMB, 7/1/28.

(98) Total income in 1828 was £4,750. PGLCAB, 1822–39.

(99) PGLCMB, 23/8/39. The transaction was financed by the creation of new shares, rather than by cash.

(100) Johnes & Clegg (1847), pp. 95–98.

(101) Bolton Gas Light Co. was obliged to pay an annual fee of £31 for permission to break open the streets. BnGLCCMB, 11/2/18.

(102) See below, pp. 139–141, for a discussion of this relationship.

(103) Johnes & Clegg (1847), p. 96.

(104) Rowlinson (1984), pp. 63–65.
(105) Paterson (1879), p. 8.
(106) These were the price ranges at Preston, Blackburn, Bolton and Wigan.
(107) BnGLCCMB, 12/2/41.
(108) Johnes & Clegg (1847), p. 96.
(109) *Ibid*.
(110) See also Wilson (1991B).
(111) See later, p. 168, for the case of Liverpool.
(112) See PGLCMB, 3/1/27, when a reduction in income was recorded because of a depression in trade.
(113) See later, p. 167, for an analysis of market breakdown in 1847.
(114) Johnes & Clegg (1847), p. 97.
(115) See later, p. 167.
(116) Evidence for Blackburn and Preston is taken from Appendix D, and for Bolton from BnGLCCMB, 10/4/29.
(117) BGLCMB, 12/2/29.
(118) Abram (1879), p. 3.
(119) See PP (1847a).
(120) See later, p. 208.
(121) See later, p. 173, for more detail on Chester. Chester Gas Light Co. sales were only £4,321 in 1845. CGLCBM, 30/6/45. See also Wilson (1991B) for a fuller version of the Chester story.
(122) Harris (1956), p. 42.
(123) In 1831 Liverpool had a population of 165,175, while that of Blackburn, Preston and Bolton was 27,091, 33,112 and 41,189, respectively, 1831 Census.
(124) Rowlinson (1984), p. 71.
(125) See earlier, pp. 23–24.
(126) Harris (1956), p. 35.
(127) See later, p. 171, for a more detailed examination of gas supply in this city.
(128) Liverpool Gas Light Co. had a monopoly of coal-gas supply, even though it had a rival in the gaslighting market.

6
The Management of Expansion

*'Gad, Sir, if it were not enough that these railways
should threaten horse-flesh! Now I cannot get my tilbury
to the Club for these infernal gas companies breaking up
Piccadilly. A scandal, Major, though the price of the
stuff be but 6 shillings a what-you-call-it!'*

Quoted in the *Gas Journal Centenary Volume,*
1849—1949.

The orientation of strategy towards the needs of influential shareholders
had been a predominant concern of most managements up to 1830, and
with the obvious exceptions of Liverpool and Manchester North West gas
undertakings preferred to serve only a limited area of their geographical
market in the hope that rewards of both a direct and indirect nature would
be forthcoming for those who had provided most of the risk capital. This
cautious approach was to remain as a distinguishing characteristic of strategy
throughout the nineteenth century, and management was ever-vigilant of
the need to control marginal costs. At the same time, while the three-tier
price structure was also kept intact, charges to all consumers were reduced
to such a significant extent that growth became the key word to describe
gas company experiences up to 1880. Management had only slowly become
aware of the price elasticity of demand for gas, but from the 1830s it was
this phenomenon which became the engine of growth, improved profitability
and made gas shares nationally one of the most lucrative investments on
the provincial scene. There were still aspects of company organisation and
strategy which inhibited more rapid growth, but in this chapter we shall
examine the reasons why gas supply expanded in the North West after
what can only be regarded as a sluggish start in most towns.

Pricing policy was the key strategic tool for Directors, helping to stimulate
sales of gas after 1830. Matthews has demonstrated how Directors were
assisted enormously in pursuing a policy of price reductions by a significant
improvement in gas meters, the reduction in wastage, and a decline in coal,
iron and labour costs,(1) but his quantitative explanation ignores the
important qualitative changes taking place in gas company management.
There had naturally been a steep learning curve over which management
had to climb before mastering the complexities in gas supply, but the
training and experience of an emerging profession of gas engineer proved
much more suited to the effective exploitation of the industry's potential,
and from the 1830s it was these influential individuals who played the
leading role in determining policy. Running parallel with the growing
preponderance of *rentiers* in the North West gas company share registers, it
is consequently apparent that a greater divorce between control and ownership was slowly occurring, bringing to an end the former dominance of

certain groups of proprietors. Other factors were more directly responsible for the rise in gas sales, but the professionalisation of gas management facilitated the process of expansion, and in any analysis of the industry's performance up to 1880 such qualitative considerations must be given some weight.

Another key issue we shall examine is the extent to which the businesses were able to operate as monopolies. We noted briefly in the last chapter how, in spite of the sole access frequently granted to gas companies monopolistic profits were not earned because management preferred initially to sacrifice dividends in the interests of serving a limited market with a regular supply. After 1830 profitability improved, indicating that belatedly Directors were learning how to exploit a market, but it is important not to interpret this development as indicative of a decisive change in strategy. Legally sanctioned monopolies were in fact never granted by parliament, and in discussing performance it is vital to bear in mind how companies coped with this situation. The statutory limits on prices and dividends imposed during the 1840s were largely ineffective, but management were constantly aware of the possibility that rival suppliers could be granted authority to supply their districts, and this potential threat always acted as an important discipline on strategy. Although expansion was very much a feature of the post-1830 era, bringing more consistent returns to shareholders, gas companies did not operate in an unfettered political environment, and the actions of management were increasingly subject to a variety of pressures.

Senior Management and Strategy after 1830

The early pattern of development pursued by most of the First Generation outside Liverpool and Manchester owed much to the dominant position taken by manufacturers in financing and managing these ventures. Although retailers and merchants had provided significant proportions of both share-holders (see Table 3.2) and Directors (see Table 5.1), they had been obliged to take a backseat in the formulation of policy, partly because they held a lower position in the local socio-political hierarchy, but principally because they did not pose as great a threat as industrialists to the company's monopoly.(2) Cognisant of a manufacturer's ability to install his own gas-making equipment, companies were quick to lay mains to the larger factories and provide substantial discounts to ensure loyalty, and the pervasive presence of industrialists on Boards of Directors (see Table 5.1) ensured this priority status. The commercial viability of this system was in theory un-questionable, although in practice returns were poor at a time when other problems prevented a more ambitious policy of market exploitation. After several years of sacrifice, however, the shareholders received some returns, and from the late-1820s dividends were recorded regularly by all the First Generation. This realisation that gaslighting could be made to pay might well have stimulated interest from a different type of investor, but not only did the finance for supply operations formed after 1826 come mainly from the same sectors which invested in the First Generation (see Table 4.2), it is also clear that similar occupational groups dominated their senior management.

In spite of the growing recognition of gaslighting's commercial viability, after 1826 the reasons for creating supply companies were still essentially 'strategic', and most of the riskier start-up capital was consequently provided by local millowners, retailers and merchants anxious to gain access to the cheapest and most effective form of artificially lighting substantial premises. Table 4.2 confirms this trend, showing how 66.0% of the shares were purchased by 'Manufacturers' and 'Services', and just as with the First Generation, it is possible to see in Table 6.1 how these two sections also accounted for 73% of the Directors in eighteen companies formed between 1826 and 1860. The similarities between Table 5.1 and Table 6.1 are equally striking, demonstrating once again that ownership and control were closely related in North West gas companies. Indeed, manufacturers, shopkeepers and merchants were even more dominant in Table 6.1, but this is indicative of the smaller numbers of start-up shares purchased by professionals and unoccupied people after 1826 (see Table 4.2), and in general the structure of both ownership and Board representation were remarkably similar to those of the First Generation.

Table 6.1 Composition of North West gas company Boards at the time of their inception, 1826—1860

	No.	%
1. *Manufacturers*		
Textiles	37	23.6
Others	5	3.2
Sub-total	42	26.8
2. *Services*		
Textile Merchants	10	6.4
Other Merchants	9	5.7
Retailers	35	22.3
Publicans	6	3.8
Transport	0	0
Builders	13	8.3
Sub-total	73	46.5
3. *Professions*		
Legal	6	3.8
Bankers	2	1.3
Clerics	3	1.9
Medical	8	5.1
Gas Engineers	0	0
Miscellaneous	7	4.4
Sub-total	26	16.5
4. *Farmers*		
5. *Unoccupied*		
Gentlemen	16	10.2
Ladies	0	0
Sub-total	16	10.2
Total	157	—

Companies analysed: Milnethorpe, Nelson, Northwich, Ormskirk, Prescot, Radcliffe & Pilkington, Stalybridge, Accrington, Buxton, Colne, Hyde, Leigh, Lymm, St. Helens, Rossendale, Kirkham, Clitheroe and Altrincham.

The control exercised by certain groups over management strategy in companies formed after 1826 was perhaps even more extensive, with Directors of the eleven companies analysed in Table 4.2 holding on average 25.4% of the issued capital, compared to 17.3% for Table 3.2.(3) We also noted in Chapter 2 how in the generally smaller communities which established gas supply operations from the 1830s prominent local businessmen were often the dominant promoters.(4) Runcorn Gas Light Co. had been created largely by two soap manufacturers, J. & T. Johnson and Messrs Hazlehurst, and they not only owned 150 of the 595 issued shares, they also provided three of the nine-man Board.(5) The Hibbert family role in creating Hyde Gas Co. had resulted in a similar kind of situation,(6) the Darwen Gas Light Co. was dominated by that town's most prominent cotton manufacturers, James and Eccles Shorrock,(7) and the Greenalls at St. Helens and John Hutchinson at Widnes typified the situation prevailing in the growing number of satellite industrial towns springing up at that time.(8)

Evidence is hard to find to demonstrate how these later companies copied the First Generation by initially targeting industrial consumers, because even fewer of their Board minutes have survived, but judging from the extensive use of discounts for larger users, it is clear that every effort was made to generate business from this sector.(9) Offering inducements of this kind was one of the most effective means of ensuring the loyalty of factory-owners, because otherwise they could have laid down their own plant, depriving the companies of a major source of custom. In the smaller industrial centres like Darwen, Colne, Runcorn and Widnes failing to acquire such business would have even more serious consequences than in the larger towns, given the relative insignificance of commercial and professional sectors in those satellites, making it imperative that factories were connected up at an early stage. At the same time, of course, the promoters, and consequently the boards of Directors, were frequently dominated by local industrialists, as we have just seen, and this ensured the pursuit of a strategy concentrating on their interests emphasising the continued importance of factory consumers in the development of North West gas supply.

The discount system will be discussed again in a later section when the whole subject of North West gas company pricing policy is analysed, but it is important to understand that the three-tier price structure so typical of the First Generation remained a prominent feature of later attempts to deal with certain types of customer. This also reveals that street lighting was invariably provided at or below cost, because of the need to maintain a good relationship with local government and secure unfettered access to the streets for main-laying purposes. In the main, then, with regard to share ownership, Board composition and management strategy, there was very little difference between companies formed either side of 1826, and apart from the cases of Liverpool and Manchester, a remarkable degree of conformity existed in the pattern of business development. On the other hand, early trading performance appears to have been better in companies created after 1826, although once again there is also evidence of poor dividends and ineffective management.

Appendix C indicates that, while the shareholders of Colne Gas Light Co. were well rewarded, the undertakings at Darwen and St. Helens performed badly as speculative investments. St. Helens Gas Light Co. was an especially bad case, failing to produce any dividend in six out of the first fifteen years of trading, and averaging returns of just 2.7% in that period. Of course, the local breweries, glassworks and commercial premises were all connected up to the works by 1840,(10) and investors would have fulfilled their 'strategic' aims, but while Barker and Harris regarded Peter Greenall as 'the hero of the piece' in the town's development at that time,(11) as Chairman of St. Helens Light Gas Co. he presided over a commercially unsuccessful operation. He even attempted to incorporate a clause into the 1845 St. Helens Improvement Bill giving the local authority powers to purchase the gasworks, but his political opponents had the provision expunged on the grounds that this would not only have compensated Greenall for his failed investment, it would also have saddled the Commissioners with an unprofitable business.(12)

St. Helens Gas Light Co. proved so unsuccessful that in 1843, after four years without dividends, the Board commissioned a study of the business, and the report concluded that the business was in dire need of 'more efficient management and benefit of the affairs of the company'. The consultant was especially critical of the poor accounting system and the 'dilapidated' state of the retort house, highlighting the need to appoint

The market-place in Warrington (c.1825). As in Preston, a gaslamp was also fitted in this town's obelisk.

a qualified professional manager capable of reversing the company's
fortunes.(13) To date, typically for such small-scale suppliers,(14) the
business had been managed on a part-time basis, and a consultant, Ralph
Spooner, had advised on major purchases of equipment,(15) but in spite of
the study's criticisms Greenall and his colleagues refused to change over to
a full-time Engineer. They did hire another consultant, George Edwards of
Liverpool, to improve the methods of controlling cash-flow, and new plant
was purchased to replace their outdated equipment,(16) but in 1846 the
Board was still able to note how 'the inefficiency of the Manufacturing
Apparatus' was holding up improved performance.(17) They finally decided
in that year to elevate William Riley from his part-time post of Clerk to full-
time Engineer, and as Appendix C illustrates, this heralded the beginning
of a more prosperous phase for the company.

The managerial weaknesses in St. Helens Gas Light Co. had certainly
contributed to the poor dividend performance up to 1846, but in general the
returns produced by Colne Gas Light Co. were more typical of the undertakings formed after 1830. Table 4.3 presents confirmation of this trend,
with the market values of all gas shares (other than those of Prescot)
improving consistently in the 1850s, while the dividends recorded by
parliamentary enquiries in 1847, 1866 and 1881 indicate that it is rare to find
similar cases to St. Helens Gas Light Co. Initially, Darwen Gas Light Co.
had not fared much better, producing an average dividend of 4.3% between
1841 and 1854,(18) but the management there had also ploughed £3,000 of
undistributed profits back into the business by 1855, reflecting a concern to
build a technically viable system. However, across the region profitability
improved after the late-1820s, and in examining performance from that time
it is apparent that a variety of forces were at play, not least a significant
improvement in gas company management and organisation at a time when
the mains system was well-established, allowing a significant reduction in
the marginal costs of new connections.

Professional Management

So far we have talked of management as if only the Directors were responsible for running gas companies, but increasingly professional officers were
coming to play a much more crucial role in influencing the decision-making
process. Indeed, the skills which these functionaries brought to management
facilitated the expansion of the post-1830 period, providing both the technical
and commercial knowledge essential in the quest for greater control over
production, distribution and cash-flow. In the early years, a severe shortage
of the required talent resulted in some poor appointments, not to mention
several cases of fraud, but by the 1830s, as a result of the industry's growth,
a better quality of recruit became available, taking the burden of functional,
and eventually strategic, management off the Directors' shoulders. This was
a vitally important development in gas company organisation, because the
Boards of North West undertakings were not always blessed with the right
kind of expertise needed to exploit the commercial and technical potential
in the product. Expansion also brought further complications, and it was
the professional officers who were principally responsible for providing the
systems capable of managing this process.

In the early years of a gas company's life Directors often outnumbered other employees. Figure 6.1 illustrates the typical management structure of a First Generation business with a Board of nine or ten people and a handful of clerical and production staff. This top-heavy structure was not a financial

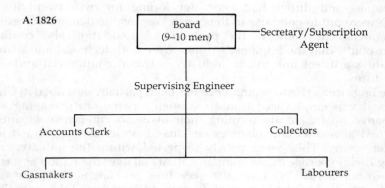

A: 1826

Board
(9–10 men) ————Secretary/Subscription
Agent

Supervising Engineer

Accounts Clerk   Collectors

Gasmakers   Labourers

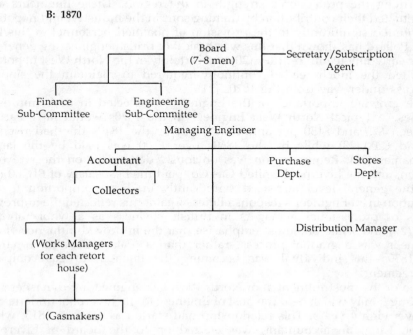

B: 1870

Board
(7–8 men) ————Secretary/Subscription
Agent

Finance   Engineering
Sub-Committee   Sub-Committee

Managing Engineer

Accountant   Purchase   Stores
                            Dept.   Dept.

Collectors

                                    Distribution Manager

(Works Managers
for each retort
house)

(Gasmakers)

Figure 6.1   Management structure of North West gas companies 1826 & 1870

burden, because rarely did Directors receive any payment for their services, but one must stress that few possessed any ability or experience in gas-making and distribution, placing a considerable burden on the resident Engineer. Up to the 1830s there were few suitably-qualified Engineers in the region, and companies had been obliged to improvise with the talent available locally.(19) Eventually, though, as we saw in Chapter 2, a recognisable gas engineering profession started to emerge, and although it was 1863 before the British Association of Gas Managers was created, a set of techniques and duties had been developing for over twenty-five years which were put to good use in the North West as the demand for gaslighting accelerated. The name of the professional association also confirms the earlier point, that the Engineer's duties were both technical and managerial, providing a direct link in the industry between commercial and planning procedures.

The Engineer's rise to prominence has been partially described in Chapter 2. There, it was emphasised how these men, apart from managing a supply company and frequently running their own gas equipment business, also designed gasworks and plant extensions at undertakings formed in many smaller towns. They were widely respected within the industry, disseminating their expertise in gas company affairs all over the region as gaslighting grew in popularity. We have also seen how St. Helens Gas Light Co. used both Ralph Spooner and George Edwards, and similarly John Rofe (Preston), George Emmott (Oldham), Orlando Brothers (Blackburn) and Alfred King (Liverpool) played equally important roles in other small undertakings. Indeed, the British Association of Gas Managers was founded in Manchester, confirming the profession's strength in the region. These Engineers also perpetuated their contribution by training sons in the industry, and nepotism contributed significantly to the provision of qualified personnel in this key area. Pollard has shown that this was typical of British engineering generally in the early-nineteenth century,(20) and certainly in the North West nepotism provided the much-needed continuity required to maintain the smooth progress under way from the 1820s.(21)

The growing importance of the Engineer is reflected in their improved salaries. A typical North West Engineer in the 1820s would have earned between £75 and £150 per annum,(22) but by the 1840s this had risen to around £200,(23) while by the 1860s over £500 was paid by the larger companies (24). Remuneration was obviously dependent on the size of a system, and the Liverpool United Gas Co. paid the best salary of £1,200,(25) but the general level increased significantly in direct proportion to the escalation in an Engineer's responsibilities. Again, this reflected the improved status of professional managers in British business as a whole at that time,(26) and while one must emphasise that the improved influence of the Engineer was a gradual process, rather than a 'Palace Revolution', from the 1830s this individual was becoming the linchpin of gas company management.

One of the most influential of North West gas engineering dynasties was the King family which held the post of Engineer to the Liverpool undertaking for over eighty years. This relationship had started as early as 1815, when Joseph King, an accountant, was elected on to the Board of Liverpool Gas Light Co., and by November 1817 he had secured the post of Sub-

Treasurer and Chief Clerk for his brother, John.(27) After the current Engineer, William Sadler, had argued with John King over the methods used to draw up accounts, the latter was appointed in his place, and for five years the *Liverpool Mercury* claimed he brought 'his activity, intelligence and practical experience' to bear in coping with the problems of building a successful operation.(28) His career was cut short by a premature death in 1826, but this simply resulted in a younger brother, Alfred, succeeding to what had already become a prestigious post. This appointment at first sight appears rather strange, Alfred King having spent the previous two years working for Taylor & Martineau as an oil-gas installation engineer, after having received a training in accountancy. Nevertheless, Alfred King became one of the leading gas engineers in the country, and not only was he responsible for successfully organising the growth of what became the region's largest gas undertaking, he also contributed several improvements to the technology. One of his most enduring achievements was the development in 1829 of efficient jointing techniques for service pipes, an innovation which earned him national repute,(29) while in later years he devised improvements to the gas meter and designed a gas cooker. He also trained a son, William, as a gas engineer, and this man succeeded his father as Engineer to Liverpool United in 1866, continuing the family's link with the business until his retirement in 1904.

The King family, and Alfred King especially, provided a major source of guidance and inspiration in the development of a highly profitable gas company. Alfred's combination of a training in accountancy and gas engineering was unusual, but it equipped him with the kind of skills necessary in filling the demanding role of Engineer. It is important to remember that the Engineer (or Managing Engineer as they were sometimes called) needed to be competent as both commercial manager and head of technical operations, advising the Board on all matters relating to these two central functions. Decisions on investment plans, prices, new appointments, and negotiations with local authorities were all taken only after the Engineer had been consulted, and his advice normally acted as the basis for most policies. In fact, by the end of our period, Harris argues that most Liverpool United Directors 'rarely rose above the "guinea pig" standard [sic]', such was the extent to which the professional officers had supplanted their role as active creators of company strategy.(30) Initially, the Board had been the source of all crucial decisions, but progressively from the 1830s their role deteriorated into a rubber-stamping of suggestions put forward by the Engineer, emphasising the key role played by this new breed of specialists.

Liverpool was by no means exceptional among North West gas undertakings as an illustration of the Engineer's growing stature, and at the larger businesses in Preston, Bolton, Blackburn, Oldham and Warrington full-time professionals soon developed into the pivot around which the whole business revolved. The advance in their salaries is a reflection of this decisive switch in the balance of power within a company's management structure, and another manifestation was the construction of elaborate headquarters for the Engineer's staff. Most of the First Generation had built special facilities for the collectors, cashiers and administrators in the early-1820s, but after a period of expansion often quite grandiose buildings were constructed as gas company offices which frequently became prominent features of their respective main streets.(31) The trend is indicative of a growing level of bureaucratisation in the industry as the incomes from an ever-increasing number of consumers placed greater burdens on the need for closer monitoring of office procedures. In this respect, however, management faced yet another problem in monitoring closely the activities of clerical officers.

Although no North West gas company Director was prosecuted for fraud, and in only two cases were Engineers sacked for committing a criminal offence,(32) there are several examples of theft at a lower level. As was common in industry generally, the Board would try to insure itself against this eventuality by insisting that those clerks handling money should provide a surety of between £500 and £1,000 from local businessmen, but even when a theft had been proven it was rare to see a company receive full compensation from the bondsmen. Employing office staff could clearly become a hazardous exercise in the nineteenth century, indicating the inability of management to supervise this aspect of the business adequately. The earliest known case of an accounts clerk being sacked for embezzling funds was at Bolton in 1824, when John Rushton was instructed 'to attend at the Works to close his accounts and that in case he neglects to do so the Sureties be called upon to make up the deficiency'.(33) No record of the actual loss was made, but Preston Gas Light Co. dismissed their managing clerk, Thomas Redmayne, in 1829 after the auditors had noticed £239 was missing from the cash-book, and his bondsmen later agreed to pay 10/- (50p) in the pound as compensation.(34) One of the factors which exacerbated the situation, apart from basic human weakness, was the low salaries paid to these officers,(35) and when they were dealing with so much money the temptation was always there to supplement their meagre wage out of company funds.

In many ways, gas companies were wide open to these abuses, and with accounting techniques so poorly developed it was relatively easy for clerical officers to siphon off money.(36) As Newbigging noted in 1883: 'confused and unsatisfactory accounts are a fruitful source of ... irregularities.'(37) The accounts clerk, however, was another functionary whose role was enhanced during the nineteenth century. Initially, accountants were rarely employed by gas companies, and in many cases a clerk would assemble the balance sheet, aided by the Treasurer,(38) but as a result of the need to improve the supply of financial information, and the later imposition by parliament of more sophisticated reporting requirements, then the position gained in importance. The accounts clerk, or Accountant, consequently became of one of the principal company officers, and by mid-century there had been significant changes to a department which had originally started out as little more than a room where the takings were counted and bills paid.

This is not the place for a detailed history of accountancy in the gas industry,(39) but between the 1820s and 1870s the function evolved from a system based on elementary double-entry book-keeping into a more elaborate attempt to produce a balance sheet which incorporated a detailed breakdown of current revenue, general revenue, capital accounts, rent accounts, and the presentation of a profit and loss account. The 1845 Companies Act laid down the first major change in this area, and all undertakings registered under that legislation were obliged to employ the model balance sheet stipulated in the legislation. We noted in Chapter 4 how the driving force behind this reform was the desire to protect shareholders from the abuses perpetrated by unscrupulous company promoters,(40) but given the non-speculative nature of North West gas undertakings the accountancy inno-vations were more important as a means of bringing greater systematisation into the analysis of business finance, although with more *rentiers* as share-holders there was also a greater demand for accurate information on company performance.

This improvement in accountancy techniques was of great significance to the expanding gas companies of the North West, bringing greater order into a key area. Problems recruiting reliable staff would continue to hamper office routines, but management was able to employ a range of new techniques from the 1840s in effecting a transformation in presenting balance sheets, bringing a greater degree of understanding to the analysis of a company's financial state. This would especially help the Engineer in his assessment of company performance at a time when demand was expanding at an un-precedented rate and expenditure on new plant was continually required, and in that capacity the Accountant became an essential member of the management team.

The evolution of management structures in many North West gas companies was consequently an important feature of the expansion recorded from the 1830s. Directors had initially been responsible for most aspects of running the business, but progressively, as both the business expanded and professional management developed the expertise to take over many responsibilities, there was a significant delegation of authority from the Board to a growing number of functionaries. Figure 6.1 depicts the gradual process of evolution through which the typical company passed between 1820 and 1880, illustrating how the structure was in effect much the same in form, but in practice the professional officers, and especially the Engineer, were much more important members of the whole team. The creation of sub-committees by the Board encapsulates the state reached by the 1860s, because in these influential bodies the appropriate officer would provide the information on which major decisions were made. Alford has pointed to the existence of 'diffused entrepreneurship' within large-scale management structures,(41) and certainly from the 1830s Directors were so increasingly dependent upon the information provided by the functional management that the Board's influence over general strategy waned significantly.

The professionalisation of gas company management was a development of great importance to the industry, and when we come to consider company strategy and the exploitation of market and technical opportunities it is vital to remember that the policies were largely conceived and implemented by people specially trained in the business of gas supply. The Engineers were enormously assisted by certain very helpful trends, but it was still necessary to seize the openings, and the part-time Directors possessed neither the skills nor the aptitude for maximising the full potential in gaslighting. The changes in strategy will be outlined later, but first we need to examine the changing circumstances in which they operated after 1830 and the impact these new factors had on the economics of gas supply.

The Environment for Growth

The emergence of an elite cadre of specialists trained to handle both commercial and technical aspects of gas company management coincided with a period in which demand was beginning to increase rapidly and regular dividends were being produced. The First Generation were all moving into a phase of profitable growth by 1830, after the early struggles to cope with the complexities of a new industry. The original intention in most cases had been to establish operations which were capable of serving the lighting needs of those who invested in the business, especially the large industrial consumers, and in consequence investment was severely restricted, while a three-tier price structure evolved which favoured those interests. Companies were also only supplying for up to seven hours each day at that time,(42) and given the seasonal nature of the demand from mills and street lighting, along with the highly inefficient method of charging customers on a rental basis, then it is not surprising that good profits were hard to make. As the 1820s had progressed, and the slowly expanding customer bases started to demand gas for longer periods, it became easier to reward shareholders directly with dividends. Directors still erred very much on the side of caution, maintaining a tight grip over marginal costs and underestimating the potential demand for gaslighting, yet it was still possible to pay regular, if unspectacular (see Appendix C), dividends. Management was acting rationally in pursuing this highly cautious strategy, guaranteeing a regular supply of gas to the limited mains system, and producing returns for shareholders, but more expansive policies appear to have been shunned. The enormous learning curve facing these pioneers was at last being overcome, or at least that is what Directors were reporting by the late-1820s, congratulating themselves and the proprietors on their enterprise and foresight, and recording how profitable the business had become.(43) After 1830, however, management was to face an even more challenging phase, leading to a series of revisions in strategy which placed even greater pressure on the ability of Directors to cope with running such a business. Fortunately, however, the new breed of professional managers emerging at that time was able to take over the direction of this expansionist phase, employing their greater understanding of the industry's technical and commercial characteristics in the development of more durable businesses.

A trend of great importance which affected gas operations directly was, as both Falkus and Matthews have noticed, the long-run decline in the cost of key items like coal and iron.(44) Representing about one-half of the capital cost of building a gas supply operation, the price of iron was an important determinant of activity within the industry,(45) and between 1810 and 1850 in Britain generally it fell from £6.80 per ton to just £2.(46) Over the same period, the price of coal in the North West was also reduced significantly, from approximately 18/- per ton to around 13/6.(47) As Figure 6.2 indicates, though, coal prices only fell rapidly in the depression years of 1827–30, 1838–42 and 1847–50, while in the relative boom years of the mid-1830s and mid-1840s they were just as likely to increase. Indeed, although the long-run trend in coal and iron prices was most definitely downward, companies would frequently be faced with more expensive commodities when the general economy was expanding, and in the early-1870s gas prices

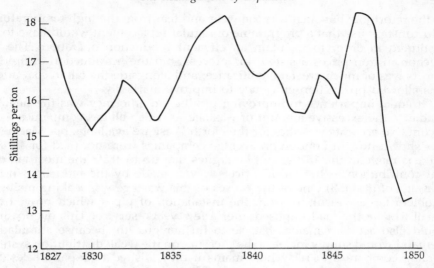

Figure 6.2   Average coal prices for selected North West gas undertakings, 1827–50. Evidence taken from PP (1847a and 1850) for works at Ashton-under-Lyne, Bury, Kendal, Manchester, Oldham, Preston and Wigan. (Only cannel coal prices have been used.)

had to be raised as a direct consequence of these short-term vicissitudes.(48)

Alongside these diminishing factor costs, the technology of gas-making and main-laying was also improving, leading to greater efficiency in the use of machinery and raw materials. Economies of scale in production were limited in the gas industry, as we have already noted, but the process of continued technical innovation could still yield advances. In the early years, because there had been few qualified people available, the organisation of gas-making had not always been efficiently managed,(49) but with the gas engineering profession taking shape, bringing a wider dissemination of new ideas and techniques, companies were better equipped to enhance their production performance. The design of retorts in particular, and how they were set in the furnace, provided a significant improvement in yields. Originally, retorts had been made of cast iron, but because this material could only operate at temperatures of up to 760°C the volume of gas obtained from a ton of coal would not have exceeded 8,000 cubic feet.(50) As early as 1820, though, John Grafton had been experimenting with fireclay retorts, and after installing these designs at his Cambridge gasworks it eventually became standard practice to replace the cast iron variety with the new material. This innovation was popular because it allowed carbonisation temperatures to rise to 900°C, improving the yield on a ton of coal until it reached 9,500 cubic feet by the 1840s.(51)

Maintaining the efficiency of retorts was one of the most demanding tasks facing the Engineer, particularly as this piece of equipment only had a productive life of no more than nine months. Another of Grafton's innovations, the exhauster, helped prevent the damaging accumulation of carbon in the retort,(52) but such was the wear and tear from the high temperatures and constant use that a programme of regular replacement would have to be instituted in order to maintain an efficient production operation. The reduction in iron prices assisted this process, but the introduction of fireclay retorts was of much greater significance, and alongside the fall in coal prices this allowed production efficiency to improve markedly.

Of equal importance to improving production efficiency was the need to eradicate the excessive amount of wastage to which all gas companies were victim. No accurate statistics for the North West are available, but Matthews has shown how in London on average companies were not paid for 45% of the gas made in the 1820s, and he argues that up to 1850 'the most important contribution to the fall in price ... was made by the reduction in the wastage of gas'.(53) One of the causes of this wastage was leaking mains, a problem largely resulting from the installation of pipes which proved too small to take the load imposed after a few years' service. This overloading could also act as a major obstacle to further growth, because stimulating demand would simply increase the pressure on the weak distribution system, forcing companies to relay new mains if they wished to expand sales.(54) Better designs for both service pipes(55) and mains helped eradicate the problem, but constant vigilance had to be maintained in this area, especially as even in the 1860s losses of up to 15% were still being recorded.(56)

The principal contributor to this problem of wastage, however, was the inefficient system of charging customers not for the amount of gas they used, but for how long they lit a certain number and type of lamps.(57) Directors constantly complained about the untrustworthiness of many customers who either burned for longer than the contracted time, or widened the jet, leading to what the Preston Directors described as 'much waist [sic]' in the system.(58) This abuse was clearly rife, adding further to the challenge of increasing the financial yield on the company's investment, and only the mass introduction of meters in the 1830s could bring any certainty into monitoring actual consumption. The unreliable nature of early meters had held up greater progress in this area, but by 1840 the First Generation had installed accurate instruments in all customers' premises,(59) and this helped enormously in eliminating much of the waste attendant on the old rental system. It is this innovation which was primarily responsible for undertakings being able to increase their revenue from a given make of gas, and in explaining the fall in prices after 1830 meters must have played a central role.

Gas technology was clearly by no means static during the nineteenth century, and although the principal stages depicted in Figure 1.1 remained unchanged, a constant series of improvements was introduced affecting everything from retorts to meters. The Engineer would have been particularly important in considering the value of each innovation, advising Directors on the most appropriate equipment to purchase, and keeping the plant and mains operating at a level commensurate with the needs of both the business and its market. At the same time, the Engineer was also responsible for an undertaking's commercial welfare, and here again he was in the best position to make clear recommendations on future policy. His knowledge of current prices for equipment, coal and labour would have given him a detailed insight into the cost side, while monitoring production and consumption, and receiving any new requests for a supply of gas, provided the intelligence on demand projections. The picture he would have gained by the 1830s would have been extremely favourable to suppliers, because, with the basic network having been established and factor costs on a gradual downward path, the marginal costs of further expansion were also falling, providing the basis for improved profitability. One cannot be too precise about the exact timing of these developments, but the combination of all these trends created an environment for growth from the 1830s which was helping Engineers to lay the foundations for a period of rapid and prosperous business development.

Pricing Policy

Arising from this favourable scenario of rising income, falling marginal and factor costs, and improved profitability, was a steady reduction in prices for all types of consumer. The three-tier price structure which came into vogue in the 1820s had been designed to stimulate sales to large consumers, resulting in a standard price which Johnes and Clegg regarded as a disincentive to take gas for the vast majority of town-dwellers.(60) This structure remained in place, where it had been in operation, but the general level of prices fell to such an extent that both the amount consumed by older customers rose, and more significantly, the number of customers connected to the mains grew, pushing the industry into a new phase of expansion. Some felt that companies were still neglecting a large part of their potential market,(61) and we shall see later how and why caution remained a prominent feature of strategy, but the general story, as Table 2.2 reveals, was one of almost continuous growth. Our task here will be to chart this process, while in the next sections the reasons behind these trends will be analysed, introducing a variety of internal and external pressures which influenced the course of management strategy up to 1880.

In the North West by 1830 standard gas prices averaged around 11/- (55p) per thousand cubic feet, having fallen from the typical starting point of between 15/- (75p) and 12/6 (62.5p) (see Table 5.2). Larger consumers paid considerably less than this up to 1830 in all towns except Liverpool, Chester, Kendal, Macclesfield and Warrington, because discounts were normally made available to assure their loyalty, and local authorities were given street lighting at or below cost as an indirect payment for granting access to the streets in all communities. Relatively little effort had gone into stimulating sales to domestic consumers, other than those located close by the mains laid to supply mills or street lights, and at those prices it was unlikely that many would have clamoured for the service. After 1830, however, North West gas prices tumbled dramatically, and in Table 6.2 we can see how by 1849 the average had fallen by almost 50%, compared to 1830. There are significant variations around this average, caused by a combination of scale and access to cheap coal supplies,(62) but even in towns like Birkenhead, Bury, Kendal and Runcorn, where the price was up to 3/1 (16p) higher than in Liverpool, reductions of at least one-third had been introduced over that nineteen year period. The region was by no means unusual in recording such a fall, and in towns across the United Kingdom gas prices were generally on a downward spiral, stimulating a rapid expansion in

Table 6.2 North West gas prices, 1830–80 (shillings per thousand cubic feet)

	1830	1849	1865	1880
Accrington	–	7/-*	N.A.	5/-*
Ashton	10/6*	5/6*	4/-*	3/10*
Birkenhead	–	7/6*	5/-*	3/6*
Blackburn	10/-*	5/-*	4/-*	3/9*
Bolton	10/-*	5/-*	3/6*	2/9*
Burnley	8/9*	5/3*	3/6*	2/9*
Bury	10/-*	7/6*	3/9*	3/4*
Congleton	–	7/-*	4/6*	3/9*
Chester	10/-	6/8	4/8*	3/9
Darwen	–	–	4/9*	4/-*
Heywood	–	5/4*	4/6*	5/-*
Kendal	12/6	7/6	5/2	3/9
Liverpool (coal)	12/6	4/6	3/-	3/1
Macclesfield	10/-	5/6*	4/-*	3/10*
Manchester	12/-*	4/9*	3/6*	2/8*
Middleton	–	5/6	5/-	4/2*
New Mills	–	–	5/10*	5/-*
Oldham	12/6*	6/-*	3/8*	4/-*
Preston	12/6*	5/3*	3/9*	3/9
Radcliffe	–	–	4/10*	4/9
Rochdale	–	6/-*	4/-*	3/8*
Runcorn	–	7/6*	5/-*	–
St. Helens	–	6/8*	5/-*	3/4*
Salford	10/-*	5/-*	4/-*	3/1*
Stalybridge	–	5/6*	4/-*	3/8*
Stockport	12/-*	4/9*	3/6*	3/2*
Warrington	12/-	6/3*	4/6*	3/6*
Wigan	10/6*	6/-*	3/9*	3/6*
Average	11/-	5/10	4/1	3/7

(*Indicates that discounts were granted to large consumers.)
Sources: PP (1847a), (1866) and (1881).

sales and income which only the most ambitious and far-sighted could have foreseen in the 1820s.

The dynamic impact of this trend in prices can be better understood by examining how it affected companies directly, and in Table 6.3 we can see how Preston Gas Light Co. was able to implement a series of reductions between 1834 and 1852, yet at the same time expand income and return healthy dividends. The company had originally set its standard price at 15/- (75p) per thousand cubic feet in 1816, reducing this to 12/6 (62.5p) in 1823, but as we saw in Chapter 5 the town's large cotton manufacturers had exacted hefty discounts from the Board in return for their custom, and in 1829 these were extended even further. Once all consumers had been provided with meters, by the mid-1830s management also started lowering the standard price, firstly to 10/- (50p) in 1834 and progressively up to 1852 by a further 55%, until it reached just 4/6 (22.5p). The Board must have been impressed

Table 6.3 Preston Gas Light Co. prices, sales & income, 1834−53

	Standard price* (shillings)	Gas sales (million cubic feet)	Income (£)
1834	10/-	N.A.	7,329
1835	10/-	N.A.	7,028
1836	10/-	23.4	7,882
1837	9/2	26.3	8,243
1838	9/2	28.2	10,747
1839	9/2	31.8	10,942
1840	9/2	35.9	12,757
1841	9/2	40.7	13,786
1842	9/2	39.7	14,483
1843	8/3	40.7	14,402
1844	7/6	43.5	16,155
1845	6/9	47.9	17,249
1846	6/-	53.6	18,009
1847	6/-	51.1	18,070
1848	6/-	50.4	14,839
1849	5/3	59.5	17,753
1850	5/3	70.8	19,996
1851	4/10	84.2	22,547
1852	4/6	96.3	22,878
1853	4/6	94.8	27,483

*Discounts of up to 25% were available to large consumers.
Sources: PGLCMB, 1834−53

with the effects of this policy, because, as Table 6.3 reveals, as soon as a reduction was announced there would be an immediate increase in consumption, compensating within the year for any possible loss in earnings arising from the price fall. A slump in income during 1847−48 was caused by the temporary closure of many local mills during the trade depression of that period, but otherwise there was an automatic mechanism at work, allowing Directors to embark on the strategy confident that returns would be improved. This also provided the basis for a period of regular 10% dividends (see Appendix C), demonstrating how companies were able to exploit their market more effectively in this period of significant growth.

The explanation behind this automatic mechanism can be found in the price elasticity of demand for gas, an elasticity which at that time exceeded unity. In simple terms, it was possible to increase sales and income by reducing prices, such was the sensitivity of demand to the cost of this product, and in all parts of the country shareholders and consumers were benefiting from the realisation that this relationship worked so effectively.(63) The evidence in Table 6.3 reveals how the mechanism worked so successfully at Preston, with sales jumping dramatically every time the price fell, and in Appendix D we can see how Blackburn Gas Light Co. was able to stimulate an expansion in sales of 263% between 1830 and 1849 by bringing the price down from 10/- (50p) to 5/- (25p). In Liverpool, where prices were the lowest in the region by 1849, the two companies had fought out a bitter struggle to dominate that market, as we shall see later, but Alfred King was still able to report in 1847 that, in response to a reduction from 8/- (40p) to 5/- (25p), the quantity of gas made by the older company had trebled over the previous seven years.(64) This case was rather unusual, given the fierce local rivalry which existed up to 1848, but in many other respects the management's awareness of demand being so price elastic was typical of developments in the region, and as a result gaslighting was becoming increasingly popular.

Market Expansion

The impact of this new pricing policy was clearly of great significance to the industry, but in spite of the drastic reductions Johnes and Clegg were still arguing in 1847 that the continued use of a three-tier price structure was preventing the emergence of a mass market for gaslighting. They were especially concerned that the majority of consumers were subsidising the larger users like factories and local authorities, because the discounts provided for the latter meant that the standard price was kept at what they regarded as an artificially higher level.(65) The companies would have responded by arguing that cheap street lighting was the price of local authority support for the venture, while industrialists would have installed their own gas-making plant had they not been given discounts, leading to the loss of a large proportion of their sales.(66) On the other hand, Johnes and Clegg felt that by the 1840s prices had fallen to such an extent that factories would have been unable to supply themselves with cheaper gas than that provided by companies, and given the price elasticity of demand for gas small consumers would have made up any losses from the industrial sector had the discounts been withdrawn and the standard prices further reduced.(67)

This debate over the justification for offering discounts was in many cases academic, because in spite of the growing importance of professional Engineers, the continued presence of industrialists on gas company Boards ensured that the *status quo* would prevail. It is also very questionable whether the arguments of Johnes and Clegg had much justification in the industrial towns, a point clarified by the information on market breakdown provided in Table 6.4. Although consumption figures are not available for Ashton-under-Lyne, industrial customers certainly accounted for half of all gas sold in the town, and taken in conjunction with the 33.2% in Warrington, and the 43.4% at Runcorn, this indicates the crucial importance of the sector to sales in such towns. Evidently, while not contributing a large number of customers, the industrial sector was a major consumer of gas in these industrial centres, and although the retailing sector provided the bulk of gas sales the companies would have suffered a significant decline in income had they not encouraged the manufacturers to remain loyal.(68) It was while giving evidence to Johnes and Clegg that Reyner made his threat in 1847,(69) and in general it seems unlikely that abolishing the discount system would have helped the companies bring prices down even further. Furthermore, they would have been faced with a rise in the marginal costs of connecting new customers had the large demand from manufacturers been reduced significantly, and this would certainly not have helped retailers, publicans or domestic consumers.

Table 6.4 Gas consumption in 1847 by type of customer for four companies

	Retail(a)		Domestic		Industrial		Public(c)		Total(d)	
	No.	million cu. feet	No.	million cu. feet	No.	million cu. feet	No.	million cu. feet	No.	million cu. feet
Liverpool (coal)	7,316	N.A.	3,065	N.A.	141	N.A.	188	N.A.	10,710	N.A.
Ashton	645	N.A.	130	N.A.	122	N.A.	40	N.A.	937	N.A.
Warrington	550	56	65	6	20	32.1	19	2.7	654	96.8
Runcorn	171	52.6(b)	20	–(b)	6	43.4	11	4.0	208	100.0

(N.A. indicates that the information is not available.)
(a) Includes public houses and offices.
(b) Taken together.
(c) Churches, chapels, workhouses and local government offices.
(d) Does not include street lamps.
Source: Rowlinson (1984), pp. 74 & 76.

The largest and most successful North West gas company in this period was clearly the Liverpool Gas Light Co., and we can see from Table 6.4 that this business was supplying almost 11,000 customers by 1847. Up to 1831 gas had been supplied at a standard price of 12/6 (62.5p) to all consumers, but even this company was obliged to introduce a discount system in 1831,(70) in order to eliminate any possible competition from its oil-gas rival in the industrial sector, and once the Liverpool Oil Gas Co. had converted to coal-gas production in 1834 prices in general started to fall. This struggle for supremacy will be described in a later section, but it is interesting to see that in 1841 the old company's discount system was abolished, and in 1844 a new method of favouring perennial customers was introduced, offering discounts to those who used gas during the summer months.(71) This was designed to attract more custom from the domestic and commercial sectors, and Table 6.4 reveals how successful they were in achieving these aims. Alfred King had described his main consumers in 1825 as 'tea dealers, spirit merchants, attorneys, ironmongers, druggists, stationers, hosiers, and publicans',(72) and while the retailing sector remained of central importance to the company, by the 1840s domestic customers were of much greater significance as a result of the policies pursued in that period.

The Johnes and Clegg prescription for even greater sales expansion does not appear to have been appropriate for all North West companies, and in general management had to tailor their policies to the requirements of their local economy.(73) Even though in industrial towns the gas undertaking was obliged to cater for the seasonal nature of demand for gas, and the trade cycle could drastically reduce demand from local manufacturers, by the 1840s supply operations could not have benefited as extensively from the general forces at work without securing industrial consumers in order to reduce the marginal costs of expansion. At the same time, having noted the disturbing influence of fluctuations in industrial activity, the growth in demand from perennial consumers like shopkeepers and publicans was helping to create an immunity from the trade cycle. This immunity had not been fully developed by the late 1840s, when most companies were obliged to cut their dividends during that depression (see Appendix C), but during the Lancashire Cotton Famine of the early 1860s most were able to maintain their 10% returns in spite of the blight affecting the region's main industry. The customer base was by then so diversified that even though income did fall (see Appendix D) such a severe depression could not affect performance severely.

In addition to the immunity from industrial depressions, from the 1840s North West gas undertakings continued to report a story of expansion, and in fact the process accelerated in the second half of the century. Fuelling the growth were further price reductions, and although these were not as dramatic as in the period 1830−49 Table 6.2 illustrates how by 1865 the average had fallen to 4/1 (21p), while by 1880 it had reached 3/7 (18p). Management was clearly intending to continue exploiting the same kind of trends operating in the earlier decades, and in achieving this aim they boosted sales even more dramatically. This impressive performance has already been described in terms of investment levels in Table 2.2, and it is interesting to remind ourselves how the average investment per undertaking in the North West jumped from £26,663 in 1847 to £88,465 in 1880, while over the same period total investment rose to nearly £8,500,000.

Unfortunately, a similar exercise for gas sales cannot be conducted, because accurate information on all undertakings only comes available from 1881, but judging from the scattered evidence still surviving there was clearly an equally impressive increase in this department after the 1840s. The incomes of the Preston and Blackburn companies are charted in Appendix D, and this depicts the post-1850 era as their most expansive, with rises of 571% and 274%, respectively. In the former's case, this represented a leap in sales from 70.8 million cubic feet in 1850 to 317 million by 1881, and many other supply operations recorded similar rates of growth.(74) Table 2.3 demonstrates the scale achieved by the region's leading businesses by 1881, and apart from the enormous undertakings at Liverpool and Manchester, where sales had reached 2,200 million cubic feet, there were several others which were as big as most of the other provincial supply operations (see Table 2.5). Total sales of gas in the North West by the end of our period were approaching 11,000 million cubic feet, and 443,742 consumers were being supplied by the 84 undertakings covered in that survey (see Table 2.4), indicating the scale achieved over these decades of rapid expansion.

This record of accelerating growth, along with consistent dividend returns, is a testimony to both the potential in the North West gaslighting market, and the ability of management to exploit the situation. The initial thrust of company development had been constrained by the 'strategic' motives behind investors' decisions to participate in these ventures, but once a group of professional engineers had emerged, with the training and expertise to perceive the possibilities open to gas suppliers, then a more ambitious policy was introduced. Realising that the demand for gas was extremely price elastic, and benefiting from both improvements in technology and reductions in coal and iron costs these professionals pushed the industry into a rapid phase of expansion. Pricing policy was very much the engine behind this growth, and the Engineer facilitated the process, providing the organisational basis for an era of comfortable profitability. But does this image of aggressive business development belie reality? Was there really such a dramatic change in management attitude? And were there any other influences on the policy of price reductions? The final question we shall answer in the next section, but we need to place in a broader context the direction of company strategy, and the impact this had on attitudes towards expansion.

Having moved from a position where investment and pricing policies were directed principally towards the needs of a limited market, into a phase when it seems that some effort was made to stimulate sales by exploiting the price elasticity of demand for gas, there appears to be evidence of a more aggressive search for customers and profits. This typology, however, can be extremely misleading, because while expansion did undoubtedly occur at an unprecedented rate, and the main force behind this trend was a decline in gas prices, management remained extremely cautious in its approach to investment. A classic illustration of this conservatism was Preston Gas Light Co.'s reluctance to sanction John Rofe's plan to extend a ten inch main from their new works in Walker St. (see Figure 5.1) to the new cotton mills built to the North West of the town. The reason given for their reluctance was a fear that the 10% dividend would be difficult to sustain if all the extensions were implemented at once, even though Rofe promised that sales would be considerably augmented if the mills were connected.(75) Rofe eventually won the argument, but due to 'the prostration of trade in this District' at that time the dividend had to be cut anyway,(76) and only in 1860 was the 10% level restored (see Appendix C).

The preoccupation with controlling marginal costs so typical of the early construction phase was consequently maintained throughout the nineteenth century, particularly when management knew that investment would not be recouped immediately from anticipated earnings. In 1848 Liverpool Gas Light Co. was considering an expansion into the suburb of Woolton, but after Alfred King reported that an outlay of £5,591 would only produce an annual income of around £600 the Board decided to encourage a group of potential consumers to establish their own supply operation.(77) Providing a supply of gas to consumers living in outlying districts usually resulted in the imposition of a higher price than in the central areas, in order to recoup the costs of laying the mains and providing additional storage and production capacity,(78) but the Liverpool Gas Light Co. was not willing to take the risk of serving Woolton in the hope that the investment would be recouped over the long term.

The concern with marginal costs was of course sound business practice, and no criticism of management should be read into this analysis, but in pursuing cautious strategies the companies were leaving themselves wide open to allegations of neglect and profiteering at the expense of public service. Most importantly, their profitable existence attracted the attentions of powerful local interests, and when considering the reasons why gas prices fell so much it is essential to bear in mind not just the technological improvements and cost reductions, but also a range of other influences which affected strategy directly. These pressures were in fact of great significance in some towns, and a balanced assessment of pricing policy must incorporate an analysis of broader issues which affected the attitudes of management towards both their consumers and their political masters. Broadening the discussion in this way also returns us to the issue of monopolistic trading, and in the examination of management strategy it is vital to understand how Directors and Engineers viewed their position in a market which was affected by a number of economic and political variables.

Competition, Regulation and Strategy

Not only was there a considerable degree of continuity in the cautious attitude of management towards the need for expansion, further evidence that after 1830 companies did not necessarily embark on an aggressive assault on the market by price-cutting can also be found by looking at some of the pressures brought to bear by consumers and local government. Although competition in gas supply rarely existed in the North West, and in theory most companies were provided with a monopoly of their market, enabling them to set prices at levels commensurate with their tightly controlled marginal costs and maintain a healthy dividend record,(79) the industry was not operating in a political vacuum. Parliament had always been uneasy about the activities of public utilities, and progressively more regulations were introduced to limit their freedom of action. The direct impact of these controls has been heavily criticised for ineptness,(80) but more importantly the refusal to grant exclusive franchises resulted in a constant awareness by companies of any implicit or actual threat posed to their monopoly. Indeed, in some circumstances this menace actually became one of the key determinants of pricing policy, indicating that, far from being a manifestation of management's aggressive search for business, the reductions were largely a defensive tool to ward off potential competition at a time when the economic environment encouraged the formation of rivals.

When considering how best to protect the public from what could have been profiteering gas companies, parliament had decided initially that they could be 'kept in check, either by the fear or by the actual existence of competition'.(81) The London gas industry was regarded as the prime example of this policy at work, with thirteen separate companies supplying overlapping districts,(82) and up to the 1850s in all major British towns at least two undertakings vied for the local gaslighting market.(83) In the North West, Manchester was an obvious exception to this rule, but after 1823 Liverpool Gas Light Co. was faced with competition from a rival, while in several other cases companies were threatened by proposed or substantive opposition. By the 1840s Parliament had moved in favour of direct controls on dividends and prices, but at no time were provincial gas companies granted sole access to their local markets, and this long-standing measure of control ensured that the possibility of competition would act as a discipline on management strategy.

(a) *Liverpool*

The formation of Liverpool Oil Gas Co. in 1823 was in fact only a small threat to the well-established Liverpool Gas Light Co., and until the former's conversion to coal-gas production in 1834 it 'was a pigmy concern compared with its older rival'.(84) Oil-gas was simply too expensive, and although the new company managed to acquire some of the coal-gas operation's consumers, as well as the contract to light the Town Hall when Liverpool Corporation decided to scrap its own plant in 1828,(85) the fierce competition only started after 1834. Gaining parliamentary permission to convert to coal-gas technology was certainly a boon to the renamed Liverpool New Gas & Coke Co., and over the next fourteen years gas prices fell by almost two-thirds as a result of the struggle for supremacy between the two businesses (see Table 6.2). Harris describes this period as 'The Battle of the Mains', and particularly in the competition to supply the wealthy districts like Everton there was intense rivalry.(86) Liverpool Gas Light Co. introduced its discount system for perennial customers in 1841 as a means of capturing this kind of market,(87) and from the evidence presented in Table 6.4 it is clear that its domestic loading was a significant part of total sales by 1847.

Competition was consequently the main reason why gas prices fell so rapidly in Liverpool. The new company's conversion to coal-gas in 1834 had resulted in an immediate reduction by both operations, bringing the price down to 10/- (50p) per thousand cubic feet, and by 1846 it had fallen to 4/6 (22.5p). When announcing a cut of 2/- (10p) in 1840 the old company wrote to its rival complaining about 'the general unfriendly and aggressive spirit

Street lamps in a Liverpool square (c.1825).

manifested by your company',(88) and during the following eight years this bitterness continued until a new solution was mooted. This competition was in fact extremely wasteful, because of the duplication of production and distribution equipment, and while the long-run fall in coal and iron costs, as well as the reduction in wastage, would have helped the companies to cut prices and maintain the 10% dividend (see Appendix C), by 1846 there were signs that these policies were beginning to cause serious problems. The companies were also concerned about the possibility that a third supplier was to be promoted, adding further to their problems at a time when Liverpool Corporation was beginning to take a much closer interest in the situation.

The third supply venture was proposed by the Liverpool Guardian Society for the Protection of Trade (hereafter referred to as the Guardian Society) in 1845, and ironically its leaders were motivated by the desire to bring prices down even further. Purporting to represent '900 and upwards of the Merchants, Bankers, Innkeepers and Tradesmen of Liverpool, consumers of gas to a considerable extent', the Guardian Society had been actively canvassing for lower prices since 1840,(89) but their intention to form a third company brought opposition not only from the existing ventures, but also from Liverpool Corporation's Watch Committee. Councillors had in fact already started to encourage a merger between the rival gas undertakings when the Guardian Society's proposal was published, and after an agreement had been reached in 1847 the Liverpool United Gaslight Co. was formed a year later to bring about the desired combination of the two supply operations.(90)

It is interesting to see how Liverpool Corporation had played a leading part in merging the two companies at a time when in other towns municipalisation was beginning to grow in popularity. A parliamentary Select Committee investigating Liverpool Gas Light Co.'s request to increase its capital in 1845 had actually suggested that the corporation should acquire the two undertakings, but this notion was rejected by the Tory majority,(91) and instead they cajoled the suppliers into a merger. Not that the Directors needed much persuading, because when the old company reduced its price to 4/6 (22.5p) in July 1845 it was revealed that the undertaking's total costs by then were 4/8 (23p) per thousand cubic feet, including 1/11 (9p) for dividends.(92) This indicated the need to call up reserves, in order to continue paying 10% (see Appendix C), and given the advantages of combining operations both managements realised that competition was no longer commercially viable.

Liverpool United's creation also coincided with the emergence of a new attitude in government circles. Contemporaries no longer felt that competition would benefit consumers, and, as Johnes and Clegg noted, many argued that 'the large amount of capital employed in founding two establishments, where one would suffice, must inevitably serve in the end to raise the general price of gas'.(93) Clearly, the fall in prices resulting from competition in Liverpool appears to contradict this view, but as costs were beginning to exceed what they were charging by 1845 then further reductions seem to have been out of the question, and had the merger not occurred one could expect the next movement to have been upwards, or alternatively the collapse of one of the companies. Parliament actually rejected the Guardian Society's proposal to form a new gas company on the grounds that a merger of the existing operations would bring greater benefits to the consumer.(94) Officials also placed much greater trust in the controls imposed on dividends and prices, anticipating that this would provide adequate protection for consumers. In effect, though, as we shall see later, these maxima did not work in anybody's interests, and the major worry for any company remained the potential fear of competition which always existed because no provincial operation was ever granted a monopoly in law. The Liverpool undertakings had experienced the direct impact of this approach since 1834, and in other towns one of the main pressures on prices and investment strategy was the indirect influence arising from the potential or actual threat from a competitor.

(b) Chester

An undertaking which suffered most from this insecurity was Chester Gas Light Co., because by 1856 it had been forced out of business by a combination of opponents intent on bringing down gas prices.(95) The company had been one of the most profitable investments among the First Generation, returning an average dividend of 9% on their original £5 shares between 1822 and 1837, after having capitalised £6,850 of undistributed profits in 1828 to double the value of each share.(96) This performance was based on a highly cautious strategy of serving a limited market contiguous to the three main streets, and maintaining prices at 10/- (50p) per thousand cubic feet right up to 1842, but the policy undoubtedly left the management vulnerable to accusations of profiteering. The reform of local government in

1835 had also resulted in a Liberal majority emerging in Chester Corporation, and the increasingly active Watch Committee diligently pursued a policy of closely monitoring the street lighting service.(97) Such was the antagonism which this caused that by 1842 the Watch Committee had recommended the construction of a municipal gasworks, on the grounds that the street lighting bill was 'very justly complained of by the public', given the poor quality of the lamps.(98) This effectively ended the company's control of the gaslighting market, highlighting the dangers inherent in an extremely volatile political and economic environment.

Although Chester Corporation rejected the Watch Committee's proposal, principally because the estimated expenditure of £10,000 might not prove remunerative,(99) Chester Gas Light Co. was warned that 'should [they] prove unwilling to serve the city on more advantageous terms' then an alternative supplier would be encouraged to establish a rival operation.(100) The company immediately decided to reduce its price from 10/- (50p) to 8/6 (42.5p), and after the Watch Committee tried unsuccessfully to seek powers in the 1845 Chester Improvement Bill to build a municipal gasworks a complete reorganisation of the gasworks and mains network was instituted as a means of improving the service.(101) A further price cut of 1/10 (9p) was also announced in 1847,(102) and by 1849 the Directors were hoping that the refurbishments would result in a 'supply of gas itself which will be of the very purest character, furnishing a further ... reason for its most extensive use in houses and private establishments'.(103) Indeed, following the general pattern, income was rising after the price reductions, from £4,321 in 1845 to £5,802 by 1850, and new customers like Chester Castle and the County Gaol were being secured as the service improved. On the other hand, the strategy resulted in a dramatic downturn in dividend performance, and as Appendix C reveals between 1838 and 1855 returns were very poor.(104)

The Tory-owned Chester Gas Light Co. had clearly made some effort to improve and cheapen its service in response to the threats raised by the Watch Committee, but even though this had been costly in terms of dividends the response did not satisfy some of their more ardent critics. Indeed, in 1850 a group of consumers took matters into their own hands and proposed 'to supply themselves as cheaply as they could'.(105) Consumer gas companies were quite a feature of the mid-nineteenth century, as we shall see later, and in Chester the mere announcement of an intention to form a Chester Gas Consumers Co., and supply gas at 4/6 (22.5p), brought the old company's price down from 6/8 (33p) to 5/6 (27.5p).(106) The threat posed by this new undertaking took an even more serious dimension when the Watch Committee passed a resolution recommending 'that the warmest support of the Corporation should be given to the proposed new company', (107) demonstrating the ease with which the rival would be granted access to the town's streets. It actually took the rebel consumers over a year to raise the estimated £18,000 required to build the new system, and an Engineer from Birkenhead, Samuel Highfield, had to be recruited to head up the operation,(108) but for Chester Gas Light Co. all their worst fears had come to pass by 1851.

The advent of competition, whether threatened or actual, had certainly precipitated a significant downturn in the fortunes of Chester Gas Light

Co., and with prices falling to 4/6 (22.5p) in 1852 the chances of producing any dividend appeared to be very slim (see Appendix C).(109) The Watch Committee had awarded the street lighting contract to Highfield's under-taking by 1853,(110) and the old company reported the loss of 'a considerable number of their customers' at a time when coal and iron costs were also beginning to rise,(111) bringing little hope of any revival in fortunes because the company's average costs were beginning to increase. Such was Chester Gas Light Co.'s parlous position by 1856 that the Directors decided to negotiate a sell-out, and reflecting their poor bargaining position they were forced to agree a price which gave shareholders just £20 for every £30 of capital held.(112) The new venture had by then been reconstituted as the Roodee Gas Co.,(113) Highfield having actually sold out himself in 1854 to a prominent local Liberal, E. G. Salisbury,(114) but after the negotiations had been completed in 1856 the Chester United Gas Co. was established, and a complete monopoly of the gaslighting market had been restored.

The history of gas supply in Chester up to 1856 provides a useful illustration of the various forces influencing the industry's viability. Changes in the control exercised by local government after 1835 had clearly played an important role in undermining Chester Gas Light Co.'s comfortable trading position,(115) but the political environment only forms part of the story, and more emphasis should be placed on the growing concern over gas prices. Matthews has attributed the failure of London companies to forestall the entry of rival suppliers to a combination of their capital structures and their reluctance to cut prices,(116) but in Chester's case only the latter seems to apply as a credible explanation for the consumer company's success. Chester Gas Light Co. had embarked upon its modernisation programme in the late 1840s when the price of iron was still falling, and in any case sunk costs should give established suppliers a competitive advantage,(117) especially if the new company was going to build its system when factor costs were actually rising. The Roodee Gas Co. was also unable to pay any dividends up to 1856,(118) demonstrating the unremunerative nature of a competitive environment, but after the merger Chester United provided consistent returns on the combined incomes (see Appendix C), and prices were maintained at 4/6 (22.5p).(119)

Chester Gas Light Co. was ultimately forced out of business by the unpopularity of its pricing policy. Even though a reduction from 10/- (50p) to 5/6 (27.5p) had been implemented between 1842 and 1851, largely as a result of local pressures, prices in Chester had been significantly higher than the North West average (see Table 6.2) until the consumers company came on the scene. There had also been a heavy political bias in the Watch Committee's actions, an issue to be taken up again, but the dissatisfaction with pricing policy was the main reason why a rival was formed, and in many British towns exactly the same scenario was being enacted. The consumers' movement was steadily gaining momentum from the 1840s, and agitators like George Flintoff travelled the country advocating the formation of rival suppliers if the established company refused to lower its price.(120) Flintoff does not appear to have visited Chester, but local consumers were capable of acting on their own initiative, and Chester Gas Light Co. felt the full impact of this increasingly influential movement.

(c) Kendal

The highest price charged for gas in the North West by 1849 was 7/6 (37.5p) per thousand cubic feet (see Table 6.2), and while in Kendal's case this can be partly explained by the cost of transporting coal up the Lancaster canal the local company was widely criticised for its approach to consumers. Up to 1844 Kendal gas consumers had actually been obliged to pay 12/6 (62.5p), and not surprisingly loud complaints were voiced about these 'extravagantly high' levels. There were also claims that 'few of the Manufactures, Warehouses, Counting Houses, and shops of the smaller class, and scarcely any private Houses are lighted by Gas', because of the company's limited mains system,(121) and a popular Kendal anecdote of the time was the claim that consumers had to 'light a candle to see whether my gas is burning or not'.(122) The Tory-owned company would have felt secure up to 1830, but just as in Chester, and in many other North West towns, after the 1835 Municipal Corporation Act the Tory oligarchy was removed from power and 'leadership of the Corporation moved down the social spectrum and became centred on the town, not on the periphery of county society'.(123) Kendal Corporation actually became the preserve of a Quaker-led radical group, and although their militancy diminished after the turbulent period associated with Chartism (1837–43) the gas company did not escape the attentions of those who wanted a significant improvement in local services.(124)

There were undoubtedly strong political overtones in the debate over gas prices in Kendal, a point confirmed by the decision of the Radical Mayor, Thomas Brindloss, to act as Chairman of the Kendal Union Gas & Water Co. formed in 1845.(125) This echoed the events of 1824, when the Tory Mayor had chaired the inaugural meeting of Kendal Gas Light & Coke Co. in the Town Hall,(126) but as in Chester it was the economic argument which prompted almost 200 local manufacturers, retailers and professionals to subscribe to the £30,000 capital of the new venture.(127) It was yet another case of consumers showing their dissatisfaction with the established company, and by the end of 1845 Kendal Gas Light & Coke Co. had agreed to a merger, a move greeted with loud applause at a public meeting held in the Town Hall to sell shares in the Union Co.(128)

The cases of Kendal and Chester demonstrate the growing effectiveness of collective consumer agitation, and both companies paid the ultimate penalty for underestimating this power. Haslingden Gas Light & Coke Co. also suffered the same fate in 1861, when 404 locals signed a memorandum attacking the venture because they claimed to have 'suffered from having gas supplied to them from the existing private company of a very inferior quality although charged at a very high rate, and some parts of the district are not supplied at all'.(129) No evidence on prices in this town has survived, but the service was extremely limited up to 1860, and the successful formation of a Haslingden Union Gas Co. in 1861, out of the old company and the consumers' movement,(130) demonstrates how undertakings were being made much more accountable to their communities. Matthews has noted how 'the huge increase in the number of middle class and enfranchised consumers brought about by the fall in prices' was provoking much wider discussion of gas prices and the quality of gaslighting by the 1840s,(131) and given the refusal of parliament to grant exclusive franchises then companies were constantly in danger of retaliatory action.

(d) General Impact

Threatened or actual competition was consequently a major reason why prices fell so consistently after 1830, indicating that North West gas companies were unable to exploit their theoretical monopoly. In one respect, Kendal, Chester and Haslingden were unusual, because where consumer pressures mounted in the region frequently this resulted in the municipalisation of the company, as we shall see in Chapter 7, but otherwise they were typical of the scenario unfolding in the country as a whole at that time. The decline in coal and iron prices up to 1851, as well as the technological innovations affecting retorts, mains and meters, had certainly contributed to the fall in gas prices, but the unwillingness to reduce them as rapidly as particularly the smaller consumers demanded was of greater significance, and the legal position with regard to monopoly certainly did not favour the companies in their attempts to withstand these pressures. This ensured that the consumers' interests were safeguarded effectively, without the need to set a maximum price, even though parliament had by the 1840s decided to insist on this additional form of protection.

The impact of government policy on gas prices, as we have already intimated, is in fact very questionable. This form of direct intervention had been instituted as a result of the growing dissatisfaction with the earlier encouragement of competition as a means of protecting consumers, but although the 1847 Gasworks Clauses Act insisted that all companies seeking a new private Act would have a maximum price imposed, management had little to fear from this system.(132) No scientific method of calculating these maxima was devised, and generally the prices were arrived at after negotiations between the company and its local authority. This could have discouraged management from applying for further statutory powers, had the revised prices been a constraint on performance, but rarely did they interfere with an undertaking's commercial prospects. The three Acts acquired at Blackburn (1853), Preston (1853) and Bolton (1854) imposed maxima of 5/6, 4/9 and 4/9, respectively, but none of these actually reduced the current price, and in Preston's case raised it by 3 pence (see Table 6.3). Each company also continued to cut their prices irrespective of statutory controls (see Table 6.2) indicating that other considerations like the threat of competition or consumer anger were of greater importance in the determination of pricing policy.

Parliamentary intervention in the field of prices, just like the attempt to control dividends, was clearly ineffective, and once the maxima had been imposed this provided legal justification for the policies followed by companies which saw no further need to expand their system. This conservative approach was the cause of much antagonism between the profitable gas companies and local authorities anxious to improve local services, but where pressure groups were willing either to form a rival venture or encourage municipalisation of the existing company then management strategy could be materially affected. In the North West, of course, as we have already seen, consumers could be extremely disruptive, and Chapter 7 will recount the growing popularity of municipal trading, re-emphasising the need for management to modify strategy in line with the vagaries of its market, but there was always the inherent danger of a company attempting to ignore these pressures.

One of the solutions devised to strengthen price controls, arising partly from the experiences of supervising the big London companies, and coming at the same time as the imposition of auction clauses,(133) was the 'sliding scale' introduced in the mid-1870s.(134) This system linked dividends inversely to the price of gas, whereby once the former had reached their statutory maximum then the latter would be reduced. In fact, no North West company came under the sliding scale regulation prior to 1880, but in practice by the 1850s most managements operated an informal system whereby, as a result of the limits imposed on dividends, they were obliged to reduce prices when the reserve account had reached its legal maximum level.(135) On the other hand, the growth in income as a result of the price elasticity of demand for gas was the basic stimulant behind the improved profitability of gas undertakings after 1830, and in this respect parliamentary controls had little influence over the trend. Moreover, if dividends were threatened when factor costs started to rise, then companies were actually allowed to raise their prices, confirming the general conclusion that controls did not interfere with the industry's commercial performance up to 1880.

Having noted the general inability of statutory maxima to reflect the economic reality of gas production from the 1840s, it is vital to remember that government policy was by no means impotent. Prices were certainly dependent on cost schedules and technological capabilities, but a powerful influence on management policy in this respect was the possibility which existed in every town that a rival could always be granted access to the same market. This threat to a company's monopoly occupied the minds of Directors constantly, providing an essential discipline on prices generally, and as Rowlinson noted of the country as a whole 'the price [of gas] fell rapidly, generally in the face of competition or the threat of competition between gas companies'.(136) Millward has also pointed out that even if most nineteenth century gas companies can be described as operating under conditions of natural monopoly, they still faced the threat of being ousted by rivals offering lower prices. Put simply, there was competition 'for the field', even though at any one time there was only a single undertaking 'in the field',(137) and as the managements at Chester, Kendal and Haslingden discovered consumer dissatisfaction could provide a serious obstacle to survival. Elsewhere in the region, where companies were confronted by an 'improving' local authority, then a similar fate could befall them, and in the next chapter we shall move on to discuss the impact of municipalisation on the industry. The environment proved increasingly unfriendly for private enterprise in this region, and progressively large parts of the industry were to fall under public ownership as a result of a variety of trends which companies were powerless to influence.

Conclusions

The North West gas industry had passed through a series of dramatic changes between 1815 and 1880, developing from a limited service into one which affected the domestic and working lives of most people. Growth had initially been sluggish in most companies, principally because of a combination of high prices and the 'strategic' motives which had influenced policy, but from the 1830s the market expanded rapidly in response to the significant reductions in gas prices. A range of factors can be called on to explain why prices fell, but companies were principally motivated by the need to prevent competition emerging in their market. Although the industry was also benefiting from lower coal and iron costs, and various technological developments improved production, distribution and metering, management was usually only willing to act when threatened by potential or actual rivalry.(138) Crucial to the success achieved in organising the response to these trends and pressures was the emergence of a gas engineering profession capable of bringing greater understanding of technical and commercial factors into the direction of company strategy. It was these specialists who were responsible for detecting the main trends and implementing the necessary changes to policy, bringing a much more sophisticated approach towards planning at a time when, in response to the price elasticity of demand for gas, the businesses were expanding at an unprecedented rate.

Having noted these refinements in company organisation, and how they facilitated the process of expansion, one must not be misled into believing that gas undertakings were aggressive in their search for new custom. In fact, as we have emphasised in this chapter, caution was a key component of management strategy, and although this approach was entirely rational for businesses which needed to control marginal costs very carefully, it could cause serious problems: firstly, collective consumer agitation could force companies to alter their pricing and investment strategies; secondly, the neglect of street lighting in working class districts would prompt criticism from local authorities anxious to improve urban living conditions; and thirdly, the profits generated from the controlled expansion after 1830 could prove attractive to local authorities in search of additional revenue to fund these improvement programmes. The resolution of this complex balancing act became one of the main challenges facing management from the 1840s, and in the final section of our study we shall see how the struggle between private and public enterprise was settled.

Footnotes

(1) Matthews (1986), pp. 246–253.
(2) See earlier, p. 124, for a detailed discussion of this subject.
(3) The figures for individual companies are: Clitheroe 15.2%; Runcorn 31%; Kirkham 21.5%; Colne 36%; Northwich 22%; Haslingden 33%; Altrincham 17.5%; Radcliffe & Pilkington 30%; Buxton 45%; Hyde 13%; Nelson 15%.
(4) See earlier, pp. 37–40.
(5) RGLCBM, 3/6/47 and RGLCSR, 1836–53.
(6) HGCBM, 12/2/55 & 18/6/55. See also earlier, pp. 39–40.
(7) DWGLC Annual Reports, 1841–54.
(8) See earlier, pp. 42–43, for a study of these towns.
(9) This subject is covered in pp. 138–141.
(10) SHGLCBM, 28/1/36.
(11) Barker & Harris (1954), p. 183.
(12) *Ibid*, p. 303.

(13) SHGLCBM, 24/5/43.

(14) See earlier, p. 42.

(15) SHGLCBM, 16/4/32 & 29/6/38.

(16) *Ibid*, 26/9/43.

(17) *Ibid*, 13/8/46.

(18) DWGLCBM, 8/3/55.

(19) See earlier, pp. 128–129.

(20) Pollard (1968), p. 94. See also Nabb (1986), p. 263 for how nepotism also worked in the south-west gas industry. For more information on the Association see Braunholtz (1963).

(21) The Brothers family ran the Blackburn gasworks between 1845 and 1874, and the Greens monopolised the position of Engineer at Bolton from 1836 to 1865.

(22) The Blackburn Engineer earned £109 per annum in 1818, the Bolton Engineer £150, and the Wigan Engineer £105 (1822).

(23) The Blackburn salary had risen to £200, as had that in Bolton, while the Wigan salary was £150.

(24) Blackburn paid £550 by 1860.

(25) Harris (1956), p. 66.

(26) Pollard (1968), Ch. 4.

(27) Harris (1956), p. 11.

(28) Quoted in *Ibid*, p. 36.

(29) *Ibid*, p. 41.

(30) *Ibid*, p. 90 for a scathing attack on these Directors. See also Nabb (1986), p. 245, for a similar view of Directors in the south-west.

(31) Those at Bolton and Preston were regarded as the best examples, with their gothic architecture and oak-panelled rooms.

(32) These were Henry Green at Bolton (BnGLCCMB, 5/12/64) and William Barratt at Accrington (*Accrington Times*, 23/5/74, p. 6).

(33) BnGLCCMB, 1/9/24.

(34) PGLCMB, 6/7/29 & 4/1/30.

(35) The typical salary in the 1820s at Blackburn, Bolton and Preston seems to have been £50 per annum for clerks.

(36) Other examples of fraud were at Rochdale (JOGL, 11/4/71) and at Rossendale.

(37) Newbigging (1883), p. 4.

(38) This was usually one of the Directors, rather than a professional officer.

(39) Detailed research on this subject has been carried out by Roydon Roberts at the Cardiff Business School, and I am indebted to him for the advice given on this aspect of the project.

(40) See earlier, pp. 96–99.

(41) Alford (1976), pp. 25ff.

(42) Although gaslighting was naturally most in demand at night, retailers also used it for display purposes during the day and publicans enhanced their premises with artificial illuminants. See earlier, pp. 85–86.

(43) PGLCMB, 5/1/29; BnGLCCMB, 8/6/27; BGLCMB, 27/6/27; WGLCMB, 4/5/26 & 3/5/27.

(44) Falkus (1967), pp. 501–502, and Matthews (1986), pp. 248–254.

(45) See earlier, p. 4.

(46) Matthews (1986), p. 251.

(47) PP (1847a).

(48) See later, p. 208.

(49) See earlier, pp. 128–129.

(50) *The Gas Engineers' Compendium* (1924), p. 22.

(51) *Ibid*, pp. 22–23.

(52) *King's Treatise* (1878), p. 53. This machine came into use after 1841.

(53) Matthews (1986), pp. 250–251.

(54) *Ibid*, p. 255.

(55) Harris (1956), p. 41.

(56) The average loss at Salford between 1868 and 1880 was 12.5% of total make of between 339 million cubic feet (1868) and 723 million (1880). (Annual Report of Gas Light Committee to Salford Council, 1868–80). And at the much smaller Darwen undertaking losses of 15% were being recorded in 1870 (DWGLCBM, 25/2/70) on a make of 47.7 million cubic feet.

(57) See earlier, pp. 136–137.

(58) PGLCMB, 1/1/21.

(59) Many of the smaller undertakings took longer to introduce meters, because of the expense, but during the 1840s almost all consumers (except street lamps) were provided with one.

(60) Johnes & Clegg (1847), p. 95.

(61) Johnes & Clegg (1847), p. 95. See later, pp. 173–177 for criticisms levelled in Kendal and Chester.

(62) Kendal coal prices were up to 33% higher than those in Liverpool, Wigan and Manchester, PP (1847a).

(63) Matthews (1986), p. 246.

(64) Harris (1956), p. 56.

(65) Johnes & Clegg (1847), pp. 95–97.

(66) See earlier, p. 138 for the arguments presented by one of the manufacturers.

(67) Johnes & Clegg (1847), p. 97.

(68) Warrington Gas Light Co. had been slow to introduce discounts, but under pressure from local glass and chemical manufacturers the Directors had given in by 1852. Paterson (1879), p. 18.

(69) See earlier, p. 138.

(70) PP (1847a). The larger customers paid 10/- (50p) per thousand cubic feet in 1831, compared to 12/6 for smaller customers.

(71) PP (1847a). The summer price was kept 1/- (5p) below the winter price between 1844 and 1846, and then prices were standardised at 4/6 (22.5p).

(72) Quoted in Rowlinson (1984), p. 71.

(73) See earlier, pp. 136–138 for a similar view of pricing policy in the 1820s.

(74) At Ashton-under-Lyne sales expanded from 30 million cubic feet to 142.8 million between 1847 and 1881, while at Warrington the respective figures were 16 million and 125.5 million.

(75) PGLCMB, 12/1/57.

(76) *Ibid*, 11/1/58.

(77) Harris (1956), pp. 60 & 131. This company never materialised until 1857.

(78) The Preston Gas Light Co. supplied the outlying districts of Fulwood and Walton at 1/- (5p) above the price for Preston customers up to the 1860s, and in Liverpool the differential was 4d. (2p) by 1865.

(79) See Matthews (1986), p. 355, for an analysis of this issue in the London context.

(80) See earlier, pp. 51–54, for a chronology and discussion of these controls.

(81) Johnes & Clegg (1847), p. 98.

(82) See Matthews (1983), Ch. 3, for a discussion of this competition.

(83) Apart from Liverpool, there were two undertakings in Birmingham, Brighton, Sheffield, Wolverhampton, Norwich, York, Edinburgh, Bristol, Tynemouth and Glasgow. Millward (1986), p. 6.

(84) Harris (1956), p. 39.

(85) *Ibid*, p. 35.

(86) *Ibid*, pp. 40–48.

(87) See earlier, p. 144.

(88) Harris (1956), p. 49.

(89) *Ibid*, p. 49.

(90)   *Ibid*, pp. 54–57.
(91)   *Ibid*, p. 56. See later, p. 211, for a discussion of the reasons why Liverpool Corporation showed no interest in imitating Manchester's experiment with municipal trading.
(92)   *Ibid*, p. 54.
(93)   Johnes & Clegg (1847), p. 98.
(94)   Harris (1956), p. 55.
(95)   For a detailed analysis of this case, see Wilson (1991B).
(96)   See earlier, pp. 143–144.
(97)   See later, p. 196, for a discussion of the impact of the 1835 Act on local democracy.
(98)   CCWC, 21/7/42.
(99)   *Ibid*, 5/12/42. By this time, Chester Gas Light Co. had started to record much lower dividends than in its first twenty years of trading (see Appendix C), and there was general concern that the Corporation would be left with a similarly unprofitable business.
(100) *Ibid*.
(101) CGLCBM, 30/6/45 & 12/8/46.
(102) *Ibid*, 20/1/47.
(103) *Ibid*, 17/8/49.
(104) Between 1845 and 1852 the company made a loss in two years (1847 and 1848), and on average recorded a profit of just £95 per annum. CGLCBM, 1845–52. Profits for the other years were not published.
(105) *Chester Courant*, 25/6/51, p. 6. This is the only known record describing the creation of a Chester consumers' company.
(106) CGLCBM, 31/3/50.
(107) CCWC, 21/3/50.
(108) *Chester Courant*, 25/6/51.
(109) CGLCBM, 20/8/52.
(110) CCWC, 1/4/53.
(111) CGLCBM, 20/8/52 & 19/8/53. Coal prices in Chester had risen by 20% in the early-1850s, according to the Directors.
(112) *Ibid*, 28/2/56.
(113) The venture was named after its location by the Roodee racecourse in Chester. None of its records have apparently survived.
(114) E.G. Salisbury, a Flintshire barrister, was Liberal M.P. for Chester between 1859 and 1865. He was to own 25% of the shares in Chester United Gas Co., and was generally regarded as the man responsible for bringing greater order into the Chester gas industry. *Chester Chronicle*, 5/7/56.
(115) See later, p. 175, for further discussion of these changes.
(116) Matthews (1986), p. 253.
(117) Millward (1986), p. 8.
(118) No direct evidence on the Roodee Gas Co. has survived, but the *Chester Chronicle* (5/7/56) indicated that neither company had received 'a fair and proper remuneration for their capital'.
(119) This was the price set by the Chester Gas Act, 1858, Cap. vi.
(120) See Matthews (1983), p. 103, where he is described as a 'paid agitator'. See also JOGL, 29/11/64, p. 804 for his activities in Brighton, and later (p. 202) for his work in Burnley.
(121) *Kendal Mercury*, 8/11/45.
(122) Curwen (1900), p. 200.
(123) Brown (1971), p. 32.
(124) *Ibid*, pp. 32–57.
(125) *Kendal Mercury*, 20/10/45 & 25/10/45.
(126) See earlier, p. 22.

(127)   Kendal Union Gas & Water Co. Registration Document, 7/11/46.
(128)   *Kendal Mercury*, 8/11/45.
(129)   Haslingden Union Gas Co. Memorial, 1861.
(130)   Aspin (1962), p. 72.
(131)   Matthews (1986), p. 258.
(132)   See Chantler (1939), pp. 65—75.
(133)   See earlier, pp. 108—109.
(134)   Matthews (1986), p. 260.
(135)   See earlier, pp. 110—111.
(136)   Rowlinson (1984), p. 73.
(137)   Millward (1986), pp. 6—8.
(138)   This was also the case in London. Matthews (1986), pp. 253—256.

7
Municipalisation and Municipal Trading(1)

'When the purchase of the Water Works comes before you it will be a question concerning the health of the town; the acquisition of the Gas Works concerns the profits of the town.'

Joseph Chamberlain (when Mayor of Birmingham, 1871–74), quoted in Waller (1983), p. 304.

The nineteenth century history of gas supply in the North West is intimately bound up with the dramatic growth in local government, and given the highly localised nature of most undertakings it would be impossible to study the industry without examining the influence of this relationship on company strategy and business development. At times, the whole story revolved around the conflict between supplier and municipality, and companies were heavily dependent upon the goodwill of councillors, commissioners or Board of Health officials. This chapter is certainly not intended to be a history of local government in the region, and even though some municipal records have been used neither will a detailed analysis of municipal management and finances be presented. Nevertheless, particularly when one considers the growing popularity of municipal trading, it is essential to fill in the background and explain the main trends. We shall be especially concerned with three themes: the impact of Manchester's experiment with municipal trading; the reasons why other towns acquired local gas companies; and how these trends affected company strategy. This will help to bring into sharper focus much of what was discussed in the last chapter, further enlightening our evaluation of the forces affecting prices by adding a new dimension to the analysis of policy.

Ultimately, beginning with the formation of a publicly owned gas works in 1817 at Manchester, almost a half of all North West gas undertakings were publicly owned by 1880,(2) demonstrating the popularity of municipal trading in the region. This was not unusual, because in most counties north of Birmingham, and in Scotland, municipalisation of gas companies became a common feature of the industry, but it is important to remember that Manchester pioneered the movement. It was Manchester's successful use of a gasworks as a subsidy to the rates that revealed the possibilities in municipal trading. In the North West, the movement spread slowly, emanating from Manchester in a ripple effect, and only from the 1860s was it beginning to influence developments in other parts of the region. There were in fact two distinct stages through which this movement passed, with 1860 acting as the dividing line (see Appendix A), but the 'Manchester Model' remained a source of inspiration for many local authorities seeking a viable financial solution to their problems.

The twentieth century experience with nationalisation of public utilities has resulted in political overtones being overlaid on to the nineteenth century movement towards municipal trading,(3) but the Manchester case illustrates how pragmatism was more important than ideology. In the North West generally, while party rivalry could often fuel the debate over 'The Gas Question', local government was concerned principally with fundamental matters like how improvement programmes were to be financed. Legislation at no time provided compulsory purchase rights for councils, but neither were exclusive franchises granted to companies, and this created an uncertain environment for private enterprise. Matthews is correct when arguing that municipal ownership 'involved no interference with the rights of property',(4) because shareholders were generously compensated when companies were taken over, but the key issue was who controlled prices and the flow of profits, and in many North West towns, by one means or another, local authorities were determined to gain the upper hand.

The Role Model

(a) *Fleming's Scheme*

When Thomas Fleming persuaded his fellow Police Commissioners in Manchester to build a gasworks,(5) they unwittingly set in motion one of the most powerful nineteenth century trends in local government. Whether or not the decision precipitated 'the most remarkable of all municipal experiments prior to 1835'(6) we shall examine later, but it certainly established municipal trading as a viable feature of local government activities, and in response to the challenges posed by an increasingly urbanised, industrial society many towns copied this example. The movement was often described, inappropriately, as 'Municipal Socialism', or 'gas and water socialism', and although it took until the 1850s to grow in popularity by 1884 the Prime Minister, W. E. Gladstone, was able to describe gas and water supply as 'two of the most elementary among the purposes of municipal government'.(7)

Ever since 1799, the Manchester Police Commissioners had been willing to undertake a range of services,(8) indicating that in fact the decision to establish a municipal gasworks was an extension of their perceived role in the community. Little had been achieved between the 1792 Act creating the Police Commission and the appointment of C. S. Brandt as Borough Reeve and Treasurer, but thereafter, under this merchant's vigorous leadership, more effort was put into cleaning, policing and lighting the streets of Manchester. They had initially been beset by financial problems during the 1790s, caused largely by an inability to raise much of their rate income, but Brandt succeeded in revamping the scheme, and by 1803 sufficient had been raised to pay for various services.(9) In 1809, the Police Commissioners even attempted to block the Bill proposing the formation of a private water company, arguing that such a venture ought to be the responsibility of local government, but in spite of spending £1,760 on the campaign parliament rejected their arguments and the Act was passed in 1809.(10) This failed attempt to create a municipal water undertaking was also expensive, because the Salford Hundred Quarter Sessions disallowed the use of public funds

T. A. Fleming (1771–1848), inspiration behind the first municipal gasworks in Manchester.

for this purpose, forcing each Commissioner to contribute to the £1,760 cost.(11) Nevertheless, in spite of this failure by 1816 they were planning 'to take into consideration the expediency of lighting the whole or any part of the Town of Manchester with Gas'.(12)

The Police Commissioners had in fact experimented with gaslighting in 1807,(13) and while the trial was regarded as an illustration of the illuminant's superiority over oil, they did not consider a permanent service because the technology for an extensive service had not yet been developed.(14) The situation had changed by 1816, however, and encouraged by what was happening in other towns a specially convened sub-committee instructed the Commissioners' Agent, Jacob Davies, to examine John Grafton's plant at Preston, leading ultimately to the decision of April 1817 to build a gasworks in their Water St. premises.(15) This instituted the first municipal gas supply in the industry, and with the necessary finance raised from an increase in the police rate from 15 pence to 18 pence in the pound the newly constituted Gas Committee was able to order all the necessary equipment from the local engineering firm of Peel & Williams.(16) The first lights were not supplied until March 1818, and initially there were just under 100 consumers connected up to the mains laid around Water St., Deansgate, Market St. and St. Annes Square,(17) but the enterprise had been firmly established as a permanent feature of local government in Manchester.

Although the Police Commissioners had been responsible for providing various services since 1799, when we come to consider why they had built their gasworks a more detailed understanding of local politics and finances is required. In particular, one must discuss the role of Thomas Fleming,(18) and what he hoped to achieve in instigating the scheme. As Treasurer to the Police Commissioners since 1810, Fleming had gained a close insight into the town's finances, and by 1816 he was convinced that the rate income would not finance the construction of the elaborate new Town Hall currently being planned. The land for this building had been purchased in 1814, but it was 1820 before the foundation stone was laid, and in the meantime Fleming hatched a plan to raise the required money by generating profits from a gasworks.(19) This indicates how in another important respect Manchester was exceptional among North West gas undertakings, because 'strategic' motives, rather than any desire for quick profits, had influenced investors elsewhere in the region,(20) while Fleming anticipated a flow of profits from the business almost immediately. He was to be disappointed with the early returns, just as other Directors in the region failed to pay dividends for several years, and even though Redford has described the move as a 'remarkable initiative' in municipal finances,(21) Fleming's actions reveal a degree of naivety which later helped to undermine his position within the Police Commissioners.

The concept of subsidising the rates from gas profits was one which gained Fleming the support of his peers in the town, and especially those who would have been faced with an increased levy on their property to pay for the much-needed improvements, but in choosing this policy the Police Commissioners inevitably aroused some opposition. In the first place, their 1792 Act did not grant any right to act as a trading venture, posing a legal problem when they decided in 1817 to supply not only street lamps, but also private consumers.(22) The issue was only settled in 1824, in circumstances to be described later, but had the business been a commercial disaster then the authorities could have been faced with a large bill for acting beyond their powers. On the other hand, the leading ratepayers were cotton and engineering manufacturers who actually made their own gas,(23) leaving the retailers and merchants to pay for the municipal service. This generated considerable resentment, because, as Prentice noted, it became general knowledge that 'in the early days ... improvements, as well as the lighting of the town, to which the whole community ought to have contributed, were effected out of the pockets of the gas consumer. At the time the consumption of gas was confined almost to the shopkeepers and publicans ... Probably not one-fourth of the ratepayers were gas consumers.'(24)

The debate was further intensified by the tendency of most gas consumers to support the Radical group in Manchester, while Fleming and his fellow-manufacturers were largely Tories,(25) and in effect Fleming seemed to be passing much of the burden of financing an improvement programme from ratepayers to consumers. This put the whole issue of gaslighting at the centre of Manchester politics, and over the next twenty years few debates did not feature a Radical attack on the way Fleming and his Tory colleagues on the Gas Committee manipulated pricing and investment policy in their own interests.

The Radicals were naturally not going to accept this situation without putting up some kind of rearguard action, and even though they were in the minority on the Police Commission they rarely missed an opportunity to raise objections at the weekly Friday Night Committee. Heading the agitation against Fleming's Tory majority were Nicholas and William Whitworth, and at meetings and in letters to Radical newspapers like the *Manchester Observer* they constantly criticised the Gas Committee for alleged discrepancies in the accounts and the way contracts were awarded. Police Commission accounts were managed in a most haphazard fashion at that time, and as Treasurer Fleming was sometimes obliged to advance his own credit to settle bills,(26) indicating the amateurish nature of local government at this time. The most sinister accusations levelled by the Whitworths concerned the Gas Committee's propensity to allocate construction and equipment contracts to fellow Tories, and rushing through payment without checking with other Commissioners.(27) This put both Fleming and Davies in a difficult position on several occasions, and in 1819 the former resigned from the post of Treasurer because of what he called 'much mental anxiety'.(28) The pragmatic approach to finances was simply too lax, and Fleming's critics were able to exploit the situation so effectively that he could not deflect all the mounting attacks. He remained an influential member of the Gas Committee for over twenty years, and in 1820 he successfully prosecuted the *Manchester Observer* for publishing a libellous statement over a contract awarded for concrete,(29) but this ended his aspirations to the Borough Reeveship.

Fleming's resignation was a moral victory for the Radicals, but having secured this gain they were unable to follow it up by preventing the continued expansion of his brainchild. Refinements in the management structure had also been introduced by 1820 to help prevent the re-emergence of Fleming's problems, and rationalise the venture's financial system. A comptroller was appointed in July 1819 to act as the accounts supervisor, and in that capacity John Thorpe brought much greater order into this crucial department, while in 1820 Jacob Davies was instructed to attend 'exclusively to the Gas Department' as Gas Agent.(30) No trained gas engineer was recruited at Manchester during this early phase, leaving Davies in charge of the production and distribution of gas, typifying the situation in much of the industry up to the 1830s. In fact, if one regards the Gas Committee as a Board of Directors, and the comptroller as Accountant, then the organisational structure of the Manchester undertaking was very close to that of its private counterparts. In another important respect, the municipal venture's performance was also typical of the period, because while profits could be made on the growing income, expenditure on new plant was so great that all the surpluses had to be ploughed back into the works, preventing greater progress on the Town Hall.

(b) *Municipal Profits*

The early results of Manchester's gasworks can be seen in Table 7.1. This indicates how income rose from just £356 to £7,557 between 1817–18 and 1822–23, producing a total profit in that period of £14,880.(31) On the other hand, by June 1823 a cumulative total of £27,430 had been invested in plant and mains, in addition to which land costing £13,783 had been purchased, bringing the overall cost to £41,213. The gasworks was not even generating enough income to fund its own expansion, still less finance the expenditure incurred in building the Town Hall, and while the Commissioners were later able to use the gas income as collateral for some much-needed bank loans the situation was certainly not what Fleming had intended.(32) The Radicals also continued to attack Davies in public, and William Whitworth was planning to prosecute the Commissioners as a whole for extending their powers into the field of trading. This threat to the legality of a municipal gasworks had worried the authorities for some time, local opinion being divided on the issue, but the event which prompted some positive action was the announcement in September 1823 of the launch of a Manchester Imperial Joint Stock Oil Gas Co.(33) With hindsight, we now know that oil-gas undertakings did not pose a commercial threat to coal-gas suppliers,(34) but in 1823 the rival seemed destined to undermine the Commissioners' entire financial strategy, and to combat this new threat they would need to formulate an effective response.

By November 1823 the Police Commission had decided that the 'act to form an Oil Gas Co. in Manchester be opposed'. They published a series of

Table 7.1 The performance of Manchester Gasworks, 1817–23

Year to 24th June	Capital expenditure (a)	Total income	Profits	Number of street lamps
1818	5,520	356	264	40
1819	8,340	2,069	1,525	50
1820	13,511	3,150	1,933	120
1821	17,935	4,778	2,882	200
1822	24,073	5,901	3,769	330
1823	27,430	7,557	4,506	460

(a) Cumulative total. Excludes land purchases of £13,783.
Source: Mitchell (1986), Appendices 8 & 9.

orders emphasising the advantages of a municipal gasworks, claiming hopefully that their venture was 'productive of a profit which ... is available for general objects and may be directed either to a reduction of the public rates or to the purposes of public improvement'.(35) Although not formally involved in what appears to have been a London-owned venture, the Radicals were initially in favour of the new project, hoping that it would undermine the Tory grip on local government. The Commissioners were consequently obliged to clear up the uncertain legality of municipal trading, and in view of the vagueness they drew up plans 'for a Bill to amend and extend the powers of the present Police Act so far as regards the lighting of the street lamps and furnishing to inhabitants an ample supply of Coal and Oil Gas'.(36) A draft Bill was ready by February 1824, and at a Police Commissioners' meeting held to sanction its provisions they also decided to petition parliament formally against the Manchester Imperial venture.(37) The rival Bill had been progressing steadily through the House of Commons, but in March 1824 the fraudulent signing of a supporting petition was discovered, and this was sufficient to see the project rejected at the committee stage.(38) This marked the first victory for the Tory majority, and after further parliamentary activity their second came in June when the Manchester Gas Act was passed.

Although the original clause seeking authority to use gas profits for improvement purposes had been expunged from the Act, and replaced by one which simply stated that surplus funds should be transferred to the Police Fund,(39) the Tory Commissioners had achieved everything they had intended. The 1824 Act effectively laid the legal foundations for municipal trading, and by interpreting the key sections concerning the appropriation of profits in a way which suited their financial predicament the Commissioners were able to embark on a policy which closely approximated to the intentions of Thomas Fleming when planning the scheme. This ruse entailed converting the capital expenditure so far undertaken into a debt which the gasworks would repay over several years, and at the same time leaving 'a fund available for defraying the charge on the general rate occasioned by the erection of the Town Hall'.(40) The newly constituted Board of Gas Directors would then be able to transfer profits to the Police Commission, and as they had also been granted rights under the 1824 Act to raise £35,000 in mortgage loans no longer would they be obliged to make demands on the general fund, providing the financial framework for a system which worked with increasing success after 1825.

The Radicals had once again been defeated by their political rivals, but undeterred by this consistent lack of success Whitworth redirected the attack on to the issue which most directly affected consumers, gas prices. This strategy was, after all, the real issue for the gas consumers who supported agitators like William Whitworth (and later prominent Liberals like Prentice and Potter), because they were the main users of the service, and the way it was managed had been their principal concern. Originally, 15/- (75p) per thousand cubic feet had been charged to all customers,(41) and although this was reduced to 14/- (70p) in November 1820 the price was still higher than in other towns, and no further changes were made until 1829, when the price was altered to 12/- (60p). Even more galling to small consumers like the shopkeepers and publicans who supported the

Radical cause, in 1826 the Directors introduced a discount system for those whose bills exceeded £200,(42) favouring the growing number of factory-owners who chose to take the public supply, rather than make their own. This pricing policy was a reflection of the significant expansion in mill-building during the 1820s,(43) and while the Tory manufacturers who had always made their own gas were not converting to the municipal service the Radicals saw the discounts as yet another manifestation of the bias in overall strategy, reflecting the tendency of the Gas Directors to favour their own class.

(c) *Expansion and Political Debate*

During the 1820s management of the gas undertaking was dominated by George Wood, the Chairman of the Gas Directors, and under his guidance the business continued to expand rapidly.(44) The Water St. works had been placed under so much pressure that in 1824 a nine-acre site off Rochdale Rd. was purchased, and what became the No.2 station was established to provide much-needed additional capacity.(45) Greater effort was also put into securing more industrial consumers,(46) and because the discounts published in 1826 led to many of the new mills built in this period preferring to use the public supply two new holder stations were constructed, in Oxford Rd. (1830) and Every St., Ancoats (1831).(47) By 1833, over 62 miles of mains had been laid in the streets of Manchester and a total of £146,946 had been invested in the business,(48) indicating how much it had grown since 1823 (see Table 7.1, p. 189). A continuous flow of profits was also generated, as we shall see, confirming the value of Fleming's initiative and irritating even further the discontented Radicals.

The failure of Radical activists to influence pricing or investment strategy in the 1820s was a sign of the Tory control over the Police Commissioners, but by 1826 new plans were afoot to change the political complexion of Manchester. At this time, to become a Police Commissioner the qualification required was that an individual had to pay a minimum of £30 in rent annually, and the Radicals realised that around 1,000 people in Manchester, principally retailers and small workshop proprietors, had failed to register.(49) These people were also more likely to be supporters of the campaign to bring prices down, and consequently during 1826 1,000 new Commissioners were sworn in, bringing the total number to 1,800.(50) William Whitworth was at the same time able to introduce secret balloting into the proceedings, but because the numbers attending Police Commission meetings leapt from 50 to 900 the Radicals found it increasingly difficult to achieve any influence over policy because the debates frequently dissolved into a shambles.(51)

The Tories responded to this new strategy by securing a new Police Act in 1829, which in theory bowed to the Radical pressure for more democratic government by lowering the minimum rental requirement for voters to £16, but as a result of insisting on a £28 level for holding office as a Commissioner, limiting the total number of Commissioners to 240, and allocating most of those seats to Tory districts, the *status quo* was reinforced.(52) This again outmanoeuvred the Radicals, ensuring that gasworks policy was not altered, and provided the finances for favourite Tory projects like the new

Town Hall. The Gas Directors were also able to continue the expansion described earlier, and by 1837, in addition to the four works already in operation, they had acquired James Fernley's Gaythorn gasworks in Chorlton-upon-Medlock, at a cost of £20,000.(53) Complete control of what under the 1838 Royal Charter became the borough of Manchester was assured when the mains laid in Cheetham by the Salford Police Commissioners were purchased.(54) Reflecting the general trend in the industry after 1830, the Gas Directors even reduced the price of gas, from 12/- in 1829 to 6/- by 1842, stimulating an increase in income to almost £61,000 by the end of this period.(55)

Davies and his staff had clearly succeeded in building a business capable of servicing the growing demand for gas in Manchester,(56) but the Commissioners had financed the venture in the hope that it would subsidise the rates, and on this criterion its performance must be judged. Up to 1823, because expenditure on plant and mains had exceeded income, the gasworks was a drain on the rates, and in the 1824 Act it had been necessary to interpret the central clauses so that the total cost of the business could be converted into a debt, in order to allow some of the profits to be transferred to the general fund. The first call on any surplus would be the interest payable on the £35,000 in mortgage loans the Gas Directors could now call upon, and then part of the remainder would be used to reduce the debt accumulated since 1817, leaving a sum for improvement purposes. They ignored many of the land purchases in calculating the debt, and settled on a figure of £31,849 as what was known in the accounts as 'Balance to Police Commissioners',(57) but this was still a substantial burden for any provincial gas undertaking in the 1820s.(58) By 1829, however, such was the profitability of the gasworks, the whole amount had been repaid,(59) and as Table 7.2 reveals the Directors still managed to provide over £25,000 for the Police Commissioners in that five year period. The business had at last achieved Fleming's objectives, and while between 1828 and 1833 transfers fluctuated markedly, in the next ten years performance indicated the faith placed in the proposal by Manchester's leading ratepayers.

(d) *Transfer to the Corporation*

By the late-1820s municipal trading in Manchester had been established on a firm footing, and Table 7.2 reveals how up to 1842 a total of £178,575 had been transferred to the rates fund, after the payment of interest. One must also remember that the cost of street lighting, nominally met by the Police Commissioners out of rates, was no more than a paper transfer of funds and no money actually changed hands. This provided a further indirect contribution which amounted to approximately £52,000 between 1824 and 1842,(60) bringing the overall subsidy to around £230,000 in that period. The funds were often transferred in a piecemeal fashion, no set dates having been determined when the Directors should pay over the cash, but such was the success of this venture that not only were the Commissioners able to finance the Town Hall project,(61) they also used the gas profits for several programmes of general value to the community. Vigier is critical of the notion that the 'municipal gasworks was the most remarkable of all municipal experiments prior to 1835', claiming that it allowed them to squander money 'on what was probably the kingdom's most expensive Town Hall', while

Table 7.2 Funds transferred by the Gas Directors to the Manchester Police
Commission Fund, 1825−42

Year to June	£	Year to June	£
1825	3,341	1834	7,127
1826	4,981	1835	10,134
1827	4,920	1836	14,199
1828	7,823	1837	11,123
1829	4,153	1838	13,837
1830	4,140	1839	18,947
1831	3,534	1840	19,020
1832	4,885	1841	21,153
1833	7,533	1842	17,725

Source: Manchester Gas Committee Minute Books, 1824−42.

squalid living conditions were allowed to persist.(62) However, the Town
Hall project had been completed by 1825, and the cost had been defrayed by
the mid-1830s, leaving most of the gas profits for use in widening St. Peter's
Square and improving the Market St. area.(63) Many of the worst evils of
early-nineteenth century urbanisation remained, but local government was
not regarded as the answer to all problems,(64) and the Commissioners
were able to finance the limited range of functions laid down in their
constitution.

Another indication of the venture's success was that by 1833 even the
Radicals were insisting that 'the inhabitants of a large town like Manchester
should have the ownership of large [gas] works'.(65) This statement was
made in the light of a proposal emanating from the Tory-dominated Gas
Directors that the business should be sold to a private company, and the
funds used to purchase the Manorial Rights to Manchester.(66) The Directors
were increasingly concerned that the proposed formation of a municipal
borough would finally end their control of local politics, and of the gas
profits,(67) and by creating a company to buy out the venture they would
be able to continue reaping a financial reward from their enterprise. On the
other hand, the Radicals were by then aware of the revenue a municipal
gasworks could generate, and they mounted a successful campaign to block
the Tory idea, keeping Manchester in the vanguard of municipal trading.
The campaign to form a municipal borough had been gathering momentum
through the early-1830s, but although the 1835 Municipal Corporations Act
provided the enabling legislation it was 1838 before Manchester gained its
Charter.(68) The Liberals had been in the forefront of this campaign sure in
the knowledge that a corporation would bring greater democracy into local
government, and in this they were not disappointed when the first elections
were held.(69). However, the creation of a borough did not lead to the
abolition of Manchester Police Commission, and as the gasworks remained
their property then two overlapping bodies were operating with legitimate
rights to perform certain functions. The Tory-dominated Commission was
naturally not keen to cede its responsibilities, and finances, to a Liberal
corporation, but in fact by May 1843 the gasworks had been transferred to
the town's increasingly powerful new governing body, and the old form of
government faded away.(70)

Since constructing the first municipal gasworks in 1817, the Manchester Police Commissioners had succeeded in establishing municipal trading as a legitimate feature of local government. The 1824 Manchester Gas Act provided parliamentary approval for this activity, and the steady flow of funds indicated to interested observers that the venture was viable. In spite of their initial opposition to the principle of obliging gas consumers to subsidise ratepayers, by the early 1830s even the Liberals were eager to acquire the use of these profits for improvement purposes, and once in possession of the gasworks in 1843 they proved just as willing as the Tory-dominated Gas Directors to charge what the *Journal of Gas Lighting* described as 'an exorbitant price in order to increase the sum applicable for improvement purposes'.(71) There is in fact no evidence that prices in Manchester were 'exorbitant' (see Table 6.2), and in general they remained consistently below the North West average, but between 1843 and 1880 on average £30,000 was transferred each year from the Gas Committee to public funds,(72) indicating how far the Corporation went in imitating its predecessor. The Police Commissioners had 'blazed a trail which no other municipal authority had the courage to follow for many years',(73) and in laying the foundations of municipal trading they provided the role model for many of the industrialised towns which looked with envy at this useful source of additional income.

The Political Environment

Local government in early nineteenth century England 'was a remarkable patchwork whose infinite variety no contemporary could fully compre-

A view inside the horizontal retort house at Bradford Rd gasworks, Manchester, in the 1880s.

hend'.(74) Even where corporations existed they were often 'narrow, in-effective and corrupt',(75) leading to a general 'indifference to the provision of such urban necessities as competent police, firemen, or clean water and lighted streets'.(76) This had resulted in 'a legacy of private initiative', with local authorities delegating the responsibility for essential public services to commercial operators at a time of unprecedented urbanisation and population growth.(77) Liverpool had taken a lead in 1748, when a group of citizens established the first body of Improvement Commissioners, but even though by 1835 almost 300 towns had copied this example, the body usually de-teriorated into 'a self-elected and self-renewing clique of principal inhabi-tants'.(78) There is evidence of some attempts at performing the functions depicted by their titles,(79) and of course Manchester's Police Commissioners had introduced the concept of municipal trading, but in general the term 'Improvement Commissioner' gave an exaggerated impression of this indi-vidual's contribution to urban change. Local government in general had yet to develop any expertise or willingness in handling the kind of problems facing industrial communities from the late eighteenth century, and in most towns private enterprise was regarded as the main vehicle for financing and managing services like water supply, transport and lighting.

Another vital characteristic of local government at that time was the control exercised by an oligarchy of wealthy Tory or Whig property-owners. Joyce has described how in towns like Blackburn, Bolton, Bury and Preston there was 'a native, employer Toryism' which had by the early nineteenth century entered 'on its inheritance of power and prestige'.(80) We have noted in earlier chapters how Tory families like the Hornbys and Fieldens in Blackburn, the Rushtons, Ormrods and Hardcastles in Bolton, the Openshaws in Bury, and the Horrockses and Pedders in Preston 'led local society by divine right of precedence', with the close correspondence of economic and political power 'expressed through the whole range of town institutional life'.(81) This dominance was manifested not only in their control of local government, it would also be reflected in the ownership of utilities created as a result of local government indifference, reinforcing the elite's position in local society.

An interesting illustration of the intimate relationship which often existed between local authorities and gas companies was the manner in which the former facilitated the latter's formation. There are cases where the Mayor would convene and chair the inaugural meeting in the Town Hall to discuss the feasibility of creating a gas undertaking, and the ventures at Wigan, Lancaster and Kendal certainly benefited from this kind of support.(82) This emphasises the hazy distinction which existed in this period between public and private interests, and clearly the picture is one of a community of Tory-dominated interests perpetuating their hold over urban society. The scenario helps to explain why gas companies were always granted per-mission to lay mains in the public highway. Of course, cheap street lighting was usually exacted as the price of this collusion, but most of the share-holders would also have been the major ratepayers, and it was in their interests to keep the cost of local government as low as possible.

In the early years of gas supply the relationship between a company and its local authority was consequently relatively harmonious, with the two bodies bonded by the political affiliations of their leading personalities.

Some undertakings sought private Acts to verify their statutory right to supply certain districts in response to the organisational confusion which reigned in some towns,(83) but this was a precautionary measure, and in other places unincorporated companies operated for many years without considering the need for legal protection. Recognising the growing popularity of gaslighting, and the tendency of private enterprise to take on the service, in 1833 parliament introduced a law which allowed the appointment of local lighting inspectors with responsibility for monitoring the situation.(84) This could have injected a new sense of discipline into the supervisory process, but as with most contemporary legislation it was permissive, and just one North West town, Colne, actually took advantage of this innovation. It was only once authorities started applying for new improvement Acts in the 1830s, and especially after the 1835 Municipal Corporations Act, that this conducive political environment altered significantly, bringing a new attitude towards the provision of certain services as a result of the changing balance of power in many towns.

The 1835 Municipal Corporations Act was of particular importance in the development of attitudes in local government.(85) Liverpool, Preston, Chester, Kendal and Lancaster were already run by fully fledged corporations, and after the 1835 Act expanding industrial centres like Stockport (1835), Manchester (1838), Bolton (1838), Salford (1844), Warrington (1847), Ashton-under-Lyne (1847), Oldham (1849), Blackburn (1851) and Rochdale (1856) were formed into municipal boroughs.(86) The movement was directly responsible for introducing greater democracy into local government by reducing the financial qualification for those eligible to vote, allowing the liberal and radical groups to make a bigger impact on the political scene, and making the council a focal point of the local power struggle. Indeed, according to Fraser, 'municipal reform was a huge Liberal accession to power', and as we saw with Manchester the old Tory oligarchy was firmly ousted after 1838.(87) This brought the issue of urban improvement into the political arena, with Liberal and Radical voices demanding a significant extension of local authority responsibility for the problems facing industrial communities at that time. After all, these were the people who actually lived in town-centres, while the old Tory elite had drifted out into the suburbs, and demands for better paving and sewerage, more effective policing, regular and improved supplies of water, and efficient street lighting would inevitably come from those most affected by the full impact of urbanisation.

It must be stressed that incorporation was not an essential step in this process, because a local improvement Act could have the same effect of reducing Tory control over a town, but whatever the case by the 1830s a decisive switch was beginning to take shape. Having secured control of local government, what Falkus describes as the 'civic consciousness' movement(88) was then faced with two problems in designing policies to deal with urban problems: a shortage of finance, and the existence of established vested interests like water and gas companies. Falkus also argues that this 'civic consciousness' movement was the leading impetus behind the acceptance of municipal trading.(89) In the first place, there was growing dissatisfaction with the price and quality of the service provided by existing private utilities, and recognising the inadequacy of government controls on gas companies, local pressure for a change in ownership mounted.

The need for additional means of funding the improvement programmes planned by the new controllers of local government provided the main impetus behind the debates over public and private ownership. The issues were rarely clear-cut, but as the Chamberlain quotation at the head of this chapter illustrates, local authorities were well aware of the financial advantages accruing from municipalising a gas company, and campaigns vilifying private enterprise were often orchestrated as a means of influencing public opinion in favour of a transfer in ownership. Party politics could also be brought into the debate, with one side (usually the liberal or radical groups) blaming the other (usually Tory) for the deficiencies of privately owned utilities, but again this was simply a means of clouding the real issue. In short, local government needed an ever-increasing amount of finance for its ever-increasing range of responsibilities and activities, and Manchester's success with its municipal gasworks provided the role model for those authorities willing to embark on urban improvement programmes. Gas companies were such a safe form of investment by the 1830s that contemporaries were well aware of the financial benefits accruing from this business, and imitating the Manchester strategy was beginning to appeal to many of the towns undergoing the political changes recorded earlier.

The reform of local government, and the resulting swing towards groups with more ambitious ideas on urban improvement, provided the background to a growing realisation from the 1830s of the need for municipal trading. It is important to stress that the movement took some time to gain widespread support, and up to 1860 only a few towns sought to copy Manchester's pioneering role, but municipal trading was becoming such a successful feature of local government that thereafter a significant number of communities either bought or established gasworks. The movement can consequently be divided into two distinct stages, but regardless of the date of municipalisation there are common features in the events unfolding in many towns, and especially in the first phase the Manchester model provided the example other towns were to follow.

The Early Imitators

Over the period 1831–60 seven towns bought up local gas companies, and it is interesting to see how most of these communities – Salford (municipalised in 1831), Stockport (1837), Rochdale (1844), Oldham (1853), Burnley (1854), and Bury (1857)(90) – were mainly concentrated around Manchester. Their geographical location was undoubtedly a common feature linking this group, but there were other characteristics which they all shared, and in identifying them we can follow the process of municipalisation with greater understanding. Each gas company had been formed by prominent local businessmen with strong links to the Tory party, perpetuating their control of the community at a time of government by oligarchy. This undemocratic system came under increasing pressure, largely as a result of its inability to deal with the pressing urban problems experienced in this heavily industrialised region, and after either a local improvement Act or the incorporation of the town, those with a vested interest in improvement policies quickly usurped the power formerly held by Tories. Coming up against both a

shortage of funds for their programmes, and widespread dissatisfaction
with the private service, these improvers looked around for a solution, and
in Manchester they found a municipal gasworks which could generate
funds and supply at a cheaper price than the North West average. There
would then follow an often bitter campaign over the 'Gas Question', and
after offering generous compensation, the local authority would persuade
the shareholders to transfer ownership. Each case has its own idiosyncrasies,
and Salford is more of an exception than the rest, but in most places the
scenario was quite standard, helping to lay the ground-rules for what
happened after 1860.

(a)   *Salford*

To illustrate how this scenario unfolded in every town would lengthen the
chapter unduly, but by taking a selection we can demonstrate the main
events in the process. Unfortunately, although Salford was the first known
example of a local authority purchasing a gas company, it highlights the
acute shortage of contemporary documentation, but there are still several
revealing aspects of this story. In particular, it is notable that almost as soon
as Salford was granted independence from Manchester, as well as the right
to appoint a self-governing body of Police Commissioners, they moved to
municipalise the gaslighting service. The 1792 Act forming the Manchester
Police Commissioners had in fact united the two towns for administrative
purposes, and only in 1828 was an Act passed which made Salford 'a body
corporate and politic'.(91) This measure was soon followed in 1830 by an
Improvement Act which bestowed on the Salford Commissioners the rights
to clean, police and regulate the town, and build a gasworks, indicating that
the example set by their former partners in Manchester was a source of
inspiration in the pursuit of financial stability. In contrast, though, the
Salford body was controlled by Liberals, and this ensured that the 'Gas
Question' did not dominate local politics there,(92) in spite of the authority's
use of the gasworks in the same way as in Manchester.

Gaslighting for general consumption in Salford up to the mid-1830s had
been provided by a limited operation established in 1819.(93) The manufacture of gas by many of the larger cotton manufacturers had inhibited the
growth of a large market, and when the Police Commissioners negotiated
the purchase in 1831 the undertaking was valued at just £6,000.(94) Unable
to generate a large income from either the rates or gas profits, in 1834
£16,500 was borrowed from local bankers to construct a much-expanded
works in Lamb Lane, and by 1836, when the new system came on stream,
they had built a business which was to provide a steady contribution to the
Police Fund. The districts of Pendleton (1838) and Broughton (1846) were
also added to the mains network, and in common with other undertakings
they significantly reduced the price of gas between 1831 and 1849, from 12/-
(60p) to 5/- (25p), stimulating a rise in sales over that period to £14,086. By
1849, £20,327 had been invested in the gasworks, and since the late-1830s,
apart from repaying all the loans taken out to expand the operation, £7,000
had been contributed to the Police Fund.(95) This represents a significantly
lower sum than the amounts generated by Manchester's undertaking, but
the Salford market was certainly much smaller, and the Commissioners had
started in 1831 from an extremely disadvantageous position. The business

also continued to expand after 1850, with sales reaching £96,967 in 1880, and between 1853 and 1880 the local Improvement Funds were given a total of £172,429 from gas profits.(96)

The Salford Police Commissioners had succeeded by 1840 in building a self-supporting gasworks which contributed to local improvements, and after the town's incorporation in 1884, the progress was even more impressive. There had been no bitter struggle over the merits of private or public enterprise, and no well-entrenched, Tory-owned gas company existed to hold up greater progress, but nevertheless the consistent Liberal majority in Salford ensured that any available surpluses would be used to help fund improvements in the town. This illustrates how the Manchester model had played a decisive role in influencing the story, and in turn Salford's use of the gasworks as a subsidy to the rates helped to spread the benefits of municipalisation, indicating the importance of the financial factor in encouraging this movement.

(b) *Stockport*

A more typical example of the scenario previously explained was the town of Stockport, because after becoming one of the first towns to take advantage of the 1835 Municipal Corporations Act, by 1837 the newly formed corporation had acquired the local gas company. Until 1835 the Stockport Police Commissioners had been dominated by a combination of Tory millowners and Nonconformist Whigs,(97) and the Stockport Gaslight Co. was also owned and managed by members of this ruling clique,(98) giving Radicals like Henry Coppock and Henry Marsland little opportunity to influence policy. These Radicals attempted in 1826 to push forward an improvement Bill which would have empowered the Police Commissioners to purchase the gasworks, pointing directly to the benefits Manchester was beginning to gain from its venture.(99) The Tories were unimpressed by this attempt to transfer ownership, however, particularly as dividends had recently reached 10%,(100) and Stockport Gaslight Co. successfully petitioned parliament to have the gasworks clause withdrawn from the 1826 Bill. Undeterred by defeat in 1826, Coppock continued to campaign for municipal ownership of the gasworks as part of his demand for much greater democracy in local government and more extensive improvement policies. Through his newspaper, the *Coppock Chronicle*, he criticised the Directors for providing a supply of poor quality for which consumers were obliged to pay what was regarded as the high price of 12/- (60p), asserting in 1834 that 'the twelve years' monopoly enjoyed by the Gas Company must be broken'.(101) The management was sufficiently sensitive to respond with a 10/- (50p) reduction in the price charged for street lamps, but in failing to implement fully the promised cut of 15/- (75p) they simply increased the support for the Radical cause. Coppock's campaign for greater local democracy also generated enough support to encourage the Radicals to make an application on behalf of Stockport for corporate status, and by immediately lowering the qualification for voting in local elections the 1835 charter provided them with the opportunity to overcome the existing Tory oligarchy. The first election reflected this change in the local balance of power, because, as in Manchester, in the 42 seats not a single Tory candidate was elected, while 25 were won by Radicals.(102).

Coppock now had his power base for the implementation of a wide-ranging programme of urban improvements,(103) and in 1836 an Act was sanctioned which extended the corporation's powers to deal with the town's major problems. The 1836 Improvement Act also granted authority to purchase the gas company, but the Directors put up such an effective rearguard action in the negotiations that it was decided in 1837 to appoint four arbitrators to settle on the price Stockport Corporation would have to pay.(104) They finally agreed on £21,494, and although it took nearly two years to raise the required loans for the purchase,(105) Coppock and his supporters had finally succeeded in eliminating the Tories from both local government and control over a key local utility.

The need for finance had been a major determinant of the desire to municipalise Stockport Gaslight Co. Party politics had played an important role in the debate, and the Radicals were naturally keen to oust their Tory rivals from power, but Coppock had also learnt in the mid-1820s how Manchester succeeded in subsidising improvement programmes from their gasworks, prompting him to imitate this strategy.(106) Coppock's instinctive move to copy the Manchester model also proved correct, because the venture provided Stockport Corporation with a consistent source of funds for the many projects undertaken in that period,(107) helping to spread even further the benefits of municipal trading as one of the most effective means of subsidising the rates.

(c)   *Rochdale*

Stockport's story reveals the pattern of events which was typical in this first phase of gas company municipalisations, and in Rochdale we have a similar story of local conflict.(108) Rochdale did not become an incorporated town until 1856, but by the 1840s the Police Commission had become the focal point of a conflict between the Tory-Anglican group and a Nonconformist/Liberal force. Garrard emphasises how party politics 'influenced relations between the public utility companies and the local authority', particularly as the Liberals had become the dominant party during the 1830s, and the Rochdale Gas Light & Coke Co. remained a Tory stronghold which provided 'the means of fighting the Liberal-dominated institutions'.(109) The gas undertaking had been formed in 1823, and over the next two decades its heavy Tory bias represented 'formidable obstacles to powers that the Police Commissioners wished to take over'.(110) Moreover, the business community was demanding a more efficient, cheaper service, and as the Liberal newspaper, the *Rochdale Spectator*, noted in 1844 with regard to the street lamps: 'Complaints were made of the deficiency of the light in various places... which, however, do not appear to have been remedied...'.(111)

Leading the campaign against Rochdale Gas Light & Coke Co. was one of the town's working class champions, Thomas Livsey,(112) and his main concern was to improve the quality of gas supply and cut the price charged in order to extend the benefits of this service to more people. The conflict came to a head in 1844, when the Police Commissioners blocked the company's application for further statutory powers to extend its capital, and at the same time they published an improvement Bill which would grant authority to 'erect Gas Works for the *sole* benefit and advantage of the public'.(113) The *Spectator* continued to launch frequent attacks on its Tory opponents, describing them as 'the fag-end of all the Tories in Lancashire. Always men, selfish and tyrannical...',(114) but Livsey's main aim was to make gaslighting a genuinely public service, as well as boost public funds.

The Rochdale Improvement Act of 1844 signalled the total victory of Livsey and the town's Liberal majority, granting authority to the Police Commissioners to purchase the gas company for £26,500.(115) They had eliminated one of the last bastions of Tory power in Rochdale, but, as the *Spectator* noted other motives were apparent, in ensuring that an 'oppressive monopoly is destroyed, a source of income to the Town's Funds is created, and a still greater benefit will result by an extended consumption of gas'.(116) It is difficult to prioritise these aims, and although Livsey actually claimed that six out of seven houses in the borough were lit by gas in 1860, and the number of consumers had increased from 904 in 1844 to 8,557, there is no evidence to support these boasts.(117) On the other hand, gas prices in Rochdale were only typical for the region (see Table 6.2), and the business produced such a good source of funds that in the 1860s Livsey, as Chairman of the Gas Committee, was obliged to set a limit of 10% on the gas profits,(118) presumably to be calculated in relation to capital employed. The service had clearly been extended to a larger number of consumers, but the need for additional funds to finance Liberal policies had been the major reason why the company had been municipalised, bringing a two-fold benefit to the town from this strategy.

(d) *Burnley*

Another illustration of how dissatisfaction with the established company could combine with pressures associated with local government finances was Burnley. Events in this town took a rather peculiar turn, but otherwise the build-up to municipalisation was typical, starting with a Tory-owned Burnley Gaslight Co. which had emerged in 1823 out of a local government which was remarkable for its inaction.(119) The Burnley Improvement Act of 1819 had been very much 'a dead letter', and the Tory oligarchy which ran the town at that time was content to allow private enterprise to provide the limited water and lighting services which prevailed until the 1840s.(120) A second Improvement Act was passed in 1846, and by allowing the growing number of Nonconformist small businessmen to vote in local elections this injected some vigour into the Commission. The progressive group started by municipalising Burnley Water Co. in 1846, at a cost of £10,500, and in the following decades they attempted to introduce a series of improvement projects.(121)

Although the water undertaking proved to be a remunerative investment, by 1853 they had accumulated a debt of £44,000 as a result of their policies. Complaints were voiced about the burden this imposed on a rate income of about £4,000,(122) and as there was also some concern about the activities of Burnley Gaslight Co. an obvious solution soon emerged. The quality of Burnley gas was described as 'very bad, very bad indeed',(123) and when Samuel Clegg was hired by the Improvement Commissioners to test its purity he reported that he had been unable even to write a letter by gaslight.(124) Burnley gas prices were actually as low as any in the region (see Table 6.2), forcing the company's opponents to concentrate on the issue of purity, but when consumers were also informed of the generous dividends paid by Burnley Gaslight Co. there was general disgust.(125) By the early-1850s 'relations between the Commissioners and the Company [were] anything but amicable',(126) and given the need to secure a stable source of income to repay the authority's mounting debts, municipalisation seemed to be the answer. The company, however, was in a very strong position, and in order to prepare the ground for a local authority take-over, a group of consumers decided to pursue the disrupting tactic of forming a rival operation.

Apart from Samuel Clegg, another leading figure in the gas industry, George Flintoff, also visited Burnley in 1853, and as the major protagonist in favour of gas consumer companies he advised a group of Nonconformist radicals on how to establish such an operation.(127) The discontented consumers, led by William Lomas, Richard Shaw and Henry Holroyd,(128) were also among the more prominent Improvement Commissioners who advocated public ownership of the gas undertaking, arguing that this would bring greater protection against profiteering, not to mention a subsidy of at least £600 per annum to the rates,(129) and clearly by creating a rival they hoped to persuade the Tory venture that whatever happened the monopoly would be severely curtailed. They had managed to raise enough local support from local businessmen to make a formal application to parliament in May 1853 for authority to form a gas company with a capital of £20,000,(130) but in November the Improvement Commission agreed to buy the old undertaking, and the rival scheme was dropped.

Lomas, Shaw and Holroyd had been mainly concerned to acquire the profitable gas company as a means of bolstering the Improvement Commissioners' finances,(131) and the consumers company had been a bargaining counter in the campaign, helping to undermine Burnley Gaslight Co.'s monopoly at a time of growing political uncertainty. A further Improvement Act was sought in 1854 to ratify the purchase, and at a cost of £30,000 the gasworks came under municipal ownership after the shareholders had given in to what by then seemed the inevitable.(132) The Commissioners discovered that the works had suffered from some neglect in recent years, probably owing to the municipalisation campaign,(133) but by pumping £40,000 into essential refurbishments over the following six years they built a business capable of subsidising the public finances.(134) By the early-1870s, an annual average profit of almost £4,200 was being transferred into the Borough Fund Account,(135) and as Bennett notes the 'new undertaking was jealously watched and every effort was made to ensure that it should be financially profitable'.(136) The Radicals had once again succeeded in eliminating Tory control over a powerful local institution, but, more importantly, a useful source of revenue had been created for the improvement projects they had been planning since the 1840s.

(e)   Oldham

The balance of power in many of the older North West towns was clearly swinging away from formerly well-entrenched Tory/Whig interests in favour of the liberal/radical groups which demanded more ambitious programmes of urban renewal.(137) Oldham provides yet another example of this decisive switch, because initially the share register of Oldham Gas & Water Co. had been 'a roll-call of the town-centre [Tory] bourgeoisie', reflecting the power of the Tory elite in that town.(138) After the incorporation of Oldham, however, in 1849, a progressive group of Liberals and Radicals gained power and implemented a series of schemes for a covered market, public baths and improved policing and scavenging services.(139) As in their close neighbour, Rochdale, they also wanted to extend the water and gaslighting service, but this resulted in a direct confrontation with the Oldham Gas & Water Co. over pricing and investment policies,(140) a conflict which would lead to the municipalisation of this business in 1853. The Radicals were, of course, aware that acquiring the company would not only eliminate the main source of opposition to their policies, it would also help finance the improvement policies currently being implemented, and after 1854 they were able to extend the services considerably, yet still generate substantial subsidies to the rates.(141)

Municipal trading had consequently gained in popularity by 1860, with seven towns having purchased their local gas company, and a further seven (including Manchester) having built their own works (see Appendix A). We shall be examining in the next section why some local authorities were obliged to initiate a service themselves, but what had happened in Salford, Stockport, Rochdale, Oldham, Burnley, Bury and Birkenhead was indicative of the dramatic changes local government had been undergoing since the 1830s. The events also illustrate how North West gas companies were faced with a growing threat to their control over gaslighting markets from increasingly powerful local authorities, and in the next section we shall see how events unfolded after 1860.

In the context of these local government changes, it is also helpful to remember what had happened in Kendal and Chester in this period, because while those companies had not municipalised they had certainly been affected by the replacement of Tory control by liberal/radical interests.(142) Allegedly exploitative prices and a low quality product had done more to precipitate the emergence of rival operations, but local political conflict had played a part in facilitating the eventual outcome, demonstrating the trends outlined in this section in a peculiar way. The scenario described earlier was being played out in full in an increasing number of towns by the 1850s (see Appendix A), and although each case had its own peculiar variation, the basic motivations of funding improvement programmes and removing political opponents from influential positions appear to have been sufficiently common to deserve some emphasis. It is now essential to discover whether after 1860 these factors continued to influence local authorities, and what impact municipalisation had on gas company strategy generally.

The Second Phase

Local government was clearly beginning to accept a wider range of responsibilities from the 1830s, and having recognised both the need to raise additional finance for new projects, and the inadequate service provided by private utilities, municipal trading was slowly being accepted as a viable proposition.(143) The success Manchester had made of its venture into gas supply also confirmed the growing belief in this radical departure. By 1860, there were fourteen local authority-owned undertakings in the North West, but over the following twenty years a further thirty-three companies were municipalised (see Appendix A), giving the public sector 65.6% of the capital invested in the region's gas industry (see Table 2.2), and over 64% of the gas sales (see Table 2.4). This represents a significant phase of expansion in municipal trading and it is important to understand why the movement spread so rapidly, and why several of the larger companies were able to withstand the onslaught on private enterprise. The answers to both questions could be closely related, but only a detailed analysis of the period will provide an adequate insight into a subject which aroused strong feelings at the local level.

The 1835 reform of municipal corporations, and the growing propensity of improvement commissioners to acquire more effective powers, had been key developments in the field of local government in the 1830s and 1840s, but the most significant move as far as the mid-nineteenth century was concerned came with the introduction of Local Boards of Health. The 1848 Public Health Act was a major breakthrough in this respect, and even though it was permissive, and parliament was obliged to revamp the scheme in 1858, local authorities could now seek wide-ranging powers to implement changes in key areas like health, sewerage, paving and lighting by creating a Local Board of Health. These new bodies largely replaced improvement commissioners as agents of urban renewal,(144) and by 1870 700 Local Boards had been formed in England and Wales, especially in communities where little had been achieved in developing effective local government.(145)

A vital implication to be drawn from the 1848 Act was that the trust formerly placed in private enterprise had been transferred to local government as the main agent in the provision of key services.(146) As the Board of Bolton Gas Light Co. was advised in 1855: 'The parties who direct the Board of Health don't like companies and they try by all means — foul or fair — to crush them.'(147) This was perhaps overstating the prevailing ethos in the new government department, but there was certainly growing support for public ownership of utilities,(148) and especially after the revisions introduced in 1858 Local Boards moved to acquire water and gas undertakings, or establish a service where none had existed previously. The new authorities were never given statutory rights to purchase companies, unless the shareholders agreed to a take-over, but in the North West especially Local Boards were the main agent of municipalisation after 1858. Table 7.3 reveals how up to 1858, with the exception of Oldham and Stockport, all the municipal gasworks had been purchased or formed by improvement commissioners, but thereafter Local Boards accounted for twenty-three of the thirty-four cases where public enterprise provided the supply. The 1875 Public Health Act further strengthened the powers of these bodies,(149) but evidently this was only reinforcing a trend already well under way, indicating the vital role played by this innovation in the development of municipal trading.

Another important feature of Local Board involvement in municipalising gas companies revealed by Table 7.3 is the typically small size of the towns affected, and this links in with a point so far neglected in our study of municipal trading, namely, the propensity of some towns to establish their

Table 7.3 Form of local government taking responsibility for gas supply, 1817–80

Improvement Commissioners	Local Boards	Councils
Manchester (1817)*	Wallasey (1858)*	Oldham (1853)
Salford (1831)	Macclesfield (1861)	Barrow (1868)
Stockport (1837)	Bollington (1862)*	Bolton (1872)
Rochdale (1844)	Tyldesley (1865)	Blackburn (1877)
Lytham (1847)*	Nelson (1866)	St. Helens (1877)
Southport (1848)*	Heywood (1867)	Warrington (1877)
Dalton (1853)*	Widnes (1867)	Lancaster (1879)
Blackpool (1853)*	Oswaldtwistle (1869)*	Chorley (1880)
Burnley (1854)	Buxton (1871)	
Newton (1854)*	Atherton (1872)	
Bury (1855)	Hindley (1872)	
Birkenhead (1858)	Lymm (1872)	
Middleton (1861)	Darwen (1873)	
Congleton (1866)	Ulverston (1874)	
	Wigan (1874)	
	Leigh (1874)	
	Ashton-in-Makerfield (1875)	
	Millom (1875)*	
	Skelmersdale (1876)*	
	Padiham (1876)	
	Clitheroe (1877)	
	Colne (1877)	
	Dukinfield (1877)	

*Indicates that the gasworks was built by the local authority.

own gasworks. It was in fact against the law for a local authority to start a gas supply where a company had already been providing the service, but clearly in the tourist resorts of Lytham, Southport and Blackpool especially,(150) as well as in the small communities of Dalton, Newton, Wallasey, Bollington, Oswaldtwistle, Millom and Skelmersdale,(151) sufficient interest in financing a gaslighting service was not forthcoming from private enterprise, and the local authority was obliged to take the initiative. This reemphasises the willingness of local government to accept responsibility for providing services like adequate lighting from the 1830s, and in small towns this would appear to have been particularly important. Improvement Commissions were just as likely to build a gasworks as Local Boards, according to Table 7.3, but the latter provided the necessary organisational structure in emerging industrial satellite communities after 1858. The Local Boards also clearly stimulated a surge in municipalisations after 1860, and they also appeared to have implemented this move for similar reasons to those outlined in the last section. To demonstrate the continuity here, the case of Macclesfield can be used.

The Macclesfield Local Board had been formed under an Act of 1852 which the existing corporation had sought to bring greater urgency into the town's improvement programme.(152) This policy had evidently worked effectively except in the field of gaslighting, where by 1860 the Local Board was 'dissatisfied with the proceedings of the [Macclesfield Gaslight] Company'.(153) The company was at that time applying for parliamentary permission to extend its capital by capitalising £18,000 of ploughed-back profits, but the Local Board successfully petitioned to have this form of bonus payment excluded from the Bill, on the grounds that it had allegedly been derived from 'excessive profits'.(154) Macclesfield Gaslight Co. had in fact been one of the more successful First Generation ventures, as we noted in Chapter 5 (and see Appendix C), recording an annual average dividend of 10% up to 1850, and paying even better returns during the following decade.(155) The opposition emanating from the Local Board, however, and especially the 1860 Macclesfield Gas Act granting permission for the authorities to negotiate a purchase, was beginning to raise doubts in the Directors' minds about the company's future viability.

By March 1861 the two sides were in detailed negotiations over a purchase, and just as in the cases of Stockport, Rochdale, Burnley and Oldham, the recurring themes of this debate were the financial benefits of municipalisation to the local authority and the general dissatisfaction with the company's policies. Party political wrangling does not feature at all in the rhetorical proclamations of either combatant, but the Local Board was convinced that a municipal gasworks could produce at least £1,000 per annum 'for the benefit of the town', emphasising the monetary value placed on the move. As one councillor noted: 'Let them look at the towns in Lancashire, where all the improvements were made from the profits of their gasworks.'(156) This was an exaggeration, of course, but the influences operating in those towns acquiring gas companies up to 1860 were clearly still at work, and by May 1861 the Macclesfield Local Board had succeeded in convincing all concerned that their town could gain similar advantages. There were some who worried that profitability might have been squeezed by the reduction in price to 4/- (20p), but the Town Council voted the deal through after having been persuaded that the price elasticity of demand for gas would stimulate both a wider use of gas and a steady flow of funds into the public coffers.(157)

Municipal Strategies

Funding requirements were consequently just as big an influence on the development of municipalisation both before and after 1860. A high level of dissatisfaction with the existing service had also been a common feature of the debate over who should control pricing and investment strategies, but whether this took the form of an anxiety over allegedly excessive charges and dividends, or the poor quality of gas and the limited area covered by the mains network, the claims were often little more than a rhetorical exercise in which local authorities indulged as a means of creating a favourable environment for municipalisation. The criticisms are certainly both persistent and consistent, in the way that they attack company policy, but one must examine what impact these claims had on the debate, and how they influenced the operation of municipal gasworks, before accepting them as a major reason why local authorities preferred public ownership.

The ineffectiveness of statutory regulations on dividends, prices and general performance has already been demonstrated, and even though the

1871 Gasworks Clauses Amendment Act tightened up on the various problems arising from street lighting contracts there was widespread concern that parliament had failed to provide controls which influenced management strategy.(158) According to Millward, this was one of the main reasons why local authorities, increasingly 'frustrated in achieving their objectives by market transactions with private companies as agents, switched instead to internal transactions' by acquiring the business.(159) Rowlinson has also emphasised how the fear of exploitation prompted more extensive municipal ownership, indicating that what was generally known as the 'Gas Question' was a primary cause behind this trend.(160) On the other hand, while the party in government might have described the Directors as monopolistic exploiters, and the quality of gas supply was heavily criticised, one needs to ask whether the transfer of ownership resulted in any decisive change in policy before accepting these arguments as a motivating force behind municipalisation. The arguments of Millward and Rowlinson might imply that local authorities wanted to do something different with prices and profits, but in fact the policies of municipal gasworks were little different from those pursued under private enterprise, and in general the 'Gas Question' was simply part of the publicity campaign leading up to municipalisation.

The course of municipal trading does not form part of this study, but in clarifying the points just made it is useful to discover how local authorities managed their gasworks. Manchester's Police Commissioners had unashamedly set out to subsidise the rates from gas profits, and in the examples we have seen so far this role model played a dominant part in determining the pattern of causation. Jones has also noted how after 1865 Birmingham councillors were motivated by the business ethic in developing a wide range of municipal services,(161) imitating the kind of strategies which had already come to the fore in North West local authority finances. Chamberlain's Birmingham of the early-1870s has often been seen as the archetypal municipal trader,(162) but other regions had been developing this so-called 'Municipal Socialism' for several decades by then, and in the North West Manchester had pioneered the movement. The term 'Municipal Socialism', however, is extremely misleading, and it is far more appropriate to talk, as Waller does, about 'Municipal Capitalism' when describing the basic ethos behind this idea.(163)

Although some local authorities claimed to have extended the gas supply to the majority of their citizens, they were still concerned to generate a surplus from the business. Even at Rochdale, where Livsey had fought the campaign to acquire the gas company as a crusade in favour of more extensive use of gaslighting, prices were kept at levels which ensured a steady profit for improvement purposes.(164) This supports Matthews's claim that 'public ownership seems to have had no impact on the price of gas or on the operating performance of the concerns', and to substantiate this he shows how in a comparison of local authority and company results for 1883, the municipal sector was actually more profitable.(165) Millward and Ward have also drawn similar conclusions from a more extensive study looking at returns in 1897−98,(166) confirming the view that municipal gasworks were run as profit-making ventures. Municipal gasworks might well have extended the service to a much larger area, but as previous chapters have pointed out, after 1850 gaslighting was in any case making major inroads into the

The gasworks at Rochdale Rd., Manchester, in the 1880s.

domestic market as a result of the fall in price, and companies were just as likely to exploit this trend as local authority operations.(167)

An interesting indication of the concern with gasworks profitability under private and public ownership is the pricing policy pursued during the inflationary boom of 1871−74, when the cost of coal, iron and labour leapt to such an extent that charges were raised across the board. Had local authorities been willing to use public ownership as a means of protecting the consumer against such vicissitudes, then they would have foregone profits in the short term and maintained prices at the same level. On the other hand, if they had wanted to protect their profits they could have raised prices, and indeed, as the *Journal of Gas Lighting* claimed when announcing a 9d (4p) increase by Rochdale Corporation, 'the corporations in the north, who will persist in making large surplus profits, must go on raising the price of gas'.(168) Always anxious to criticise public ownership, this trade journal had also noted that 'corporations seem, in most cases, at all events, to be able to do pretty much as they please with gas prices when they have the supply in their own hands',(169) and while companies were just as likely to raise prices in these circumstances, the move to municipal trading had clearly made no impact on this crucial area of management strategy.

In their attempts to cope with the rapid pace of industrialisation and urbanisation, improvement commissioners, councillors or local board officials in a growing number of towns eagerly bought up the private ventures to boost the income at their disposal, placing the financial incentive behind this move in a central position. So keen were local authorities to acquire these profitable utilities, and so reluctant had parliament been to provide compulsory rights of purchase, that generous compensation was often meted out to persuade shareholders of the benefits arising from a transfer in ownership. The payments took a variety of forms, from a simple cash payment to the provision of annuities paying the same returns as the old gas shares,(170) but the authorities were invariably obliged to pay the full market price. Table 7.4 reveals the prices paid by twenty-three towns, and while there is a large difference between the £300 received by Burnley Gaslight Co. and the £150 paid at Nelson, in general the shareholders were well compensated for agreeing to the take-over. Bolton Gas Light Co., for example, was able to negotiate perpetual annuities of 10% and 6% in respect of its two classes of fully paid up equities, as well as a £2 bonus per share on completion of the deal, an inducement the *Bolton Chronicle*, with some understatement, described as 'one which prudent investors, one would think, would not be disposed altogether to overlook'.(171)

The case of Bolton indicates just how extensively the municipal trading movement had spread by the 1870s, because it was a Tory-controlled council which in 1872 acquired the gas company. Until that time all North West municipalisations had been executed by bodies dominated by either Liberal

Table 7.4 Price per £100 of share capital paid by local authorities to purchase North West gas companies (£)

	Year of Purchase	Price
Ashton-in-Makerfield	1875	160
Atherton	1873	160
Birkenhead	1858	220
Blackburn	1877	235
Bolton	1872	204
Burnley	1854	300
Bury	1859	250
Chorley	1871	250
Clitheroe	1878	210
Colne	1877	237
Dukinfield	1877	250
Heywood	1867	208
Hindley	1872	298
Macclesfield	1861	250
Nelson	1866	150
Oldham	1858	250
Over-Darwen	1873	188
Padiham	1876	200
Rochdale	1844	167
St. Helens	1876	272
Tyldesley	1865	167
Warrington	1877	240
Wigan	1874	208

Source: T. Newbigging, *Gas Managers' Handbook*, pp. 302–303.

or Radical groups, and although the party political factor has been under-played, it is interesting to see that such was the growing popularity of municipal trading that even Tory councillors were willing to envisage this move. In fact, a Liberal majority had emerged in Bolton Corporation during the 1850s,(172) after many years of Tory control, and in 1861 an Improvement Act was secured, after a bitter battle, allowing municipalisation of the gas company. However, the Tory-dominated undertaking was able to thwart this attempt at a take-over,(173) because three-fifths of the shareholders had to agree to the sale, and during the 1860s Garrard claims that it 'remained a major source of constraint' on Liberal improvement policies.(174) There were all the usual complaints about the quality of service and high prices, but the political *impasse* remained until control of Bolton Corporation reverted to the Tories in 1870, and the shareholders succumbed to the financial temptations offered by their political allies.(175)

In assessing the reasons why a Tory council acquired the local gas company it is interesting to note that by 1870, echoing the Manchester case, grandiose plans to build 'a wedding cake of a Town Hall' costing £70,000 had been drawn up, and in general municipal spending on improvement programmes had continued to expand.(176) This provided strong financial justification for the acquisition of Bolton Gas Light Co., and, just as in many other North West towns, gas profits were to become an essential component in local government finances. The political persuasion of the party in power was not a major issue here, a point further illustrated by looking at Blackburn, where another Tory council purchased the local gas company in 1877. Even though the compensation paid at Blackburn was more generous than at Bolton (see Table 7.4), the Mayor was still convinced that municipal owner-ship would bring 'immense pecuniary advantages' for a town currently embarking on an extensive policy of urban improvement.(177)

Municipal Capitalism

The high prices paid for North West gas undertakings, averaging almost £210 per £100 of share capital for the twenty-three cases listed in Table 7.4, are indicative of the eagerness with which local authorities sought access to these lucrative businesses. They were clearly convinced that gas profits were such a guaranteed form of income that they would be able to repay either the loans taken out to compensate shareholders, or meet the annual annuity charges, and still subsidise the rates. In achieving these aims they were certainly not disappointed, and in the late nineteenth century muni-cipal gasworks were run as commercial ventures which provided a constant stream of funds for local improvements projects. This was indeed 'municipal capitalism', as Waller argues,(178) and after 1860 a growing number of towns realised the advantages to be gained from such a policy at a time when local government was taking on a much-increased range of responsi-bilities.(179) Evidence is not always easy to find, but the twenty-six North West local authorities which made returns in 1881 revealed that they had transferred a total of £153,554 from the gasworks to various improvement funds in the previous financial year, and although Manchester accounted for 33.9% of this sum (£52,000) the other towns earned an average of almost £4,100 from their enterprise.(180) One should also emphasise that municipally owned gas undertakings were in a much stronger position to exploit their monopoly of the local industry, because, while they were not granted exclusive rights to a particular market, the threat of competition was minuscule, given the need for local authority permission to break open the streets. The communities consequently derived a considerable benefit from municipal trading, subsidising the rates from a low-risk operation at a time of greater local government action in various fields.

A final issue to settle in this analysis of municipalisation is the uneven distribution of public ownership in the North West. There was also a distinct north—south divide in the general attitude towards municipal trading: most of the undertakings below a line drawn between Cardiff and King's Lynn remained in private hands, while in the Midlands, Yorkshire, Lancashire, the North East and Scotland, local authorities owned most of the industry.(181) The southern towns were naturally much less affected by the dual forces of industrialisation and urbanisation, and having developed an established structure of local government financed out of rates and other forms of levies, the need for municipal trading was not going to be felt as extensively.(182) On the other hand, North West towns like Liverpool, Preston, Ashton-under-Lyne, Stalybridge and Accrington were directly affected by rapid population growth and industrial development, yet they retained private gas undertakings up to 1880 (see Appendix A).

In fact, the Accrington Local Board, after several rejected entreaties between 1854 and 1873,(183) finally persuaded the shareholders of the local gas and water company to transfer ownership in 1893,(184) and in 1885 the Stalybridge Local Board had also purchased that town's utility.(185) This fits in with the pattern of municipalisation already outlined, but it still seems strange that some of the larger companies in the region, as well as the county towns of Chester and Kendal, were supplied by private companies up to nationalisation in 1949.

In a detailed quantitative analysis of the municipalisation movement in England and Wales, Millward and Ward confirm the view expressed in this study that finance was a key factor influencing local authority strategy. They conclude that 'towns with relatively high population growth but not an especially strong revenue base' were more likely to buy gas companies for their profits,(186) emphasising the link between the need for improvement policies and a shortage of finance to follow through the policies. Conversely, Millward and Ward also argue that towns with a good revenue base and low population growth were less likely to indulge in municipalisation,(187) and this would help to explain why in the south the movement was not very popular, while applying this thesis to the peculiar turn of events in Kendal and Chester would rationalise the actions of the respective local authorities there. In general terms, the relatively affluent (and Tory-dominated) corporations of Liverpool and Preston would also have seen no financial need to acquire trading interests to bolster their funds,(188) confirming in an indirect manner the arguments presented above. Access to adequate finance for local government became the key determinant of an authority's willingness to buy gas companies, and because of the dramatic change in attitudes towards the provision of essential services, a growing number of under-funded North West towns responded by municipalising the most profitable utilities in their district.

Conclusions

A study of the North West municipalisation movement illustrates how gas
company management came under mounting pressure to improve the quality
of its service and reduce the price of gas. We noted in the last chapter how
potential or actual competition had been a major reason why gas prices had
fallen so significantly after the 1830s, and the refusal of parliament to grant
exclusive franchises to any provincial operation ensured that Directors and
Engineers would always have to keep a wary eye on the activities of
disenchanted consumers or local opportunists. When the local authority
started to take a hand in mobilising public opinion against the company
then it was often only a matter of time before municipalisation was mooted,
particularly in towns where public finances were severely stretched. The
emphasis on service, however, was simply a means of generating antipathy
towards the company, because the utility was usually municipalised for its
profitable business, and once under public ownership prices were not
reduced any faster than those of private companies, but in general the
situation forced management to keep a watchful eye on local pressure
groups. Indeed, the dramatic transformation in attitudes towards local
government responsibilities which took place over our period became a
major determinant of management strategy. Directors had always been
careful to maintain a good relationship with the authorities, granting generous discounts for street lighting in order to secure unfettered access to the
public highway. Although the annual negotiations over prices were later
characterised by a 'state of vexation, endless disputes, and turmoil',(189)
and the 1871 Gasworks Clauses Amendment Act laid down even more
stringent regulations governing this service, it was advisable to keep in
favour with whatever form of government prevailed in the town. However,
the changing approach towards the provision of essential services in towns
most affected by the dual forces of industrialisation and population growth,
often accompanied by a decisive swing in power away from Tories towards
groups with ambitious improvement policies, would frequently result in
municipalisation, emphasising again how gas companies in most North
West towns were faced with a wide range of influences which were beyond
their control. Demand for gaslighting was certainly accelerating appreciably
from the 1830s, and even more so after mid-century, bringing a period of
prosperity to the industry after the early struggles, but mounting pressures
prevented management in the region from pursuing complacent strategies
not attuned to the economic and political realities of their locality. This re-
emphasises the difficulties experienced by management in exploiting their
local gaslighting market at a time when traditional attitudes were changing
and the concept of a 'public' utility was emerging.(190)

Footnotes

(1) This chapter could not have been written without the research assistance of
     Mr. T. M. Mitchell of British Gas North Western, and I am heavily indebted
     to him for the guidance provided over the last three years.
(2) See earlier, pp.55−58, for a detailed breakdown of the North West gas
     industry by 1880.

(3) Robson (1939), Ch. 14.
(4) Matthews (1986), p. 261.
(5) For a description of the build-up to this decision, see above, pp. 15—16.
(6) Webbs (1922), p. 258
(7) Quoted in Falkus (1977), pp. 137—138
(8) See Redford (1939), p. 210, and Vigier (1970), pp. 120—122.
(9) Redford (1939), pp. 210—212, and Webbs (1922), pp. 258—260.
(10) Webbs (1922), p. 261, and Vigier (1970), p. 125.
(11) Vigier (1970), p. 126.
(12) The Police Commissioners' minutes for 1816—17 have been lost, and any references for this period have been taken from Mitchell (1986).
(13) *Ibid*, pp. 15—19.
(14) *Ibid*, p. 18.
(15) PMPC, 18/4/17 & 30/4/17.
(16) Mitchell (1986), pp. 28 & 42. This contract was later to cause some problems for Fleming, because his political opponents alleged that Peel & Williams tendered at a higher price than their competitors, and the Gas Committee still gave them the contract. It was claimed that the Gas Committee had acted in this way to suppress the criticisms of the project voiced by George Williams.
(17) *Ibid*, pp. 30—34.
(18) See earlier, pp. 15—16, for an insight into this man, and Redford (1939), pp. 241—274.
(19) *Ibid*, pp. 283—286.
(20) See earlier pp. 84—90.
(21) Redford (1939), p. 262.
(22) PMPC, 3/4/17.
(23) Most of the major manufacturers in Manchester made their own gas by this time. See above, pp. 6—8, and evidence of J. Davies to the 1823 Select Committee, p. 264.
(24) Prentice (1851), p. 121.
(25) Webbs (1922), pp. 265—267.
(26) Redford (1939), p. 271.
(27) For a full discussion of these accusations, and the public debate surrounding the Police Commission finances, see Mitchell (1986), pp. 41—71, Redford (1939), pp. 268—272, Vigier (1970), pp. 144—146. William Whitworth became Fleming's main opponent after 1821, when his brother emigrated.
(28) Letter from Fleming to the Gas Directors, on his retirement, MGCM, 12/11/41.
(29) Mitchell (1986), p. 65.
(30) *Ibid*, p. 64.
(31) No attempt was made to depreciate the plant at that time.
(32) £22,000 had been borrowed from local banks between 1824 and 1826. Redford (1939), p. 293.
(33) *Ibid*, p. 290.
(34) See earlier, pp. 23—25.
(35) PMPC, 5/11/23.
(36) *Ibid*.
(37) *Ibid*, 11/2/24.
(38) *Ibid*, 7/4/24. The Radicals had also withdrawn their support for the venture by this time, because little information on pricing policy could be gleaned from the London promoters.
(39) *Ibid*, 16/6/24, and Redford (1939), p. 290.
(40) PMPC, 16/6/24.
(41) Mitchell (1986), p. 33.
(42) MGCM, 21/7/26. The discounts ranged from 20% for bills between £200 and

£225 up to 25% for those exceeding £250.

(43) Lloyd-Jones & Lewis (1988), pp. 103–124, recount how the Manchester popu-
      lation of manufacturing premises expanded from twenty-five to fifty-seven
      wholly occupied factory firms, compared to the earlier preponderance of firms
      sharing part of a mill.

(44) Baines had claimed that Wood (later an M.P. for South Lancashire) had 'the
      merit of originating these works on the present liberal plan' (Quoted in
      Webbs (1922), p. 262), but this exaggerates his role and understates the vision
      of Thomas Fleming. Wood was also replaced as Chairman of the Gas Directors
      by H. H. Birley in 1831. MGCM, 11/11/31.

(45) MGCM, 23/7/24.

(46) *Ibid*, 25/3/25, 26/5/26 & 28/7/26.

(47) City of Manchester (1949), pp. 21–22.

(48) PMPC, 1/12/33.

(49) See Redford (1939), pp. 295–305, for a description of the political manoeuvrings
      at this time.

(50) *Ibid*, p. 297.

(51) At one meeting in January 1828 it took four hours to appoint a Chairman, and
      in the end nothing was discussed of substance. *Ibid*, p. 301.

(52) *Ibid*, p. 312.

(53) MGCM, 20/3/35. This works had started out as the premises of the ill-fated
      Provincial Portable Gas Co. See earlier, pp. 24–25.

(54) *Ibid*, 31/1/34.

(55) *Ibid*, 23/12/42.

(56) By this time the mains network was 90 miles long (including the six miles
      purchased from James Fernley). *Ibid*, 21/10/42. This was not as extensive as
      the 150 miles of mains laid by Liverpool Gas Light Co. (Harris (1956), p. 56)
      by 1846.

(57) MGCM, 2/7/24.

(58) At least the private companies were not obliged to pay dividends on their
      share capitals, but the Manchester gasworks was legally committed to repaying
      both the debt and the loans.

(59) This particular date is an estimate, because the Board minutes for that year
      do not exist, but by 1828 the debt had been reduced to just £5,510 (MGCM,
      25/1/28), and it is not mentioned again in the 1830s.

(60) No consistent set of figures for this period can be found, and the figure of
      £52,000 is based on an average of £2,880 per annum spent on street lighting.
      The average is based on figures in PMPC, 23/1/34.

(61) Redford (1939), p. 325.

(62) Vigier (1970), p. 150, quoting Webbs (1922), p. 256.

(63) Redford (1939), p. 326.

(64) See later, pp. 203–205.

(65) Speech by a prominent Radical, Thomas Hopkins, quoted in City of
      Manchester (1949), p. 16.

(66) MGCM, 13/12/33.

(67) Redford (1939), p. 344.

(68) For a discussion of this campaign, see Redford (1940), Ch. 1.

(69) Of the forty-eight seats contested, not a single Tory candidate was elected on
      to Manchester Corporation in 1838. Fraser (1976), p. 124. By the 1830s the
      Radical interests had been assimilated into the Liberal party.

(70) Redford (1940), pp. 73–74.

(71) JOGL 20/9/64, p. 647.

(72) The total transferred over the period 1844–87 amounted to £1,367,641. City of
      Manchester (1949), p. 17.

(73) Redford (1939), p. 262.

(74) Fraser (1979), p. 1.
(75) Gill (1948), p. 256.
(76) Smellie (1968), pp. 29—30.
(77) Fry (1979), pp. 91—92.
(78) Smellie (1968), p. 21.
(79) Falkus (1977), pp. 138—139.
(80) Joyce (1980), pp. 1—3.
(81) *Ibid*, pp. 9—16, and see earlier, p. 72.
(82) WGLCMB, 21/2/22: *Lancaster Guardian*, 24/8/27; *Westmorland Gazette*, 16/10/24.
(83) See earlier, pp. 74—76.
(84) Lighting and Watching of Parishes in England and Wales Act, 1833.
(85) Falkus (1977), p. 138.
(86) Fraser (1979), p. 150.
(87) Fraser (1976), p. 124. The 48—0 victory achieved by the Radical/Liberal group at Manchester was matched by a similarly impressive defeat of the Tories in their other major stronghold, Liverpool, by 43 seats to 5. The Tories, however, had regained control of Liverpool by 1841.
(88) This label can be used to describe those groups which were concerned with improving the urban environment. Falkus (1977), p. 152.
(89) This section is based on *Ibid*.
(90) Birkenhead Gas & Water Co. was also municipalised in this period. See Appendix A.
(91) The basic chronology can be found in County Borough of Salford (1920), pp. 9—14.
(92) For an insight into the Salford political scene, see Garrard (1983), pp. 208—220, and Fraser (1976), p. 100.
(93) See earlier, p. 27.
(94) See Appendix B for a comparison of sizes in 1826.
(95) Information gleaned from *Reports of the Gaslight Comittee*, 1831—1843, and *Gas Committee Reports to the Council*, 1844—49.
(96) By the Salford Extension and Improvement Act, 1853, the townships of Pendleton and Broughton were brought within the Borough of Salford, but they retained their self-governing status, and were given a share of the gas profits. Between 1853 and 1880 Pendleton received £38,277, and Broughton £28,768, out of the £172,429 total. *Gas Committee Reports to the Council*, 1853—80.
(97) The voting qualification up to 1835 was the unusually high figure of £35 annual rental, and only about 150 people were eligible under this rule. Giles (1950), pp. 543—544.
(98) *Ibid*, p. 597.
(99) *Ibid*, p. 600.
(100) Heginbotham (1890), p. 411.
(101) Quoted in Giles (1950), p. 622.
(102) *Ibid*, pp. 622—666. See also *Stockport Advertiser*, 6/1/37.
(103) Coppock was appointed the first Town Clerk for Stockport.
(104) *Stockport Advertiser*, 6/1/37.
(105) Stockport Watch Committee minutes, 1/12/37 & 7/12/38.
(106) Giles (1950), p. 600.
(107) In the early 1850s approximately £1,500 per annum was transferred to the Improvement Fund (Stockport Borough Gasworks special minute book, 1851—54), and by the 1880s this had risen to £6,500 per annum (Heginbotham (1890), p. 413).
(108) For a review of the Rochdale political scene, see Garrard (1983), pp. 109—156.
(109) *Ibid*, pp. 111 & 120.

(110)   *Ibid*, p. 120.
(111)   *Rochdale Spectator*, 1/3/44, p. 3.
(112)   See Garrard (1983), pp. 127−129.
(113)   *Rochdale Spectator*, 1/3/44, p. 3.
(114)   *Ibid*, 1/7/44, p. 2.
(115)   *Ibid*, 1/6/44, p. 2.
(116)   *Ibid*, 1/1/45, p. 4.
(117)   Garrard (1983), p. 149. Only in the *1980*s did six out of every seven houses in Rochdale receive a supply of gas, and in all probability Livsey was referring to the availability of street lighting in most parts of the town.
(118)   *Ibid*.
(119)   *Burnley Express* (1897), p. 45.
(120)   No Improvement Commissioners were appointed or elected at this time. Bennett (1948), p. 354.
(121)   The voting qualification was reduced to £20 in rates per annum. *Ibid*, pp. 356−361.
(122)   *Ibid* and *Burnley Mentor*, 15/1/53, p. 1.
(123)   *Burnley Express* (1897), p. 50.
(124)   *Burnley Advertiser*, Apr 1854.
(125)   Dividends since the mid-1820s had been paid out ranging between 11% and 15%. *Burnley Express* (1897), p. 50, and Bennett (1948), p. 356.
(126)   *Burnley Mentor*, 18/6/53, p. 1.
(127)   *Ibid*, 8/6/53. See Nabb (1986), p. 85, and earlier, p. 175, for more on Flintoff.
(128)   A Burnley Gas Consumers' Co. Executive Committee Minute Book has survived, and these are the leading characters in the discussions.
(129)   *Burnley Mentor*, 15/1/53.
(130)   Burnley Gas Consumers Co. Registration Document, 11/5/53. George Flintoff is described as 'Engineer' to the new operation.
(131)   Bennett (1948), p. 359.
(132)   See later, p. 209, for the generous compensation provided.
(133)   *Burnley Advertiser*, July 1854.
(134)   The £40,000 was raised in loans from the public. Bennett (1948), p. 362.
(135)   Reports of Burnley Corporation Gas Works, 1870−75.
(136)   Bennett (1948), p. 362.
(137)   Fraser (1976), p. 124.
(138)   Foster (1974), p. 185. The dominant families of Dunkerley, Chadwick, Clegg, Heywood, Lees, Platt, Shaw, Whittaker and Wrigley were all represented as shareholders. Oldham Gas Act, 1825, 6 Geo. IV.
(139)   Bateson (1949), pp. 131−134.
(140)   *Ibid*, p. 133.
(141)   By the mid-1850s an average transfer of over £9,000 was made from the gas and waterworks profits to the corporation. Oldham Gas & Waterworks Committee, 13/9/54.
(142)   See earlier, pp. 173−177.
(143)   Falkus (1977), pp. 138−139.
(144)   Local Boards were often operating side-by-side with existing bodies, but the new forms of local improvement were usually more powerful.
(145)   Fraser (1979), pp. 110−125.
(146)   Falkus (1977), p. 139.
(147)   This advice came from the London-based lobbying organisation, the Private Enterprise Society. BnGLCCMB, 15/3/55.
(148)   Johnes & Clegg had recommended public ownership as a means of bringing down prices. Johnes & Clegg (1847), p. 99.
(149)   Compulsory purchase rights were still not provided though. Falkus (1977), p. 139.

(150) See earlier, pp. 44−46.
(151) For a history of the Skelmersdale undertaking, see Harris (1956), pp. 228−229.
(152) *Macclesfield Courier & Herald*, 16/3/61, pp. 7−8. Macclesfield had become a borough in 1835.
(153) *Ibid*, 2/3/61, pp. 4−5.
(154) *Ibid*.
(155) Dividends of 15% were paid in the 1850s, according to local sources like the *Macclesfield Courier & Herald*, 16/3/61, p. 7, but this cannot be corroborated by company records.
(156) *Ibid*, 13/4/61, p. 5.
(157) *Ibid*, 4/5/61, p. 7.
(158) The 1871 Act laid down more stringent regulations on the provision of lamps within 50 yards of any mains, better testing facilities, improved lighting quality, and standardised prices. See earlier, pp. 51−53, for a study of parliamentary controls in general.
(159) Millward (1986), p. i.
(160) Rowlinson (1984), pp. 192−193.
(161) Jones (1983), p. 247.
(162) Fraser (1979), pp. 135−50.
(163) Waller (1983), p. 300.
(164) Garrard (1983), p. 149.
(165) Matthews (1986), p. 262.
(166) Millward & Ward (1987), pp. 719−737.
(167) See earlier, pp. 166−170.
(168) JOGL 19/5/74, p. 685.
(169) *Ibid*, 20/1/74, p. 74.
(170) Cash was paid at Buxton, Colne and Nelson, for example, and at St. Helens and Warrington Twenty-Five Year Annuities were paid.
(171) *Bolton Chronicle*, 1/11/71.
(172) For a review of the Bolton political scene, see Garrard (1983), pp. 159−205.
(173) See Hacking (n.d.), Ch. 2, for a detailed discussion of this attempted take-over.
(174) Garrard (1983), p. 198.
(175) *Ibid*.
(176) *Ibid*, pp. 203−205.
(177) *Blackburn Standard*, 15/7/76, p. 4. The Mayor at this time was William Coddington.
(178) Waller (1983), p. 300.
(179) Falkus (1977), pp. 151−153.
(180) PP (1881).
(181) See earlier, p. 56.
(182) Other forms of local government finance included market tolls, port dues, warehouse rents and turnpike income.
(183) *Accrington Times*, 13/2/69, p. 5, & 6/3/75, p. 6, and Singleton (1928), p. 115.
(184) Accrington District Gas & Water Board Act, 1894.
(185) Stalybridge & Mossley Gas Act, 1885.
(186) Millward & Ward (1991), pp. 26−28.
(187) *Ibid*.
(188) These towns had both a good revenue base from rates and additional income from market and port tolls. *Ibid*.
(189) JOGL, 30/10/66, p. 783.
(190) See earlier, pp. 51−53.

8
Lighting the Town

By 1880 the gas industry had come a long way since its birth in 1805. At the beginning of the century only a few amateur scientists and jobbing engineers were aware of the potential in gaslighting, but by the end of our period millions had come into contact with the illuminant at work, school, home or just in the streets. Almost all communities of any size had built a gasworks, and in the major centres the businesses responsible for this service had grown into some of the leading manufacturing operations in their area. This was a story of growth, from relatively humble origins into a multi-million pound industry employing thousands of people in hundreds of locations. The utility was not as significant as some of the other public utilities emerging in the same era, particularly the railways, and its impact on service industries may not have been as great, but the gas industry's contribution was by no means insignificant. We have seen in this study that, for example, in terms of investment gas companies were part of the learning process which eventually resulted in the growing popularity of joint stock companies. This was certainly one of the industry's most important contributions to capital formation, and although the actual supply companies were usually much smaller than railway undertakings they helped to introduce the middle classes to the practice of investing in public utilities. The profitability of the gas companies after 1830, and the handsome premiums to be earned, confirmed the contemporary impression that here was a lucrative haven for surplus cash, and certainly in the North West gas shares became highly prized features in investment portfolios.

The generally acceptable performance of North West gas companies by the mid-nineteenth century contrasted with the poor earning potential demonstrated by the First Generation of undertakings established prior to 1826. With the exceptions of Manchester and Liverpool, most experienced difficulty in producing dividends in their early years, and the inadequacy of management must take some of the blame for these failings. Obviously, they were dealing with a new technology which was still developing, and an acute shortage of experienced gas engineers contributed to this weakness, but poor planning, inaccurate accounting and cautious decision-making compounded the problems faced when establishing such a service. It was only from the 1830s that gas company management woke up to the commercial potential in their product, and this major step forward came largely as a result of the emergence of a group of specialist gas engineers who superseded the Board of Directors as the source of strategy and expertise. These Engineers, or Managing Engineers as they came to be known, evolved a recognisable set of standards and techniques which set them apart from the typical gas company Director, who was most likely a local cotton manufacturer or an attorney with little knowledge of gas manufacture or distribution. It was the Engineers who were responsible for planning the North West gas industry's expansion after the 1830s, bringing a new sense of organisation and efficiency to operations which in the past had lacked system.

The Engineers apart, however, North West gas undertakings were highly localised phenomena. They were initiated by local businessmen and professionals, financed from local resources, organised by local attorneys, and in many cases taken over by local authorities. This localisation was inevitable, given the state of gas technology and a contemporary desire for independent municipal operations, and in consequence it is easy to see the early business as the preserve of the local hierarchy. Indeed, in terms of management and ownership most early North West gas companies were characterised by their heavy Tory-Anglican bias, and when local government was opened up to the strong Nonconformist/Liberal influences in the region there was often an intense conflict over the issue of street lighting and gas prices generally. Local government had always been an important influence over gas supply, because the companies required permission to open up the streets to lay their mains, and in return for this privilege the authorities had exacted a cheap supply of gas for the public lamps. In conjunction with the generous discounts offered to large (factory) consumers, this subsidised street lighting service became a permanent feature of the pricing structure. Gas prices were generally reduced after 1830, in many cases significantly, but the bulk of the population could still not afford to use the illuminant in their homes, while manufacturers and local authorities were given subsidised services in order to prevent the emergence of rival suppliers. Contemporaries focused in on prices, frequently using them as a key issue in what came to be known as 'The Gas Question', and this was often at the heart of the conflict between increasingly active local authorities and North West gas companies after the 1840s.

Once the old Tory-Anglican hierarchy had been replaced in the 1830s and 1840s, gas companies started to fall prey to local government pressures. Some authorities (for example, at Chester and Kendal) felt obliged to break the supplier, usually by creating, or helping to create, a rival operation, but in most cases in the North West municipalisation was seen as the most suitable alternative to a privately owned service. The rise of civic consciousness, the need to solve pressing social problems, and the fear of exploitation by gas companies have been seen as some of the reasons behind this fashion, but above all it was the need for additional sources of revenue to fund essential improvement programmes which prompted local authorities in the North West to purchase these profitable businesses, and the shareholders were tempted with generous terms to sell their equities. In the south private suppliers were allowed to continue unhindered by the threat of, or actual, municipalisation, but in the North West (as in much of the country north of Birmingham) management lived with this feature of the local political scene and there is no doubt that it affected their planning process. In addition, the refusal to grant exclusive franchises to gas companies forced management to pursue policies which were essentially cautious, forcing down prices to levels at which the local gaslighting market would not be contested. Competition was a constant threat to all companies, and when combined with the emergence of more effective local government this placed a considerable strain on decision-making. The result in many towns was the municipalisation of local utilities, bringing a growing proportion of the North West industry into public ownership.

Irrespective of the changing pattern of ownership, up to the 1880s the gas industry held a tight grip on the lighting market, and even the advent of electricity posed few problems for an industry which had grown rapidly since the Napoleonic Wars. Gradually, of course, electric lighting was to eat into its market share and eventually eliminate gas from this sector altogether, but these developments were a long way off and shareholders or ratepayers could anticipate many years of sound returns on their investments. The North West gas industry had benefited enormously from the region's expansion as an industrial and commercial centre to rival any in the world at that time, and clearly this was the key to its success. Only the London gas industry could boast a larger market, but the North West variant had been able to build successfully on the roots firmly laid down by Samuel Clegg and William Murdoch in 1805. This study has attempted to enliven the story surrounding the establishment of these foundations, and while many aspects have been ignored new light has been shed on areas which demanded to be illuminated. Further research is required if we are to open up other avenues, but in the fields of management, investment and local government interference we now have an insight into how the nineteenth century pioneers coped with many of the problems associated with founding one of the region's major industries.

Appendix A

A Chronology (relating to the year in which it was decided a public gas supply operation should be established, and when it was municipalised, where applicable). N.B. Those undertakings with a * were formed by that town's local authority.

Creation	Municipalisation	Creation	Municipalisation
1815 Preston Liverpool		**1826** Heywood Lancaster	
1816		**1827**	
		1828 Bury	
1817 Chester Macclesfield			
	Manchester*	**1829** Stalybridge	
1818 Blackburn Bolton		**1831**	Salford
		1832 St. Helens	
1819 Salford Chorley		**1833** Prescot Ormskirk Congleton	
1820 Stockport Warrington		**1834** Northwich Leigh Ulverston	
1821		**1835** Bacup Atherton	
1822 Wigan			
1823 Rochdale Liverpool New Burnley		**1836** Runcorn Clitheroe New Mills & Hayfield	Provincial Portable (by Manchester Police Commissioners) Stockport
1824 Kendal Ashton-under-Lyne Provincial Portable		**1837**	
1825 Oldham		**1838** Colne Kirkham	

1839

1840
Darwen
Birkenhead
Fleetwood
Accrington

1841
Haslingden

1842
Crewe

1843

1844
                    Rochdale

1845
Poynton
Marple
Radcliffe/
Pilkington

1846
Kendal Union
Altrincham
Middleton

1847
Padiham
Sandbach   Lytham*

1848
Liverpool United
Tyldesley

1849
Hindley
Todmorden
Kirkby Lonsdale   Southport*

1850
Roodee (Chester)
Buxton

1851
Vegetable Oil

1852

1853
Cheadle   Oldham
                        Blackpool*
                        Dalton*

1854
Ramsbottom   Burnley
Hyde
Stretford
Rossendale Union
Farnworth/
Kearsley
Middlewich

1855
                        Newton*

1856
Great Harwood
Widnes
Woolton
Huyton/Roby
Chester United

1857
Droylsden   Bury

1858
Morecambe   Birkenhead
                        Wallasey*

1859

1860
Milnethorpe
Nelson

1861
Lymm   Macclesfield
Haslingden Union   Middleton

1862
Leyland
Windermere   Bollington*

1863
Barrow

1864		

1865		
Dukinfield	Tyldesley	
Littleborough		

1866		
Longridge		
Grange		
Ashton		

1867		

1868		
Ambleside	Barrow	

1869		
Westhoughton	Droylsden (by	
Milnrow	Manchester Corp)	
	Oswaldtwistle*	

1870		
Rainhill		

1871		
	Buxton	

1872		
Carnforth	Atherton	
Wilmslow	Bolton	
	Lymm	
	Hindley	

1873		
		Darwen

1874		
		Leigh
		Wigan
		Ulverston

1875		
		Ashton
		Millom*

1876		
St. Annes		Padiham
Blackrod		
		Skelmersdale*

1877		
Formby		Clitheroe
		Blackburn
		St. Helens
		Warrington
		Colne
		Dukinfield

1878		
Hoylake/		
West Kirby		

1878		
Garstang		Lancaster
Knutsford		

1880		
		Chorley

Appendix B

Capital invested in North West gas undertakings in 1826, 1847, 1865 and 1881 (£)
The companies are listed in order of date of establishment.

	1826	1847	1865	1881
Preston	30,177	52,500	150,000	300,579
Liverpool	101,504	200,000	861,000	1,118,308
Liverpool New	40,000	160,750		
Chester	15,000	24,000	75,000	105,500
Macclesfield	10,000	20,000	50,000	49,000
Manchester	55,014	235,786	481,065	962,541
Blackburn	13,120	50,000	131,664	590,000
Bolton	15,000	49,500	187,688	491,268
Salford	6,000	52,519	250,000	467,806
Chorley	1,300	6,500	15,000	20,084
Stockport	15,000	34,200	70,000	192,956
Warrington	15,000	18,000	45,000	194,057
Wigan	12,500	20,000	100,000	187,812
Rochdale	12,000	29,395	68,375	203,350
Burnley	8,100	19,946	51,326	83,199
Kendal	5,000	8,000	18,630	39,600
Ashton-under-Lyne	27,000	42,500	60,000	70,391
Provincial Portable	5,000	–	–	–
Oldham	24,000	50,000	100,000	271,680
Heywood	2,700	2,700	32,724	60,690
Lancaster	8,000	17,766	43,000	97,200
Bury	–	12,800	62,356	101,930
Stalybridge	–	15,000	54,000	83,000
St. Helens	–	7,200	38,000	152,835
Prescot	–	6,000	8,000	12,070
Ormskirk	–	5,000	9,807	14,085
Congleton	–	5,000	19,068	19,990
Northwich	–	4,800	5,565	21,800
Leigh	–	4,000	39,000	66,332
Ulverston	–	5,000	10,000	34,769
Bacup	–	5,000	–	–
Atherton	–	2,000	5,000	24,906
Runcorn	–	8,000	13,800	25,000
Clitheroe	–	3,000	13,450	38,131
New Mills/Hayfield	–	2,000	4,600	5,400
Colne	–	5,000	25,000	34,000
Kirkham	–	2,000	4,000	6,765
Darwen	–	8,000	37,910	54,608
Birkenhead	–	28,500	183,314	246,642
Fleetwood	–	10,000	10,000	10,450
Accrington	–	6,000	115,812	226,285
Haslingden	–	3,240	23,775	31,999
Crewe	–	3,000	5,000	10,000
Poynton	–	2,500	5,000	10,000
Marple	–	2,000	4,000	8,000
Radcliffe/Pilkington	–	9,000	31,745	124,893
Altrincham	–	40,000	50,000	80,000
Middleton	–	5,000	26,000	100,000
Padiham	–	1,155	4,990	12,928
Sandbach	–	4,240	5,000	5,640
Lytham	–	5,000	10,000	9,200

	1826	1847	1865	1881
Tyldesley	–	–	12,000	38,189
Hindley	–	–	15,000	52,500
Todmorden	–	–	10,000	29,886
Kirkby Lonsdale	–	–	2,000	5,000
Southport	–	–	20,000	157,025
Buxton	–	–	7,390	52,500
Cheadle	–	–	3,000	5,000
Blackpool	–	–	10,000	29,886
Dalton	–	–	2,000	5,000
Ramsbottom	–	–	15,611	47,201
Hyde	–	–	36,000	43,000
Stretford	–	–	25,000	67,000
Rossendale	–	–	63,923	124,893
Farnworth/Kearsley	–	–	21,000	59,500
Middlewich	–	–	2,500	5,000
Newton	–	–	2,000	10,170
Widnes	–	–	20,000	56,540
Woolton	–	–	5,000	14,500
Huyton/Roby	–	–	6,000	14,200
Droylsden	–	–	16,000	–
Morecambe	–	–	5,000	16,600
Wallasey	–	–	15,000	57,800
Milnethorpe	–	–	2,000	5,000
Nelson	–	–	6,500	47,980
Lymm	–	–	3,200	9,150
Leyland	–	–	5,000	8,896
Windermere	–	–	6,000	8,952
Bollington	–	–	5,500	10,120
Barrow	–	–	10,000	81,115
Dukinfield	–	–	22,476	92,000
Littleborough	–	–	20,000	22,500
Longridge	–	–	–	4,802
Grange	–	–	–	6,490
Ashton	–	–	–	13,983
Ambleside	–	–	–	5,000
Westhoughton	–	–	–	21,900
Milnrow	–	–	–	14,700
Oswaldtwistle	–	–	–	27,105
Rainhill	–	–	–	12,000
Carnforth	–	–	–	5,000
Wilmslow	–	–	–	21,500
St. Annes	–	–	–	20,000
Blackrod	–	–	–	11,435
Skelmersdale	–	–	–	9,770
Formby	–	–	–	5,684
Hoylake/West Kirby	–	–	–	7,800
Garstang	–	–	–	1,955
Knutsford	–	–	–	11,000

Sources: Most of this information has been taken from either company balance sheets or parliamentary returns for 1847, 1866 and 1881. *Sources and Bibliography* provide the exact location of that information, but it must be emphasised that it simply amounts to an assessment of capital issued and loans at the time of sampling. Only in rare cases for the years 1826 and 1847 can information on ploughed-back profits be found in the records, but given the practice of capitalising this sum it is likely that the figures for 1865 contain money reinvested from undistributed earnings. Where no information on capital has survived an estimate of expenditure has been made on the basis of population figures.

Appendix C

Dividend performance of selected companies (%) (N/A. Indicates that the information is not available)

	Preston (1815)	Bolton (1818)	Blackburn (1818)	Liverpool (1815)	Liverpool Oil (1823)	Wigan (1822)	Macclesfield (1817)	Darwen (1840)	Colne (1838)	St. Helens (1832)	Chester (1817)
1816	0	—	—	0	—	—	—	—	—	—	—
1817	0	—	—	0	—	—	—	—	—	—	—
1818	0	—	—	0	—	—	0	—	—	—	—
1819	0	0	0	9	—	—	0	—	—	—	0
1820	0	0	0	6	—	—	0	—	—	—	0
1821	6	0	0	8.5	—	—	0	—	—	—	0
1822	6	6	5	5	—	0	15	—	—	—	5
1823	6	6	7.5	5	0	7.5	14.8	—	—	—	6
1824	6	6	5	10	0	0	14.4	—	—	—	7
1825	7.5	6	5	10	0	5	14	—	—	—	6
1826	7.5	6	5	10	5	10	8.2	—	—	—	7.5
1827	7.5	10	5	10	5	10	11	—	—	—	8
1828	7.5	7.5	5	8	5	10	10.2	—	—	—	6
1829	7.5	5	5	10	5	7.5	8.2	—	—	—	6
1830	7.5	5	5	10	6	5	8	—	—	—	5
1831	7.5	10	5	15	7	10	8.2	—	—	—	5
1832	7.5	10	5	15	5	0	11	—	—	—	6
1833	7.5	10	6	15	5	7.5	8.4	—	—	5	6
1834	7.5	10	6.5	10	1.5	5	7.8	—	—	0	6
1835	7.5	10	7.5	10	6.5	5	7.1	—	—	5	6
1836	7.5	10	7.5	10	8.75	7.5	8.4	—	—	5	5.5
1837	7.5	10	7.5	10	10.1	5	8	—	—	5	0
1838	7.5	10	7.5	10	9.5	7.5	9.2	—	—	2.5	2.5
1839	7.5	10	7.5	10	12	5	10	—	0	0	2.5
1840	7.5	10	7.5	10	12	7.5	9.8	—	10	0	3.75
1841	7.5	10	7.5	10	12	10	9.5	0	10	0	3.75
1842	8.75	10	10	10	11	7.5	9.4	5	10	0	7.5
1843	10	10	10	10	10	10	9.2	0	8	2.5	5
1844	10	9	10	10	10	7.5	10.2	0	15	0	5
1845	10	10	10	10	10	5	10	5	12.5	5	5

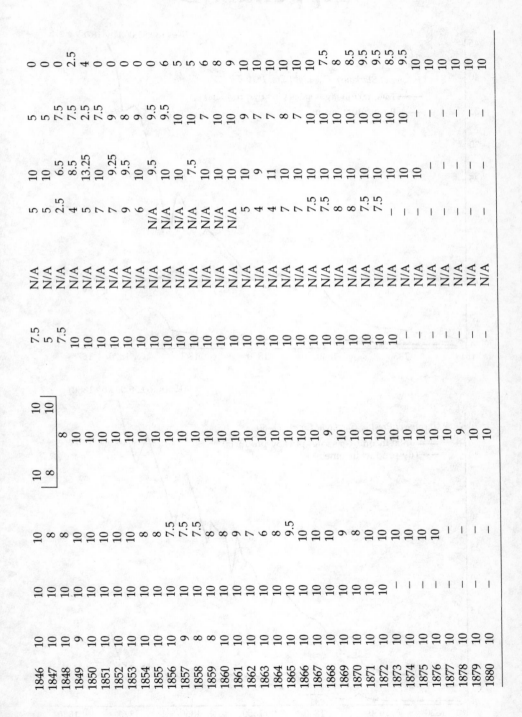

Appendix D

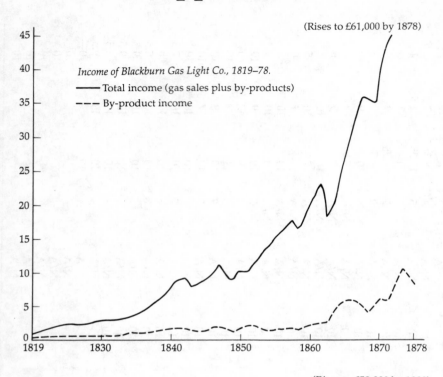

(Rises to £61,000 by 1878)

Income of Blackburn Gas Light Co., 1819–78.
—— Total income (gas sales plus by-products)
- - - By-product income

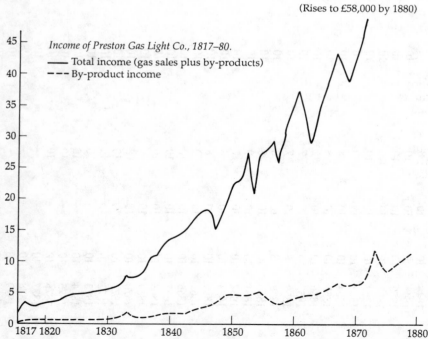

(Rises to £58,000 by 1880)

Income of Preston Gas Light Co., 1817–80.
—— Total income (gas sales plus by-products)
- - - By-product income

Sources and Bibliography

This is an itemised list of all the records which were used to write this history, with an abbreviated reference to their location (see *Abbreviations*) where appropriate. Further advice on this subject is available from the author. (Place of publication is London, unless otherwise noted.)

A. Parliamentary Papers (PP)

1823,   Report from the Select Committee on Gas-Light Establishments, v, 195—285.
1847a,   Returns from Gas Companies established by Act of Parliament in the United Kingdom, xliv, 360—407.
1847b,   General Report on the existing System Towns with Gas, by Messrs. Johnes and Clegg, xxii, 96. (Referred to in the text as Johnes & Clegg Report, 1847).
1850,   Return, or Statement, from every Gas Company established by Act of Parliament in the United Kingdom, xlix, 28—45.
1850,   Report of the Select Committee on Investments for the Savings of the Middle and Working Classes, xix, 508—509.
1866,   Return from every Gas Company established by Act of Parliament in England and Wales, lvii, 519.
1867,   Return of number of shareholders in each of the thirteen Metropolitan Gas Companies, lvii, 585.
1881,   Return of authorised Gas Undertakings in England and Wales, lxxxiii, 288—369.
1945,   The Gas Industry: Report of the Committee of Enquiry, Cmd, 6699.

B. Statutes

Lighting and Watching of Parishes in England and Wales Act, 1833.
Accrington Gas and Water Acts, 1841 and 1894.
Companies Clauses Consolidation Act, 1845.
Gasworks Clauses Act, 1847.
Sale of Gas Act, 1859.
Stalybridge and Mossley Gas Act, 1885.
Gasworks Clauses Amendment Act, 1871.
Public Health Act, 1875.

C. Printed Primary Sources

(i) *Books*

Abram, W.A. (1878), *History of the Blackburn Gas-Light Company*, Blackburn.
Abram, W.A. (1877), *A History of Blackburn, Town and Parish*, Blackburn.
Accum, F. (1819), *Description of the Process of Manufacturing Coal Gas for the lighting of Streets, Houses, and Public Buildings.*

Clegg, J. (1872), *The Bolton Gas Company, 1818–1872: an historical perspective*, Bolton.
Clegg, S. (1841), *A Practical Treatise on the Manufacture and Distribution of Coal-Gas.*
Hemingway, J. (1831), *History of the City of Chester from its Foundations to the Present Time*, Chester.
Matthews, W. (1832), *An Historical Sketch of the Origin and Progress of Gas-Lighting.*
King's Treatise (1878), T. Newbigging & W.T. Fewtrell, eds, *King's Treatise on the Science and Practice of the Manufacture and Distribution of Gas.*
Newbigging, T. (1870), *The Gas Manager's Handbook.*
(1822) *New Manchester and Salford Directory for 1821/2*, Manchester.
Paterson, J. (1877), *Brief Sketch of the History of Gas-Lighting in Warrington*, Warrington.
Peckston, T.S. (1819), *The Theory and Practice of Gas Lighting.*
Ralph (1818), *Gas-Light: or, the inside of a cotton factory*, Manchester.

(ii)   *Newspapers*

Accrington Times, 1867–75.
Blackburn Standard, 1874–76.
Blackburn Mail, 1818–20.
Bolton Chronicle, 1830–71.
Bolton Free Press, 1836–44.
Burdett's Official Intelligence, 1880–90.
Burnley Advertiser, 1853–54.
Burnley Mentor, 1853.
Chester Chronicle, 1816–20 and 1853–56.
Chester Courant, 1851.
Gas Journal Centenary Volume 1849–1949, 1949.
Journal of Gas Lighting, 1849–80.
Kendal Mercury, 1845.
Lancaster Guardian, 1925.
Macclesfield Courier and Herald, 1855–62.
Manchester Stock Exchange Daily Lists, 1836–90.
Pilot and Rochdale Reporter, 1847.
Preston Chronicle, 1815–20.
Rochdale Spectator, 1844–45.
Stockport Advertiser, 1837–40.
Westmorland Advertiser and Kendal Chronicle, 1825.
Westmorland Gazette, 1824–28.

D.   Company and Local Government Records

Altrincham:
      Deed of Settlement, 21 Feb 1846. HGA.
      Miscellaneous Correspondence, 1850–51. HGA.
      Altrincham Gas Co. Board Minutes, 1859–64. HGA.
      Altrincham Gas Co. Secretary's Notes, 1854–57, HGA.
      Altrincham Gas Co. Shareholders' Register. HGA.
Ashton:
      Ashton Gas Act, 1847.
Barrow:
      Barrow Gas Co. Registration Document, 21 Feb. 1862. PRO BT 31/616/2586.
Blackburn:
      Blackburn Gas Light Co. Board Minutes (Abram, 1878).
      Articles of Association, 1818. BL (Local History).
      Share Certificates, 1818–77. BM, UDBBN, 2/6/7.

Bolton:
    Bolton Gas Co. Minutes Books, 1818−71 (8 Volumes). BnL UGB/1/1−5/1.
    Bolton Gas Co. Finance Committee, 1861−71. BnL UGB/5/1.
    Register of Calls, 1861−71. BnL UGB/6/1.
    Bolton Corporation Bill, Minutes of Evidence, 1861 and 1871. BnL UGB/7/1 & 2.
    Bolton Gas Acts, 1820, 1843, 1853 and 1864.
    Bolton Corporation Act, 1872.
Burnley:
    Burnley Gas Consumers Co. Executive Committee Minutes. BlyL P5.
    Burnley Gas Consumers Co. Registration Document, 11 May 1853. PRO BT41/110.
    Reports of Burnley Corporation Gas Works, 1870−75. HGA.
    Burnley Gas Act, 1826.
Buxton:
    Buxton Gas, Coke & Coal Co. Registration Document, 3 Dec 1850. PRO BT31/1085/2027C.
Chester:
    Chester Gas Light Co. Board Minutes, 1845−56. HGA.
    Chester United Gas Co. Board Minutes, 1856−80. HGA.
    Chester Corporation Watch Committee Minutes, 1835−56. ChCRO OCB/15.
    Chester Town Council Assembly Book, 1817−40. ChCRO CCB.
    Chester United Gas Act, 1858.
Chorley:
    Chorley Gas Light Co. Articles of Agreement, 20 Oct 1819. ChL Q54.
    Deed of Settlement, 9 April 1849. ChL Q54.
    Share Register, 1820−49. LCRO MBCh 5/1.
    Registration Document (1871). PRO BT31/144/448.
Clitheroe:
    Clitheroe Gas Light Co. Articles of Agreement, 1836. HGA.
    Clitheroe Gas Light Co. List of Shareholders, 1836. HGA.
    Miscellaneous Papers. LCRO DDX 177 & 1525.
    Accounts, 1836−81. LCRO QDB/1.
Colne:
    Colne Gas Light & Coke Co. Articles of Agreement, 1838. CnL.
    Dividend Book, 1838−70. CnL.
    Inspectors for Lighting the Town of Colne Minute Book, 1838−50. CnL.
Darwen:
    Darwen Gas Act, 1854.
    Darwen Gas Light Co. Minute Book, 1859−72. DwnL.
    Annual Reports, 1843−60. LCRO DDBd 15/2.
Droylsden:
    Droylsden New Gas Co. Memo of Association, 1857. HGA.
Farnworth & Kearsley:
    Farnworth & Kearsley Gas Co. Registration Document, 9 March 1854. PRO BT41/236/1346.
Fleetwood:
    Fleetwood Gas Co. Correspondence, 1840−80. HGA.
    Miscellaneous Records. LCRO DDX 1135.
Garstang:
    Garstang Gas Co. Register of Members, 1879. HGA.
Haslingden:
    Haslingden Gas Light Co. Deeds and Papers, 1841−63. LCRO DDWo.
    Haslingden Union Gas Co. Memorial, 1861. LCRO DDWo.
Hyde:
    Hyde Gas Co. Board Minutes, 1855−80. HGA.

Register of Mortgagees. HGA.
Sales Ledger, CCRO DDG/2/2/18.
Correspondence, CCRO DDG/2/2/2.
Kendal:
Kendal Union Gas & Water Co. Registration Document, 1846. PRO BT41 328/1910.
Statement of Receipts and Expenses, 1859–1878. CuCRO WD/ag box 51.
Kendal Gas and Water Act, 1846.
Kirkham:
Kirkham Gas Co. Register of Transfers, 1838–40. HGA.
Board Minutes, 1838–65. HGA.
Lancaster:
Lancaster Gas Co. List of Shareholders, 1879. LrL.
Lancaster Gas Act, 1856.
Liverpool:
Liverpool Oil Gas Co. Board Minutes, 1822–28. LplCA Acc 2103.
Liverpool Gas Light Co. Board Minutes, 1845–48. LplCA Acc. 2103.
Manchester:
Manchester Gas Committee Minutes, 1824–43. MCAD M27/1/1/1–4.
Proceedings of the Manchester Police Commissioners, 1815–43. MCAD, Vols 4–7.
Nelson:
Nelson Gas Co. Memo. of Association, 1860. LCRO DDX 617.
Registration Document, 10 Aug 1860. PRO BT31/489/1933.
Northwich:
Northwich Gas Light & Coke Co. Registration Document, 10 Aug 1863. PRO BT31/816/614C.
Oldham:
Oldham Gas Act, 1825.
Oldham Corporation Gas and Water Act, 1853.
Oldham Gas & Water Co. Committee of Management Minute Book, 1826–33. OLIC PCO 1/5.
Oldham Police Commissioners' Committee Minutes, 1827–32. OLIC PCO 1/1.
Oldham Gas & Waterworks Committee Minutes, 1854. HGA.
Oldham Corporation Gasworks Statistical Tables, 1862. HGA.
Ormskirk:
Ormskirk Gas Light Co. Articles of Association, 2 Oct 1833. HGA.
Preston:
Preston Gas Acts, 1839, 1853 and 1865.
Preston Gas Light Co. Minute Books, 1815–70. (6 Vols.) LCRO DDX 256.
John Abraham's Diary and Account Book, 1815–17. LCRO DDX 256/10.
Share Registers, 1817–80. LCRO DDX 256/Item 23 and HGA.
Account Books, 1817–79. LCRO DDX 256/Item 38.
Radcliffe & Pilkington:
Radcliffe & Pilkington Gas Co. Deed of Settlement, 17 July 1845. LCRO DDS1 6/1.
Rochdale:
Rochdale Gas Act, 1823.
Rochdale Improvement Acts, 1825 and 1844.
Rochdale Corporation Gas Committee Minute Book, 1854–59. RL LA D/2/8.
Statistical Report of the Rochdale Gas Works, 1870–71. HGA.
Rossendale:
Rossendale Union Gas Act, 1854.
Rossendale Union Gas Co. Board Minutes, 1854–58. RtlL.

Runcorn:
    Runcorn Gas, Light & Coke Co. Register of Shareholders. HGA.
    Account Book, 1840−49. HGA.
    Minute Book, 1847−64. HGA.
St. Helens:
    St. Helens Gas Acts, 1832 and 1852.
    St. Helens Gas Light Co. Minute Books, 1832−65. HGA.
    Accounts. StHL ST 1/11
    Dividend Book. StHL ST 1/10.
    St. Helens Improvement Act, 1862.
Salford:
    Reports of the Gaslight Committee to Salford Council, 1831−80. SCL.
    Proceedings of Salford Council, Annual Reports, 1854−80. SCL.
Stockport:
    Stockport Borough Gasworks Special Minute Book, 1851−54. SpL B/EE/3/18.
    Stockport Corporation Minutes, 1836−38. SpL.
    Stockport Watch Committee Minutes, 1835−40. SpL.
Warrington:
    Warrington Gas Act, 1847.
    Warrington Gas, Light & Coke Co. Articles of Association, 1820. WL.
    Minutes of Evidence for 1847 Bill. WL p8079.
    Corporation Report on Gasworks, 1877. WL p1863.
    Subscription List, 1820. WL p824291.
Wigan:
    Wigan Gas Light Co. Board Minutes, 1822−72. (6 Vols.) LRO F3/1/1−6.
    Wigan Gas Act, 1822.

E. Secondary Sources

Alford, B.W.E. (1976), 'Strategy and structure in large scale companies', in L. Hannah (ed), *Management Strategy and Business Development*.

Anderson, B.L. (1969), 'The attorney and the early capital market in Lancashire', in Crouzet, F. (ed), *Capital Formation in the Industrial Revolution*.

Aspden, J.P. (1947), *Warrington Hundred*, Warrington.

Aspin, C. (1962), *Haslingden, 1800−1900: a history*, Haslingden.

Awty, B.G. (1975), 'The introduction of gas-lighting to Preston', *Transactions of the Historic Society of Lancashire and Cheshire*, 125.

Bailey, F.A. (1955), *A History of Southport*, Southport.

Baines, E. (1924), *History of the Cotton Manufacture in Great Britain*.

Barker, T.C. & Harris, J.R. (1954), *A Merseyside Town in the Industrial Revolution: St. Helens, 1750−1900*, Liverpool.

Barton, B.T. (1973), *History of the Borough of Bury*, Manchester.

Barton, B.T. (1987), *History of Farnworth and Kearsley*, Bolton.

Bateson, H. (1949), *A Centenary History of Oldham*, Oldham.

Bennett, A.S. (1986), 'Dolphinholme, 1811', paper presented to the Manchester District Junior Gas Association.

Bennett, A.S. (1986B), *Samuel Clegg and Stoneyhurst College*, BGNW.

Bennett, W. (1948), *The History of Burnley, 1650−1850*, Burnley.

Bennett, W. (1957), *The History of Marsden and Nelson*, Nelson.

Bland, E. (1887), *Annals of Southport and District*, Manchester.

Bowman, W.M. (1960), *England in Ashton-under-Lyne*, Ashton-under-Lyne.

Braunholtz, W.T.K. (1963), *Institution of Gas Engineers: the first 100 years*.

Broadbridge, S. (1970), *Studies in Railway Expansion and the Capital Market in England, 1825−73*.

Brown, S.M. (1971), 'The growth of middle class leadership in Kendal society and its influence on politics, 1790–1850', Lancaster M.A.

Burnley Express (1897), *Burnley in the nineteenth century*, Burnley.

Chaloner, W.H. (1950), *The Social and Economic Development of Crewe, 1780–1923*, Manchester.

Chandler, D. (1947), *Outline of the History of Lighting by Gas*.

Chandler, D. & Lacy, A.D. (1949), *Rise of the Gas Industry in Britain*.

Chantler, P. (1939), *British Gas Industry: an economic study*, Manchester.

Chatfield, M. (1977), *A History of Accounting Thought*, New York.

City of Manchester Gas Dept. (1949), *143 Years of Gas in Manchester*, Manchester.

Co. Borough of Salford (1920), *The Salford Gas Undertaking*, Salford.

Cotterill, M.S. (1980–81), 'The development of Scottish gas technology, 1817–1914: inspiration and motivation', *Industrial Archaeology Review*, v.

Cottrell, P.L. (1980), *Industrial Finance, 1830–1914*.

Crouzet, F. (1972), 'Capital formation in Great Britain during the Industrial Revolution', in Crouzet, *op.cit.*

Curwen, J.F. (1900), *Kirkbie-Kendal*, Kendal.

Davies, C.S. (1961), *A History of Macclesfield*, Manchester.

Dickson, P.G.M. (1967). *The Financial Revolution in England*.

Eastwood, K. (1988), 'Preston Gas Light Co.: a story of faith and determination', paper presented to the Manchester District Junior Gas Association.

Evans, G.H. (1936), *British Corporation Finance, 1775–1850*, Baltimore.

Everard, S. (1949), *History of the Gas, Light & Coke Co.*

Falkus, M.E. (1967), 'The British gas industry before 1850', *Economic History Review*, second series, xx.

Falkus, M.E. (1977), 'The development of municipal trading in the nineteenth century', *Business History*, xix.

Falkus, M.E. (1982), 'The early development of the British gas industry, 1790–1815', *Economic History Review*, second series, xxiii.

Finer, H. (1941), *Municipal Trading. A Study in Public Administration*.

Foster, J. (1974), *Class Struggle in the Industrial Revolution*.

Fraser, D. (1976), *Urban Politics in Victorian England*, Oxford.

Fraser, D. (1979), *Power and Authority in the Victorian City*, Oxford.

Fraser, D. ed (1982), *Municipal Reform and the Industrial City*, Leicester.

Fry, G.K. (1979), *The Growth of Government*.

Garrard, J. (1983), *Leadership and Power in Victorian Industrial Towns, 1830–80*, Manchester.

Gas Engineers' Compendium (1924).

Giles, P. (1950), 'Economic and social development of Stockport', Manchester M.A.

Gill, C. (1948), 'Birmingham under the Street Commissioners', *University of Birmingham Historical Journal*.

Golisti, K. (1984), 'The gas adventure and industry in NEGas, 1802–1949', paper presented to NEGas, Bradford.

Hacking, B. (n.d.), *The Municipalisation of Bolton Gas Co., 1818–1872*, HGA.

Harris, S. (1956) *The Development of Gas on North Merseyside: 1815–1949*, Liverpool.

Harrop, S.A. & Rose, E.A., eds, (1974), *Victorian Ashton*, Tameside.

Heginbotham (1890), *Stockport: Ancient and Modern*, Stockport.

Hodson, J.H. (1974), *The Old Community: a portrait of Wilmslow*, Wilmslow.

Hudson, P. (1988), *The Genesis of Industrial Capital. A Study of the West Riding Wool Textile Industry c.1750–1850*, Cambridge.

Hunt, B.C. (1936), *The Development of the Business Corporation in England, 1800–1867*, Camb., Mass.

Hunt, J.R. (1958), 'The Widnes Gas & Water Co.', *Transactions of the Historic Society of Lancashire and Cheshire*, 110.

Ingham, A. (1879), *A History of Altrincham and Bowdon*, Altrincham.

Jones, L.J. (1983), 'Public pursuit of private profit? Liberal businessmen and municipal politics in Birmingham, 1865−1900', *Business History*, xxv.

Joyce, P. (1980), *Work, Society & Politics*.

Killick, J.R. & Thomas, W.A. (1970). 'The provincial stock exchanges, 1830−1870', *Economic History Review*, second series, xxiii.

Lloyd-Jones, R. & Lewis, M. (1988), *Manchester in the Age of the Factory*.

Lockwood, A. (1980), 'The origins of gas in Leeds', *Proceedings of the Thoresby Society*.

Macclesfield Courier & Herald (1888), *A Walk through the Public Institutions of Macclesfield*, Macclesfield.

Mackenzie, C. (1947), *The Vital Flame*.

March, J.W. (1957) *Borough of Stalybridge Centenary, 1857−1957*, Stalybridge.

Marshall, J.D. (1958), *Furness and the Industrial Revolution*, Barrow.

Matthews, D. (1983), 'The London gasworks: a technical, commercial and labour history', Hull, Ph.D.

Matthews, D. (1985), 'Rogues, speculators and competing monopolies: the early London gas companies', *London Journal*, ii.

Matthews, D. (1986), 'Laissez-faire and the London gas industry in the nineteenth century: another look', *Economic History Review*, second series, xxxix.

Middleton, T. (1932), *The History of Hyde and its Neighbourhood*, Hyde.

Millward, R. (1986), *The Emergence of Gas and Water Monopolies in Nineteenth Century Britain: Why Public Ownership?*, Salford Papers in Economics, 86−4.

Millward, R. & Ward, R. (1987), 'The costs of public and private gas enterprise in late-nineteenth century Britain', *Oxford Economic Papers*, 39.

Millward, R. & Ward, R. (1991), 'From private to public ownership of gas undertakings in England and Wales, 1851−1947: chronology, incidence and causes', Working Papers in Economic and Social History, University of Manchester, No. 1.

Mitchell, T.M. (1986), 'What Manchester did yesterday', paper presented to the NWGHS.

Morgan, E.V. & Thomas, W.A. (1962), *The Stock Exchange: Its History and Functions*.

Mountfield, D. (1979), *The Railway Barons*.

Musson, A.E. & Robinson, E. (1970), *Science and Technology in the Industrial Revolution*, Manchester.

Nabb, H. (1986), 'A history of the gas industry in the South West of England before 1949', Bath Ph.D.

Neill, R.S. (1958), *Song of Sunrise*.

Pollard, S. (1968), *The Genesis of Modern Management*.

Porter, J. (1876), *History of the Fylde in Lancashire*, Fleetwood.

Prentice, A. (1851), *Historical Sketches and Recollections of Manchester*, Manchester.

Pressnell, L.S. (1956), *Country Banking in the Industrial Revolution*, Oxford.

Redford, A. (1939), *The History of Local Government in Manchester*, Vol I, Manchester.

Redford, A. (1940), Vol II.

Roberts, D.E. (1978), *The Leicester Gas Undertaking, 1821−1921*, EM Gas, Leicester.

Roberts, D.E. (1979), *The Sheffield Gas Undertaking, 1818−1949*, EM Gas, Leicester.

Roberts, D.E. (1980), *The Nottingham Gas Undertaking, 1818−1949*, EM Gas, Leicester.

Robson, B.T. (1973), *Urban Growth: an approach*.

Robson, W.A. (1939), *A Century of Municipal Progress*.

Rowlinson, P.J. (1984), 'Regulation of the gas industry in the early-nineteenth century, 1800−1860', Oxford Ph.D.

Schofield, M.M. (1946), *Outlines of an Economic History of Lancaster, 1680−1860*.

Shaw, J.G. (1889), *History and Traditions of Darwen and its People*, Blackburn.

Shercliffe, W.S. et al. (1983), *A History of Poynton*, Manchester.

Singleton, J.W. (1928). *The Jubilee Souvenir of the Corporation of Accrington, 1878−1928*, Accrington.

Smellie, K.B. (1968), *A History of Local Government.*

Smith, Rev. (1921), *Illustrated Chronicles of Nelson and District from Human Times until Now*, Nelson.

Smith, R.N. & Lefevre, N.S. (1932), *Domestic Utilisation of Gas.*

Stewart, E.G. (1962), *Samuel Clegg, 1781–1861. His Life, Work and Family.*

Thomas, W.A. (1973), *The Provincial Stock Exchanges.*

Thompson, S. (n.d.) *The Municipalisation of Bolton Gas Co.*

Turner, B. & Palmer, S. (1981), *The Blackpool Story*, Blackpool.

Vigier, F. (1970), *Change and Apathy: Liverpool and Manchester during the Industrial Revolution*, Camb., Mass.

Waller, P.J. (1983), *Town, City and Nation: England, 1850–1914*, Oxford.

Walton, J. (1987), *Lancashire, a social history, 1558–1939*, Manchester.

Ward, J.R. (1974), *The Finance of Canal-Building in Eighteenth Century England*, Oxford.

Webb, S. & B. (1922). *English Local Government: statutory authorities for special purposes.*

Wilson, J.F. (1991A). 'Ownership, management and strategy in early North West gas companies, 1815–1830', *Business History*, xxxiii.

Wilson, J.F. (1991B), 'Competition in the early gas industry: the case of Chester Gas Light Co., 1817–1856', *Transactions of the Lancashire and Cheshire Antiquarian Society*, 86.

Winstanley, M.J. (1983), *The Shopkeepers' World, 1830–1914*, Manchester.

Index

N.B. In addition to the references listed here, all the companies are mentioned in Appendices A and B.